The Origin of
ENGLISH
PLACE-NAMES

by

P. H. REANEY

Routledge and Kegan Paul
LONDON

First published 1960
by Routledge & Kegan Paul Limited
Broadway House, Carter Lane, E.C.4

Printed in Great Britain by
Lowe & Brydone (Printers) Limited, London

© *P. H. Reaney 1960, 1964*

Second impression 1961
Third impression (with some corrections and
additions to the bibliography) 1964
Fourth impression 1969

SBN 7100 2010 4

CONTENTS

	PREFACE	*page* vii
	ABBREVIATIONS	ix
One	INTRODUCTORY	1
Two	METHODS OF PLACE-NAME STUDY	17
Three	DIALECT AND PLACE-NAMES	43
Four	PERSONAL-NAMES AND PLACE-NAMES	49
Five	THE CELTIC ELEMENT	71
Six	THE ENGLISH ELEMENT	99
Seven	THE SCANDINAVIAN ELEMENT	162
Eight	THE FRENCH ELEMENT	192
Nine	LATIN INFLUENCE	203
Ten	FIELD-NAMES	207
Eleven	STREET-NAMES	226
	FOR FURTHER READING	243
	INDEX OF SUBJECTS	247
	INDEX OF PLACE-NAMES	250

MAPS

THE CELTIC ELEMENT	78
EARLY ENGLISH SETTLEMENTS	105
THE SCANDINAVIAN SETTLEMENT	178

PREFACE

'OXSHOTT, where the ox was shot.' This remark, overheard from a stranger passing through the town, might well be taken as a text and a justification for this book. It reveals an interest in place-names and a realisation that they must have a meaning, but the explanation is a popular etymology which ignores all the essentials. The speaker was unaware of the necessity of tracing the history of the name which proves it has nothing to do with the ox, whilst the *shott* was a piece of land and had no connexion with shooting. A long experience of lecturing on place-names to local Antiquarian and Historical Societies has proved not only that there is a wide interest in the subject, but also that this interest is increased when the principles underlying the study are explained with illustrative examples. The real difficulty is that whilst the general principles and the simpler problems can be explained to the non-expert, the interpretation of difficult names involves a knowledge of philology and languages not possessed by the many and much must be taken on trust, just as the layman can appreciate the results of atomic science although he is ignorant of the physics and higher mathematics on which they are based. The purpose of this book is first to give the general reader an indication of the way in which explanations of place-names are arrived at, and secondly to give him some idea of the general results already achieved.

Many place-names can be explained without difficulty; for some more than one interpretation is possible; others have so far defeated the experts. In selecting examples, every effort has been made to indicate where doubt exists. Early forms have been given, where necessary, to show that the name has changed. Dates have been added, but it has not been considered essential to give the source of these early forms. Those interested who wish for more detailed information will find it in the books listed in the bibliography.

PREFACE

In a work covering such a wide field as this, it is not always possible to acknowledge specific debts. Long ago, I found H. C. Wyld's *Historical Study of the Mother Tongue* (1906) an invaluable introduction to method. His *History of Modern Colloquial English*, too, contains much which throws light on the development and pronunciation of place-names. I learned much from the late Sir Allen Mawer, quite apart from his published works. For the rest, I am particularly indebted to the publications of Professor Eilert Ekwall, Professor A. H. Smith and Sir Frank Stenton, and more recently to those of Professor Kenneth Jackson, whilst a general acknowledgement is due to the authors of the works included in the bibliography as well as to numerous specialist articles not given there. To Mr. J. E. B. Gover and Professor R. M. Wilson of the University of Sheffield I owe a special debt. Both have unselfishly devoted much of their time to reading the manuscript and their comments have purged it of errors and inconsistencies, though they must not be held responsible for statements as they stand. Mr. Gover has also given me access to his collection of place-name material, relating particularly to Hampshire and Cornwall.

For permission to reproduce the maps, my grateful thanks are due to the Edinburgh University Press (from K. Jackson, *Language and History in Early Britain*), the Oxford University Press (from R. G. Collingwood and J. N. L. Myres, *Roman Britain and the English Settlements*) and the Cambridge University Press (from H. C. Darby, *A Historical Geography of England*).

P. H. REANEY

Hildenborough
November, 1959

In the third impression some misprints and errors have been corrected and additions made to the bibliography.

P. H. R.

Birchington
July, 1964

ABBREVIATIONS

a	*ante*	Herts	Hertfordshire
AFr	Anglo-French	Hu	Huntingdonshire
AN	Anglo-Norman	IOW	Isle of Wight
Beds	Bedfordshire	Ir	Irish
Berks	Berkshire	K	Kent
Bk	Buckinghamshire	L	Lincolnshire
Brit	British, Brittonic	La	Lancashire
c	*circa*	Lat	Latin
C	Cambridgeshire	Lei	Leicestershire
Ch	Cheshire	m.	masculine
Co	Cornish	ME	Middle English
Co	Cornwall	MHG	Middle High German
Cu	Cumberland	MIr	Middle Irish
D	Devonshire	Mon	Monmouthshire
Da	Danish	MW	Middle Welsh
dat.	dative	Mx	Middlesex
DB	Domesday Book	Nb	Northumberland
Db	Derbyshire	Nf	Norfolk
Do	Dorsetshire	nom.	nominative
Du	Durham	NRY	North Riding of York-shire
ERY	East Riding of York-shire	Nt	Nottinghamshire
Ess	Essex	Nth	Northamptonshire
f., fem.	feminine	O	Oxfordshire
Fr	French	OBret	Old Breton
Gael	Gaelic	OCo	Old Cornish
gen.	genitive	ODa	Old Danish
Gl	Gloucestershire	OE	Old English
Ha	Hampshire	OESc	Old East Scandinavian
He	Herefordshire	OFr	Old French

OG	Old German	sg.	singular
OHG	Old High German	So	Somerset
OIr	Old Irish	Sr	Surrey
ON	Old Norse	St	Staffordshire
ONFr	Old Northern French	Sx	Sussex
OSc	Old Scandinavian	W	Welsh
OW	Old Welsh	W	Wiltshire
OWSc	Old West Scandinavian	Wa	Warwickshire
pl., plur.	plural	We	Westmorland
PrOE	Primitive Old English	Wo	Worcestershire
PrW	Primitive Welsh	WRY	West Riding of York-shire
R	Rutland		
Sa	Shropshire	Y	Yorkshire
Scand	Scandinavian	*	a postulated form
Sf	Suffolk		

Chapter One

INTRODUCTORY

Mᴏʀᴇ nonsense has been written on place-names than on any subject except, perhaps, that of surnames. Nor is this surprising. Names, whether of persons or places, are a perpetual source of interest but their interpretation demands a knowledge of languages, and of the sound-changes which took place in them, not possessed by the many. The modern spelling of a name is often a dangerous snare; its earliest forms may be difficult to find and, when found, must be explained in the light of the language spoken when the name was given. The man-in-the-street can hardly be blamed when he tells us that Barking got its name because there could be heard the barking of the dogs in the Isle of Dogs. He has no means of knowing that the name occurs in a Saxon charter of 695 as *Berecingas*, that there is another Barking far away in Suffolk, found in a charter of c1050 as *Berchinges*, and that this was originally the name of a community 'dwellers by the birch trees', later given to the place where they lived.[1] Tradition has it that after the defeat of the Armada, Queen Elizabeth I went down to Purfleet to watch her victorious fleet sail up the river. Overcome by the sight of torn sails, damaged rigging and other signt of conflict, she exclaimed, 'Alas, my poor fleet!' and so Purfleet got its name, a pretty fiction which will never die, in spite of the fact thas

[1] Ekwall prefers to explain the name as 'the people of Berica.'

1

the name existed at least 300 years earlier, in 1285, and was then spelled *Purteflyete*, which can certainly have no connexion with *poor*; the *fleet* was a creek and no assembly of warships.[1]

Journalists and topographers are great sinners in perpetuating fictitious and impossible derivations and for them there is no excuse. They ought to be aware of the existence of standard books of reference which it is their duty to consult and they have no more right to discard etymologies merely because they do not like them than they have to falsify facts.

No place-name student claims infallibility. He admits that some etymologies are difficult and doubtful and that, at present, some names cannot be explained. But when a writer rejects an etymology, it is his duty to give his reasons and to support his alternative with evidence. When we are told that Teddington (Mx) means 'Tide-ending town', we are entitled to know why the Saxons called the place *Tudincgatun* 'the farm of Tuda's people' in 970, a time when *tide* was *tid*. There was also a Teddington in Worcestershire, recorded in 780 as *Teottingtun* 'Teotta's farm'. In spite of the identity of the modern spellings, the two names are clearly of quite distinct origin. When we read that the Isle of Dogs was named 'possibly because so many dogs were drowned in the Thames here', and that Akeman Street, an ancient road passing through Bath, 'received in Saxon times the significant name of Akeman Street from the condition of the gouty sufferers who travelled along it', we begin to wonder what Chinaman put the *Ching* in Chingford, and whether Tooting owes its name to the hideous cacophony made by impatient Anglo-Saxon motorists in some pre-Conquest traffic jam.

Yeavering

Often these fanciful etymologies are due to the smug self-assurance of writers obsessed with pre-conceived theories they are determined to support by hook or by crook. One such, a columnist in a once-popular journal now defunct, delighted in debunking the experts. After citing from 'the august pages' of the *Oxford Dictionary of English Place-names* a long list of derivations of which he disapproved —no reasons given—he continues: 'A guessing-game at a Sunday School picnic could do as well as that; and I shall reserve for later pillorying some even sillier "scientific" findings by other experts.

[1] A different, and impossible, derivation 'the port at the mouth of the fleet' is given in *The Essex Countryside*, vol. 7, No. 28 (1958), p. 66.

Here I will refer only to the omission of Bel.' And here we have Ekwall's real crime, the 'inadequacy' of his derivations: he gives no support to the worshippers of the 'fires of Bel that blazed forth on Celtic hill-tops' as at Belsay (Nb) and 'vulgarizes the Sun-god' by explaining the name as 'Bill's ridge'. In further support of his views, our columnist calls in Yeavering Bell in the Cheviots. 'Some historians maintain that this is Bel-ad-Gabron, or Mount of the Sun, a title common in Syria and ancient Babylon. The venerable Bede refers to it when writing of a visit by Paulinus as "Ad Gebrin (at this day Yeverin)". Bell, of course, is derived from Bel or Baal, as it still survives in Beltane, the old Mayday of Scotland, when the fires of Baal, the Sun God, were kindled as sympathetic magic.' To this he adds an undated cutting with the heading, 'Village pays fire tribute to the god Baal', which records that 'at the touch of a torch a twelve-foot-high paraffin-impregnated pile of tree branches and motor-car tyres burst into flames at Whatton last night. It was a signal for more than 300 inhabitants of this picturesque old Northumbrian village and crowds of visitors to pay tribute to the pagan god Baal. The ceremony goes back through the centuries and is now observed only in one other spot in the British Isles.' Later, returning to the fray, he asks what the etymologists who deny the Semitic Bel make of the latter part of its ancient name, *Ad Gebrin*. 'This is certainly derived from Gib, the Syrian word for hill. I begin to suspect that the "orthodox" refusal to concede a derivation which is clear beyond cavil is because, once having conceded it in this instance, half the foundations of their "science" will be undermined and there is no telling what might happen. Yeavering Bell has traces of ancient occupation so far unidentified. Apparently by reason of its extreme isolation this district was one of the last strongholds of the ancient Britons, and the guttural in the north Northumberland dialect is supposed to be the last trace of their language. It is quite different from the Scottish guttural, and De Quincey, in his travels, remarked on it as a "shibboleth".' A misquotation of Bede, two mutually exclusive derivations, one incomplete—*Gebrin* wrongly divided as *Gib-rin*—the second element unexplained—a Syrian place-name containing an imaginary guttural (presumably the *Y* of Yeavering), last relic of the language of the ancient Britons, twentieth-century Northumbrian villagers offering to Baal the smoke and incense of paraffin and burning rubber tyres—all this 'a derivation which is clear beyond cavil'! From this cloud-cuckoo land let us descend to Ekwall—a simple, unadorned statement behind which lie years of close study and research: '*Gefrin* is evidently the old name of Yeavering Bell, a prominent hill at the place. The name is derived from Welsh *gafr* "goat" or a compound containing the word, e.g. a name with Welsh *bryn* (mutated *fryn*) as second element.' Bede gives two forms: *Adgebrin* and *Adgefrin*. The *Ad* is the Latin preposition 'at' or 'to'. At the end of the Roman occupation Romano-British *b* was pronounced something like *v* and the *v*-sound was written *f*. *Gebrin* thus preserves an old spelling; *Gefrin* gives the approximate pronunciation. Far from being 'one of the last strongholds of the ancient Britons' modern excavation shows that Yeavering was the site of a palace of the Anglian kings of Northumbria.

Tonbridge

The historical section of the official guide to Tonbridge is by D. C. Somervell, a historian of repute, who should be aware of the value of evidence and the importance of checking his facts, but he flounders badly once he enters on the dangerous path of etymology. He begins with a derivation. 'What's in a Name? First of all, why is it called Tonbridge? The notion that it means "town-bridge" *must* [1] be wrong. The syllable "ton" when it means a township or a collection of dwellings comes at the end of the name. For example Paddington means the "ton" (settlement, township) of the "ing" (family, clan) of a gentleman called *perhaps* Padda. Secondly, "bridge" at the end of a name is, *I believe*, generally a corruption of burg (borough) which means a hill or fortress. *Perhaps* Ton or Tun is a variant of Dun, which means hill, and survives in "Downs" and "Dunes", Dunstable, etc. *If so*, Tonbridge = Dunborough = Hill-hill, each syllable meaning the same thing in a different language, a common feature of place-names.'

It is true that names with *Tun-* as a first element are not common. There are some twelve places named Tunstall 'site of a farm, farmstead', two of which are now Dunstall: Tunstead in Derbyshire, Lancashire and Norfolk 'farmstead'; Tonwell (Herts), *Tunwelle* 1220 'farm-spring', and Tunworth in Hampshire. This latter is *Tuneworde* in Domesday Book, which Ekwall explains as 'perhaps Tunna's farm'. But he notes a lost place in Middlesex in a charter of 957 which occurs both as *Tuneweorðe* and *Tunwæorðinga gemære* 'boundary of the dwellers at *Tunweorð*' which seem to have as first element

---

[1] These italics are mine.

OE *tūn*. '*Tūnworð* might be "farm with a fence". If Tunworth is from *Tūn-worð*, the -*e*- of the early forms is intrusive.' This is of importance, as he explains Tonbridge (DB *Tonebrige*) as 'Tunna's bridge', chiefly because in 1230 it appears as *Thunnebrigge*. There is no other form with -*nn*-, though the medial -*e*- is common. Insertion and omission of an unstressed medial -*e*- is frequent in medieval documents and the topography confirms Wallenberg's etymology 'village-bridge'. The strategic importance of this bridge, carrying, as it does, the Hastings–London road over the Medway at the only point passable in time of floods, was emphasised by the building here of the Norman castle of Tonbridge. The place-name reappears in Two Bridge in Writtle (Ess), *Tunbrygge* 1274, *Tonebrigge* 1276, 'the bridge by the Town Quarter' of Writtle, and in a place in Kingston (So) called *Tonbrugge* alias *Tobryge* in 1340.

Now back to our historian. ME *burg* does, at times, occur as -*brug*, -*brigge*, but it is uncommon and very rarely does it survive in that form. There is no trace of this in the forms of Tonbridge. The OE word for 'fortress' was *burg*, modern *borough*, that for 'hill' was *beorg*, which gives a modern Barrow or Berrow. Its confusion with -*borough* is late. If Tonbridge is to be derived from *Dun-*, it is essential to produce medieval spellings with *D-* and to show that names like Dunham and Downham 'hill-farmstead', Dunmow 'hill-meadows', and Dunton 'hill-farm', occur also as *Tunham, Tunmow* and *Tunton*. Neither has been done. The final justification of the tautology—two syllables meaning the same thing in a different language—is sheer nonsense. Tonbridge = Dunborough = Hill-hill: every topographical term used is Anglo-Saxon. Tonbridge 'village-bridge' is a Saxon name, older than the Castle Hill, which is Norman and artificial.

At the risk of weariness or boredom, we must accompany our historian a little longer. He continues 'As for the spelling, Ton, Tun, in really early days one spelt anyhow but in the eighteenth century and onwards both our town and its neighbour of the Wells had settled down to Tun. Then, about a hundred years ago, our town decided to be different and officially rechristened itself Tonbridge. Why the change was made I do not know, but it is reasonable to regret it. The two towns share the same name, "the Wells" taking the name of the older town because its springs, which became fashionable in the seventeenth century, were within the civil parish of Tonbridge. To write "Tonbridge" and "Tunbridge Wells" is much as if one wrote "London" and "Lundon Bridge", though in our case it is the "o", not the "u" that is the intruder. Also the present spelling leads the ignorant to pronounce the first syllable as if it rhymed with "on", which is very deplorable.'

The common assumption that the variation in the spelling of place-names and surnames and of common words, too, is a sign of ignorance and illiteracy is unwarranted. We are apt to forget that it is less than a century since education became compulsory, and even within the last twenty years there have been official lamentations at the surprisingly large number of illiterates. Speech is older and more important than writing. Without speech there would be no need for the written word, and the original purpose of writing was to record in permanent form some ordinance or law, some instruction, advice or warning which it was desired to preserve for record or to pass on to those at a distance who had no opportunity to hear the oral statement. To understand this document, the recipient must be able, on seeing it, to reproduce the actual sounds of the original speech. To meet this need, a system of symbols was in time devised, each symbol representing a distinct sound or syllable. These could be grouped to represent words, and written communication was possible—so long as writer and reader interpreted the symbols in the same way.

From about 500 A.D. to the Norman Conquest the language spoken in England was Anglo-Saxon or, as it is now more commonly called, Old English. But, just as today the dialects of Yorkshire and Lancashire, Somerset and Devon, Kent and Staffordshire preserve distinct characteristics of their own, so Old English had its dialects, Northumbrian, Mercian, West Saxon and Kentish, each with its own peculiarities of pronunciation. As spelling was reasonably phonetic, the place of origin of a document was often obvious from its dialect, and, as pronunciation changed, so, in time, did the spelling. Errors and anomalous forms inevitably occur, but throughout the Old English period phonetic spelling prevailed, although it always lagged behind the actual pronunciation.

With the Conquest came a great change. For some three centuries two languages, the Anglo-Norman of the conquerors and the native English of the defeated, fought for supremacy until English prevailed, an English which was the direct descendant of Old English, but greatly changed and altered by the impact of its continental rival. The documents with which we are concerned were usually written in Latin, often by clerks whose native language was French. Their spelling—adapted to French pronunciation, and different from that

6

previously used in England—they retained. They knew little or no English. Its sounds were strange to them; they found difficulty in pronouncing them, and they had no symbols for those sounds which did not occur in French. Hence they had to improvise. English names often appeared in strange forms, especially when misunderstood or imperfectly heard from the mumbling lips of some uncouth peasant from Yorkshire or Devonshire. As time went on, English itself, too, changed. Dialectal varieties are found more frequently in the writings of the period and their pronunciations developed in different ways. Place-names, in particular, are often found in a bewildering variety of spellings, some local, some official, some undoubtedly erroneous, but all attempts at expressing the pronunciation. On such material as this must philologists work. They have to interpret these spellings, eliminate errors and determine the original form of the name and then, and only then, can they attempt an explanation. The older the forms and the greater their number, the more hope there is of success. It was only after the invention of printing that any attempt was made to establish a recognised system of spelling, and printers long continued to use their own discretion. But for the place-name student, forms found first in print are of little value except to supplement earlier material or to throw light on the later developments of pronunciation.

To return to Tonbridge, the cause of this digression. The name derives from the Saxon *tūn*, and the normal modern spelling would be Tunbridge. It was a common practice of Norman scribes to write *o* for the Saxon *u* (shortened in the compound), and the name is spelled *Tonebrige* in Domesday Book. The strategic crossing of the Medway was defended by the Norman castle and Normans must have been numerous in the neighbourhood and their influence paramount. Hence the Norman spelling Tonbridge is the most common form and has survived. When Tunbridge Wells began to grow in importance, the spelling with *u* was adopted, partly, perhaps, from a knowledge of the derivation, but more probably from a deliberate desire to distinguish between the two places. The French spelling of Tonbridge did not affect the pronunciation, which is identical with that of Tunbridge Wells.

The serious student of local history, too, is liable to err. He is anxious to establish the meaning of a place-name with which he is familiar not only in its modern form but in a variety of earlier spellings which he has found in printed documents or in manuscripts. He is aware there is a problem, he knows how to consult authorities and has discovered and used books on place-names, but he has no knowledge of the history of language. He misunderstands and misinterprets, does not like the etymology he finds and tries to explain it away.

Brightlingsea

Dr E. P. Dickin, in the second edition of his *History of Brightlingsea* (1939), devotes four full pages to a discussion of the etymology of the parish-name. He has collected 404 different spellings, prints 90 and refers to the *Place-names of Essex* (1935), where a selection of some 80 forms is given. There is no lack of material. The sole problem is one of interpretation, a difficulty of a somewhat unusual kind in that the Domesday form, simple and easily explained, but with very little later support, does not fit in with the vast majority of later spellings. In 1086 the name occurs as *Brictriceseia*, a type of which only three other examples are known, the latest in 1212. In 1096 the form is *Brihtlingeseya*, and from this are derived all other forms, both medieval and modern. What follows will be better understood if we reproduce here the etymology to which Dickin took exception: 'The two earliest forms seem to stand for OE *Brictrices-eg* and *Brihtlinges-eg* respectively. If so, we must believe that the settlement was first named after one *Beorhtric* and then one *Brihtling* (perhaps a descendant of his), or that *Brihtling* was a pet-form for *Brihtric*. An alternative possibility is that the DB form represents the Anglo-Norman scribe's attempt to render a difficult *Brihtlingeseg* or that *Brihtlingeseg* is a later perversion of original *Brihtriceseg*. Confusion of *l* and *r* is specially common in early ME.' [1]

On this Dickin comments: 'The derivation presents no difficulty to some writers. To them the Domesday form Brictriceseia represents an OE *Brictrich* (sic), a man's name, and *eg*, an island, Brictric's island. The name followed the rule in which '*r...r*' became '*l...r*'. Thus arose the form 'Bricklesey'. The '*ing*' got in at a later date, because it was a usual part of place-names. Thus it is that Domesday *Torinduna* and *Widermondefort* became Thorington and Wormingford. It is not quite so simple.'

This is misleading. The etymology criticised points out a distinct difficulty and suggests two possible explanations. Dickin then proceeds to flog a phantom horse. Nothing has been said of a 'rule in

[1] P. H. Reaney, *Place-names of Essex* (1935), 331.

which *r...r* becomes *l...r*', the form *Bricklesey* has not been discussed, no mention has been made of Thorington or Wormingford, whilst the statement about *ing* is simply ridiculous. Apart from mere inaccuracy, there is conclusive proof of a complete lack of understanding of the problems involved. Place-names do not develop according to preconceived rules. Grammatical rules simply state facts observed. Syllables like *ing* don't 'get in' to names. If it is not there at the beginning, it is the result of a change of pronunciation, a change which is gradual and not deliberate and has been in use long before it comes to be written. Other inaccuracies may be noted, inaccuracies of detail, but of essential detail, points so fundamental that the expert takes them into account without comment, the very matter of place-name study, where inaccuracy can falsify a derivation. 'This is the OE genitive *-gas*, later *-ges*.' The reference is to forms like *Brightlingeseye*. *-as* is the OE nominative plural, *-es* the genitive singular. The *g* is not part of the ending.

Dickin sums up possible explanations:

'1. The Domesday form means Brictric's Island. This became *Brictlicesea*, then *Bricklesey*. The -ing- of Brightlingsea was introduced as a matter of fashion.

'2. The first syllable was one of the OE forerunners of "Bright" *Bric, Brich, Brid, Bright*,[1] and *Beorht* (Searle, 114). All of which forms except the last, appear in the name at times.[2]

'3. The -ling- had the meaning of (*a*) the people connected with the tribe of *Bright*. (*b*) A colony of *Brights* separated from the main tribe of *Bright* (*Essays and Studies*, V, 81).

'The last two paragraphs contain the more likely explanation.'

His results are vague and inconclusive. The pronunciation *Bricklesey* is more likely to arise from *Brightlingeseye* than from the rare *Brictriceseia*, not found after 1212. The only possible connexion *Beorht* can have with the name is that it is the simple name from which *Beorhtric* and *Beorhtling* are derived. 'The tribe of Bright' is misleading; *-ling* is another error due to wrong division of syllables. *Beorhtingas* would mean 'sons, descendants, or people of *Beorht*' and cannot be the origin of Brightlingsea. *Beorhtlingas* would mean

---

[1] *Brich* and *Bright* are impossible OE spellings and *Brid* must be a different name.

[2] This impossible etymology 'Brich's island' is repeated in *The Essex Countryside* vol. 7 .No. 28 (1958), pp. 60, 61.

9

'people of *Beorhtel*'. If this were the source, the name would be *Beorhtlinga-eg* 'island of the Beorhtlingas' and would become a modern *Brightlingey*. The personal-name must be singular, either *Beorhtlinges-eg* 'island of Beorhtling' or *Beorhtrices-eg* 'island of Beorhtric', which leaves us where we began.

Walthamstow

For many years a schoolmaster of my acquaintance began his local history course with a derivation: Walthamstow, *wald, ham, stow* 'the stockaded town in the forest', an etymology which would have been unexceptionable if only the name had contained the three elements given and if these had had the meaning attached to them. *Wald* means 'forest', *ham* 'homestead, village, and *stow* 'place'. The place-name consists of two, not three elements; it began life as *Wilcumestou* and was nearly 400 years old before it reached the form *Walthamstow*. The non-expert finds it difficult to believe that we are dealing with only one name which by the cumulative effect of a series of gradual changes of pronunciation ultimately became *Waltamstow*, which was regarded as a spelling error and was assimilated in form to the better-known and not-far-distant Waltham Abbey.

In 1921 and 1922 the present writer dealt with the history of this name in lectures to the Walthamstow Antiquarian Society and not altogether successfully, for in 1929 G. F. Bosworth, the local historian who had presided over those lectures, discussed the name in print.[1] He warns his readers against dogmatism in dealing with the etymology of place-names, 'especially with that of the first name of our town—Wilcumestou'. He clearly believes there was a change of name and is not content to accept my etymology. He appeals to C. T. Martin of the Public Record Office and author of *The Record Interpreter*, who gives an impossible derivation from Latin *welcomare* 'to welcome'. He continues 'Mr. Reaney, an authority on Essex Place-names, writes Wilcumestou—welcome-place. This is so simple that one would like to feel that it is historically correct. If the word *welcome* is the secret enshrined in our place-name, the following note by Professor Ernest Weekley will be apposite. He writes, "the A.S. form of welcome was *wilcuma*, one coming according to "will", i.e. an acceptable gift."

'But there is another conjecture as to the origin of Wilcumestou, and this leads us to the opinion expressed by some that the name of

---

[1] *Chapters in the History of Walthamstow* (1929).

the Abbess Wilcuma is therein commemorated.' To this we will return later; for the moment we will accompany Bosworth. He refers vaguely to 'some other alleged origins of this word', cites J. H. Round, who 'in the end had regretfully to admit, "I do not know the origin of Wilcumestou",' and 'there, for the present, we will leave this tantalizing question, and hope that a solution one day will be found.'

But, he continues, 'when we come to consider the origin of *Walthamstow* we are on safer ground. Wilcumestou continues to occur as Welcomestowe, Wolcomestowe and Wolkhomestowe through the two or three centuries following the Conquest. Then the new name comes into use in the Fourteenth Century, and Dr Round remarks, "It is obvious that the modern Walthamstow is a corruption due to the near neighbourhood of the great parish of Waltham", and he thinks that "this is a striking illustration of the strong tendency to the corruption of the true form to a neighbouring but distinct name". Professor Blackie writes that Walthamstow = the dwelling-place near the wood. Other names occur, as Weald, and Saffron Walden in England; Walstadt, Waldheim, Waldorf, Waldan, Unterwalden, and Waldsassen in Germany. Anyhow, Walthamstow is a good old English name, and its meaning, unlike that of its predecessor, is not disputed.'

In an attempt to clear up these uncertainties, in 1930 I accepted an invitation to devote a whole lecture to this one name and in the same year published a full collection of forms and discussed at great length their spelling, pronunciation and development, and their meaning,[1] a treatment reproduced in more concise form in *The Place-names of Essex* (1935). To summarise briefly: The Domesday *Wilcumestou* is a compound of *wilcume* and *stow*. The first element is either a descriptive term, OE *wilcuma* ' a welcome person or thing', an element rare in place-names, or a woman's name, *Wilcume*, recorded twice as the name of an abbess, 'Wilcume's place'. In place-names, *-stow* when compounded with a personal name usually has some religious signification, the personal name often being that of the saint to whom the church is dedicated, as in Michaelstow (Ess) and Bridstow (He), from St Bride or St Bridget, in 1138 Latinised as *Ecclesia Sancte Brigide virginis*. Peterstow (He), dedicated to St Peter, occurs c1150 in the Welsh form *Lann petyr*. No saint named Wilcume is known. Round has suggested that Walthamstow was a

---

[1] *The Place-names of Walthamstow* (1930).

daughter church of Waltham Abbey, and some support is given to this theory by the statement of John of Salisbury that Waltham Abbey claimed tithes in Walthamstow and by the fact that part of the manor of Higham Bensted in Walthamstow was held of Waltham Abbey. 'If therefore, there were a close connexion between Waltham and Walthamstow, we have something of the religious meaning often associated with -*stow*. The church on the hill would be a welcome resting-place on the way to Waltham Abbey. Whilst, therefore, we cannot state categorically either that this was "Wilcume's place" or "the welcome place", the probabilities, in view of the cumulative evidence above, are distinctly in favour of "welcome place".' Ekwall (1936) says simply 'Wilcume's *stow* or holy place'. My own hesitation to adopt this was due to the fact that only two examples of the personal-name are known, from Durham and Paris. I have recently discovered that William Thorne, the Canterbury chronicler, gives some particulars of Wilcume, abbess of Chelles, near Paris. According to him, she did her utmost to induce Mildred, daughter of Eormenburg, a Kentish princess, one of her nuns, to break her vow of chastity and to marry. So harshly and cruelly did she treat the future saint and abbess of Minster—she even baked her in an oven from which she came out alive—that Mildred persuaded her mother to allow her to leave the monastery and to return to England. Wilcume was certainly no saint.

'With regard to the development of the name *Walthamstow*, it is important to remember that we have to deal with *one* name, not with two. *Walthamstow* is the direct descendant of the Domesday *Wilcumestou*. There was no violent or sudden change of name, but a normal phonetic development, very similar to that of the common word *welcome*, which was at a later stage influenced by popular etymology.' Up to the middle of the fifteenth century the name was spelled *Wilcume-*, *Welcume-* or *Wolcumestowe*, with slight variations, such as *k* instead of *c*, which did not affect the pronunciation, and *t* for *c*, which is rare and is probably due to an error on the part of the scribe or transcriber, as these letters were very similar and are often confused. Towards the end of the fourteenth century we find forms beginning with *Walcam-*, *Walcume-*, *Walcom-*, and these *a*-forms find no parallels in the development of *welcome*. They may be due to the unrounding of *o* in *Wolcume-* or to the analogy of words with normal variation of *welc-*, *wolc-* and *walc-*. The variation between *um*, *om* and *am* in *Welcumstow*, *Welcomstow*, *Walcamstow* is

12

due to lack of stress. There is very little evidence of the medial *-ham-* before the sixteenth century. In the 1263 *Welchamstowe* the *ch* is probably a common Norman spelling for the sound of *k*. *Waltham-stow* is so printed in 1312, where it is an error of transcription for *Wlfhamston* (Woolston Hall in Chigwell), and in 1315, now shown to be a similar error for *Wolcomesteuwe*. The only certain examples of the medial *-ham-* before the sixteenth century are *Wolkhamstouwe* in 1309 and four examples of *Welk(e)ham(p)stowe* between 1337 and 1397, where any association with Waltham is impossible owing to the form of the first syllable, and in the 1446 *Walthamstowe*, at present an isolated form 80 years earlier than the next example of this spelling.

To the end of the fifteenth century, then, the first element has developed without any certain influence from the name *Waltham*. From the sixteenth century the modern spelling begins to creep in and to become more and more common. In local documents it occurs 86 times between 1526 and 1588. But side by side with this we still find 158 forms in *Walc-* and *Walk-* in the same documents and for the same period. There is great variety in the spelling, even in the same document, and, in general, in the sixteenth century the local spelling seems to have been *Walc-*, *Walkhamstowe*, whilst *Waltham-stow* was more common in official documents written by non-local people. It is at least curious that the spelling *Walthamstow* only became common in the reign of Henry VIII, just before the time of the suppression of the monasteries, at the very end of the long history of Waltham Abbey. Why at this late period should the name of the Abbey affect the name of Walthamstow? The correct explanation probably is that we are concerned with a further phonetic change and not with a variation due to popular etymology. A change of *lc* to *lt* is found elsewhere in Essex: Walter Hall in Boreham, *Walcfara* in 1086 'passage (ford) used by Britons', and in Pilt Down (Sx), *Pylkedoune* 1455, *Peltdowne* 1582 'Pileca's hill'. Once an inorganic *h* had got into such forms as *Walkamstowe* (1445) and *Waltamstow* (1498), the medial *-ham-*, a common topographical term, tended to persist. A similar unetymological *-ham-* appears in the early forms of Alphamstone, *Alfelmestune* 1086, *Alfhampston* 1318, 'Ælfhelm's farm' and in Woolston in Chigwell, *Ulfelmestuna* 1086, *Wolfhamston* 1296, 'Wulfhelm's farm'. 'The influence of Waltham on the name of Walthamstow was probably limited to crystallising and preserving the modern spelling once it had been reached.'

13

In spite of this evidence, Bosworth, in his *History of the Parish Church of Walthamstow* (1938), repeats that 'the first name' *Wilcumestou* 'continued through the Domesday Book of the eleventh century, was changed to Walthamstow in the fifteenth century and so continues to the present time'. And now we are promised a book on *The Origin of Walthamstow* [1] by a prospective author who roundly declares that 'Wilcumestowe is not the original name of Walthamstow but is only a name recorded by the Domesday scribe, probably under compulsion. Moreover, this name has no connection with a "welcome place",' and, with naïve optimism, he continues: 'It will probably be agreed, when the evidence is produced, that the village of Walthamstow is actually the "home of the dead".'

POPULAR ETYMOLOGIES

This urge to explain place-names is no modern growth. We find it in the Bible and in Virgil, and, in England, as early as the eighth century in Bede. Rendlesham in Suffolk, once the site of a palace of Redwald, king of East Anglia, he explains as *mansio Rendili* 'the home of Rendil', a personal-name otherwise unknown, but clearly a diminutive of some compound of the stem *rand* 'shield'. This stem, originally common to the whole Germanic world, must have become obsolete in England within a few generations of the settlement. It survived among the Franks, passed from them to the Normans, and was brought to England by them at the time of the Norman Conquest in the compound Randulf. Bede's reference to the name proves the high antiquity not only of such compounds but also of Rendlesham itself.

Ely, he says, owed its name to its resemblance to an island, surrounded as it was on all sides by marshes and streams in which innumerable eels were caught, an etymology supported by the form *Elige* in the Anglo-Saxon Chronicle (c900), in a manuscript of Bede of c1000, and regularly thereafter. But two eighth-century manuscripts of Bede record the name as *Elge* and *Elgae* and describe the place as a *regio* 'province'. Hence the real meaning is 'eel-district'. The meaning of the archaic OE *gē* 'province, district' had already been forgotten. The correct form occasionally survived but from the tenth century the original *ēl-gē* 'eel-district' had been changed to *ēl-īg* 'eel-island' to fit the popular etymology, frequently repeated,

[1] *The Essex Countryside*, Vol. 6, No. 24 (1958), p. 157.

occasionally with more fanciful alternatives. The Ely chronicler improves on Bede by explaining the name as 'the house of God', from two Hebrew words—*el* 'God' and *ge* 'land'—'the land of God', 'a name', he says, 'suited to the island'.

The author of a life of St Oswald tells us that the island of Ramsey n Huntingdonshire is fittingly so called from the Latin *ramis* 'branches' and the English *īg* 'island', 'for the island is as it were hedged around by great trees', an etymology aptly described by Mawer as 'a monstrous hybrid',[1] exceeded only by that of Prior Fossour for Findon Hill near Durham. He states that after the Battle of Neville's Cross the pursuit of the Scots continued as far as Findon, which may have been prophetically so called as there the *fin* had been finally *doune* to the wars between the English and the Scots.[2]

Tradition explained Barnwell All Saints (Nth) as 'children's springs' because 'about the town are seven or eight wells, from which, and the custom of dipping *Bernes* or children in them, the town is supposed to be named'. In the middle of the site of Barnwell Priory, Cambridge, were several springs of fresh, pure water from which the place was said to be named 'the children's springs' because, according to the chronicler of the priory, each year, on the eve of the Nativity of St John the Baptist, boys held sports there and sang and played musical instruments. Some local tradition probably lies behind each of these stories but the reference cannot be to children. OE *bearn* would give a ME *Barnwell*, whereas the normal form for each name is *Bernewell*, both also occurring as *Beornewelle*, probably 'warriors' springs', though *beorn* is used only in poetic texts in OE.

At an inquisition held in 1340 to decide whether the port of Orwell belonged to Harwich or to Ipswich, the jurors declared that the port took its name from a well called *Erewell* in Rattlesden, 15 leagues from Ipswich, which formed a running river through the midst of that town, which was first appointed the capital of Suffolk because of the port by a pagan king 'Ypus', who called the town *Ypeswich*. Nothing more is known of this king and no such name is on record. The earliest form of Ipswich is *Gipeswic* (993), later *Ipeswich*, for which two explanations have been offered: 'the village of Gipe', a personal-name, for which no evidence is known, or 'the village on the *Gip*', an early name for the estuary of the Orwell, from an

---

[1] The first element is OE *hramsa*, 'wild garlic'.
[2] *Fin* is from OE *fīn* 'heap (of wood)'.

unrecorded OE *gip*, from the root of *gipian* 'to yawn', meaning 'gap, opening'. It may well be that behind this statement of the jurors lay some folk-memory of a long-forgotten king of East Anglia. Some of these early popular etymologies may be demonstrably false but others may contain an element of truth, and each must be judged independently on the basis of all the evidence available.

Chapter Two

METHODS OF PLACE-NAME STUDY

GENERAL PRINCIPLES

THE essential principles upon which all place-name study must be based were laid down over 50 years ago by Skeat. The student must first make as wide a collection as possible of the early forms of each name and then deal with the special problems before him in the light of a thorough knowledge of the history of English sounds from the earliest times to the present day. But his assertion that the phonetic laws governing the history of place-names were precisely the same as those governing the history of other words needs some modification. The etymologist deals with words which have retained a definite meaning throughout their life. They may, and do, change in spelling and in pronunciation, but the speed and the extent of these changes are checked by the need for mutual understanding. Writer and reader, speaker and hearer must interpret the words and meaning in the same way. The place-name student, on the other hand, is dealing with names which in the wear and tear of everyday speech have lost the meaning which they originally had and have become mere unintelligible names, subject for still further centuries to the inevitable processes of phonetic change, unchecked by the need to preserve the meaning, changes often increased by deliberate attempts to give the name some semblance of sense.

We have already seen that within 300 years of the Saxon Conquest the origin of a name could be forgotten and the spelling changed to suit a new interpretation. Most of our parish-names—and many others—are first recorded in Domesday Book. They were given some time between 450 and 1086, and many had already undergone considerable change during these six centuries: *Peginga burnan* 843, *Pangeborne* 1086 (Pangbourne, Berks), 'stream of Pæga's people'; *Ecelesford* 969, *Exeforde* 1086 (Ashford, Mx), either 'Eccel's ford' or 'ford through the *Eccles*', perhaps an old name for the Ash river. Many were to undergo still further changes in the next eight centuries: *Tingdene* 1086, *Tindena* 1167, *Thingdene* 1200, *Thingdon* alias *Fyndon* 1606 (Finedon, Nth), 'valley where the "thing" (the assembly or council) met'; *Witingham* 1086, *Hwithingham* 1175, *Whyttynham* alias *Whycham* 1573 (Whicham, Cu), 'homestead of Hwīta's people'; *Sabrixteworde* 1086, *Sabrihteswrde* 1118, *Sabrichewurth* 1248, *Sabrigeworth* 1338, *Sabrysford* alias *Sabrysworth* 1475, *Sabbisford* 1489, *Sapsworth* 1565, *Sapsforth* alias *Sabridgeworth* 1607, *Sabridgeworth* alias *Sawbridgeworth* 1770 (Sawbridgeworth, Herts), 'farm of Sæbeorht or Sæbriht'.

It is with such material that the place-name student has to deal. He is concerned to find the original meaning, and for this the earlier the forms, the better. The actual development of the name may not be revealed by the chronological order of the forms. A scribe may copy the spelling of a much earlier document. He may make mistakes. A sound etymology must take account of all the variant spellings, eccentric or not, and interpret them in the light of the known history of the pronunciation and development of the language, and this includes a knowledge of inflexions and grammatical forms, a subject to which we shall return later.

Since Skeat laid down these essential principles, all reputable scholars have followed them and, in course of time, others have been added. Wyld and his pupils rigidly adhered to these principles and extended them to include a study of the development of the pronunciation of place-names from the earliest times to the present-day form. But he took up an impossible position when he asserted that the problem was purely linguistic and that the work was 'not concerned with the question whether the names fit the places to which they are attached, nor whether they ever did so'.

The historian bristled when Roberts explained Hamsey (Sx) as 'OE *hammes ea*, stream bordering the enclosures, or *hammes eg* island or marshy land in the bend of a river', on the basis of a 1321 form *Hammes Say*, when we learn from the document itself that the manor was then held by Geoffrey de Say.[1] And when the same writer, to explain Rackham (Sx), postulated a personal-name *Raca*, a short form of a personal-name *Raculf*, inferred from *Raculf* and *Raculfcestre*, the OE forms of Reculver (K),[2] the archaeologist and the expert on Roman Britain smiled derisively, for they knew that *Raculf* was no personal-name but an anglicising of the Romano-Celtic place-name *Regulbium*. Mawer notes that Linshields (earlier *Lyndesele*) on the Coquet in Northumberland may, from the phonological point of view, be either 'lime-tree shiels' or 'shiels by the lynn or pool' (with epenthetic *d*) and, since there is a lynn there and no lime-tree could possibly stand the climate, the choice is obvious. Wyld explains the first element of Cockersand and Cockerham in Lancashire as the genitive of a hypothetical Norse name *Kókr*, but there can be little doubt that the real meaning is 'sands and homestead by the Cocker'. Both places are on a River Cocker, a river-name found also in Cumberland and in Cocker Beck in Durham from which are named Cockermouth and Cockerton respectively.

IMPORTANCE OF GEOGRAPHY

No place-name student would deny the importance of testing his etymologies on the ground, and if the interpretation proposed does not fit the topography, an explanation must be found or the etymology must be rejected. Rivers may have changed their course, forests may have been cleared and marshes drained, the sea may have receded or encroached on the land. The Yare once flowed straight out to sea in a wide estuary of which Breydon Water is now an inland relic. In this estuary a sand-bank was formed, increased in size, and is now occupied by the town of Great Yarmouth. The river turned south and flowed into the sea at Gorleston—the present outflow, with its right-angled bend, is artificial—and in course of time the whole parish of Newton, on the seaward-side of Gorleston, was engulfed.[3] Since the Anglo-Saxon settlement the whole coast of Suffolk

[1] R. G. Roberts, *Place-names of Sussex* (Cambridge, 1914), p. 78; A. Mawer, *English Place-name Study* (Oxford, 1921), p. 8.

[2] Roberts, *op. cit.*, p. 262.

A village named *Reston* in Gorleston has also disappeared.

has suffered a series of changes. Ports have disappeared. The ancient town of Dunwich, once the seat of a bishopric, is now beneath the sea.

Around the Wash the sea has receded, in places as much as ten miles. Wisbech was once a port on the coast-line of Cambridgeshire. It is now known that the Fens were not always the inhospitable waste of uninhabited swamp they were once thought to be. Aerial photography and excavation have revealed the existence in Romano-British times of many sites of native villages and groups of associated Celtic fields, particularly in the silt areas and certain islands. Towards the end of the third century, conditions seem to have deteriorated, possibly through a slight subsidence in the whole fen basin or through a breach in the natural silt defences the sea had built against itself round the southern shores of the Wash. By the fifth century, it seems clear, the general abandonment of the district was inevitable. Rivers did not flow on their present courses and for centuries they meandered, silted up and forced new channels. Many of these decayed rivers can still be traced on the ground in the form of silt ridges, once the bed of the river, now raised above the level of the old banks of peat which has dried and shrunk. They have, at times, been mistaken for Roman roads.

A knowledge of such changes is essential if we are to understand the conditions under which the Anglo-Saxon settlement was made. The facts are not always easy to find and the chronology of the changes is difficult to establish. Occasionally place-names can throw some light on the problem. An Anglo-Saxon charter mentions a river flowing from Peterborough to Elm and Wisbech which can safely be identified as the Nene. It flowed past Throckenholt and so must have followed the course of the stream now variously known as Muscat, Cat's Water, Shire Drain and Old South Eau, forming for some distance the boundary between Cambridgeshire and Lincolnshire. The 'fair stream called *Bradanea*' (the broad river) of the same charter clearly refers to the earlier course of the Ouse, now called on the Ordnance map 'Old Course of the Nene', on which lie Bradney House in Benwick and Bradney Farm in March.

The former coast-line of Cambridgeshire is marked by a huge earthen embankment now known as the Roman Bank. There is no evidence of Roman work and its attribution to the Romans is due to seventeenth-century antiquarian speculation. It is first called *the old Roman Bank* in 1696. Earlier it was called *le Seediche* or *Seadike* from 1221 to 1570, *the ould and auncyent Seabancke* in 1617, *the great Sea banke of Ouse* in 1657 and *The Old Country Banck against the sea* in 1706. It was clearly built as a protection against the sea and its course can still be traced on the map through Long Sutton and Tydd St Mary (L), where we have 'Roman Villa', into Cambridgeshire through Tydd St Giles, past Tydd Gote and the Four Gotes, through Newton, where there was a 'Chapel of the Sea' (a name preserved in Chapel Grove), a lost *Segate* and *Semylle* and also Bank Barn, through Leverington (with Roman House, Sea Field and Horseshoe Lane, named from a bend in the Roman Bank, shaped like a horse-shoe), to Wisbech St Peter, where part is known as Mount Pleasant Bank. Passing round the inside of Crabb Marsh (on the seaward side of the Bank, named from the crab-grass or glasswort, a medicinal plant common in saltmarshes) and Turnpike Marsh, it turns north into Norfolk through Walsoken, West Walton (*Old Roman Bank* 1829), Walpole St Peter and St Andrew, Terrington St Clement and Clenchwarton (*fossa maris de Klenchworton* c1210). Here it must once have been called *weall* 'wall', from which Walton and Walpole are named, and must have been in existence before the earliest mention of Walpole c1050.

NEW MATERIAL DEMANDS REVISION OF EARLIER ETYMOLOGIES

The establishment of the pedigree of a place-name does not necessarily solve the problems. Some names are easy to interpret, some difficult, others, at present, are complete mysteries. New material may turn up from some unexpected source, necessitating a revision of previously accepted views. The student must be prepared to learn from his own mistakes and to profit from the work of others. Time and again a satisfactory solution of a problem has been reached by the combined application of a number of scholars. In 1923 Ekwall derived Epping (Ess) from a personal-name *Eoppa*, a derivation accepted by Stenton, who in 1924 explained the personal-name as a shortened form of *Eorpwine*. When, in 1935, the full forms for the place-name were assembled, there was, curiously enough, a solitary *Erpinges* (1231), but the common form was *Eppinges* (from 1086), with an isolated *Upping* (1227) and a late *Iphing* (1436). Whilst an original *Eorpingas* could have become *Eppinges*, it could not develop into *Upping*. In Essex, OE *y*, an *i*-mutated form of *u*, usually became *e*, occasionally *i* or *u*. Consequently, an original *Yppingas would explain the variation between *Eppinges, Upping* and *Iphing*. This would mean 'the upland dwellers' and is clearly correct. The original settlement was high up near Epping Upland Church and not on the site of the modern Epping Town which has grown up there since the sixteenth century on the new road made by a bequest of John Baker in 1519. In 1936 Ekwall adopted this etymology.

Theydon (Ess) is usually found as *Teidana* (1086) or *Theydene* (1236), with occasional forms *Taindena* (1086) and *Theyndon* (1205). In a thirteenth-century copy of an Anglo-Saxon charter of 1062 the name occurs as *þecdene*. In 1935 this was rejected as an error and inconsistent with the later development. The name was regarded as identical with a lost *þegna dene* 'thanes' valley' in Twyford (Wo) and compared with Thenford (Nth) 'ford of the thanes'. In 1936 Ekwall preferred Thorpe's reading *þetdene* to Kemble's *þecdene* and explained the name as 'apparently OE *þēot-denu*, identical with Thedden, Hants', from OE *þēot* 'water-pipe', perhaps also 'stream', and adds that the sound-development offers difficulties. In 1939, Mawer discovered that Braydon Hook (W), *Brayden* 1257, is found as *bræcdene* in a thirteenth-century copy of a charter of 968. This is clearly from OE *bræc* and *denu* 'valley in which there is land broken up for cultivation' and the development suggested an immediate parallel with Theydon. A new examination of the Essex charter showed that, though *c* and *t* are hard to distinguish in this handwriting, the probabilities are all in favour of Kemble's *þecdene*, so that the name must be derived from OE *þæc* and interpreted as 'valley where thatch (material) grows' and the occasional forms in *Tain-, Theyn-* regarded as eccentric.

Scholars have long differed about the origin of the names Ludgershall (Bk, W), Luggershall (Gl) and Lurgashall (Sx). All are clearly identical in origin, the earliest example being a genuine OE form (*æt*) *Lutegaresheale* in a document of 1015 of which there are two contemporary texts. Early forms are *Lutegareshale*, with variant *Lote-*; forms with *d, Ludegarshal, Lodegareshale*, are clearly a late development. It was at first suggested that the names derived from OE *lȳtel-gærshealh* 'little grass nook' or *hlyte-gærshealh* 'grass-land in a *healh* assigned by lot'. Mawer pointed out that the almost invariable *u* (with occasional *o*) in the ME forms was inconsistent with the development of OE *y* in the counties concerned, that no other example of *gærshealh* has been found, that the usual form is *-gares-*, not *-gers-* or *-gars-*, and that it is at least curious that this compound, if it ever existed, should always be compounded with *lȳtel* or *hlyte*. In 1939 he repeated the suggestion he had first made in 1925 that these names mean 'Lutegar's nook of land' and derive from an otherwise unknown personal-name. He cites as a parallel an eleventh-century *Lutsige* and postulates an OE **Luthere*, found in Lotherton (WRY) and Lutterworth (Lei). But that a personal-name *Lutgar* should regularly occur as *Lutegar* is open to the same objection as the derivation of *-gares-* from *gærs*, and that this personal-name should be compounded only with *healh* in such widely separated counties is at least as suspicious as that *gærshealh* should always be compounded with *lȳtel* or *hlyte*. It is doubtful, too, whether an OE *Luthere* ever existed. Ekwall derives both Lotherton and Lutterworth from a river-name *Hlūtre*, from OE *hlūttor* 'clean, pure'. In 1940 Tengstrand re-examined all the evidence and made an entirely new suggestion which seems to solve the problem. He takes *gar* in the compound to have its ordinary sense 'spear' and the first element as an OE **lūt(e)*, related to OE *lūtian* 'to lie hid, to be concealed', which may well have meant 'hiding-place, ambush, trap'. **Lūtegār* would thus mean ' trap-spear', a spear set as a trap for wild animals, an impaling trap. The custom of killing animals by means of a spear or arrow which shoots itself off when the animal passes is known from various parts of the world. In England it may have been customary to set the trap in a hollow in a hill-side, in a remote, narrow valley or in a cave, all possible meanings of *healh*.

A similar problem arises in the group of names including Windsor (Berks), Broadwindsor and Little Windsor (Do) and Winsor in Yealmpton (D) and in Eling (Ha). The Berkshire name is found as *Windlesora* 1061, *Windesores* 1086, and similar forms occur for the other names. Further examples of Windsor are found in Hemyock and in Luppitt (D), in Lanreath (Co) and in Lamphey (Pembroke) and a Winsor in Lansallos (Co). These are less well documented and occur only in late forms. But the frequency of this compound of *windles* with *ora* 'bank' makes it difficult to believe that the first element is, as suggested by Mawer, a personal-name which is not on record in OE or the recorded *windel* 'basket' which is also found in a different sense in *windel-strēaw* 'a long withered grass' and *windel-trēow* 'a willow'. Nor is Mawer's suggestion that one or more of the places may have been deliberately named in imitation of the famous Berkshire Windsor at all probable. Much more likely is the suggestion of Ekwall that here we have early examples of *windlass* (found from c1400) which goes back to an OE *windels*, a derivative of OE *windan* 'to wind'. A meaning 'shore, bank or landing-place with a winch for pulling up boats' might well be repeated and would suit the topography. The Berkshire Windsor is on the Thames, the Dorset places on a stream, the Devon Winsor near the mouth of the Yealm and that in Hampshire in Eling near Southampton Water. Support for such an interpretation is forthcoming from Oxfordshire, where we find three field-names *Winchcroftes*, *Winchcomb* and *Winch Mead*. In a description of how a barge was navigated through Whitchurch Weir, we read: 'When the water was low enough a stout hawser was fixed to the barge and it was drawn up through the opening by means of a winch which stood on the left bank . . . in a field still called the "Winch Field" ' [1]

York

The ancient city of York bears a name which conceals centuries of its history. The name is first mentioned c150 A.D. by the Greek geographer Ptolemy in the form 'Εβόρακον. In 79 A.D. Agricola made it the headquarters of a Roman legion and it became the military centre from which the North was controlled. The name was Latinised as *Eburacum* and *Eboracum*. It has long been recognised as Celtic and is found in ninth-century Welsh sources as *Cair Ebrauc*, from an Old British *Eborācon*, either from a British personal-name *Eburos* or from *eburos* 'yew', from which this name is derived. By the end of the Romano-British period *b* had come to be pronounced very much like *v*. The Angles, who controlled the city in the seventh and eighth centuries, adopted the name and spelled it *Eferwic* (c897) and *Euorwic* (c1150), replacing the meaningless suffix -*ac* by the common OE *wīc* 'village, town'. The first element, too, was assimilated to their own speech-habits and associated with the common *eofor* 'boar', *Eoforwic* (1053–66), which made sense of a sort, 'boar-village'. In 865 York was captured by Scandinavians and in 876 became a Danish kingdom under Halfdan, and in the tenth century an Irish–Viking kingdom under Rægnald. Like their predecessors, these Scandinavians adopted the name, pronouncing it in their own fashion and spelling it *Iórvík* (962), which later became *Iórk*, *Ʒeork*, *Ʒork*, and finally *York* in the thirteenth century. The modern *York* is the Celtic *Eborācon*, modified in the course of centuries in the mouths

[1] R. J. Godlee, *A Village on the Thames* (London, 1926), p. 55. *v.* also L. F. Salzman, *English Trade in the Middle Ages* (Oxford, 1931), pp. 210–11.

of successive Anglian, Danish and Irish–Scandinavian invaders and masters of the city.

Cambridge and Grantchester

Cambridge and Grantchester provide problems of a different kind. Both are on the Granta, and had the names developed normally we should now talk of the University of Grantchester and Rupert Brooke would have been associated with Granset. The earliest reference to Cambridge is found in Bede, where he describes how monks from Ely found in the desolate little city of *Grantacaestir* a beautifully fashioned coffin of white marble which they took to Ely for the re-interment of St Etheldreda. This was the site of the original Roman fort on the Granta, clearly abandoned and disused in the eighth century, the site on which was later built the Norman castle, now also in ruins, the site which gave name to Chesterton 'the farm by the camp'. It was the oldest part of Cambridge. The castle was built on ground taken from the Saxon town and added to the king's manor of Chesterton. Thus the castle, although topographically in the borough, was legally outside it, in the county, in Chesterton. The name was seldom used after the Conquest, and then only by historians. Had it survived, it would have become Grantchester. The modern name first occurs c745 as *Grontabricc* and became the name of the settlement which grew up near the bridge over the Granta. Grantchester first occurs in DB as *Granteseta*, originally the name of its inhabitants 'the settlers on the banks of the Granta'. The development of the two names is best seen by placing the forms side-by-side:

Cambridge		Grantchester	
Grantanbrycge	925	Granteseta	1086
Grantebricge	1050	Gransete	1199
Cantebrigie	1086	Grancestre	1208
Crantebr'	1219	Cantesete	1218
Cauntebrig'	1230	Crantesete	1260
Caumbrigge	1348	Granseste	1272
Cambrugge	1378	Granteceste	1272
Caunbrige	1386	Granteseter	1327
		Granchester	1643

The eccentric development of both names is due to the strong Norman influence in Cambridge, with its Norman castle and a priory founded by a Norman, the chief town of the county, the centre of its

25

fiscal and legal business. The Normans appear to have had a difficulty in pronouncing names beginning with *Gr-*, which they sometimes pronounced *Cr-*; at others they simply dropped the *r*. Hence *Grantebrige* became *Crantebrige* and *Cantebrige*, a form which long survived. The difficult group of medial consonants was simplified, giving *Cantbrige*, *Canbrige* and finally *Cambridge*. With the change in the first element, the name of the river also changed. *Cantebrige* was taken to mean 'bridge over the Cante' (1340) and *Cambridge* that over the Cam (1610), a form which must have been in use earlier as members of the University had Latinised it as *Camus* forty years earlier.

In Grantchester the second element *-seta* was early confused with *-cestre*, the Anglo-Norman pronunciation of *-chester*. The consonants were simplified in various ways, giving *-seste*, *-seter*, etc. Of the 70 or so English place-names ending in *-chester*, some 16 appear in a French garb. From the twelfth century such spellings as *Glouceter*, *Leyceter*, *Worceter* are common and survive in Exeter, Wroxeter and Mancetter. Most are pronounced with only two syllables, as *Bister* for Bicester (O), and the local pronunciation is often preserved in the spelling of surnames: Worster, Wooster; Gloster; Lester, Lessiter, Laister and Lassiter. *Granseter* (1349) did not survive. The whole name was at one stage regarded as French, the *Grant-* being interpreted as OFr *grant*, *grand* 'great' and as early as 1287 translated by *Magna Cestre*. This, perhaps, accounts for the ultimate victory of *Grantchester*. Such alternatives as *Gransete immo Grandesete* (1287) reveal official uncertainty as to the real form of the name which occurs as *Graundcester* (1549) and *Grandchester* (1655), whilst *Grandesete* (1299) actually developed into *Grandcittie* (1563).

Harringay and Hornsey

For over 150 years historians and philologists have exercised their wits on the problem of Hornsey (Mx), formerly *Haringeie*. Have we a single name with divergent developments or two distinct names? Is the first element descriptive or a personal name? Is the second element meadow, wood, island or enclosure? The two standard modern authorities agree that we have only a single name. In the *Oxford Dictionary of Place-names* (1936) Ekwall writes:[1] 'The original

---

[1] *s.n.* Hornsey. He would now substitute *Hǣring* for *Hāring* and *(ge)hæg* for *ēg. v. Etymological Notes on English Place-names* (Lund, 1959), pp. 69–71.

name may have been OE *Hāring-ēg*, the second element being OE *ēg* "island, land on a river". The first might be the name of a wood, derived from *hār* "grey" and meaning "grey wood".' The editors of the *Place-names of Middlesex* (1942) explain the name as 'the woodland enclosure (OE (*ge*)*hæg*) of a man named Hæring' or, possibly, *Hæringa*(*ge*)*hæg* 'enclosure of Hær's people', with occasional development of an inorganic medial -*es*-.

In his *Origin of the Name of Hornsey* (1936), based on a collection of over 2,000 forms, S. J. Madge, after a full discussion of the whole problem, confirmed an etymology he had first published in 1921, differing from Mawer's first suggestion only in the form of the personal name (*Hering*). As a resident of long standing in Hornsey, Hon. Sec. of the Middlesex Archaeological Society and Secretary of the British Records Society, he had a unique knowledge of the topography, records and history of the district and was able to dispose of etymologies based on corrupt, mistaken and mis-dated forms and on 'ghost-words' due to invention, confusion, wrong identification and errors of transcription. His account of the different etymologies advanced at various times and discarded with the discovery of new evidence and of the two schools of interpretation, descriptive and personal, is a fascinating excursion into the history of place-name study. He himself began as a 'descriptionist'. Skeat put forward two and Anscombe four different derivations between 1907 and 1919. Some indication of the thrust of debate and the persistent pursuit of truth may be gathered from the paragraph in which Madge summarises his account: 'Charnock, Edmunds, and Hone discussed the relative merits of "haringe", "haraney", and "horn" as derivations, and later Bardsley and Anscombe found agreement in "Horn"; but the views of Taylor and Skeat were divergent where tribal names like "Hearings" and "Herrings" were concerned. Anscombe and Skeat were in opposition, however, over *Heringa-eg, "island of the Herings", and Anscombe and myself over his theory of *Hæferinga-hege, which he subsequently modified into *Haringa-hege, "at the stronghold of the Harings". In the end Mr Anscombe was convinced that the two names, Harringay and Hornsey, were interchangeable, equal in origin and identical in meaning, and his letter to the "Journal" (19 August, 1921), when I put forward the solution of *Haringes-hege* for both names, is in itself a graceful tribute to the fine scholarship, generosity, and great personal charm of the man.'

27

In 1795 Lysons derived Harringay, then called as now Hornsey, from *Har-inge* 'the meadow of hares', an etymology which long held the field and was supported by some very late hunters of hares. 'One would scarcely look for hares in Hornsey at the present day', wrote Sherington, a historian of Hornsey in 1904, 'but some time after the formation of Finsbury Park, I remember a present of a hare being made from the island in the lake, which towards the close of the sixties was still teeming with wild-fowl. Somewhat before then—in April 1866—a fine hare one morning caused considerable amusement to the passengers waiting for the 8.45 train at Hornsey station, poor puss being chased about for a time, but ultimately getting clear off across the meadows to what was then Haringhey Park.' So impressed was he with the importance of the 'very ancient, most respectable, fascinating and peaceful sport' of hunting the hare, that he elaborated Lysons' derivation, quoting Nimrod, Cervantes and medieval monarchs and ended by declaring that 'the vicinity of the village of Hornsey was originally a place set apart for those devoted to hunting the hare'! When Hornsey became a borough in 1903, the design for the mayoral chain included a series of hares in the decorative work of the links; and in 1935, when the new Town Hall was opened, it was discovered that hares formed a prominent feature in the design over the entrance.

For 400 years, from the beginning of the thirteenth to the end of the sixteenth century, the most common form was *Haringeie*. This would suggest as the second element, OE *ēg* 'island', which does not suit the topography; the final element says Madge, 'cannot be OE *ea*, meaning "water, stream, river", or even *eg*, *ieg* "island", for the rivers, marshes, and "watery places" are not notable features, nor are islands or peninsulas characteristics of this inland parish'. The river marked on the maps, which may have led some astray, is the New River, an artificial water-course constructed by Sir Hugh Myddelton in 1609–13 to bring water from springs near Amwell (Herts) to London. The ending must be OE *(ge)hæg* 'enclosure', as in *Harengheye* (1232), which in the unstressed position often loses its *h* and appears as *-eie*, *-eye*. Less common are forms with *e*, *Heringeye* (1241–1397), *Heringheie* (1274), ignored by Ekwall, but important as the variation between *a* and *e* points to an original *æ* or *ǣ*.

In 1243 we find a form *Haringesheye* and in 1274 *Haringeseye*, forms less common than those without the medial *s*, but clearly in frequent use, as contracted forms become common from the fifteenth century: *Harnsey* (1392), *Harynsey* (1400–1524), *Harensey* (1461–1577), *Harnsey* (1464–1634). The modern form is reached in the sixteenth century, *Hornesey* (1539), and is equated with Harringay in numerous alternative forms, as *Haryngay alias Harnsey* (1520), *Hornesey alias Harynghay* (1549).

Throughout the thirteenth century *Haringeye*, with its variants, invariably refers to the modern parish of Hornsey, its manor, the church, or the park and woods there of the Bishop of London. *Hornsey* is first used of the Park (1410) and the Down (1461), of the manor in 1547, the church in 1553 and of the parish not until 1609. The name *Hornsey* developed quite regularly from *Haringeseye* to *Harynsey* and *Harnsey*, and in the sixteenth century the *a* was rounded to *o* and the name became *Hornsey*. It seems clear that this was the popular pronunciation, though older spellings long continued to be used in documents. It is first used of the park and the woods, but, as one would expect, officials were conservative and persisted in using the customary forms in referring to manor, church and parish.

Today both names Hornsey and Harringay are in use, but the latter is a resurrected name. In the manorial court-rolls there are 130 examples of the forms *Hornzey* and *Hornezey* between 1629 and 1680. *Haringeye* had become nothing but a name of legal memory until it was rescued by an eighteenth-century landowner and a nineteenth-century company of builders. After 1600 it occurs only once on the maps before 1810. About 1792 Edward Gray, a linen-draper of Cornhill, erected 'a capital messuage or mansion house called Harringay House', so named on Greenwood's map of 1819 and on the ordnance maps as *Harringhay* (1822) and *Haringey* (1864). In 1881 'Harringay House in Hornsey' was bought by the British Land Company and the estate was called 'Harringay Park'. With the Tithe Award of 1883, this 'District No. 2' in Hornsey Parish was styled 'Harringay House District' and later was divided into the double ward of 'North and South Haringey', with a third ward called 'Harringay' in Tottenham. The Town Council and its Education Committee use variant forms in writing to North and South 'Harringay' Schools in the 'Haringey' Wards.

In short, Hornsey derives from *Haringesheye*. The modern Harringay, with its variants, is a deliberate, late eighteenth-century resurrection of the old name from a variant *Haringeie*. The most probable meaning is 'woodland enclosure of Hæring', OE

29

Hǣringes(ge)hæg, with a variant *Hǣring(ge)hæg*, a non-genitival compound, for which parallels can be found.

SURVIVAL OF PREPOSITIONAL FORMATIONS

Farnborough 'fern-clad hill', Hertford 'stag-ford' and Broomfield 'open-country covered with broom', were originally nature-names from which later settlements near-by took their names. Tuddenham 'homestead, estate or village of Tudda', Edwardstone 'enclosure or farm of Ēadweard' and Hawksworth 'enclosure of Hafoc' were habitation-names. The nature-names consisted simply of a compound of two nouns, *fearn-beorg*, *heorot-ford*, *brōm-feld*, but in the habitation-names the second element is preceded by a personal name in the genitive singular, *Tuddan-hām*, *Ēadweardes-tūn*, *Hafoces-worð*, and each of these still preserves the *n* or *s* of the genitive.[1]

These are simple names. Both classes include other types, often much more difficult to explain. The simplest nature-names were nouns in the dative case preceded by a preposition. They would be used chiefly in such expressions as: (he lives) by the stream, beyond the river, above or below the wood, etc. In many modern names the preposition is preserved, in whole or in part.

OE *bī*, *bē* 'by, near': Bythorn (Hu), *Bitherne* c960 '(place) by the thorn-bush'; Byfleet (Sr), (*æt*) *Bifleote* 1062 '(place) by the fleet or stream'. Already by the eleventh century the name had become a real place-name, before which the preposition *æt* could be used, and even earlier with Bygrave (Herts), (*æt*) *Bigrafan* 973 'by the entrenchments', remains of which survive; Biddick (Du), *Bidich* c1190 'by the ditch'; Bure (Ha), *Beora* c1200, *Boure* 1316, OE *bē ōfre* '(place) by the sea-shore'; Beaute Fm (K), *Byholte* 1327, OE *bī holte* '(place) by the grove'.

OE *begeondan* 'beyond, on the other side of', is particularly common in Devon. In modern names the *be* has disappeared; Henwood, *Byundewode* 1333, *Indewood* 1650; Indicombe, *Beyendecoumbe* 1314, *Hyndecomb* 1330, *Yundecomb* 1333, 'on the other side of the coomb or deep valley'. Such names were probably given by the people of the nearest village. Indicombe is about a mile from West Buckland, on the slope of a hill above an intervening valley. Indio in Bovey Tracy, *Yondeyoe* 1544, *Indeho* 1765 '(place) beyond the

---

[1] But not always, *e.g.* Padworth (Berks), *æt Peadanwurðe* 956; Edmondthorpe (Lei), *Edmerestorp* 1086.

water' would have been named by the villagers of Bovey, as the farm is directly opposite Bovey on the other side of the river. Indicleave 'beyond the cliff'; Yendamore, *Beyundemyre* 1333 'beyond the miry place'; Yonderlake, *Byundelake* 1333 'beyond the streamlet' (OE *lacu*); Yondhill, *Yundehill* c1556 'on the other side of the hill'.

OE *betwēonan, betwēonum, betwīnum* 'between, amongst', usually compounded with *ēam*, dative plural of *ēa* 'stream': Twyning (Gl), *Bituinæum* 814 '(place) between the rivers' (Severn and Avon), identical with Twineham (Sx) and *Twinham*, the old name of Christchurch (Ha), *æt Twynham* 738, and, in Devon, Twinyeo, *Betunia* 1086, *Bitweneya* 1263; Tweenaways, *Twyneweye* 1567 'between the ways'; Tinhay, *Bituinia* 1194 'between the waters'; Twinney Creek (K), *Twineneia* 1166 'between the streams'.

OE *binnan* 'within': Benwell (Nb), *Bynnewalle* c1050 '(place) inside the wall'. It is between the Roman Wall and the Tyne. Bembridge (IOW), *Bynnebrygg* 1316, *infra pontem* 1324, is situated at the end of a peninsula about three miles long, formerly called the Isle of Bembridge. Before the construction of the present embankment in 1877–80 it could be reached only by boat or across a bridge at Brading. Hence 'the land (lying) inside, on the other side of the bridge'. Bindon Abbey (Do), *Binnedon'* 1204, *Binenedon'* 1209, 'surrounded by downs', an apt description of Little Bindon, the original site of the monastery.

OE *bufan* 'above, over': Bowcombe (IOW), *Bovecome* 1086, *Bowcombe* 1299 '(place) above the valley' on Bowcombe Down, where there were tumuli and an Anglo-Saxon cemetery, and where the hundred-moots were probably held; Bowood (Do), *Bovewode* 1086 'above the wood'; Burton End (C), (field called) *Bouetoun* 1232, 1340, *Burton End* 1825 'above the *tūn* or hamlet'. It lies farther up the hill than West Wickham.

OE *under* 'under, beneath, below': Underhill (K), *Vnderhelde* 1332 'below the slope' (OE *helde*); Underly (He), *Hunderlithe* 1242 'at the foot of the slope' (OE *hliþ*). Underriver (K) lies below River Hill (OE *yfre*) and Underskiddaw (Cu) is at the foot of Skiddaw.

OE *uppan* 'higher up, upon': Upnor (K), *Upnore* 1374 'upon, above the bank' of the Medway (OE *ōra*)'

Northway and Southway in Widdecombe (D) were *Bynorthewey* (1330), and *Bysoutheweye* (1333). They are not on different roads, but lie respectively to the north and the south of the road over the moor. So, too, Norway and Southway in Whitestone are north and south of the main road which passes between the two farms. Thus, some names (at least) like Eastwood and Westwood are probably to be interpreted not as the east or the west wood, but as shortened forms of old compounds, *bī ēastan* (*westan*) *wuda* 'to the east (west) of the wood'. Eastchurch in Crediton has no church, but Walter *Byeste-church*, who was living there in 1330, was so called because he lived just to the east of Hittisleigh church in the next parish. Westwood Court in Preston (K) is *Beuuestanuudan* in a charter of 805. In some names the preposition is preserved: Bestwall (Do), *Beastewelle* 1086, *Biestewalle* 1293, lies just outside the east wall of Wareham. The Beesons (C), *Estounesende* 1302, *Beestoun* 1348, was *bī ēastan tūne* 'to the east of the hamlet' as opposed to a lost *Westounesende de Sutton* (1324).

Similarly elliptic are names such as Eastington (D, Do, Gl, Wa), Ashington (So), *Estinton* 1186, *Astynton* 1291, Norrington (Herts, W, Wo), Southington (Ha), Siddington (Gl) and Sodington and Leigh Sinton (Wo). These were originally *ēast, norð* or *sūð in tūne* '(place) east, north or south in the village', forms which may also have become Easton, Norton or Sutton. At quite an early stage they were regarded as real place-names from which surnames could develop: John *de Sothynton, de Sutingthun* 1296 (Sx). Sindon's Mill in Suckley (Wo) was a place 'south in the village' as opposed to another to the north, now Norton Farm.

Haulgh, Hallow, Hale, Heale, Hallam

Many nature-names consist simply of a noun which may be used in the singular or the plural, in the nominative or the dative. Very common is OE *halh* 'nook or corner of land', with a dative singular *hale*, nominative plural *halas*, dative plural *halum*. The corresponding West Saxon forms were *healh, heale, healas, healum*. In place-names the word developed a number of special meanings (i) 'a secluded hollow in a hill-side', as at Birdsall (ERY), or 'a small steep valley on the side of a larger one', as at Halton (WRY), or, most commonly, 'a remote narrow valley'; (ii) 'a nook of land in the corner of a parish', as at Hale in Hendon (Mx), North Hills in Horningsea (C), *Northalefeld* 1313, and Rableyheath in Codicote (Herts), *Wrobbeleye-hale* 1263; (iii) 'a piece of land almost enclosed by the bend of a river', as at Heale House in Woodford (W), in a well-marked bend of the Avon, Hensall and Roall (WRY), or 'a tongue of land between two streams' as at Hallow (Wo); (iv) 'a piece of flat, low-lying land by a river, a haugh', as at Edenhall (Cu), Hallows (La), Haughton (L), a sense very common in the north. The nominative singular survives as Haugh, Haulgh (La), Hollow Wood in Harringworth (Nth), *wood of Halgh* 1306, and in Haughton (Ch, La, Nb, Sa, St), Haughton le Skerne (Du), Hallaton (Lei), Halloughton (Nt, Wa), Halton (La, L, Sa, WRY), Little Houghton in Eccles (La), Westhoughton and Haighton (La); the dative singular is frequent as Hale and as Hail(e) (Cu, ERY), whilst the West Saxon *æt heale* is very common in Devon as Heal, Heale and Hele and is found occasionally in Somerset and Wiltshire. The nominative plural survives in Hales (Nf, Sa, St, Wo), and the dative plural in Halam (Nt), Hallam (Db) and Hawne (Wo). As a second element it has various forms and often appears as *-hall*, *-all*, and occasionally as *-hill*, *-ell*, as in the Lancashire Halsall, Red-vales, *Rediveshale* 1185, Rivenhall (Ess), Lattersey (C), *Latereshale* 1285, Pookhill (Sx), *Poukehale* 1350 'goblin nook', Bibbill Farm (ERY), *Bibbehale* 13th, Ellel (La), *Ellhale* 1086. Northolt (Mx) is *æt norð healum* (960) 'at the north angles of land', as opposed to Southall, *Sudhale* (1204). Nipnose, surviving as the name of a field by the Thames in Thorpe (Sr) is a salutary warning against speculation on the meaning of late forms of field-names. Had we, as so often, nothing but the modern spelling and the 1701 *Knipp Knowles*, only an inspired genius could have guessed that the *nose* concealed a second element *-hale*. The name occurs in a thirteenth-century copy of a charter of 675 as *Nippenhale*, was *Nypnall* in 1525 and *Nypnowle* in 1579, probably '*halh* of Nippa', a short form of OE **Niðbeorht*.

OE burh, beorg, bearu

The various case-forms of OE *burh*, whether used alone or as a first or final element, have produced a variety of modern spellings in place-names. The primary meaning is 'fortification' and it is used of pre-English earthworks, Roman camps, Anglo-Saxon forts, and later of a fortified house, manor or town. The nominative is found as Burgh, variantly pronounced *Borough* or *Bruff*, Burrough, Burrow (La, Lei), and Brough, and in such names as Burbage (Db, Lei, W), Burford (Sa), Burham or Burgham (Sr), Burghill (He), Burham (K), Burwash (Sx) and Burwell (C, L), whilst the dative singular became Bury (Hu, La, Sf), Berry Pomeroy and Berrynarbor (D). The genitive singular had two forms: (i) *burge* in Burghley (Nth), *Burgelai* 1163; Burley (Ha), *Burgelea* 1178; Burley (R), *Burgelai* 1086 'wood belonging to the fort'; Burstead (Ess), *Burgestede* c1000 'site of an old fort';

(ii) *byrh* in Boarhunt (Ha), *Byrhfunt'* 10th 'spring by the fort'; Burton Joyce (Nt), *Bertune* 1086, *Birtona* c1170, *Burton* 1222, and Burton on Trent (St), *Byrtun* 1002.[1] The dative singular *byrig*, which became ME *buri, biri, beri*, survives in Sudbury (Db, Sf), Fowberry (Nb), etc., and is particularly common in Essex, Hertfordshire and Middlesex, and to a lesser extent in Buckinghamshire in the later sense of 'manor'. Fuller, in his *Worthies of England*, writes of Hertfordshire: 'Surely no county can shew so fair a *Bunch of Berries*, for so they term the fair *Habitations* of *Gentlemen* of *remark*, which are called *Places, Courts, Halls* and *Mannors* in other Shires.' This may be added to the name of a parish or Domesday manor (Feeringbury, Quickbury), or be preceded by a descriptive element (Eastbury, Greenberry, Newbury), or by a manorial owner's name (Earlsbury, Mascallsbury, Monksbury).

Owing to these numerous variations of spelling, *burh* has been confused with other elements similar in form and because of its frequency has often been substituted for them. OE *beorg* 'hill, barrow' became ME *bergh*, later *bargh, barf*. The normal development survives in Barrow (R, So), *Berc, Berghes* 1206 and *la Bergh* 1232 respectively; Barugh (NRY, WRY), both *Bergh* 1086, now pronounced *barf*, and Berrow (Wo), *la berge, la Berwe* 1190; the modern form is confused with *burh* in Burgh Apton (Nf), *Berc* c1050; Burgh (Sr), *Berge* 1086, and Burf (Wo), *la Bergha* 1212. The OE dative *beorge* became ME *berwe*, later *berrow, barrow*, as in Rowberrow (So), but is usually confused with *burh*: Farnborough (Berks, K), Finborough (Sf), Finburgh (St), Modbury (D, Do), Blackberry (Lei), Blackborough (D), etc., in all of which the early forms prove derivation from *beorg*.

A similar confusion arises with OE *bearu* 'wood, grove'. The dative *bearwe* develops normally to Barrow (Ch, Db, Gl, Lei, Sa, Sf, So), several of which are recorded early, the earliest, Barrow upon Humber (L), in Bede: *Adbaruae* i.e. *ad nemus* 'at the grove', *Æt Bearwe* c890. In compounds it occurs as Harrowbarrow (Co), Sherbarrow (WRY), Sedgeberrow (Wo), Crowborough (St), *Crowbarwe* 14th; Timsbury (So), *Timesberua* 1086, *Timberbarewe* 1200, which had already been confused with *burh* in 1086: *Timesberie*. Timsbury (Ha), *Timbreberie* 1086, is from *burh*, and Crowborough (Sx), *Crowbergh* 1390, from *beorg*. In Devon, *bearu* had a dative *beara*, ME *beare, bere*, found in Shebbear, (*of*) *Scaftbeara* 1050–73, the only OE

---

[1] Burton is usually from OE *burhtūn*, '*tūn* by a *burh*' or 'fortified manor'.

form for one of the very numerous names Beare, Beer, Beere (41, apart from compounds). The final -*a* of the OE dative inflexion is preserved in Beara, Beera, and in Berry in Thornbury, *de la Beara* 1316.

DATIVE PLURALS

Many place-names were originally dative plurals: Bath (So), *æt Baðum* 'at the baths', Lydd (K), *ad Hlidum* 774 'at the slopes'; some preserve old folk-names or tribal names: Hitchin (Herts), *ad Hiccam* 996; Ripon (WRY), *Inhrypun* c730. The ending -*um* was either weakened to -*e* and finally disappeared, or was assimilated to common second elements such as -*ham* or -*holm*. In the south this type of name seems to have become obsolete early. It is confined, on the whole, to Anglian England, particularly east of the Pennines, from Northumberland to Yorkshire, being especially frequent in the North and East Ridings; it is found sporadically as far south as Hitchin (Herts) and as far west as Lindon (Wo), Lidham (St) and Oaken (Sa). In Cumberland, Lancashire and other western counties it is uncommon. Typical examples are: Newsham (L, NRY), Newsholme (ERY, WRY), both from (*æt þæm*) *nīwum hūsum* '(at the) new houses'; Windersome (ERY), *wind-hūsum*; Woodsome and Wothersome (WRY), *wudu-hūsum*; Burnham (L), *Brunum* c1115 'at the streams or springs'; Carham (Nb), *Carrum* c1050 'at the rocks'; Eyam (Db), *Eyum* Hy 3 'by the streams'; Fenham (Nb), *Fennum* c1050 'in the fens'; Yarm (NRY), *Iarun* 1086 'by the fishing-weirs' (OE *gear* 'dam'); Acomb (Nb, NRY, WRY), *Acum* 1086 'oaks'; Thornholme (ERY), *Thirnon* 1086 'thornbushes'; Haslam (La), *Haselum* 1235 'hazels'; Hipperholme (WRY), *Huperun* 1086 'osiers'; Salome Wood (Hu), pronounced *Sollem*, *Salne* 1227, (*æt*) *sealum* 'at the willows'; Stockham (Ch), *Stoccum* 1288 'by the stocks or stumps'; Escombe (Du), *Ediscum* 10th 'by the enclosed pastures' (OE *edisc*); Leam (Nb), *Leum* 1176, Lyham (Nb), *Leum* 1242, *Leyum* 1279 'by the glades or clearings' (*æt lēam, lēagum* respectively, dative plural of OE *lēah*); Kilham (Nb, ERY), *Killum* 1177, *Chillun* 1086 'by the kilns (OE *cylen*); Lealholm (NRY), *Lelun* 1086 'by the withies or willows' (OE *læla* 'twig, withe').

Coate, Cot, Cote; Coates; Coton, Cotton; Coatham, Cottam

The varied forms of simplex names derived from OE *cot(e)* 'cottage' raise different problems. There were two forms of the word in OE, *cot* (neuter), with dative singular *cote* and nominative plural *cotu*, and *cote* (feminine), with dative singular *cotan*, nominative plural *cotan* and dative plural *cotum*. As both *cote* and *cotu* became ME *cote*, it is impossible, without other evidence, to decide whether the name is singular or plural, nominative or dative. Except for some few very late forms of insignificant places, a singular modern form is found only in Cote (O), Coat (So) and Coàte (W), all of which occur also as *Cotes*, which can be explained only as a new ME nominative plural formed on the analogy of strong masculine plurals. This is the only form found for Coates in Sussex (from 1142) and for that in Nottinghamshire (from 1200), but for many modern names with a plural form, *cotes* and *cotun* are found side-by-side, and here we must have an interchange between the strong and weak nominative plurals: Great and Little Coates (L), *Cotes*, *Sudcotes* 1086, *Cotis*, *Cotun*, *Sut Cotun* 1115. The problem is complicated by the fact that some of these names preserve the weak plural form and are thus liable to confusion with survivals of the dative plurals: Coton (C), *Cotis* 1086, *Cotene* 1293, *Cotton* 1404; Coton (Nth), *Cota*, *Cote* 1086, *Cotes* Hy 2, *Cotene* 1285, where *Cota*, *Cote* must be from the nominative plural *cotu*; Claycoton (Nth), *Cotes* 1175, *Claycoten* 1330; Coton (Lei), *Cotes* 1235, *Cotene* 1327; Nun Coton (L), *Cotes* 1086, *Cotun* 1115; Cotton End (Nth), *Cotes* 1199, *Cotun* 13th.

The element is common in the Midlands, especially in the West Midlands and in the south, except in Sussex and Dorset, increasing in use towards the west in Devon. It is least common in Essex, East Anglia and Lincolnshire. Many of the names are not recorded in Domesday Book and are those of minor places, as would be expected from its meaning 'cottage' or 'shelter', often referring to sheds for manufacture or storage or shelters for livestock: Glascote (Wa), Salcott (Ess) 'salt', Sapcott (Wo) 'soap-maker', Lumbercote (ERY), Bulcote (Nt) 'bulls', Lamcote (Nt) 'lambs'. The general distribution of simplex names with plural forms only or with alternation of strong and weak plural forms is, on the whole, more southerly than those in the dative plural. It would seem that there was a belt along the boundary between Mercian and Saxon England where the two types overlapped. Some names are clearly from dative plurals: Cotton Abbots (Ch), *Chotam* 1100, *Abbotescoten* 1288; Coton in the Elms (Db), *Cotune* 1086, *Cotene* 1242; Coatham Mandeville (Du), *Cotum* Ric I; Cottam (La), *Cotun* 1230; Cottam (ERY), *Cottun* 1086, *Cotum* 1285; Coatham (NRY), *Cotum* 1231. The ending of the dative plural (-*um*) is preserved only in the counties of Durham, Lancashire, Nottinghamshire and Yorkshire. *Cot(t)on*, from *Cotum*, is found in the Midlands, from both nominative and dative plurals. *Cotton* may also have an entirely different origin: Cotton in Derbyshire and Suffolk are both recorded in Domesday Book as *Codetune* 'farm of Cod(d)a'.

This variation between strong and weak nominative plurals is common in Devon, especially in the south-east, in names such as Hayes (6) and Hayne (22) and in various compounds. In ME the forms vary between *heghes* and *heghen* from OE (*ge*)*hæg* 'enclosure'. Many of the names are compounded with a personal-name of ME origin, as Alexanderhayes in Hemyock, which probably owes its name to the family of William Alexander (1244), and the word had probably come to mean 'farm' or 'holding'. In Cottarson Farm in Awliscombe (D), *Cotterilleshegges* 1622, the suffix varied between the strong and weak plural form, the latter being finally weakened to -*on*: *Cottershaies* alias *Cottershene* alias *Cotterson* 1836.

Nash, Noakes; Ray, Ree, Rye, etc.

Many medieval place-names arose from such collocutions as '(place) by the ash, oak, elm', etc. OE *æt þæm æsce* 'by the ash' or *æt þæm æscum* 'by the ash-trees' became ME *atten ashe*, which, in colloquial speech, came to be pronounced *atte nashe*. Later, in the place-name, the preposition was dropped. Hence arise such common place-names as Nash, Noke, Noakes, Nelmes, Naldretts (Sx) 'by the alder-copse', Nechells (St, Wa), from OE **ēcels* 'land added to an estate', Nyland (Do) and Nayland (Sf) 'island', Nempnett (So) (OE *emnet* 'plain'), Knockholt (K), OE *āc-holt* 'oak-copse', Nasty (Herts), *atten ast hey* 'at the east enclosure', Nasthyde (Herts) 'at east hide'.

The OE dative feminine singular (*æt*) *þære* survives in Thurleigh (Beds) 'by the wood'. OE *ēa* 'river, stream' had two forms for the dative singular. OE *æt þære ē* became ME *atter e, atte re*, whilst *æt þære īe* became *atter ie, atter ey, atte rie, atte rey*, which was indistinguishable from ME *atte rey* from OE *ēg* 'island', 'land partly surrounded by water'. Consequently, with the confusion of forms, etymological certainty is not always possible, especially as it is often, too, doubtful whether the reference is to a stream or to low-lying land close by. Ray (W), Rea (Wo) and Rhee (C) are river-names (*ēa*). Rye (Sx) is clearly from *ēg*, as the town was originally built on a rock-promontory separated from the mainland by marshes overflowed by the sea. Rye House in Dunton Green (K) is near the Darenth, in a flat district liable to flooding. Rye Farm in Berrow (Wo) is between two streams on land which must formerly have been called *ēg* 'island'. Ray Island (Ess) is clearly from *ēg*. Walter *at Reghe* in 1287, and John *ate Ree* in 1332, both lived near Ray Bridge in Lingfield (Sr), i.e. 'by the stream' (*ēa*). Rye End in Kimpton (Herts), *Reefeld* Ed I, is named from the Mimram River (*ēa*) on which it lies, but Rye House in Stanstead Abbots, *Eia* 1086, is from *ēg*, nearly surrounded, as it is, by the rivers Stort and Lea. To these examples may be added: Rivar (W), River (Sx) and River Hill (K), from OE **yfer* 'edge, brow of a hill'; Rill and Rull (D), from OE *hyll* 'at the hill'.

In addition to this confusion of forms, we have also, in ME, a confusion of genders. By the side of Rye and Ray, we have Nye (So) and Neigh Bridge (W), from *atten ee* 'by the stream', and alongside Noak, we have Rock (Wo) and Rook (D), *atter ok* 'by the oak'. Occasionally, a fuller form of the preposition is preserved, in the Devon Terley, Traymill, Tredown and Trehill, all from *atter*; at other times nothing survives but the *t* of *æt*: Tiddingford (Bk), Taldbridge (La), '*at Aldbrycg*'; Tipperton (Co).

In other names the loss of initial *T* presupposes the loss of an original *æt*. Elstree (Herts) is *Tiðulfes treow* in 785, 'Tidwulf's tree'. It is *Idolvestre* in 1254, a form due to wrong division of *æt Tidwulfestreow*. Similarly, Adlestrop (Gl), *Tatlestrop* 11th 'Tætel's thorp'; Arracott (D), *Tadiecote* 1327 'toad-cottage'; Acton (Do), *Tacatone* 1086 'sheep-farm'. So, too, in place-names beginning with an initial *Th*, *æt Th-* was assimilated to *att-* and the preposition was then dropped, as in Ede Way (Beds), *ðiodweg* 926 'people-way'; Evegate (K), *æt þeofa gadan* 993, *Thevegate* 1246 'thieves' gate'; Elbridge (K), *æt þæl brycge* 948, *Elebregge* 1332 'bridge of planks' (OE *þel*).

GENITIVE PLURALS

Traces of the genitive plural survive in Bolnhurst (Beds), *Bolneherst* 1240, OE *bulena hyrst* 'bullocks' wood', as formerly in Bulmer (Ess), *Bulenemera* 1086 'bullocks' pool'; in Calverton (Bk, Nt), OE *calfra-tūn* 'farm where calves were kept', Calverley (WRY) 'pasture for calves', and in Childerley (C) 'wood of the children', here, perhaps, the landowners' sons, to whom the land may have been allotted during their father's lifetime. In 1066 Childerley was held by four *sochemanni*. One Ælfsi *cild* was described as a *sochemannus* or 'one under a lord's jurisdiction'.

ADJECTIVAL INFLEXIONS

In compound place-names adjectives generally appear in the weak form. Newton is always *Nīwatūn*, dative *Nīwantūne* in Old English sources. But -*hām* is frequently compounded with an uninflected adjective. This cannot always be proved, for it is generally impossible to decide the original form of the adjective in names recorded only after the Norman Conquest. But Higham is a valuable test-word. It is a common place-name, found at least six times in Kent, twice in Suffolk and Northamptonshire, and also in Bedfordshire, Derbyshire, Essex, Leicester, Northumberland and Yorkshire. In OE it was *Hēah-hām*, a form found in 765 for Higham Upshire (K), *Heahhaam*, and clearly reflected in such eleventh-century forms as *Hehham*, *Hecham* and *Heihham*. On the other hand, when compounded with *tūn*, the adjective is always in the weak form, the dative *Hēan-tūne* surviving as Hampton [1] in Cheshire, Shropshire, Hampton in Arden, Warwickshire, and Great and Little Hampton in Worcestershire, the latter being *æt Heantune* in 780; in Heanton Punchardon, Satchville and Kingsheanton (D); Hempton and Henton (O); Hinton Waldrist (Bk), *Heantunninga gemære* 958 'at the boundary of the people of Hinton', Hinton St Mary (Do), Hinton (Gl), Hinton Admiral, Ampner and Daubney (Ha), Hinton in Eardisland (He), Hinton Blewett and Bower Hinton, Hinton Charterhouse and St George (So), Broad and Great Hinton (W). [2] In the north, the dative was *Hēa-tūne*, which survives as Heaton five times in the West Riding, four times in Lancashire and thrice in Northumberland. Higham (*hēah-hām*) is clearly a very old formation, but *hēa(n)-tūne* is not necessarily late, as *Heantune* is found as early as 780. Twice, in Essex and in Suffolk, we find Henham, from OE *Hēa-hām*, dative *Hēanhām*, which shows that *hām* continued as a living place-name element until the period when place-names were usually compounded with weak adjectives. Hence such names as Newnham, Nuneham,

[1] Hampton (Gl, O) and Hampton Lovett (Wo) are from *hām-tūn* 'home-farm, village'; Hampton (He, Mx) and Hampton Lucy (Wa) are from *hamm-tūn* '*tūn* in a *hamm*'.

[2] Some Hintons are from OE *higna-tūn* 'farm of the monks or of the nuns': Hinton Martell (Do), *þare hina gemære* 946, *Hinetone* 1086; Hinton on the Green (Gl), *Hinhæma gemæru* 1042, *Hinetune* 1086; Hinton (He, Sa, Sf. W).

from *Nīwan-hām*, dative of *Nīwa-hām*. The very meaning 'new *hām*' shows that it is a comparatively late name. A village founded by the earliest Anglo-Saxon settlers would not be called 'the new village'. As with *-tūn*, the weak form of *hēah* is used in Handley (Ch, Db, Do, Nth), Hanley (St, Wo) and Henley (O, Sf, So, Sr, Wa) 'high wood', with the northern dative *hēa* in Healaugh (NRY, WRY), Healey (La, Nb, NRY, WRY) and Heeley (WRY). OE *nēowan-tūne* has kept its inflexion in Newnton (W) and, with a different development, in Naunton (Gl, Wo), and is common as Newington (Gl, K, Mx, O, Sr).

VOWEL SHORTENING IN COMPOUNDS

The modern spelling is a clear guide to the meaning of some place-names, e.g. Ashfield, Ashley, Martindale, Woodbridge and Wood-ford. Others offer little more difficulty, provided we keep in mind changes of pronunciation and spelling found in common words. OE *āc* and *stān* have become *oak* and *stone* and survive in place-names as Oake and Stone. In compounds, the long vowel may be shortened: *Know, knowledge*; *sheep, shepherd*, etc.; and in place-names, Ackton, Acton; Stanford, Stanley, Stanton, Stanway; Shipbourne, Shiplake, Shipden, Shipmeadow and Shipway, all from *sheep*. In names like Occold (Sf), *Acholt* 1050 'oak-copse', Stondon (Beds, Ess), Stonham (Sf) and Stonton (Lei) this shortening did not take place until later, after *ā* had been rounded to *ō*. In the final element of a compound, lack of stress often led to a weakening of the vowel, represented pho-netically by [ə], the final sound of butt*er*, gutt*a* percha, thor*ough*, with consequent confusion of such elements as *-don* and *-den*, *-hale*, *-hall* and *-hill*, etc. Strethall (Ess), Panshill (Bk), Finchale (Du), all derive from *halh* 'nook', whilst Warnell (Cu), Ryal (Nb), Shucknall (He) 'goblin-hill', are from *hyll* 'hill'. From OE *-denu* 'valley', we have Dipton (Nb) 'deep valley' and Croydon (C) 'crow-valley', whilst OE *-dūn* has given Malden (Sr) by the side of Maldon (Ess) 'hill with a cross', Darmsden (Sf) 'Dēormōd's hill', Longden and Longdon upon Tern (Sa), both 'long hill'. Haydon (W), *Haydon* 1242 is 'hay down', but Haydon Bridge (Nb), *Hayden* 1236, is 'hay valley'.

CONSONANTAL CHANGES

In ordinary colloquial speech consonants are dropped or assimilated to neighbouring sounds, as in Sandford, Sampford, Santon, all from *sand*; Haddon, Hadleigh, Hatton, all from *heath*; Southall, Sudbourne, Sudbury, Suffield, Suffolk, Sutton, all from *south*. Conversely, intrusive consonants are often introduced to facilitate pronunciation, as in thimble (OE *þ̄ymel*), thunder (OE *þunor*), empty OE *ǣmetig*), and in numerous place-names: Ambleside (We), *Amelsate* 1275 'shieling on a sandbank by a river' (ON *á* 'river', *melr* 'sandbank', *sætr* 'shieling'); Deptford (K, W), both originally *Depford* 'deep ford', but both pronounced *Detford*, where the intrusive *t* has absorbed the original *p* to simplify the pronunciation of the difficult *-ptf-*; Grindle (Sa), *Grenhul* 1190 'green hill'; Impney (Wo), *Ymeneia* 1176 'Imma's island'; Kempsford (Gl), *Cynemæresford* 800 'ford of Cynemǣr'; Thimbleby (L), *Timlebi* 1115 'Þymli's farmstead'; Thunderfield (Sr), 'open-land dedicated to Þunor'.

In addition to such changes, more than one of which may occur in a single name, there has always been a marked tendency to shorten long names by dropping unstressed vowels, with subsequent assimilation and simplification of difficult groups of consonants. The development of Abram (La) from the OE *Ēadburgeham* 'farmstead of a woman named Ēadburh' can easily be traced in the forms *Adburgham* 1199, *Abburgham* 1246, *Abraham* 1372, *Abram* 1461. The development of other names is less simple. Birmingham is found in a long and complicated series of forms. It is *Bermingeham* in 1086 and *Birmingeham* in 1206, forms which may mean 'homestead of the people of Beorma', a possible pet-form of such OE names as *Beornmǣr*, *Beornmund*, etc. Or the name may have been originally *Beornmundingaham* 'homestead of Beornmund's people', with reduction to *Bermingeham* already by 1086. The old local pronunciation *Brummagem* (with a *j* sound) derives from a variant with metathesis of *r*, found early in the twelfth century in *Bremingeham* 1166, *Brumingeham* 1189. From the thirteenth century there is evidence that the medial *-inge-* was pronounced *-inj-* and that later the *n* was lost: *Burmincham* 1260, *Byrmycheham* 1285, *Brimygham* 1377, *Brymycham* 1469, *Bromecham* 1515, *Bromegem* 1650. Thus, both the spelling *Birmingham* and the pronunciation *Brummagem* derive from a single source.

Innumerable examples of similar developments could be given, but one or two must suffice: Battersea (Sr) 'Beadurīc's marshy island': *Badrices ege, Batrices ege* 693, *Batricheseye* 1200, *Batriseye* 1366, *Batersey* 1408; Elstree (Herts) 'Tīdwulf's tree': *Tiðulfes treow* 785, *Tidulvestre* 1188, *Idolvestre* 1254, *Idelestre* 1320, *Illestre* 1487,

THE ORIGIN OF ENGLISH PLACE-NAMES

Elstre 1598; [1] Arlington (D) 'Ælfheard's farm', *Alferdintona* 1086, *Alfrintone* 1262, *Alrington* 1284, *Arlyngton* 1550; Bicester (O), pronounced *Bister*, OE *beorna ceaster* 'fort of the warriors': *Bernecestre* 1086, *Berecestria* 1152, *Bircestre* 1382, *Bysseter* 1517, *Bister* 1685.

NAMES OF DIVERGENT ORIGIN

One result of these various changes is that modern names of the same form may have different origins:

Alston (Cu): *Aldenestoun* 1208, *Haldeston* 1279, *Aldeynston* 1356 'Halfdan's farm'; (D), in Holbeton: *Alnatheston* 1228, *Aylnetheston* 1244 'Æþelnōð's farm'; (D), in Malborough: *Alwinestona* 1086 'Ælfwine's farm'; (D) in Chardstock: *Alwoldestone* 1201 'Ælfweald's farm'; Alstone (Gl): *Ælfsigestun* 969 'Ælfsige's farm'; (St): *Aluerdestone* 1086 'Ælfrēd's farm'.

Kimberley (Nf): *Chineburlai* 1086 'wood of a woman named Cyneburg'; (Nt): *Chinemarelie* 1086 'Cynemǣr's wood'; (Wa): *Kinebaudelege* 1230 'Cynebeald's wood'.

Woolston (D): *Ulsistone* 1086 'Wulfsige's farm'; (Ha): *Olvestune* 1086 'Wulf's farm'; (So), in Bicknoller: *Wolwardeston* 1225 'Wulfweard's farm'; Woolstone (Bk): *Wlsiestone* 1086 'Wulfsige's farm'; (Berks): *Olvricestone* 1086 'Wulfrīc's farm'.

NAMES OF DIVERGENT DEVELOPMENT

Conversely, names identical in meaning have developed differently:

OE *Beorhtelmes-tūn* 'farm of Beorhthelm' now appears as Bricklehampton (Wo), Brighstone or Brixton (IOW), Brighthampton (O), Brighton (Sx) and Brislington (So).

Dēorlāfes-tūn 'farm of Dēorlāf': now Dalston (Mx), Darlaston (St), Darliston (Sa).

Duddingtūn 'Dudda's farm' becomes: Doddington (C, K, L, Nth), Dodington (Gl, Sa, So), Duddington (Nth), Diddington (Hu), Dunnington (ERY), Derrington (St), Dunton (Bk) and Dotton (D).

Þūrstānes-tūn 'Thūrstān's farm': now Thurstaston (Ch), Thurston in Hawkedon (Sf), Thuxton (Nf), Thrislington (Du), Thrussington (Lei).

[1] For the loss of the initial *T*, *v.* p. 38.

Chapter Three

DIALECT AND PLACE-NAMES

THE origin of the Germanic tribes which invaded and settled in England in the fifth and sixth centuries A.D. is too complicated and controversial a subject to be discussed here. Traditionally, they consisted of Angles, Saxons and Jutes. But they were called collectively *Angelcynn* 'the Angle race', whilst the country was always *Englaland* 'the land of the Angles' and their language *Englisc*. Bede himself tells us that Kent was conquered by the Jutes but calls these very invaders *Anglorum sive Saxonum gens*, whilst Wilfrid, bishop of York, an Angle of noble birth, writes to the Pope as *Episcopus Saxoniae* and abbot Hwætberht addresses a letter from Wearmouth in Northumbria *de Saxonia*. What is clear is that they were of Germanic origin and came from the continental sea-board facing eastern and south-eastern Britain. They probably spoke a single language but one with varying characteristics which later developed into different regional dialects.

When the mists of illiteracy finally clear, we find four distinct dialects: Northumbrian, Mercian, West Saxon and Kentish. Kent always differed from the rest in its dialect as in its customs and system of land-tenure. In the south, West Saxon differed from the dialects of the Midlands and the North, both areas of Anglian settlement, which shared certain characteristics not found in West Saxon.

43

But, roughly north of the Ribble and the Humber, Northumbrian had its own pecularities not found in Mercian. Linguistic barriers did not coincide exactly with the boundaries of the kingdoms or the later counties. There was no abrupt change from one dialect to another. There were border areas with mixed dialects. In passing north from Cumberland and Northumberland the dialect gradually changed until it possessed what we now regard as specifically Scottish characteristics. Lowland Scots is an English dialect derived from Northumbrian.

After the Norman Conquest the position changed. The old kingdoms had disappeared and administration was based on the counties. Dialects continued to change and in the Danelaw had undergone a marked Scandinavian influence. The increasing importance of London as the centre of trade and of Westminster as the seat of government strengthened the influence of the East Midland dialect, which was the dialect not only of the Court but of both the Universities of Oxford and Cambridge and ultimately became the foundation of modern standard English.

The words and personal-names used in place-names were inevitably pronounced in the dialect of those who gave the names, but at a later period, when these came to be written, there was a tendency for official scribes to use official forms and so to obscure their local origin. But the real local form can be established from the numerous field-names, now often long disused, which are found in such documents as court-rolls, surveys and extents, written by local clerks. It is a matter of interest to know that the south-west Yorkshire Hoyland is identical in origin with the Essex Holland, and that in the Kent Helsted, the North Riding Hilton and the Staffordshire Hulton, we have dialectal developments of OE *hyll* 'hill'. But these dialectal place-name forms are of greater value to the linguistic historian in helping to delimit the area of the Old English dialects and so to locate the place of origin of Middle English works of literature. Useful results have already been obtained, but much still remains to be done. Here we are concerned only with surviving place-names whose forms preserve evidence of characteristic dialectal developments.

In the Midlands and the South, OE *ā* was rounded in ME to *ō*, but in Northumbria remained and was later fronted to *ǣ*, was often written *ay*, and became *eea* or, initially, *ya*: Aike (ERY), pronounced *Yack*, as opposed to Oake (So); Acomb (Nb, NRY) 'at the oaks', pronounced respectively *Yeckam* and *Yackam*; Rae Burn (Cu), Raydale (NRY), Raylees (Nb), from OE *rā* 'roe'; but Roecombe (Do).

In East Sussex and the adjoining parts of Kent an unmutated OE **hāð* 'heath' is found instead of the normal *hǣð*: High-hoad, Hoads, Hoath, Hoards, Hoadley, Hoathly, Hoddern 'heath-hill', Hodore 'heathy bank', Hodsherf, Hodshrove, probably 'steep slope covered with heath', all in Sussex; Hoad, Hoath, Hoades, Hode, Hothe, Hoaden 'heath-hill', Hothfield, all in Kent.

In Essex and the south-eastern counties from Bedford to Kent and Sussex certain OE words like *fenn, ende,* ME *wente* 'path, way', have forms with *an*. In Essex we have Fan, Fanns, Fanners, Fandown, Fambridge, Farmbridge 'fen-bridge', Vange 'fen-district', Bulphan 'fen by the fort' and Broadfans; Bran End and Brannetts from *brende* 'burnt'; Four Wantz 'four ways'. Both Mile End and Myland Lodge were so named because they were about a mile from Colchester. OE *denu* 'valley' is found as Dane (End, Farm, House) in Bedfordshire, Cambridgeshire, Hertfordshire, Surrey and Kent, and is often wrongly regarded as a relic of Danish occupation. In compounds we have Danehurst (Sr), Danaway (K), Danehill and Danhill (Sx).

In Devon, OE *ēa* frequently became a rising diphthong in ME and survives with initial *y*: Yalland, Yelland, Yellowland, Yelloways, Yollacombe, Youlden and Youldon, all from *eald* 'old'; Yarnacombe, Yarnaford, Yarner, Yarnicombe, Yarninknowle, Yarnscombe, all from *earn* 'eagle'. OE *ēa* 'river' became ME *yā, yō*, and is now found 21 times in the county as Yeo. A similar development is also found in Yafforth (NRY) 'ford through the river', Yaldham and Yalding (K), from *eald* 'old' or *Ealda*, Yarlet (St) 'eagle-slope', and Yen Hall (C), *Eanhale* 974 'lambs' valley'.

OE *ēast* is common in compounds such as Eastbridge, Eastbury, Eastcott, but in the Midlands is frequent as *Ast-*, both in the common Astley and Aston, and also in Astall (O), Astcote (Nth), Ascot (Berks, O), Ascott (Bk), Astey (Beds), Astle (Ch) 'east hill', Astwell (Nth), Astwick (Beds), Astwood (Bk, Wo).

Anglian *wald* originally meant 'forest, woodland' and was used especially of high wooded land; when the forest was cleared the name survived, and came to mean 'open upland ground, waste ground', as in the Yorkshire and Lincolnshire Wolds and the Cotswolds. It survives also in Wold (C), Wolds (Wa), Upton Wold (Wo) and in Old Hurst (Hu), *Waldhirst* 1227. The West Saxon form *weald*

survives as Weald in Oxfordshire, Sussex, Kent, Essex, Buckinghamshire and Huntingdonshire, as Wield in Huntingdonshire and in
Weildbarns in Essex. The best-known example is the Kent and
Sussex Weald. This became *weild*, pronounced *weald*; the vowel was
shortened and pronounced as in *filled* and *killed*. The name was then
spelled *Wilde* (1667), associated with the common word *wild*, and
pronounced like it. The spelling *Weald*, with the resultant modern
pronunciation, was an antiquarian revival of the sixteenth century
due to the Kentish topographer Lambarde. The same process
accounts for the form Wild found in Hertfordshire, Buckinghamshire and Northamptonshire, and Westbury Wild (Bk) and Croydon
Wilds and Hatley Wilds (C).

Anglian and Kentish *wella* 'well, spring' is found as Well (NRY,
Sx), Wells (Nf), Welham (Nt) 'at the springs', and in numerous
compounds such as Welborne (NRY), Weldon (Nth), and also frequently in Saxon territory, through the influence of standard English.
The West Saxon *wiella* became ME *wille*, *wulle*, the former surviving
in Will, Halwill, Holwill, Willhayne, Wilcombe and Wiltown in
Devon, Wilton (So, W) and Wilcote (W), whilst the latter is preserved in Wool, Woolbridge, Woolcombe and Woolcombe Farm in
Toller Porcorum in Dorset, and in Woolley (So). Mercian *wælla*
'spring' became ME *walle* and is difficult to distinguish from *wall*.
It is most common in the West Midlands, South Lancashire and
South-West Yorkshire, but is found also in field-names as far east
as Bedfordshire, Cambridgeshire and Suffolk. It survives in Wall
under Haywood, East Wall and Walltown (Sa), Wallingwells (Nt)
'bubbling springs', Aspinwall (La), Bradwall (Ch), Childwall (La),
Caldwall (Wo), Chatwall (St), Colwall (He), Crabwall (Ch), Etwall
(Db) and Heswall (Ch).

OE *y* became *i*, *e* or *u* in different ME dialects and standard
English has been selective in its choice of survivals: ridge, hill (OE
hrycg, *hyll*); rush, hurst (OE *rysc*, *hyrst*); merry, knell (OE *myrige*,
cnyll). In *bury* and *busy* the spelling preserves the *u*-type, but the
words are pronounced as if spelled *berry* and *bizzy*. In general, ME
i was the prevalent type in the North and the East Midlands; *e* in
the South-east and the South-east Midlands; *u* in the West Midlands,
the Central Midlands and the southern counties, excluding Kent. In
place-names containing common words the standard form has now
usually replaced that of the dialect, but some survivals of the local
form are found, especially in unstressed syllables. The south-eastern

46

e remains in Herne, Pett, Petlands and Petham in Kent; Herst-monceux, Pett, Petlands, Petley, Petworth and Redgeland in Sussex; Heron, Boucherne; Redden and Woodredon, from **ryden* 'clearing'; and Mell House 'mill', in Essex. The old harbour of Colchester is still Old Heath, from ME *hēthe* 'hythe', but the standard form has now been substituted in the neighbouring Old Hythe Meadow and for the new harbour at Hythe. The West Midland and South-Western *u* survives in Huyton, earlier *hȳð-tūn* 'farm by the hythe' (La), Hurn (Ha, Nth), Hurst, Hull, Rodge and Rugg's Place 'ridge' (Wo), Hulton (La), Hulls, Solihull (Wa), Rudgwick (Sx), Rudge (Gl, Sa, W), Rull 'by the hill' (D), and Culham, from *cyln* 'kiln' (Berks). OE **cnyll* 'knoll, hillock' is found as Knell (Sx) and Nill Well (C). The northern *i* survives in Dovehirn (L) and Hirst (Nb, WRY).

Standard English *cold* and *calf* are from Anglian *cald* and *calf*, but *chalk* is from the West Saxon *cealc*. Here we have a marked dialectal difference between Anglian and Saxon England and, though Anglian forms like Calcote (W), Coldham (Ess), Collecot (D) have penetrated into the south, a considerable number of Saxon forms have remained in use. Calverton 'calves' farm', Cauldwell 'cold spring' and Caulke 'chalk' (Nt) are typical Anglian forms. Calke (Db) and Cawkwell (L) both derive from *calc* 'chalk'; Calthwaite (Cu), Calveley (Ch), Calverley (WRY), Calvington (Sa) and Calwich (St), from *calf*; Caldecote (C, Nf, Wa), Callow 'cold hill' (Db), Cauldwell (Beds), Caudle 'cold spring' (C) and Coldwell (Nb), from *cald*. Similar names in Saxon and Kentish districts begin with *Ch-*: from *cealc*: Chalk (K, W), Chalford (O), Chalgrave (Beds), Chalton (Ha); from *ceald*: Chalfield (W), Challacombe near Linton (D), *Celdecomba* 1086 'cold valley', Chaldecotts, Chalcot (W), Chadwell, Chardwell and Shadwell (Ess), Chardle (C), all 'cold spring or stream', Cholash (D), Cholwell (So); from *cealf*: Chaldon (Do, Sr), Challacombe in Combe Martin (D), *Cheluecumba* 1168, Challock (K) 'calves' enclosure', Chalvey (Bk, So), Chawleigh and Chelfham (D), Chawton (Ha), and Choulden (W).

In ME initial *f* became *v* in the South, still preserved as *v* in south-western dialects, and surviving in place-names from Devon to Essex and Kent: Varracombe 'fair valley', Venn, Voaden, from *fāg* 'variegated', possibly with reference to the colour of the soil, Vole-house 'fowl-house', all in Devon; Vobster (So) 'Fobba's tor'; Frome Vauchurch (Do), Vowchurch (He) 'variegated, coloured church';

47

Verwood 'fair wood' (Do); Vasterne (OE *fæsten*) 'stronghold'; Venn, Venny (W); Venniscombe (IOW) 'marshy valley'; Verney, Vann 'fen', Vanhurst (Sr); Varndean, Varncombe 'fern', Venns, Verridge 'fern-ridge', Vuggles Farms, from a surname 'Fowl', Vox End, from *feax* 'hair', used of coarse grass, shrubs, etc. (Sx); Vexour, from *feax*, 'bank overgrown with rough grass' (K); Vange 'fen district', Venmore, Voucher's Farm, named from William ffowcher (Essex).

This pronunciation of *v* for *f* led to a misunderstanding, and every initial *v* in place-names was liable to be regarded as a dialectal pronunciation of *f*. The name was then often re-spelled and *f* wrongly substituted for *v*. Hence, in Essex, the former holding of Robert de Vals or de Vaux in Belchamp Otton in 1086, still *Vauces* as late as 1484, came to be called Fowe's Farm, and *Videlowes* (1493) in Little Baddow, which owes its name to the family of John *Vis de Lu* (1248) 'wolf-face', is now Phillow's Farm. The normal development of *Vis de Lu* would be to *Vidlow*, which would be pronounced *Vidler*. This was regarded as a dialectal form of *Fidler*, the form taken elsewhere for this family's holdings in Fiddlers Dykes in Shelfhanger (Nf), Fidler's Hall in Cransford and Fiddler's Hall in Tannington (Sf). Similarly, Filston Hall in Shoreham (K) preserves the surname of Simon *Vele* de Shorham (1292).

In Southern Middle English *s* was also voiced, but survivals are less numerous: Zeal (D), Zelah (Co) and Zell House Farm (Ha), from OE *sele* 'hall', Zeaston 'at the seven stones' (D) and Zeals (W).

In words like *parson, north*, etc., the *r* is no longer pronounced and such spellings as *ar, or*, etc., have long been used to indicate that the preceding vowel is long. This inorganic *r* is found in some place-names: Armoury Farm in West Bergholt (Ess), *Almerey* 1468, *Amerie* 1596, from OFr *aulmosnerie*; the farm was formerly part of the endowment of the almonry of St John's Abbey, Colchester; Chardwell 'cold spring', Farmbridge 'bridge by the fen', Harmes Farm in Lambourne (Ess), from Robert de *Hageham*, Marles Farm in Epping, from William le *Masle* 'male, masculine', Norsey Wood, *Nossesheye* 1250 'Nōðsige's wood', Portsmoorhall, *Possemore* 1240 'Possa's moor', all in Essex. Parsloes in Dagenham derives from Hugh *Passelewe* 'cross the water', with the same spelling as in Drayton Parslow (Bk), where already in 1086 Ralf *Passaquam* held the manor. Similarly, Marsworth (Bk) is from *Mæssanwyrð* 1012, 'Mæssa's enclosure'.

Chapter Four

PERSONAL-NAMES AND PLACE-NAMES

M ORE than once already, in giving a brief etymology of a place-name, we have silently assumed that one element is the name of some former owner, occupier or other early inhabitant. We still call at the Smiths', shop at Harrod's and lunch at Simpson's. A surname like Vickers often appears in medieval records as (Agnes) *atte Vicares*, Agnes who was the servant at the vicar's (house). Similar possessive formations have given rise to place-names from the earliest days of the Saxon invasion, but always combined with some word defining the actual possession, *-hām* (homestead), *-tūn* (farm), *-lēah* (wood), etc. Few medieval spellings are needed to show that Alderton (Nth), Harrietsham (K) and Whiteoxmead (So) contain the OE personal-names *Aldhere*, *Heregeard* and *Hwituc* respectively, or that Aslockton (Nt), Kettlestone (Nf) and Thurstaston (Ch) are derived from the Scandinavian personal-names *Áslákr*, *Ketil* and *Þorsteinn*. Nor is there any doubt, in spite of their Scandinavian ending, that Allonby (Cu), Johnby (Cu) and Jolby (NRY) were named from men who bore the post-Conquest names of *Aleyn*, *John* and *Johel*, whilst Jordanthorpe and Waterthorpe Farm (Db) were clearly the outlying farms of *Jordan* and *Walter*, both OFr names. In the

49

south-western counties we find the English *-ton* compounded with a Norman surname. Lovistone (D) was held by William *Lovel* in 1303, Puxton (So) by Robert *Puckerel* in 1158, and Sarson (Ha), *Savageston* 1363, by Richard *le Salvage* in 1203.

A full appreciation of the significance of English place-names must, therefore, require a close examination of the personal-names they contain, Celtic, whether Old British or Old Irish, Old English, Scandinavian, whether Danish or Norwegian, with all their various types and diminutives where they can be distinguished, and, for the later periods, the new names brought over from the Continent by the Normans, a subsidiary but by no means unimportant source.

OLD ENGLISH PERSONAL-NAMES

Old English personal-names are of two types: compound names formed from two distinct elements, as *Æðelwine* 'noble friend', *Gōdgifu* (f) 'good gift', *Gārmund* 'spear-protector', and simple names like *Beocca, Sibbi, Ubba*. These simple names, too, may be divided into two classes. One consists of short forms of compound names, *Goda, Lēofa, Wulfa*, from such names as *Godwine, Lēofmǣr, Wulfbeald*, etc. Others are derived from adjectives, *Brēme* 'famous', *Frōda* 'wise', *Hwīta* 'white', or names of animals, *Hengest* 'stallion', *Eofor* 'boar'. Some it is impossible to classify definitely. *Dēor(a)* may be from OE *dēor* 'wild animal', *dēore* 'dear', or from such compounds as *Dēorwine* or *Dēormund*. Some we cannot explain.

Originally, Old English compound names had a meaning, *Wulfweard* 'wolf-guard', *Beorhtsige* 'bright victory', *Sǣmǣr* 'sea-famous', but the Anglo-Saxon system of indicating relationship by giving a child a name beginning with one or other of the elements contained in his father's name, or by combining one element from the father's name and one from the mother's name, soon resulted in meaningless compounds. Early in the seventh century, for example, *Hererīc* 'army-ruler', nephew of King Edwin of Northumbria, and his wife Bregu*swīþ* 'ruler-mighty', gave their daughter the name *Hereswīþ* 'army-mighty', a name more suitable in meaning for a son. According to his biographer, St Wulfstan, Bishop of Worcester 1062–95, who was born c1012, was given a name compounded of the first theme of his mother's name, *Wulf*gifu 'wolf-gift', and the second theme of his father's, *Æþel*stān 'noble stone'. Their son's name, *Wulfstān* 'wolf-stone', had no more meaning as a name than had the names of his parents. Their sole concern was to give their son a name which would indicate his parentage—there were no hereditary surnames at this period. They were no more concerned with the meaning of the name than were those who called their children *Friþuwulf* 'peace-wolf' or *Wīgfriþ* 'war-peace'. Traces of the persistence of this method of name-giving can still be found as late as 1200 in pedigrees of villeins cited in the Norman King's Court. In Hertfordshire a certain *Sǣgār* had a brother *Sǣgēat* and an uncle *Sǣmann*; in Sussex one *Æðelwine* had an aunt *Æðelgifu*, who named her younger son *Æðelwine*. Her brother *Wulfrīc* gave his daughter *Wulfgifu* a name compounded of the first theme of his own name and the second of that of his sister.

These compound names were often shortened in every-day use. Bede tells us that *Sǣberht*, king of Essex, was commonly called *Saba* or *Sæba*, whilst Symeon of Durham refers to an eighth-century Northumbrian abbot called both *Edwine* and *Eda*. The full name of *Sicga*, bishop of Selsey 733–c760, was *Sigefrið* or *Sigehelm* and that of *Ælle* or *Ælli*, bishop of Lichfield c920–38, was *Ælfwine*. Difficult groups of consonants were often simplified: *Ælfgār* son of *Æffa*; *Totta*, bishop of Leicester 737–64, was called also *Torhthelm*; in the letters of St Boniface, *Bucge* is a short form of the women's names *Ēadburg* and *Hēaburg*; in the seventh century *Tuma* was used as a short form of *Trumwine*; in Domesday Book one *Wulfwine* in Cornwall occurs also as *Wine*; the real name of the countess *Goda* was *Godgifu*.

Whilst some short names consist simply of the first element of the compound, as *Wine* from *Winebeorht* and *Cēn* from *Cēnweald*, others are formed by the addition of *-a* to the first element, as *Cūða* from *Cūðbeorht*, *Hūna* from *Hūnbeorht* and *Utta* from *Uhtrǣd*. In the early period, a suffix *-i*, which had generally become *-e* by the eighth century, gave such names as *Tīdi* and *Tili* by the side of *Tīda* and *Tila*. This *-i* often caused mutation of the preceding stem vowel, as in *Brȳni*, a short form of compounds like *Brūnheard*.

Many difficult place-names can be explained from short forms of compound names which contain not only the first element of the compound, but also the initial consonant of the second element, often combined with assimilation of the two consonants. Wormleighton (Wa), 'Wilma's kitchen-garden', contains an unrecorded OE *Wilma*, probably a pet-form of *Wilmund* or *Wilmǣr*. Cubbington (Bk, Wa) and Cubwell (Db) derive from *Cubba*, a short form of a name like

Cūþbeorht; Massingham (Nf), Messingham (L) and Marsworth (Bk), from *Mæssa*, an assimilated form of *Mǣrsa*, a pet-form of *Mǣrsige* 'glorious victory'; and Tubney (O), from *Tubba*, a short form of such names as *Tūnbeorht* or *Tūnbeald*.

Numerous diminutives of these short forms are recorded in OE documents and are found in place-names: *Berhtel*, from names like *Beorhtrīc*, and, with mutation, *Dyddel*, *Tyrhtel*, from stems in *Dudd*- and *Torht*-; *Hwituc*, *Hereca*, *Lēofeca*; some with less common suffixes, as *Monnede*, *Wipped*; *Cymen*, *Cūðen*; *Piper(a)*, *Lippor*. Some of these are rare and must have become obsolete early, but their existence seems proved by their occurrence in such place-names as Cuddesdon (O), Peppering and Lippering (Sx).

One other type of personal-name, that ending in *-ing*, is of importance, e.g. *Lulling* in Lullingstone (K), *Hearding* in Hardingstone (Nth), *Billing* in Billingshurst (Sx) and Bellingham (W). They were originally patronymics, descriptive, but not personal-names: Wulf *Wonrēding* 'Wulf the son of Wonred', and the formation is common in genealogies: *Ida wæs Eopping* 'Ida was the son of Eoppa'. Later, such formations became a kind of byname and were then used as independent names. The patronymic *Dēoring*, originally 'the son of *Dēor*', might well be associated with the adjective *dēor* 'brave, bold', was then regarded as a parallel to the noun *dēorling* 'darling' and, like *Dēorling*, was employed as a distinct name.

Our knowledge of OE personal-names is both limited and abundant. We are dependent on the surviving literature and on the lists of witnesses to charters which are not only rare for the period before 750 but are very unevenly distributed over the country, most of them relating to Wessex and southern Mercia. In addition, we know little of the names in common use among the lower classes. Most of the names on record are those of the upper classes. Many names in use during the period of the migration ceased to be used within a few generations. Apart from this, up to about 900 there was little change in the character of the names used. From the tenth century there is a marked difference. Uncompounded names became rare, the compound names in use tended to become stereotyped and by the end of the century we find a marked preference for a limited number of some dozen stems, particularly names in *Ælf-*, *Æðel-*, *Ēad-*, *Lēof-*, *Sige-* and *Wulf-*. But in an eleventh-century list of peasant names at Hatfield (Herts) we find short names for both men and women, *Dudda*, *Brada* and *Wine* (m), *Tate*, *Dudde*, *Lulle* and *Dunne* (f), side by side with the common *Ælfstān*, *Wulflāf* and *Wulfsige* and such names as the unique *Dryhtlāf*, with *Tilewine* and *Cēolmund*, once common but rarely found after the ninth century, and the feminine *Hereðrȳð*, of which the only other example is from the seventh century. There is no parallel to these Hatfield short names elsewhere. Among the numerous Suffolk freemen named in Domesday Book, we find only compound names, with a marked preference for stems in *Lēof-*, *God-* and *Wulf-*, the same name occurring more than once in the same parish, so that the clerk was driven to differentiate by writing *et alter Godwine* 'and another Godwine'. At the same time, both in DB, in a list of over 600 names of peasants on the Suffolk manors of the abbot of Bury St Edmunds, and in scattered post-Conquest sources, we find many compounds unrecorded in OE, with others not recorded after the seventh–ninth centuries.

UNRECORDED PERSONAL-NAMES IN PLACE-NAMES

At one time the results of place-name study were received with some scepticism, chiefly on the ground that too many unrecorded personal-names were postulated to explain too many place-names. Many scholars found it difficult to believe that Alresford (Ha) could mean 'ford of the alder-tree' or that Ashdown (Berks), OE *Æscesdun*, meant 'hill of the ash-tree'. Ekwall still explains the Berkshire name as 'the hill of a man named *Æsc*' and discards Asser's *mons fraxini* as a popular etymology. Thirty years ago Mawer wrote:[1] 'It is clear therefore that a genitival form in the first element of a place-name does not necessarily imply a personal-name. We have ceased to use inflexional genitives in Modern English in the case of words denoting objects without life, and it is repugnant to our speech-instinct to think that people could ever have spoken of the "mapletree's *denn*" [as in Maplesden (Sx)], but our ancestors felt no such inhibition and could use such inflexional forms, though they clearly preferred to use on most occasions the uninflected form "mapletree-*denn*".' Tengstrand, more recently, has shown that these genitival compounds are more common than has been thought.

When every allowance has been made for such names as Beaconsfield (Bk), for which no reasonable explanation can be offered except that this high 'open land of the beacon' was long used as a site from which signal-fires blazed forth far and wide their messages and

[1] A. Mawer, *Problems of Place-name Study* (1929), pp. 98–9.

53

warnings, there still remain numerous place-names which appear to contain some unknown personal-name. If this personal-name conforms to one or other of the types of well-established OE names, its probable existence can be accepted, especially if it is found in more than one place-name. Similarly, in place-names of an early type, if the personal-name postulated can be shown to have existed on the Continent, we may regard the name as one which became obsolete before written records began. When Bede explains Rendlesham as *mansio Rendili*, he clearly shows that this mutated diminutive *Rendil*, for which we have no other evidence, was a personal-name his contemporaries would accept without reserve. So, too, although we have no record of men in England called *Mealla*, *Healla* or *Basa*, personal-names postulated to explain Malling (K, Sx); Halling (K), Hallingbury (Ess), Hallington (L); Basing (Sr, Ha), Basingstoke (Ha) and Basford (Nt), the fact that we find parallels in OHG *Malo*, *Mallabaudes*; *Halo*, *Hello*, *Halabold*; and *Baso*, *Basulo*, suggests the possibility that these names really were brought to England, whilst the occurrence of each in more than one English place-name makes their existence at least probable.

Recent work has shown that post-Conquest records reveal the use of OE personal-names never found in pre-Conquest documents, many of them still surviving as modern surnames. Some few of these prove conclusively that certain names postulated to explain place-names were actually in use in the eleventh or twelfth centuries, or even later, and must, therefore, have been in use for a long period in spite of their absence from OE documents. Particularly interesting is *Pacchild*, the name of a woman living in Essex in 1166. The first element must be connected with OE *Pæcc*, *Pæcci* or *Pæcca*, the second is *-hild*, a common second theme in women's names. *Pæcc(i)* has been postulated to explain Patching, Patcham and Pashley (Sx), Patching Hall (Ess), Paxford (Wo), Patchill and Paschoe (D), Paxlet (W) and Packsfield (IOW) and *Pæcca* has been assumed for Patchendon (Herts) and Patchecott (D). A diminutive *Pæccel* occurs in Patchway (Sx), Paglesham (Ess), Paddle Brook (Wa) and Paxcroft (W), whilst *Pæccīn* is found in Pachesham (Sr). Related to these personal-names is *Pacc(a)*, also unrecorded, but found in Packington (Lei, St, Wa), Packmores and Packwood (Wa), Pakefield and Pakenham (Sf). The two Patchings are names of an ancient type in *-ingas*, where we should expect derivation from a personal-name; Patchway, on record in the eighth century, was the site of a heathen temple clearly owned by a man *Pæccel*, whilst names in -*hām* and -*tūn* are frequently combined with a personal-name. No common noun is known which would explain the first element, and the accidental survival in the twelfth century of *Pæcchild*, in the very county in which is Patching Hall, confirms the conclusion that *Pæcc(i)* was familiar to the early Saxon immigrants, that the name flourished and produced derivatives, was widely spread and persisted in use throughout the OE period.

In a document of 1198 copied into the Cartulary of St John's Abbey, Colchester, there is a reference to land formerly held by a certain *Hauer*, who was probably living in the first half of the twelfth century. This is the sole example known of OE *Hæfer*, probably a nickname from *hæfer* 'he-goat', which has long been accepted as the personal-name contained in Havering-atte-Bower (Ess), Haveringland (Nf), Haversham and Averingdown, with the neighbouring Hearndon Wood (Bk), and Azores in Tavistock (D), *Haverisworthy* 1353. A diminutive *Hæferic* is found in Hersham (Sr).

One other example may be noted. Ekwall derived the names Worsthorne and Worston (La), Worthing (Sx) and Worthington (La, Lei) from an unknown personal-name *Wurð*, from the root of *weorð* 'worth' or *wyrþe* 'worthy'. A personal-name *Werth* has since been noted twice in twelfth-century London, a compound *Weorðgifu* (f) in Bury St Edmunds (Sf) c1095, in Bedfordshire in 1212 and in Essex in 1222, and a derivative *Weorðing* twice as a christian name in Essex as late as 1240. The variant forms suggest that *Weorð* was the original form both of the personal- and of the place-names. Seldom does such confirmation of his theory await the scholar.

SCANDINAVIAN PERSONAL-NAMES

Numerous place-names and field-names not now on the map prove that the Irish–Norwegians continued to use Scandinavian personal-names, but many of these are not recorded before the twelfth century and some, like Gamblesby (Cu), derive, not from the settlers of the tenth century, but from their twelfth-century descendants. Elsewhere, Scandinavian personal-names are due to the conquest of eastern England by Danes in the ninth century and the parcelling out of the land among their armies, especially in the counties of Yorkshire, Lincolnshire, Leicestershire, Nottinghamshire and Derbyshire, and in East Anglia. With the reconquest of the Danelaw by the descendants of Alfred and the control of the kingdom by the Danish Cnut (Canute), we begin to find men with Scandinavian names in the southern counties, some of sufficient importance to give their names to places, but such place-names have no bearing on the strength and extent of the earlier Scandinavian settlement.

These Scandinavian personal-names are inadequately recorded in OE sources and their number and importance cannot be fully appreciated in the absence of a full collection. For the majority of the personal-names of the Danelaw, our earliest source is Domesday Book, which records names which may have been formed at any time between 876 and 1066, most of them belonging, probably, to the first half of this period. The vitality of the Scandinavian nomenclature of the Danelaw in the twelfth century has been revealed by Sir Frank Stenton, and light has been thrown by others on that of East Anglia. Many of the names are of an ancient type; some are not recorded in Scandinavian sources; new and otherwise unknown diminutives were being formed, and many are to be found in place-names found in Domesday Book or are still in use as surnames. But with these personal-names we have the added complication that some are known to have been used also in Normandy; they often appear in forms clearly due to French clerks and it is not always easy to decide whether we are concerned with an Anglo-Scandinavian name in Norman guise or a Scandinavian name brought over direct from Normandy. Alstonby (Cu), first recorded as *Astinebi* c1210 in the Lanercost Cartulary, with similar forms thereafter, is derived by Ekwall from ME *Austin* (the vernacular form of *Augustine*) and by Dickins from Anglo-Scandinavian *Asten*, the name of a ninth-century moneyer. About 1210 a grant of land in *Astinebi* was made to Lanercost by Willelmus *filius Astini*, and there can be no reasonable doubt that this is another of the place-names in *-by* formed in Cumberland in the late twelfth century and that the place owed its name to William's father *Astin*, a name which survives today in the surnames *Askin* and *Astins*, from a Norman form of ON *Ásketill* or *Áskell*, the origin of the modern surnames *Ashkettle*, *Askell* and *Astell*. The name was common in England both before and after the Conquest, and was also popular in Normandy in the forms *Anschetel* and *Anketell* and elsewhere in northern France as *Anquetin* and *Asketin*. The various forms were used in England of the same man: *Aschetinus* de Houkesgard (c1145) is also called *Aschetillus*, *Astillus* and *Astinus*. Alstonby clearly derives from a French name of Scandinavian origin.

Asselby (ERY) and Exelby (NRY), each recorded in DB as *Aschilebi*, are villages founded by a Scandinavian. Exelby, *Eskelby* 1252, preserves the Danish form *Eskil*, Asselby, that of Norwegian *Áskell*, though it also occurs as *Eskilby* in 1198.

Most of the Scandinavian personal-names were common to both East and West Scandinavian, and in England it is impossible to decide whether they came from Denmark or Norway. But a certain number can definitely be identified as Danish: *Api* (Apethorpe, Nth), *Esi* (Easby, NRY), *Flik* (Fleecethorpe, Flixter (Nt), Flixborough (L), Flixton (La, Sf, ERY), *Kære* (Kearby (WRY), Kirby Muxloe (Lei), Cold Kirby and Kearton (NRY), *Toke* (Toxteth (La), Tugby, Lei), *Tove* (Towthorpe (ERY), Towton (WRY), Toton, Nt).[1] *Sumar-liði* 'summer warrior', which appears to be purely Norwegian, is found in Somerby (L, Lei), Somerleyton (Sf), Somersby (L) and Somerton (Sf).

Like the Anglo-Saxons, the Scandinavians had both short names and compounds. Among the former are: *Áli* in Ailby and Althorpe (L), Alby (Nf) and Oulton (Sf, WRY); *Bǫrkr* in Barkby and Barkestone (Lei) and Barkston (L, WRY); and *Siggi* (Sigston, NRY). ON *Ketill*, an early and popular byname from *ketill* 'cauldron', an apt nickname for a round-headed man, was in frequent use in Iceland before 900 A.D. In England it became very popular in the Danelaw and had given rise to ten place-names before 1066: Kedleston (Db), Ketsby and Kettleby (L), Ab Kettleby and Eye Kettleby (Lei), Kettlestone (Nf), Kettlethorpe (L, ERY), Kexmoor (WRY) and Keyston (Hu); and to others later: Kettleshulme (Ch), Keskadale (Cu). In the ninth century it was also used to form new compound names, some of which became widely popular and survive in numerous place-names: *Ketilbiǫrn* (Kettlebaston, Sf), *Ketilgrímr* (Kellamarsh (La), Kilgram, NRY), *Ásketill* (Asselby, ERY), *Úlfketill* (Oakerthorpe (Db), Ouston, Du, Nb), *Ylfketill* (Ilketshall, Sf).

Compounds of *Thor-* were common: *Þóraldr* (Thoralby, NRY, Thorlby, WRY, Torrisholme, La), *Þorgeirr* (Thurgarton, Nf, Thurgoland, WRY), *Þorgils* (Thirkleby, ERY), *Þorgrímr* (Thorganby, L, Thornthorpe, ERY), *Þorketill*, *Þorkell* (Thirkleby, NRY, Thirtleby, ERY, Thurcaston, Lei, Thruxton, Ha, He), *Þorleifr* (Thurlaston, Lei, Wa), *Þorleikr* (Thurloxton, So), *Þormóðr* (Thormanby, Thornaby on Tees, NRY, Thrumpton, near Nottingham,

---

[1] This is not a complete list.

Nt, Thurmaston, Lei), *Þórólfr* (Tholthorpe, NRY, Thulston, Db, Thurlby, L, Thurlston, Sf, WRY), *Þorsteinn* (Thrislington, Du, Throxenby, NRY, Thrussington, Lei, Thurstaston, Ch, Thurston, Sf, Thuxton, Nf).

Among other compound names, some of which are ancient, are: *Ásgautr* (Osgarthorpe, Lei, WRY, Osgodby, L, ERY, NRY, Osgoodby, NRY), *Ásgeirr* (Asgarby, L), *Áslákr* (Aislaby, Du, Aslockton, Nt), *Ásmundr* (Osmotherley, La, NRY), *Bǫðvarr* (Battersby, NRY), *Gunnhildr* (f) (Gunthorpe, Nt), *Gunnólfr* (Gonalston, Nt, Gunby, ERY), *Gunnvarðr* (Gonerby, L, Gunnerton, Nb), *Hrómundr* (Romanby, NRY), *Ingvarr* (Ingarsby, Lei), *Ingialdr* (Ingoldisthorpe, Nf, Ingoldmells, L), *Sigólfr* (Sigglesthorne, ERY, Sileby, Lei), *Solmundr* (Salmonby, L).

Unlike the Anglo-Saxons, the Scandinavians used the same personal-name in different generations and in different branches of the same family. It was a common practice, too, for a man to give his son the name of some prominent chief or of some intimate friend. The result was that, in time, there were so many men of the same name in the same district that it became necessary to distinguish them by some byname. Some of these were complimentary, some derogatory and derisive, characteristic of the gross humour and acute realism of the Vikings. By the end of the ninth century many of these bynames had come to be used as independent names and still lie concealed in our place-names: *Blanda* 'the man who mixes his drinks' (Blansby, NRY), *Bróklauss* 'the man without breeches' (Brocklesby, L), *Feitr* 'fat' (Faceby, NRY), *Hari* 'the hare' (Hareby, L), *Hraði* 'quick or rash' (Raithby, L, Rearsby, Lei), *Kári* 'curly-haired' (Careby, L, Carthorpe, NRY, Caythorpe, ERY, Corton, Sf), *Káti* 'the cheerful' (Cadeby, Lei, L, WRY, Caythorpe, L, Nt), *Kausi* 'tom-cat' (Cowesby, NRY), *Keptr* 'jaw, chump or chop' (Kexbrough, WRY, Kexby, L), *Kisi* 'cat' (Keisby, L), *Klakkr* (Claxby, L, Claxton, Du, Nf, NRY, Long Clawson, Lei, Claythorpe, L, Glassthorpehill, Nth) and *Klyppr* (Clippesby, Nf, Clipston, Nt, Nth, Clipstone, Nf, Nt, Clixby, L), both meaning 'lump or clod', *Loðinn* 'hairy' (Londesborough, ERY, Lonsdale, NRY), *Lútr* 'bent' (Lusby, L), *Skammbein* 'short-legged' (Scammonden, WRY), *Skammlauss* 'shameless' (Scamblesby, L), *Skarfr* 'cormorant' (Scarsdale, Db), *Skarði* 'hare-lipped' (Scarborough, NRY), *Skúma* 'squinter' (Scunthorpe, L), *Skyti* 'archer' (Skeeby, NRY, Skidby, ERY), **Slengr* 'idler' (Slingsby, NRY), *Slóði* 'good for nothing'

(Sloothby, L), *Snípr* 'miser' (Snibston, Lei), **Spilli* 'waster' (Spilsby, L). *Sumarliði* 'summer warrior', noted above, *Vestliði* 'one who has travelled west', found in Westlaby (L) and Westleton (Sf), and *Víðfari* 'the far-traveller' in Weaverthorpe (ERY), were tributes to achievement, but *Náttfari* 'wanderer by night' in Nafferton (Nb, ERY) is ambiguous. Few of these personal-names were common in medieval England and many were probably obsolete by the time of Domesday Book.

POST-CONQUEST PERSONAL-NAMES AND SURNAMES

Some thirty places recorded in Domesday Book contain the name of the undertenant who held the manor in 1066, among them, Blackmanston (K), from OE *Blæcmann*, Brigmerston (W), from *Beorhtmær*, Afflington (Do), from the woman's name *Ælfrūn*, Shearston (So), from *Sigeræd*, Goodcott (D), from *Godgifu* (f), Osmaston (Db), from *Ōsmund*, and Carleby (L), from ON *Karli*. Of the chief elements denoting habitation, the Scandinavian *-by* was still in living use in the north-west in the twelfth century, whilst compounds of the English *-tūn* continued to be formed, especially in the south-west, for two centuries or more after 1086. The personal-names used to form these compounds are extremely varied. Both Old English and Scandinavian personal-names continued to be used, but in the twelfth and thirteenth centuries we are faced with a new problem. Does the place-name contain the name of a man who, like the Anglo-Saxons, had only one name, or is it a christian name or a sur name? All three types are found, and it is only when the individual in question can be identified that we can be certain. ON *Grípr*, recorded in Dorset in 1086 and as a surname in Yorkshire in 1195, is found in Gripstone (D) 'the farm of Grip', of whom nothing further is known. He may have been a Scandinavian from the Midlands who had come south and left his name in the farm he had established some time in the eleventh or twelfth century, but, as the place is first mentioned in 1244, *Grip* might by that time have become a surname. Cruxton (Do), originally a part of Frome, is called simply *Froma* in DB, but is *Fromma Johannis Croc* in 1178 and certainly takes its name from John's surname, itself deriving from ON *Krókr*, a personal-name which may have reached England from either Denmark or Normandy and was already a surname in Hampshire in 1086. The modern name of the place first appears as *Crocston* in 1195, when the manor was held by William *Croc*, probably a son of John Croc.

59

Neither the John of Johnstone (D), the Jordan of Jurston (D), *Jordaneston* 1238, nor the Robert of Rabscott (D), *Roberdescote* 1238, can be identified. But Rawstone in the same county is named from *Ralph* de Nimet (1198) and Richardson (W) from one *Ricard* (1168). All these are from Norman christian names, as is Vielstone (D), from French *Viel*, Latin *Vitalis*, and Jesson Farm (K), *Geffreyeston* 1254. But Filston Hall (K), *Vielston* 1203, is a doubtful example. It is named from an ancestor of Simon *Vele* (1292), whose surname must be derived from an ancestor named simply *Viel*, but we cannot decide whether the name had become a surname before 1203.

Clear examples of Devonshire place-names derived from surnames include Gambuston, from Geoffrey *Gambun* 1238, the modern *Gammon*, a diminutive of AN *gamb* 'little leg'; Corstone, *Corbineston* 1242, from Peter *Corbin*, a French nickname 'raven'; Faunstone, identical with Fonston (Co), from Simon *le Enfaunt* 'the child', found as *Fant*, *Faunt* and *Font* in modern surnames; Harpson, *Herbertyston* 1270, from Walter *Herbert*; Mountshayne, *Maundeuillesheghs* 1330 'the farm of Robert *de Maundevill*' (1299), a Norman family. In Dorset we have a christian name *Walter* in Waterston (1227) and surnames in Herrison, from Philip *Hareng* 1224 (OFr *hareng* 'herring'), Quarlston, from William *Quarel* 1232, metonymic for an arbalester, from OFr *quarel* 'bolt for a crossbow', and Pulston, from Bernard *Poleyn* temp. Henry II (OFr *poulain* 'colt'). Austle in Cornwall was originally *Austineswelle* and Cripstone, *Crispinston*. In Cumberland we have christian names of varied origin, Norman in Isaacby, Johnby, Moresby (*Maurice*) and Rickerby (*Richard*), Breton in Allonby, Ellenby and Wiggonby, and a surname in Aglionby, from Walter *Agullon* (1130).

When we turn to Essex, we find that, although -*ton* is found in a number of field-names, none of these contains a post-Conquest personal-name and not one survives. On the other hand, some dozen names of OE origin, five of them Domesday vills, have been replaced by the surnames of later holders: Coupal's Farm (DB *Celuestuna*) from Hugh *Curtpeil* (1232), a French nickname 'short hair'; Bigods (DB *Alferestuna*) from Bartholomew *le Bigod* (1235), another French nickname; Rockell's Farm (DB *Wyggepet*) from Humphrey *de Rokell* (1205), who came from a French place, la Rochelle; Culvert's Farm (DB *Richeham*) from Richard *de Coleworde* (1253), whose family came from Culworth (Nth); and Hunt's Hall (DB *Polheia*) from Simon *le Hunt* (1312), an English occupation-name 'huntsman'. In addition, 13 manorial names derive from Domesday land-holders bearing French nicknames or surnames from French towns: Fowe's Farm (Robert *de Vaux*), Mark Hall in Latton (Adelolf *de Merc*, from Marck, Pas-de-Calais), Spain's Hall (Hervey *de Ispania*, from Espinay, Ille-et-Vilaine). Robert *Gernon* (OFr *gernon* 'moustache'), who held many manors in 1086, has (with his descendants) left his name in 11 Essex places: Garnons, Gernon Bushes, Garnetts, Garnish Hall, Garlands (Farm) and Gallant's Cottages. This type of name is particularly common in Essex and many, even of the minor names, are more or less anglicised forms of famous family names, e.g., Poor Park from William *lepuier* (1171), OFr *Pohier* 'a Picard'; Brimstone Hill from John *de Brinzun* (1240), who came from Brien-çun in Normandy; Blamster's Hall from William *de Blauminister* or *de Albo Monasterio* (1285) whose family came from Whitchurch (Sa).

Essex, too, is a county where the strength of Norman feudalism is still revealed in aristocratic and often mellifluous village names like Layer Breton, Layer de la Haye and Layer Marney, villages still distinguished by the addition of the surnames of twelfth-century lords of the manors, Lewis Brito 'the Breton', Maurice de Haia and Hugh de Marinni, the Bretons retaining their possessions here for 300 years and the Marneys for some 400. Similar names are found in most counties even where they are now rare, and many have disappeared. They are thinly represented in the north, save in Yorkshire, and in the east, with the noteworthy exception of Essex, but increase in numbers as we go west and south, becoming most frequent in Wiltshire, Devon, Dorset and Somerset. The attributes are of varied types, occasionally English, but chiefly French, including both christian names and surnames of every kind and they range in time over some five centuries, from 1066 to 1500 or later. The attribute is sometimes prefixed, Cockayne Hatley (Beds), more often suffixed, Dunton Basset (Lei), occasionally combined, Boscastle (Co), 'the castle of (William) Boterel' (1130). Famous names rub shoulders with those less well-known or obscure: Melton Mowbray (Lei), Holme Lacy (He), Wharram Percy (ERY), side by side with Langton Herring (Do), Morton Bagot (Wa), Stoke Orchard (Gl), held by John *le Archer* in 1244.

One reason for the development of this type of name was to distinguish between the numerous places with such common names as Combe, Compton, Sutton, Stoke and Weston, as in Combe Martin (D), held by Robert, son of *Martin*, in 1133; Compton

Dando (So), from Alexander *de Alno* (temp. Hy 2), who came from Aunou (Orne); Sutton Mandeville (W), from Robert *de Mandevilla* (1224); Stoke Doyle (Nth), from Henry *de Oilli* (1189), who came from Ouilly (Calvados), and Weston Corbett (Ha), from Thomas *Corbet* 'raven' (1203). The tendency of some English vills to throw off daughter vills of the same name and the later division of a single vill into two or more manors also led to the need for a distinction of name, as did the multiplication of vills named after a single river. But at times the reason for the difference is not clear at first sight. Churston Ferrers (D), held by Hugo *de Fereris* in 1303, is the only place in Devon called Churston. But there are three places in the county called Cheriton, two with attributes, Cheriton Bishop and Cheriton Fitzpaine (from its lord in 1256, Rogerus *filius Pagani*). All four names mean 'church farm', and it may well be that, though the recorded forms of Churston are quite distinct from those of the Cheritons, the identity in meaning was realised and a need felt for distinction.

The three Wiltshire parishes now named Winterbourne Dauntsey, Winterbourne Earls and Winterbourne Gunner, all named from the old name of the river Bourne, are all included in Domesday Book under the simple name *Wintreburne*. In 1242 one manor was held by Roger *Danteseye*, whose family came from Anisy (Calvados), the second in 1281 by the *Earl* of Salisbury, whilst in 1249 the lady of the third manor was *Gunnora* de la Mare, whose christian name is of Norman–Scandinavian origin.

The four modern parishes lying along the Essex Colne were already distinguished in 1086 as *Colun* and *Parva Colun*. Great Colne was given by William I to Aubrey de Vere and is variously called from him *Aubrey's Colum* (1152) and *Culn de Ver* (1238). It is also called *Colne Chepingge* (1309), from its market, *Colum Oxon'* (1254), and *Erlescolne* (1358), which survives, commemorating the rank of his descendants, *Earls* of Oxford. Little Colne, now Colne Engaine, preserves the surname of Viel *Engayne* 'trickery', but was also occasionally named from his christian name *Culn Vital* (1238), Colum *Viel* (1254). Wakes Colne was *Colum Malot* (1227), from Robert *Malet* (1086), Colne *de Quency* (1240) and *Colum Saer* (1254), from *Saer de Quincy* (1210), who came from Cuinchy (Pas-de-Calais), and whose niece married Baldwin *de Wake* (d. 1282). White Colne was Colum *de Miblanc* in 1163 and owes its attribute to an under-tenant who held land here in 1086. His nickname *Demiblanc*, a small coin, was contracted first to *Miblanc*, then to *Blanc*, and finally translated into English 'White'.

Many similarly varied examples can be found; occasionally the whole manorial history of the place can be traced in its varying names. Tolleshunt D'Arcy (Ess) was held in 1086 by Robert *Gernon*, in 1141 by William *de Tregoz* and in 1292 by John *de Bois*, whose family intermarried with that of *D'Arcy*. Robert Darcy had land in the parish in 1441. The place-name is found as *Tolleshunte Gernon* (1248), *Tolleshunte Tregoz* (1303), *Tolshuntboys* (1412) and *Tolshunt Darcy* (1472). Virley (Ess) has undergone a series of interesting and unusual changes. Originally *Salcota* 'salt cottage', it later acquired a feudal addition, *Salcote Verly* (1291), from its Domesday lord, Robert *de Verli*, and is now known only by that feudal addition. In Cornwall, too, the feudal elements of *Venton Vacye* and *Venton Hurlefrenche* now survive alone in Vacye and Hollafrench.

In the south-west these names had a development of their own. The Dorset river Tarrant has given name to eight villages on its banks, all, except one, originally named Tarrant. In the exception, Tarrant Crawford, the old name was Crawford 'crow ford', to which the river-name was prefixed, partly, perhaps, because Tarrant Abbey was in this parish, partly on the analogy of the other Tarrant parishes. Tarrant Hinton and Tarrant Monkton, though feudal names, do not strictly belong here, as the former was given by Alfred the Great to Shaftesbury Abbey and was called *Hyneton* 'farm of the monastic community', a name later combined with the river-name as Tarrant Hinton. Tarrant Monkton, which belonged to Tewkesbury Abbey in 1107, is called *Tarente Monachorum* in 1291. As with the Shaftesbury manor, this, too, was given a name of its own, *Monketon* 'farm of the monks', and the parish later became Tarrant Monkton. Tarrant Launceston is a doubtful example. The attribute *de Lowyneston* (1285) suggests the name of a former owner, but none such is known and the remaining forms might mean 'Lēofwine's farm'. Tarrant Rawston is *Tarente Willelmi de Antioche* 1242, *Tarente Antioch* 1291, *Auntyocheston, Tarente Auntyocheston* 1399, *Tarrant Rawston* 1535. Curiously enough, in 1086 the DB under-tenant was named *Ralph*, which would satisfactorily explain *Rawston*, but it is unlikely that he would suddenly reappear after 500 years in a name previously associated only with the Antioch family. *Tarrant Rawston* is probably a corruption due to the difficulty of pronouncing *Tarent Auntyocheston*. Similar forms are found for Tarrant Rushton,

Tarente Petri de Russell 1242, *Tarente Russeals* 1289, *Tarente Russ-cheweston* 1307, *Russheston* 1326, *Tarente Russhton* 1340. Peter *de Rusceaus* came from one of the French places named Rousseaux. The manor of Tarrant Keynston (with similar forms) was held in 1199 by William *de Cahaignes*, whose family came from Cahaignes (Eure).

Among the compounds of this type are Ashwater (D) and Bridg-water (So), both from *Walter*; Berrynarbor (D), from Philip *de Nerebert* (1172), probably from Narberth (Pembroke); Bridgerule (D), from its DB holder *Ruald* Adobat; Clevancy (W), now named by a late owner, Cliffansty House, the *Clive* 'cliff' held by Robert *de Wancy* in 1249 who came from Wanchi (Seine-Inférieure); Herst-monceux, Hurstpierpoint and Horselunges (Sx), *Hurstlyngeore* (1346), held by William *de Lyngyver* in 1318; Stogursey (So), *Stok Curcy* 1212, a manor of William *de Curcy* (temp. Hy 1), who came from Courcy (Calvados); Stourpaine (Do), from Berthinus *Payn* (1303); Teigngrace (D), from Geoffrey *Gras* 'the fat' (1352).

OE personal-names are found in Edith Weston (R) and Stoke Edith (He), both among the possessions of Queen Edith at the time of the Conquest; Preston Gubbals (Sa), held in 1086 by *Godebold* the priest, probably an Englishman. Scandinavian personal-names occur in Wootton Wawen (Wa), held by *Wagene* de Wotton c1050 (ODa *Vagn*), Crosby Ravensworth (We), from ON *Hrafnsvartr* 'raven black', and Crux Easton (Ha), held by *Croch* the huntsman (ON *Krókr*) in 1086. The Irish *Patrick* is found in Weston Patrick (Ha) and the Welsh *Madoc* in Sutton Maddock (Sa). Brampton Bryan (He) and Milton Bryant (Beds) are from Breton *Brian*.

French personal-names are more numerous: Beer Hackett (D), from *Haket* de Bera (1175), an Anglo-Norman diminutive of ON *Haki*; Tolleshunt Major (Ess), from its Domesday holder *Malger* (OFr *Maugier*, from OG *Madalgar*, *Malger* 'council-spear'); Pap-worth Everard (C), from *Everard* de Beche (c1165). This was also called *Pappeworthe Petri* (1254), from the dedication of the church to St Peter, which led to the assumption that the *Pappeworthe Anneis* of the same document had a similar origin, with the result that the *Agnes* de Papewurda, who held the manor in 1160, has been wrongly canonised in the modern Papworth St Agnes. Another uncanonical saint is found in Sawtry St Judith, where Judith, niece of the Con-queror and widow of Waltheof, who held the manor in 1086, has been raised to a dignity level with that of Sawtry All Saints and Sawtry St Andrew. Burton Agnes (ERY) owes its attribute to *Agnes* de Albemarle (c1175), Lydiard Millicent (W) to *Millisent*, who held the manor for life in 1199. Sutton Benger (W) was held in 1086 by *Berenger* as under-tenant. The christian name is OFr *Berengier*, from OG *Beringar* 'bear-spear', but this had become a surname before it was added to Shipton Bellinger (Ha), held by Ingelram *Berenger* in 1296.

The great majority of these attributes are French surnames, from both nicknames and place-names. Among nicknames may be noted: Acaster Malbis (WRY), from William *Malebisse* (12th) 'evil beast'; Milton Malzor (Nth), from William *Malesoures* (1202) 'evil deeds'; Berwick Maviston (Sa), from Henry *Malveisin* (1166) 'bad neighbour'; Goadby Marwood (Lei), from William *Maureward* (1316) and Norton Malreward (So), from William *Malreward* (1235) 'evil eye'; Hope Mansell (He), *Hope Mal Oysel* 1242, 'ill-omened bird'; Hill Farrance (So), held by Robert *Furon* (1182) 'ferret'; Martyr Worthy (Ha), from Henry *la Martre* (1201) 'weasel'; Bentley Pauncefote (Wo) 'round belly'; Kirby Bellars (Lei) 'ram'; Farnley Tyas (WRY) 'the German'.

The family of Ralph de Toesny, lord of Tosny (Eure) and standard-bearer of Normandy, who preferred the hurly-burly of the fight at Hastings, has left its name in Saham Toney (Nf), Newton Toney and Stratford Toney (W). Tihel de Herion, a Breton follower of the Conqueror from Helléan in Morbihan, was rewarded with the manor of Helion Bumpstead (Ess), and descendants of his are found in 1242 at Upton Hellions (D). With a knowledge of family history and the origin of surnames, there is little difficulty in identifying many of these attributes: Sampford Courtney (D), Compton Verney (Wa), Manningford Bohun (W), Swaffham Bulbeck (C) and Carlton Colville (Sf). But the appearance of many is deceptive. Hatley St George (C) has no connexion with either the christian name or the saint. It was held in 1236 by William *de Sancto Georgio*, who owed his surname to one of the French places named St Georges. Hinton Admiral (Ha), Stoke Damarel and Sydenham Damarel (D), all derive from a family which came originally from Aumale (Seine-Inférieure), earlier *Alba Margila*, whence the title of the Duke of Albemarle. Stoke Farthing (W), held by Rois *de Verdun* in 1242, like Newbold Verdon (Lei), held by Bertram *de Verdon* in the reign of Stephen, derives from a family from Verdun (La Manche) or possibly Verdun (Eure), not from the better known Verdun in the Vosges. Stoke Bliss (Wo) derives from William *de Bledis* (1212), a family name probably from Blay (Calvados). The attributes of Carlton Curlieu (Lei), Charlton Musgrove (So) and Compton Greenfield (Gl) were originally *de Curly* (1175), probably from Cully, *de Mucegros* (temp. John), from Mussegros, both in Normandy, and *de Greinvill* (1228), from a French place Grainville. Occasionally, the attribute is from an English place: Thorpe Bulmer (Du), probably from the North Riding Bulmer; Berrick Salome and Britwell Salome (O), pronounced locally *Sollem* (*Brutewell Solham* 1320), from the family of Aumaric *de Suleham* (1236) which came from Sulham (Berks).

CELTIC PERSONAL-NAMES

That there was a Celtic strain in the earliest OE personal-names is certain, but its extent is difficult to determine, in spite of its historical importance. OE *Ceadd(a)* is undoubtedly of Celtic origin, from British *Caduc*, OW *Catuc*, though the OE form proves that it must have been adopted at a very early period and it became so acclimatised that from it was formed the diminutive *Ceadel(a)*. Its popularity may, in fact, be due to the veneration of St Chad, for in Cheshire we find Chadkirk, whilst the Lancashire Chadwick is in Rochdale, where the church is dedicated to this saint. Elsewhere we have Chadwick (Wo), Chadsworth (Sr), Chadstone (Nth) and Chaddesden (Db), whilst the diminutive *Ceadel(a)* is found in Chaddleworth (Berks), Chadlington (O), Chillington (D), Chadshunt (Wa), Chadwich (Wo), Chalfont (Bk) and Cheldon Barton (D). The name *Tūda*, recorded as the name of a bishop of Lindisfarne in 664 and of a priest in the diocese of Rochester in 803, is meaningless as a Germanic name, but intelligible if it derives ultimately from the Old Welsh stem *tūd* 'people'. It is curious, however, that in place-names it is found only in the eastern counties, in Tuddenham (Nf), and twice in Suffolk, near Mildenhall and near Ipswich, in Tudhoe (Du), Tudworth (WRY), Toddington (Beds), Teddington (Mx) and in Tedfold (Sx). Chadbury (Wo) is 'the fort of *Ceadwalla*', an OE name corresponding to Welsh *Cadwallon*, but it does not follow that there is any connexion with the early West Saxon king of this name, who may have been so called because some near ancestor had married a Welsh princess.[1] Chertsey seems to contain a British *Cerotus*, whilst OW *Branuc* is found in Branxton (Nb), Branscombe (D), Branksome (Do) and Braintree (Ess).

[1] It is significant that his brother was called *Mūl* 'the mule, the half-breed'.

In the Welsh border counties, where Welsh influence is by no means negligible, the Celtic personal-names in English place-names are chiefly those of saints, often obscure, and sometimes otherwise unknown, e.g. in Herefordshire: Dewchurch 'church of Dewi or St David', Kenderchurch 'church of St Cynidr', Kentchurch 'church of St Keyne', St Devereux 'church of St Dyfrig', St Weonards 'church of St Gwennarth', whose history is obscure. Early forms are not seldom in Welsh, and the Welsh form sometimes survives: Llancloudy 'church of Loudeu', presumably a saint, of whom nothing is known; Llandinabo 'church of Junabui', an early bishop of Llandaff, to whom the church is dedicated; and in Gloucestershire, Lancaut 'church of St Cewydd'.

Cornwall

Cornwall, separated from Wales at an early period, with its linguistic affinities with Brittany, preserved its native language until the eighteenth century and with it, its characteristic place-names. Those compounded with *trev*, *tre* 'homestead, village, town' very often, and those with *bod*, later *bos* 'house, dwelling' nearly always contain a personal-name: Trevarthian 'homestead of *Arthgen*' 'bear-born', Tresillian (*Sulgen* 'sun-born'), Bodbrane (*Bran* 'crow') Boswyn (*Gwin* 'the fair'). Well-known names found also in Old Welsh appear in Tredrustan (*Tristan*), Trenearne (*Aneirin*), Trevanion (*Eineon*, Latin *Anniānus*, the source of the modern surnames *Ennion*, *Eynon*, *Anyan*). As in Old English, personal-names may be simple or compound; adjectives as *Caradoc* 'beloved' (Tregardock), *Gweri* 'active' (Trewerry); diminutives as *Ruthan* 'little red one' (Bedruthan), *Bescan* 'little short one' (Trevescan); or names of animals and birds used as nicknames: *Ceneu* 'whelp' (Tregenna), *Blethic* 'little wolf' (Treblethick). Other nicknames include *Mael* 'prince' (Treveal), *Gwas* 'servant' (Boswase), *Lew* 'chief' (Trelew). Among the compounds we may note: *Cadwith*, a compound of *cad* 'battle', in Tregaswith; *Conhoiarn*, from *Cyn* 'chief' in Polkinghorne; *Iudnou*, from *iud* 'lord' in Trudnoe; *Tudwal*, from *tūd* 'people, folk', in Tredudwell, and *Tudur* in Lesteuder. Diminutives are formed by the addition of -*oc* or -*an*; *Cadoc* (Tregaddock), *Maeloc* (Trevellick), *Cadan* (Rosecaddon) and *Conan* (Tregonning).

A number of Cornish personal-names derive ultimately from Latin, and some from Greek or Hebrew, but are difficult to identify, partly because of the changes they have undergone in the course of centuries and partly through the working of the laws governing lenition: *Æmiliānus* (Trevillian), *Cyriacus* (Tregerrick), *Constantinus* (Strickstenton, formerly *Tregestentin*), *Cornelius* (Trekernell), *Elias* (Trevillis), *Felix* (Bephillick, formerly *Bodfilek*), *Iacobus* (Trago), *Iulius* (Bodilly), *Iuliānus* (Trellian), *Paulinus* (Trebowland), *Samuel* (Tresamble), *Saul* (Tresawle), *Saturnus* (Tresadderne), *Victor* (Trewether), *Vitalis* (Boswhiddle, Trewhiddle).

Whilst Cornish personal-names are found in such names as Cargenwyn 'fort of Cenwyn', Carveddras 'fort of Modred', and Treveryan 'Merchion's homestead', the most striking feature is the great number of its villages named from the saint to whom the church is dedicated. Many of these are peculiar to the county or associated with Brittany. Some, like Probus (St Probus), Mawgan (St Maugan), Mullion (St Melan) and Mylor (St Melor), are used alone; others are prefixed by *llan* 'church', as Lamellan (St Maylwen) and Linkinhorne (St Cynheorn); others are anglicised, like St Ives. Landewednack is 'the church of St Gwennock or Winnoc'. In its earliest reference it is called *Ecclesia Sancti Wynewali* 'the church of St Wynewalo', a name identical with Breton *Guenole*, earlier *Win-waloe*, which survives also in Gunwalloe. *Winnoc* was used as a short form of *Wynwalo*. In addition to such well-known saints as St Germans and St Neot, we have Breton saints in St Eval (Breton *Uvel*), St Just, St Kew, St Mawes (Breton *Maudez*) and St Wenn (Breton *Guen*); Irish saints in St Erth, from St Ercus, bishop of Slane; St Kevern, earlier *St Achebrannus*, from Ir *Aed Cobhran*; St Nighton (Ir *Nechtan*); and unknown Cornish saints in St Breward, St Endellion, St Gluvias, St Veep, and others. Mevagissey is from a double dedication, Co *Mew ag Ida* '(the church of SS) Mewa and Ida', the latter commemorated also in St Issey.

Such names are much more common in the west than in the east of the county, where more than half the parish names are ordinary place-names. In the west many of the parishes had an earlier name, now lost, or surviving only in that of a farm or tenement adjoining the 'church town'. St Issey, for example, was earlier *Egloscruc*, St Blazey has replaced *Landraeth* 'the church on the shore', whilst *Nansfonten* 'valley with a spring' is now Little Petherick. In Cornwall, as Mr Gover suggests, were material available, the names of farms and hamlets could probably be traced to the time when the inhabitants first abandoned their hill-forts and strongholds and came to dwell in scattered settlements among their fields and pastures, at any

time before the fourth or fifth centuries A.D. The churches are obviously of much later date, and if, as was often the case, they were
built at a distance from the nearest habitation, they would often
come to be known simply by the name of the saint to whom they
were dedicated.

Cumberland

One aspect of the racial complex of Cumberland 'the land of the
Cymry or Welsh' is revealed by the British personal-names surviving
in its place-names. Carwinley, near Arthuret, a difficult name, probably contains OW *Gwendoleu*, the name of a British leader at the
battle of Arthuret (573 A.D.), whilst Carnetley 'cairn of *Teiliau*',
modern Welsh *Teilo*, may well date from the same period. Dunmail
Raise, according to a tradition which may well be correct, was 'the
cairn of Dunmail', one of the last of the kings of Strathclyde. It is
seldom possible to assign a date to the origin of a place-name, hence
it is impossible to decide whether Castle Hewin owes its name, as
suggested by earlier historians, to Owain, king of the Cumbrians, or
to the Ywain of Arthurian legend, or to some unknown Ewein. But
Tarn Wadling 'the tarn of Gwyddelan', an old Welsh name meaning
'little Irishman', compounded with the ON *tiorn*, cannot have
received its name before the Irish–Scandinavian settlement of the
tenth century. Similarly, Maughonby, 'the farm of Merchiaun', a
compound of the Scandinavian *by* and an Old Welsh personal-name,
must have arisen in the twelfth century. It is in the parish of Glassonby, to which is now added that of Gamblesby, and we have proof
that these represent the land held by Gamel, son of Bern, and
Glassan, son of Brictric, in 1130, an interesting example of the mixture
of races in the district. *Gamel* and *Bern* are Scandinavian, *Brictric* is
OE *Beorhtrīc*, *Glassán* Old Irish and *Merchiaun* Old Welsh.

Early in the tenth century Scandinavians from Ireland settled in
Cumberland and made their way over the Pennines into Yorkshire,
where they have left their mark in place-names showing signs of
Irish–Scandinavian influence. They adopted Irish words and names
and had become so far Celticised that, instead of the normal Scandinavian type of patronymic, *Orm Gamalsuna*, they had adopted the
Irish form, *Thorfynn Mac Thore*, even when both father and son bore
Scandinavian names. In addition, they had adopted the Irish method
of forming compounds by placing the defining element last, as in
the Irish Downpatrick and Ballymurphy, and a number of these

inversion compounds are still found on the map in Cumberland: Aspatria 'Patrick's ash', Brotherilkeld 'Úlfkell's booths', Dalemain 'Máni's valley', Gillcamban 'Cambán's ravine', Setmurthy 'Murdoch's pasture', Greysouthen 'Suthán's rock or cliff', Kirkandrews, Kirkbride, Kirkoswald and Kirksanton, the churches of St Andrew, St Bride, St Oswald and St Sanctán respectively, the latter the name of more than one Irish saint.

Irish personal-names survive in Cumberland in Glassonby (*Glassán*) and Corby (*Corc*); in the North Riding in Brettanby (*Brettan*), Carperby (*Cairpre*), Coldman Hargos and Commondale (*Colmán*), Gatenby (*Gaithan*) and Melsonby (*Mælsuithán*); in the East Riding in Duggleby (*Dubhgall*), and in the West Riding in Feizor and Fixby (*Fíach*) and Mankinholes (Mancan). OIr *Dubhán* is found in Dovenby (Cu) and Dowthwaite (NRY), *Lochán* in Laconby (Cu) and Lackenby (NRY), and *Maelmuire* in Melmerby (Cu, NRY).

Chapter Five

THE CELTIC ELEMENT

CERTAIN of the most familiar English place-names were well known on the Continent long before the first Saxon invaders set foot on these shores, and must therefore be pre-English in origin. The Thames is mentioned by Caesar and Tacitus, Kent by Caesar, Diodorus Siculus and Strabo, London by Tacitus and Ptolemy, the Isle of Wight by Pliny and York by Ptolemy. All these are probably Celtic in origin, but all are difficult and more than one etymology has been put forward for each. York we have discussed above.[1] London may be a derivative of a stem *londo- 'wild, bold', from which a personal-name or tribe-name may have been formed. Kent has been derived from Celtic canto- 'rim, border' ('border country') and from canto- 'white' in the sense 'clearing'. This is the origin of Kenn (D, So), both DB Chent and both situated on streams called 'white' or 'brilliant'. Wight, Vectis in Pliny, Gueith in Nennius, Wiht in Bede, is probably identical in origin with Welsh gwaith 'work', a word cognate with Lat vectis 'lever' (lit. 'the act of lifting') and OE wiht 'weight', derived from the root of Lat vehere 'to carry'. The meaning might have been 'what has been raised', 'what rises above the sea', 'an island'. The same element may occur in Penwith (Co), with

[1] v. p. 24.

reference to the hilly Land's End peninsular separated from the rest of the county by a flat neck of land.

The earliest forms of Thames, *Tamesa, Tamesis*, point to a British *Tamesā*, which was adopted by the Anglo-Saxons as *Tamis* or *Temes*. What is most noteworthy here is the preservation of the inter-vocalic *s* which has disappeared in other British loan-words such as Trent (*Trisantona* in Tacitus, *Treenta* in Bede), possibly 'the trespasser', river liable to floods. We must assume that the Thames was known to the Anglo-Saxons at a very early period, before *s* had disappeared and before they had settled in Britain. The common ME *Tamise* is a French form, as is the modern spelling with the French *Th-* for *T-* (*Thamis'* 1220). The pronunciation is from the OE *Temes*. The name is considered to be related to the Sanskrit *Tamasā*, 'dark water', the name of a tributary of the Ganges.

Stour, a fairly common river-name in England, is derived by Ekwall, after considering various possibilities, from a Primitive Celtic **Staur-* or **Steur-*, which would give British **Stūr-*, and this an OE *Stūr*, a form common in OE documents, with a meaning 'strong, powerful river', which would suit the English Stours.[1] On this, Jackson comments that there is no known stem remotely like it in the Celtic languages and there is actually the very word in Norwegian, Dutch and Low German, but, because it was lacking in Anglo-Saxon, Ekwall rejects it and gives a Celtic etymology. 'We should not lose sight of the possibility', he adds, 'that some names which have an Indo-European look and are not obviously either Germanic or Celtic may be due to non-Celtic Indo-European elements among the pre-historic immigrants to Britain.'[2]

The etymology of these pre-English place-names is a difficult and complicated problem. Very rare indeed is the scholar who is equally at home in Celtic and Germanic philology. The Celtic languages involve problems of pronunciation, loss of consonants, affection and lenition unknown in Germanic, whilst the history of the development of the modern Celtic languages from Common Celtic is far from well-known, and we have no full and comprehensive modern treatment of the place-names of Wales. Little wonder is it, then, that scholars differ and that we are often concerned with possibilities or probabilities rather than with definite etymologies. This is particularly unfortunate, as an agreed solution of many of these problems would be

---

[1] E. Ekwall, *English River-names* (1928), 378–82.
[2] K. Jackson, *Language and History in Early Britain* (1953), 195, n.1.

invaluable in discussing the extent of the survival of a British population after the Anglo-Saxon conquest.

Apart from scattered and valuable contributions by Henry Bradley and useful material from Max Förster, we are particularly indebted to Professor E. Ekwall, whose *Scandinavians and Celts* (1918) threw a flood of light on Celtic personal- and place-names in the north-west. His *English River-Names* (1928), still the standard work on the subject, has been supplemented by numerous articles on pre-English place-names in his *Dictionary of English Place-Names* (1936).[1] Recently a newcomer has entered the field. Professor Kenneth Jackson of Edinburgh, in his *Language and History in Early Britain* (1953), has made an outstanding contribution to the subject. He is concerned not with individual etymologies so much as the fundamentals on which future research must be based—the pronunciation of Latin and Brittonic in Roman Britain, the development of Common Celtic to Welsh, Breton, Irish and Gaelic, and above all with the dating of the various sound-changes. In future we shall have a means of judging the pronunciation of a British name at the time of its introduction into OE and shall be better able to distinguish between early and late borrowings. What follows may appear more dogmatic than is warranted. We shall concentrate on what may be regarded as reasonably agreed, avoiding technical and hypothetical discussions which would be largely unintelligible to the non-expert.

BRITISH NAMES OF HILLS AND WOODS

Comparatively few of these British names are found in early sources, but where they do occur, the forms are important and instructive. Kinver and Morfe (St), e.g., appear in an original eighth-century charter as *Cynibre* and *Moerheb, Moreb* respectively. This makes it clear that the second element of Kinver is late Brit **bre(ȝa)* 'hill', whilst without this charter form Morfe would be an unsolved mystery. It is clearly a British name, corresponding possibly, as Ekwall suggests, to a reduction of an OW *mor-dref* 'big village'. Brit *Corinium* (Circencester) must have developed to something like *Cerin* before it was adopted, otherwise the pronunciation of the *C* in OE would be inexplicable. OE *Cirencester* (577), the origin of the present spelling, should have become a modern *Chirenchester*, a form actually found in Layamon. The local pronunciations *Sissiter, Sister*,

[1] 4th edition, 1960.

and the spelling pronunciation *Syren-sester*, are due to the AFr pronunciation of *ch* as *ts*, later *s*.[1] Wrekin (Sa), *Wreocen-* (855), a hill to which was transferred the British name of Wroxeter, the *Viroconium* of the Antonine Itinerary, goes back to a British form with loss of *i* between the *v* and the *r*, but the etymology is obscure.

A common term for 'mountain' is Co *meneth*, OW *minid*, W *mynydd*, which usually became OE *myned*. It survives in Mynde (He), Longmynd (Sa), a long, broad ridge, near which are Myndtown and Minton, where OE *tūn* has been added to the hill-name, Minn (Ch) and Meend (Gl, He, Sa). In Mindrum (Nb) it has been compounded with *trum* or *drum* 'ridge', and in Mendip, *Menedepe* 1185, with an element suggested to be OE *hop* 'valley'. Minehead (So) is situated by a hill on which are East and West Myne (*Mene* 1086). This hill is *Menedun* in 1225, 'the hill (OE *dūn*) called *Mene*', which is probably a simplification of *Myned-dūn*, later *Myne-dūn*, interpreted as 'Myne Hill'. Hence Myne and Minehead, *Mynheafdon* 1046, *Menehewed* 1225, where OE *hēafod* has been added, 'Myne Head' or 'Myne Hill'.

Brit **caito-* 'wood', later **cēto-* (W *coed*) remained in OE as **cēt*, which became *cīet* c600 and later *cīt*, *cȳt*, and survives in Chute, Chitterne ('house in the wood', a hybrid compounded with OE *ærn* 'house'), Chittoe (possibly 'yew wood'), all in Wilts, perhaps in Chiddingly and Chithurst (Sx), and in the derivative Chideock (Do) 'wooded'. In Anglian districts it was adopted as *cēt* in Cheetham (La) and Cheadle (Ch, La), whilst in the south-east it is found as *cæt* in Chatham (Ess, K), and probably in Chattenden (K), *Chatindone* 1281, which is not far from Chatham, on the opposite side of the Medway, and was probably an outlying part of Chatham. Here, too, belongs Penge (Sr), *Penceat* 1067, *Pænge* 957 (a wood), 'chief wood'. As a second element, **cēto-* usually appears as *-chet*: Melchet (Ha), perhaps 'bare wood', Lytchett (Do) 'grey wood', Watchet (So) 'lower wood', and, with popular etymology, in Morchard (D) 'great wood', corresponding to W *mawr-coed*, and in Orchard (Do), *Archet* 939, identical with the Welsh Argoed, 'shelter of wood'. Culcheth (La) and Culgaith (Cu) are both from a PrOE **Cȳlcēt* 'narrow wood', the first element being Brit **coilo-* 'narrow'.

Many surviving village names of British origin were originally names of natural features, of rivers, hills and forests, which had already been adopted by the Anglo-Saxons and were afterwards given to the villages which grew up in the neighbourhood. Only

[1] Cf. p. 199.

exceptionally, and in the parts settled late, were they inhabited by Britons. Among the most common British or Primitive Welsh elements found in such names are: *barr 'top, summit' in Great Barr (St); *bre(ʒ) 'hill' in Bray (D) and in compounds with the synonymous OE dūn or hyll, Bredon (Wo), Breedon on the Hill (Lei), Brill (Bk), Brehull 1198, and, as a final element, in Clumber (Nt), Mellor (Db, La), Kinver (St); *brynn 'hill' in Bryn (Sa), Brynn (La); *carrec 'rock' in Cark (La), Cargo, Carrock Fell (Cu), Liscard (Ch), Lisecark 1260, 'hall on the cliff'; Brit *crouco-, late Brit *crūgo- 'hill, mound, barrow' in Creech (Do, So), Crich (Db), Crook (D, Do), Crutch (Wo), in compounds with British elements, as Evercreech (So) 'yew', Penkridge (St), Romano-British Pennocrucium, 'hill summit',[1] and with OE elements in Christon (So), Crucheston 1197, Cruchfield (Berks), Crewkerne (So), 'hill-house', and in the tautological Churchill (So, Wo) and Crichel (Do), with the addition of OE hyll; *mēl (W moel) 'bald' in Malvern (Wo), 'bare hill', Melchet (Ha) 'bare wood', Mellor (Db, La) Melver 1246, from *mēl-bre(ʒ) 'bald hill', to which ON stǫng 'pole' has been added in Mallerstang (Cu) and W blaen 'top' prefixed in Plenmeller (Nb); *penno- 'head, end, hill' in Pendle Hill, Pendlebury and Pendleton (La) and Penhill (NRY), in all of which a tautological hyll has been added to an original penn, and in the Lancs names a second Hill, beorg 'hill' or tūn, Pensax (Wo) 'Saxons' Hill', identical in meaning with Sixpenny Handley (Wo). Names beginning with an original Pen- are difficult, as there was also an OE penn 'enclosure, fold', which was not uncommon, but the above examples seem to be certainly British in origin. *ros 'moor' occurs in Roos (ERY), Roose (La), Ross (He, Nb), and in Moccas (He), 'swine moor'.

RIVER-NAMES

On the banks of the Essex Colne lie four villages, Colne Engaine, Earls Colne, Wakes Colne and White Colne, which owe their names to their situation on the banks of the Colne, a British river-name of doubtful etymology, identical with the Herts Colne and the Clun. Such village-names are rare in the eastern counties but common in

[1] The Roman station was on rising ground near the place where Watling Street crosses the stream now called the river Penk. By the 10th century, the name had been transferred to the stream (Penchrich), which later gave name to the village on its bank, so that the original 'hill summit' became the name of a village in the bottom of a shallow valley.

the south-west, where Brixton, Hill, Kingston, Longbridge and Monkton Deverill are all simply *Devrel* in Domesday Book, 'river of the fertile upland region', so called from the river along which they lie. The farm-names Deveral in Gwinear and Deveral in Sancreed (Co) are similarly named from small streams near by. Frome St Quentin, Vauchurch and Whitfield, with Chilfrome (Do), Bishops, Castle and Canon Frome (He) and Frome (So) all similarly owe their names to their situation on the banks of a river Frome, a British name identical in origin with Ffraw in Anglesey, from a root meaning 'fair, fine, brisk'.

Such village-names are usually found in areas thinly populated and settled late. The Anglo-Saxons adopted the river-name which came to be applied to the villages in which they lived. At a much later period it was found convenient to distinguish the villages by distinctive additions to the names, but in the early days the river-name alone was used. This would not be so confusing as might at first sight appear. The actual name of the river would seldom be used locally. It would be of more importance to people at a distance. Even today the Londoner goes for a stroll along 'the Embankment' and the countryman for a walk along or a swim in 'the river'. In medieval documents it is not uncommon to read that a man was drowned in the 'aqua de Wautham' (the Lea) or the 'ripa de Abiton' (the Granta), where the name of the river was of less importance than the part where the tragedy occurred. But such important rivers as the Severn, the Thames or the Humber would be well known to sailors and traders from abroad and it would be important for them to know the name of the river for which they were making.

The farther west we go, the greater the number of British river-names which have survived. By the time these areas were reached the full force of the invasion was spent, the Saxons were concerned rather with occupation than with conquest, and there can be little doubt that for some time Briton and Teuton lived side by side and this intercourse resulted in the adoption of numbers of British names. But in the east, where the full brunt of the Saxon onset was felt, those Britons who were not slain or did not escape by flight lived on only as serfs, a subdued minority, crushed and despised. Here only the more important rivers and the large Roman towns preserved their British names. In Kent, Cray, Medway and Darent are pre-English names; in Essex only Lea, Pant and Colne. In Sussex the only British river-name still in use is the Lavant. In these eastern counties some river-names are of English origin, the Kent Swale and the Essex Black-water.

Place-names prove the former existence of now lost British river-names, the *Limen* in Kent, preserved in Lyminge and Lympne, the *Tarrant* in Sussex, the old name of the Arun, surviving in Tarrant St in Arundel, and the *Hyle*, now the Roding, from which Ilford (Ess) was named. But a noteworthy feature of the river-names in the east is the large number of back-formations. An eleventh-century charter shows that *Beadewan ea* was then the name of the Chelmer, and this survives in the names of two parishes on its banks, Great and Little Baddow near Chelmsford. A. H. Smith unhesitatingly explains this as 'the battle river', from OE *beadu* 'battle', but long ago Ekwall remarked that 'such a name would be absolutely without English parallels', and the etymology is best left open. No other name of the river has been noted before the sixteenth century, when the map-makers call it the *Chelmer*, clearly a back-formation from Chelmsford (*Celmeresfort* 1086, 'the ford of Cēolmǣr'). Similar back-formations are the Eden, from Edenbridge (K), the Rom from Romford (Ess), the Brain from Braintree and others in Essex, the Wandle from Wandsworth (Sr), and a number in Norfolk and Suffolk, including Thet (Thetford), the Bure from Briston (*Burstuna* 1086) or Burgh near Aylsham (*Burc* 1086), or both, Alde (Aldeburgh), Bret (Bretten-ham), Deben (Debenham) and Ore (Orwell).

It is a noteworthy fact that the same British name is frequently applied, often in a slightly varied form, to more than one river or stream and that many of these names mean simply 'water' or 'river', e.g., Avon (cf. W *afon* 'water, stream'), found only in the south-west and Scotland; Axe, Exe, Esk, Usk, Wiske, all forms of Brit *Isca* 'water'; Dour, the river from which Dover (K) is named, Dover Beck (Nt), Doverdale (Wo), Dore (He), from *Dubrā* (cf. W *dwfr* 'water'), found also in compounds such as Calder (La, Y), Conder (La), Deverill (W), Andover (Ha), an old name of the Anton, and Condover (Sa), identical with Conder. Some names are derived from descriptive adjectives: Cam (Gl), Cam Beck (Cu), Wiley (W) 'crooked', 'winding'; Cray 'clean, pure'; Lugg 'white, bright'; Devy, Dove 'dark, black'. Others derive from names of trees or plants: Derwent, Darent, Dart 'oak'; Leam, Lemon, Lymn, and *Limene*, the old name of the Rother (Sx, K) 'elm'.

That the Celts worshipped rivers is suggested by the name of the French Marne, Gaulish *Matrona* 'mother'. The *Matronae* were the

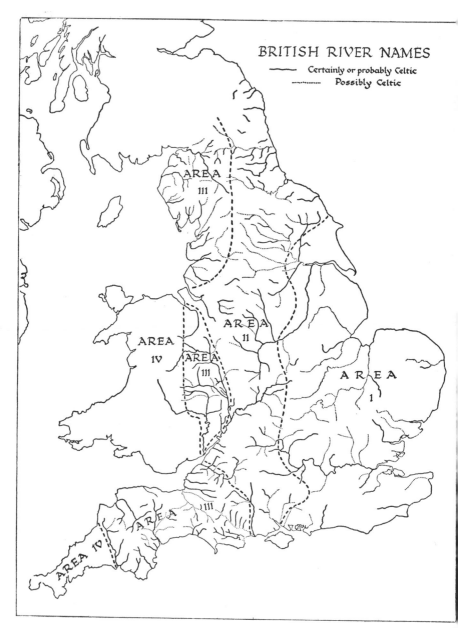

BRITISH RIVER NAMES

——— Certainly or probably Celtic
·············· Possibly Celtic

AREA
111

AREA
11

AREA
IV

AREA
111

AREA
1

AREA
111

AREA IV

The Celtic Element

From Kenneth Jackson's *Language and History in Early Britain* (Edinburgh University Press, 1953)

Gaulish mother-goddesses. Dee, earlier *Deva*, is from Brit *Dēuā* 'the goddess', 'the holy one', an interpretation confirmed by the alternative Welsh name *Aerfen* 'the goddess of war'. Giraldus Cambrensis tells us that in his life-time the Dee was still supposed to indicate in advance the result of the wars between the Welsh and the English by eating away its bank on the Welsh or on the English side. It was clearly regarded as a holy river dedicated to or identical with the goddess of war. Dee may be a later name than *Aerfen* and came to be commonly used because the real name was regarded as too sacred for everyday use. It may be that such a belief lies behind the frequency of names meaning simply 'water' or 'river' and that some, at least, of these once had sacred names. The Bean, on which are situated Bengeo and Bennington (Herts), 'the ridge and the village of the dwellers by the R. Beane', derives from a Brit *ben*, identical in origin with Ir *ben* 'woman' and with the second element of *Aerfen*. As this clearly means 'goddess', the Beane was probably also a sacred river. Lea is probably a derivative of *Lugus*, the name of a British god, whilst some of the names containing *Camel* are probably derived from the name of another deity named *Camulos*, found also in *Camulodunum*, the British name of Colchester.

ROMANO-BRITISH TOWNS

Even if the old British cities or Roman stations were destroyed by the Anglo-Saxons, the names would often remain associated with the sites, and a number of these still survive. London has preserved the Romano-British *Londinium* almost unaltered. The process by which *Eburacum* became York has been discussed above.[1] Carlisle appears in the Antonine Itinerary as *Luguvalio* 'belonging to *Luguvalos*', a personal-name meaning 'strong as (the Celtic god) *Lugus*', whose name apparently occurs in *Lug(u)dunum*, from which Leiden (Holland) and Lyons (France) derive. By the ninth century the name had become *Luel*, to which OW *cair* (W *caer*) 'city' was prefixed, *Carleol* 1108, *Cairleil* 1129, from which comes, somewhat irregularly, the modern Carlisle.

Some of these names were adopted with the addition of OE *ceaster*: Mancetter (Wa), Brit *Manduessedon*, Manchester (La), Brit *Mamucion* and Wroxeter, Brit *Viroconion*, all mentioned in the Antonine Itinerary and all obscure in meaning. The first element of

---

[1] *v.* p. 24.

Winchester, originally *Venta Belgarum*, is identical with *Venta Icenorum* (Caister), *Venta Silurum* (Caerwent, Mon) and *Gwent*, the name of an old district in Wales. Gloucester, Brit *Glevum*, is perhaps the 'bright, splendid place', whilst Worcester, *Uueogorna civitas* 692, *Uueogorna ceastre* 889, was 'the Roman fort of the tribe called *Wigoran* or *Weogoran*'. The tribal name is also found in Wyre Forest and in Wyre Piddle (Wo) and may be derived from a river-name identical with Wyre (La), on which is Wyresdale, and the Gaulish *Vigora* (now Vière and Voire in France), possibly meaning 'winding river'. *Wyre* may have been the old name of the Piddle (of English origin), on which Wyre Piddle stands. In other instances the Saxons added *-ceaster* to the river-name: Doncaster (Don), Exeter (Exe), Colchester (Colne), Lancaster (Lune), etc.

Old names of this kind are common in Kent, where we have Dover and Lympne from river-names, with the British name of Canterbury, *Durovernon*, probably 'the swamp by the fort'. Other names provide difficult problems. Richborough occurs as 'Ρουτουπίαι in Ptolemy, *Rutupina litora* in Lucan and *Portus Ritupis* in the Antonine Itinerary. By the time of Bede the name had been contracted and *-ceaster* added, *Reptacæstir*. In the Domesday Monachorum it is found as *Raetta*, apparently a development of *Repta*, which seems, like *Rutupiae*, to have been used without addition. To this was finally added OE *-burg* 'fort', *Ratteburg* 1197. The modern form descends from a genitival compound, *Retesbrough* 14th, 'the fort of *Rætta*'. The exact meaning cannot be determined, but it may be from a root meaning 'to tear out', 'to dig', hence 'a ditch or trench'. Reculver is *Regulbium* in the *Notitia Dignitatum*, from Brit *ro* 'great' and **gulbio-* 'beak', 'the great headland'. By 669 this had come to be pronounced *Reculf*. The modern form derives from *Raculvre* 1276, in which an inorganic *r* has been added by Anglo-Norman scribes, as in the Domesday *Dertre* for the R. Dart (D), etc. Here, exceptionally, this *r* has been retained. Rochester has had a curious and complicated history. In the Antonine Itinerary it is *Durobrivis*, a British name, 'bridges of the stronghold'. This became a PrW *D'robrīw*, the *u* being lost before the name was adopted into OE. The Saxons found this difficult to pronounce and turned it first into *Hrofri* and then into *Hrofi*, the name appearing in Bede both in Latin as *ciuitas Hrofi* and in English as *Hrofæscæstræ*, 'the Roman fort of *Hrofi*'. Then the initial *H* was dropped and the DB *Rovecestre* developed normally into *Rouchestre* and finally to Rochester.

Eccles

Some village-names of British origin may have denoted places of some importance. Eccles (La) goes back to a Brit *eclēs* 'church', whence W *eglwys*, OCo *eglos*, from Lat *ecclesia*. A survival of Britons in the Eccles and Manchester district is suggested by such British names as Cheetham, Cheetwood, Pendleton, Pendlebury and, perhaps, Worsley, which seems to have been a British name ending in *cēt* 'wood' to which was added OE *lēah*. Two further examples of Eccles in Norfolk and two of Eccles House in Derbyshire may similarly point to British villages, but Eccles in Kent has quite a different origin and is purely English. It is *Aclesse*, *Æcclesse* in the eleventh century, *Aiglesse* in 1086 and *Eccles* in 1208, probably 'oak-pasture', OE *āc-lǣs*, *ǣc-lǣs*, with variation between the nominative singular *āc* and the genitive **ǣc*.

This same element *eclēs* may also occur in such names as Ecclesfield and Ecclesall (WRY), Eccleshall (Wa), Eccleshill (La), Eccleston (La, Ch), etc., names found chiefly in the north-west Midlands. The forms of some may point to a late Brit **eglēs*, e.g., Eccleshill (WRY), *Egleshil* 1086, Eccleston (La), *Eglestun* 1086, Eccleswall (He), *Eggleswalle* 1274, but we cannot be certain that this was not an English development. Exhall occurs twice in Warwickshire, near Coventry and near Alcester, both appearing as *Eccleshale*, which had become *Exhall* by 1535. Each is also found as *Egelyshale* (1228) or *Egleshale* (1291), whilst that near Alcester is *Echeleshale* in 1291. Here *ch* may represent a *k*-sound; it might, however, represent the *ch* sound, surviving from a personal-name *Eccel*, which should normally become *Etchel-*, but, with early syncope of unstressed *e*, the genitive *Ecceles-* would become *Eccles-*, where the *c* would not be palatalised. Thus Exhall may be either 'church-nook' or 'Eccel's nook', and a similar explanation is possible in other compounds. The early forms of Ashford (Mx) clearly had a palatal *c*, *Ecelesford* 969, *Echelesford* a1066, but later forms are similar to those above, *Exforde* 1062, *Eglesford* 1445. The meaning is probably 'Eccel's brook', but it is also possible that this (and other names) may contain a stream-name *ec(c)les*, as in Ecchinswell (Ha), originally the name of the stream there, called *Ec(c)lesburna* in 931,[1] and identical with the river-name Ecclesbourne (Db).

[1] O. G. S. Crawford (*The Andover District* (1922), p. 79) takes the first element as *eglwys*. 'At the spot where the spring rises stood the old church, of which the remains can still be seen.' But he gives no evidence that these were those of a church, or of their date.

FOREST-NAMES

Forest-names are often of British origin and etymologically obscure, as in Blean (K) and Chiltern (O). Berkshire is named from an old forest, OE *Bearruc*, from Brit **barrǫg* 'hilly'. In Lancashire and Cheshire, place-names provide evidence of the extent of an old forest-area called Lyme. To distinguish the Lancashire lands of the Honour of Lancaster from those in other counties, it became usual to describe them as *infra Limam* or *infra comitatum* as distinct from those *extra Limam* or *extra comitatum*, 'the lands within or those beyond the Lyme'. The name is preserved in Ashton-under-Lyne, where there is a Lyme Wood (1246), Limehurst (1379) and Lyme Park (1337). In Cheshire we have Lyme Handley; Church Lawton was formerly *Lauton under lyme*, whilst Audlem, *Aldelime* 1086, is either 'old Lyme' or that part of Lyme held by one Alda. In Staffordshire we have Newcastle-under-Lyme, Whitmore, formerly *Wytemore under Lyme* 1243, and Burslem, *Barcardeslim* 1086, *Burwardeslym* 1297, 'Burgweard's Lyme'. In Shropshire, Betton-in-Hales, near the Staffordshire boundary, was *Betton under Lime* in 1182, whilst the neighbouring Norton-in-Hales is described as situated next the wood called *Lima* in 1126 and as *Norton subtus Lime* in 1225.

The name is a difficult one. It was clearly applied originally to a very extensive forest-area in Lancashire, Cheshire, Staffordshire and Shropshire, but ceased at an early period to be applied, at least officially to the whole area, though it continued to be used for various parts of it. As most of the places containing the word are on or near a county boundary, the name was interpreted as 'boundary'. The lands of the earls of Chester *extra Lymam* referred originally to those 'beyond the forest of Lyme', which then formed the eastern boundary of Cheshire. Though Lyme Forest formed only a small part of the boundary of Lancashire, it did separate the Lancashire lands of the honour from those in Derbyshire, etc. Thus, *infra, extra Limam* came to be used to mean 'inside or outside the (county) boundary', an interpretation perpetuated in the alternative *Lyne* of Ashton-under-Lyne, from a substitution of *line*, used from at least 1595 in the sense 'limit, boundary'. *Lyme* was clearly a name in use in OE and it is impossible to derive it either as an OE or a British word from Latin *limes* 'boundary'. It appears to have been the name of an old forest of which Macclesfield Forest was a survival and probably belongs to a Celtic stem **lemo*, **limo* 'elm', hence 'elm wood'.

THE SURVIVAL OF A BRITISH POPULATION

Apart from the well-known names familiar to the Teutonic invaders before their departure from the Continent, Celtic place-names were borrowed at different times according to the date when the Anglo-Saxons came into contact with the native Romano-Britons. In the course of the conquest enclaves of Britons might be left in forests or on moors, surrounded by English settlers, and might retain their British language long after the tide of conquest had passed them by. Ultimately they would be absorbed and their place-names taken over, but both languages would by this time have developed and changed from those spoken when the adjacent areas were first occupied. Thus the Celtic place-names in the wilds of the Pennines between Cumberland and Northumberland or on the Yorkshire moors reveal a linguistic stage later than that in the names on either side.

The western part of Yorkshire, the British kingdom of Elmet, which included Leeds, remained unconquered until it was overwhelmed at the beginning of the reign of Edwin (617–32). Elmet is a British name identical with *Elfet*, the name of a cantred in Wales, but its etymology is obscure. It still survives as an addition to two names, Barwick in Elmet and Sherburn in Elmet. Leeds has been derived by Max Förster from a Celtic river-name *Lotissa*, from **luto-* 'mud'. Jackson disputes this and does not fully accept Ekwall's explanation from a root **plōd* 'flowing', an assumed early name of the Aire. He considers the name is more likely to be a tribe-name than a river-name, from a Brit *Lātenses* which may well contain a river-name *Lāta* 'the boiling or violent one' and that Leeds 'very likely' means 'the Folk living round the *Lāta*'.[1]

Further evidence of British survival is found in the West Riding names Wales and Waleswood. Wales is identical with the name of the country, OE *Walas* 'the Britons', used for the place where they lived. Place-names compounded with this element are not always easy to interpret. They are seldom recorded early and are liable to confusion with *weald* 'forest', *weall* 'wall' and *wælle* 'spring or stream'. Even an unequivocal OE *weala-tūn* or *weala-cot* 'village or cottage of the Britons' would not necessarily point to a British survival, for the word also meant 'serf, slave'. These serfs may well have been

---

[1] *Antiquity*, vol. xx (1946), pp. 209–10. The Kent Leeds is a different name, of English origin, probably the name of the stream there, OE *Hlȳde* 'loud brook'.

Britons; most probably were; but some may have been of some other nationality, and there is no proof that the names go back to early Saxon times. Caution is needed in using these names as a proof of British survival. Zachrisson maintained that the majority, if not all, of the Waltons and Walcotts contained *weall* not *wealh* and admitted only Walworth (Sr) and Walden (Herts), the only names with pre-Conquest forms, as derivatives of *wealh*. Of 11 such names in East Anglia, Schram finds *wealh* only in Walpole (Sf) and Walcott (Nf). The fact that *worð* is an element found in early place-names, combined with its situation, suggests that Walworth was a village of Britons, just as Walbrook points to a British survival in London. The field-name Walfords in Finchingfield, *Walewurth* Hy 3, and Walter Hall in Boreham, *Walhfare* 1062, similarly suggest the survival of groups of Britons in the woodlands of central Essex. Saffron Walden (Ess) is almost certainly the 'valley of the Britons'. It is situated in the far north-west corner of the kingdom which the East Saxons would reach last and Sir Cyril Fox is of opinion that a neighbouring cemetery was that of 'Christian Romano-Britons who continued to occupy the site for some time after the conquest of the district as a whole was completed'. But Walsoken, West Walton and Walpole St Peter's and St Andrew (Nf) are undoubtedly named from the sea-wall now known as Roman Bank, just as Walton on the Naze (Ess) must owe its name to another sea-wall which failed of its purpose. The sea has been encroaching here for centuries and the original church has long been swallowed up by the waves. The Cumberland Walton is by the Roman Wall, whilst that in Suffolk was near the site of one of the forts of the Saxon Shore, now beneath the sea, and may owe its name either to its situation near the walls of the fort or to a sea-wall. Each name needs consideration in the light of all the available evidence. The massacre of the Britons at Anderida is not now regarded as typical of their fate in general. Many of them undoubtedly did survive, but their chance of survival would be less in the districts which felt the full force of the first Anglo-Saxon incursions.

Wallasey in Cheshire is *Walea* in 1086 'the island of the Britons'. Later, a second ME *ey* was added to the genitive of this name, *Waylayesegh* 1362, 'the island of *Walea*'. Liscard, now part of the borough of Wallasey, is a British name 'hall on the cliff'. There is some other evidence of British settlement in Cheshire in Crewe 'ford', Landrican 'church of St Tecan', and there are clusters of British names in certain parts of Lancashire, the most interesting of which are Treales, *Treueles* 1086, identical with Treflys (Carnarvon), from *tref* 'village' and *llys* 'court', 'the township of the court', and Wigan, perhaps identical with Wigan in Anglesey, which appears to be elliptical for *Tref Wigan* 'Wigan's homestead', a personal-name found also in Wiggonby (Cu).

Place-names such as Walton do not necessarily prove the survival of a British language. They suggest rather that British villages were sufficiently rare to be worthy of note. Nor do they of necessity point to a late survival of a British element. More important in this respect are Scandinavian place-names containing ON *Bretar* (gen. pl. *Breta*) 'Britons'. This is used chiefly of Britons of the north-west and Strathclyde and is found in Bretby (Db), Birkby (Cu, La, NRY, WRY), olim *Brettebi*, Brettargh Holt (La), 'shieling of the Britons' and Briscoe (Cu), *Brethesco* 1203, 'wood of the Britons' (ON *Bretaskógr*). Two examples of Bretton (Db, WRY) are doubtful. These places are all in Scandinavian districts, none south of Derbyshire, all in areas where, on other grounds, a late survival of Britons would be expected. They are all, too, in areas of Irish–Norwegian settlement and, as all are compounded with a Scandinavian element, they must point to the existence of groups or villages of Britons in the ninth and tenth centuries. Brettargh contains the Irish loan-word *ergh* and suggests the presence of Gaels from Ireland. According to the *History of St Cuthbert*, Ecgfrith, king of Northumbria (670–85), gave Cartmel 'et omnes Britannos cum eo' to St Cuthbert. This implies a British population living on after the Anglian invasion. Near Cartmel is a place Walton Hall, *Walletun* 1086. This, in spite of the form, may represent a village of these Britons (*Walatūn*). In the same parish is Birkby Hall. The situation of both places, fairly high and away from the broad valley, suggests that these Britons were compelled to settle in the more remote parts on the less fertile land. Whether they were Irishmen who accompanied the Scandinavians who named Birkby or whether these latter gave a Scandinavian name to a village of Britons in existence before their arrival, we cannot say. Unfortunately, none of these names throws any light on the problem of the survival of Britons in the eastern and southern districts first settled by the Anglo-Saxons.

Devonshire

The name Devon is identical with the tribal name *Defnas* which came to be used as the name of their territory. It is Brit *Dumnonii*, the name of the Celtic aborigines, which was transferred to their Saxon conquerors. Denbury (D), *Deveneberie* 1086, 'fort of the men of Devon', is the site of an old earthwork which may once have been a stronghold of the Dumnonii. This would tend to support the common belief in a strong Celtic element in Devonshire, but the most remarkable fact brought out by the full survey of the Place-names of Devonshire is 'the prevailingly English character of the local nomenclature. The British element is much more evident in the place-names of Dorset and Somerset than in most parts of Devon'.[1] It would appear that the Saxon occupation of eastern Devon may have begun soon after 658, that the Saxons reached Exeter before the end of the seventh century, and that the west and the north of the county were opened to them by the battle of 710 between Ine king of the West Saxons and Geraint king of the Britons. It is clear that the Saxon conquest of Devon cannot be regarded as the imposition of the rule of an alien minority upon a large British population. The whole topographical vocabulary of the region is English. Archaeologists are of opinion that 'Devon was thinly inhabited during the Romano-British period'. The Breton kingdom of Domnonia, it appears highly probable, was colonised in the sixth century by migrants from the Dumnonia which has given its name to Devon. A large number of the Celts of Devon must have withdrawn from Britain a century or more before the arrival of the Saxons, who in the late seventh century found only a sparsely settled Celtic kingdom. When the resistance of its kings had been broken, the Saxons, now dominant and outnumbering the natives, proceeded with their settlement and by the eleventh century had created a distinctive local nomenclature which extended over every part of the county. But there was no extermination of the Britons. They lived side by side with the conquerors, probably as serfs in such places as Walland and Wallover, but possibly as a free and independent community at Walreddon (OE *Wealaræden* 'community of Britons'). In Lifton Hundred a group of British place-names suggests the late survival of a British-speaking population: Breazle, Carley, Dunterton,[2] Kelly (cf. Co *celli* 'wood') and Trebick, perhaps a parallel to Trebeigh (Co), 'little homestead'; cf. W *tref, bychan*). This element *tref* is found also in Treable and Trellick; Dunchideock is a purely British name 'wooded fort or camp', as is Penquit 'end of the wood', whilst there are a number of

---

[1] v. *Place-names of Devon*, xiii–xxiv.
[2] v. *Place-names of Devon*, 174, 189, 182.

hybrids such as are found where different races intermingled: Breadon, Penhill, Countisbury, *arx Cynuit* c894, a hill-name from **kuno-* 'high', etc. Brit *nemeton* 'holy place, sanctuary', used also of a 'holy' river, is found in George, Bishop's and King's Nympton, Nymet Tracy and Nymph, as also in Nymphsfield (Gl) and Lanivet (Co) 'church on the site of an earlier heathen sanctuary'. These British names are widely spread throughout the county but form only a small proportion of the whole.

BILINGUAL BRITONS AND MONOGLOT SAXONS

During the Roman occupation British place-names consisted either of uncompounded names such as *Eburacum* or *Londinium* or of true compounds in which the defining element preceded that defined, as *Lētocētum* 'grey wood' or *Moridūnum* 'sea-fort'.[1] Such compounds survive both in Wales and in England (e.g. Lytchett (Do) 'grey wood', Malvern (Wo) 'bare hill', Wendover (Bk) 'white water'), but the medieval Brittonic languages formed their place-names on a different pattern, in which a noun was followed by a defining adjective or a dependent noun, as in *Coed Mawr*, lit. 'wood big' or *Penn Brynn* 'head hill'. Such late compounds are common in Brittany as in Wales and Cornwall and are found in England, chiefly in the western counties, in areas of late Anglo-Saxon settlement, e.g. Coedmoor (He) 'great wood', Maisemore (Gl) 'great plain', and in Cumberland, Blencarn 'summit-rock', Cumrew 'valley-slope', Glendhu, lit. 'valley dark', these latter due, perhaps, to the British re-occupation of north Cumberland in the tenth and eleventh centuries.

The British population was nowhere completely exterminated, though it certainly survived more fully in some areas than in others. Brittonic was still spoken in Somerset and Dorset at the end of the seventh century for Creechbarrow Hill (Do), the hill from which Creech St Michael took its name, is described in a charter of 682 as 'the hill which is called in the British language *Cructan*, but among us (i.e. the Saxons) *Crycbeorh*'. Symeon of Durham, too, quotes a document of 877 describing Selwood Forest as 'the forest which in English is called *Mucelwudu*, in Latin *Magna Silva* and in British *Coitmawr*'. The modern name is English, 'sallow wood'. The existence in OE of such personal-names as Cædmon and Cædwalla, undoubtedly of

[1] Probably the origin of Merthen (Co), *Merðin* 1186, *Meredin* 1195, where there is a large camp by the Helford estuary.

Celtic origin, implies intermarriage and interfusion between the two races, presumably on a considerable scale, and therefore some degree of bilingualism.[1]

As a rule it is the aboriginal population and not the newcomers who are responsible for the handing on of place-names. The Britons learned the language of their conquerors and acquired their sound-system and vocabulary very completely. For a time they could speak both Anglo-Saxon and British, but this bilingual period is not likely to have lasted long, especially in the east. It is not probable that the conquerors learned much of the language of the conquered. They had difficulties with the pronunciation of the names they borrowed and had recourse to popular etymologies, as when they turned *Ebrauc* into *Eoforwic* (York) and *Domnoc* into *Dunewic* (Dunwich). Some British place-names undoubtedly came into English through the mouths of bilingual Britons, as is proved by translations and by some of the hybrid names, and more particularly by the preservation of the plural forms of Dover, Lympne and Rochester in Kent, where British place-names are few, but where much of the Romano-British civilisation was preserved. Others were taken over by uncomprehending monoglot Saxons, especially the tautological compounds.

Place-names like Cheetwood, Penhill, Bredon and Crichel, which consist of a combination of a Celtic word with an English word identical in meaning, are hardly likely to be due to bilingualism. It looks as if the Britons called a certain wood *ir cēd* 'the wood', and the Anglo-Saxons, hearing, but not understanding this, took it for a name and added their native word, hence *Cētwudu*, and similarly added *hyll* to a PrW *penn*, etc. Bilingual Britons would hardly have coined such names.

THE DISTRIBUTION OF BRITISH PLACE-NAMES

A clear picture of the distribution of surviving British place-names can best be obtained from a summary of Jackson's division of the country into four areas, based largely on river-names, the largest and most significant class. *v.* Map, p. 78.

Area I includes the country east of a line from the Yorkshire Wolds to Salisbury Plain and the New Forest, including the East Riding of Yorkshire, Nottinghamshire, Leicestershire, Oxfordshire, east Berkshire and south Hampshire. Here Brittonic names are rare and are

[1] For Celtic personal-names in place-names, *v.* pp. 66–70.

confined almost exclusively to large and medium-sized rivers like the Trent, Thames, Thame and Darent. Names whose Celtic origin is doubtful form the majority, and these include the Witham, Soar, Welland, Ouse, Granta and the Stours. The area corresponds fairly closely with the extent of primary English settlement up to the first half of the sixth century.

Area II is an intermediate central strip, west of the line described above and east of one running approximately along the eastern borders of Cumberland and Lancashire to the Ribble, and thence south-west to the flat country round Wigan, and to the sea. It is taken up again near Chester, passes by the valley of the Dee and south to the Severn, which it follows to the Bristol Channel; crossing this, it runs along the northern boundary of Somerset and down the eastern boundary through Selwood to the south-west corner of Wiltshire, where it turns east down the Wiley valley and thence along the boundary between Hampshire and Dorset. Brittonic names are markedly more common than in Area I and the proportion of certainly Celtic names is higher. They include more names of small rivers. The area agrees pretty well with that of the expansion of Anglo-Saxon occupation in the second half of the sixth century in the south and the first half of the seventh in the north.

Area III includes Cumberland, Westmorland and Lancashire to the west of the line described above, a strip between that line and the present Welsh border, comprising most of Shropshire, west Worcestershire, all Hereford north of the Wye, and Gloucestershire west of the Severn, with all south-western England between the same line and the Tamar. Here Brittonic names are especially common, including often those of mere streams, and the proportion of certainly Celtic names is highest of all. The sections agree remarkably well with the third and final stage of Anglo-Saxon conquest: in the middle and third quarter of the seventh century in the north, the middle and second half of the seventh century on the Welsh Marches and the middle of the seventh and the early part of the eighth centuries in the south-west.

Area IV consists of Wales and Monmouthshire with the corner of Herefordshire south-west of the Wye and Cornwall. The whole character of the nomenclature is overwhelmingly Celtic since these lands all remained Brittonic in speech until at least the Norman Conquest, most of Cornwall until the end of the Middle Ages and part of it until the eighteenth century, and much of Wales until the present day.

The names of Romano-British towns, the larger rivers and some hills and forests are preserved in all parts of England, even in Area I. Area II differs in including not only these but also more and smaller rivers, and more hills and forests. To these Area III adds the names of villages, homesteads and even small brooks, with compounds of the later type.

The Welsh Marches

In Herefordshire and Shropshire we are faced with special problems. It was not until the second half of the seventh century that the Mercians became firmly established in Herefordshire, and even then their occupation was sporadic and incomplete. In the eighth century Offa's Dyke was made to mark the boundary and serve as a defence against the Welsh, the line adopted clearly abandoning English territory to the Welsh. As late as the Norman Conquest the Wye between Hereford and Monmouth still separated the English shires of Hereford and Gloucestershire from the Welsh territory to the west. This district, now represented by the Deanery of Archenfield, bore a Welsh name, *Erchin* or *Ercing* (c1150), a survival of the Romano-British *Ariconium* of the Antonine Itinerary. Its derivation is obscure, but the name was adopted by the Mercians as *Ircingafeld* (918) 'the open country of the men living in *Erchin*', and modern place-names still differentiate the areas of Welsh and English settlement separated by the Wye. On the eastern side we have such English names as Brockhampton, Fawley, Brampton, Walford and English Bicknor, on the west side is Welsh Bicknor, with Celtic names like Kilforge; Treyseck, Llanfrother, said to be the site of Dubricius's monastery and explained as *Llanfrawtur* 'church of the friars', Caradoc, *Cayrcradoc* 1292, *Cradoc* 1329, 'the fort of Caradoc', now preserving only the personal-name, Daffaluke, *Diffrinluke* 1478, a corruption of W *dyffryn-llwg* 'valley of the marsh', Ganarew, W *genau rhiw* 'pass of the hill', and Moccas, *Mochros, locus porcorum* c1150 'swine moor'. Elsewhere in the county we have pure Celtic names in Dinmore, W *din mawr* 'great stronghold', Ewyas 'sheep-district', Kilpeck, containing W *cil* 'corner, retreat', Pencoyd 'end of the wood', Pengethley, containing W *celli*, with the same meaning, with numerous names beginning with *Llan-*, as Llanfair 'church of the Virgin'. The mixture of races has produced interesting examples of translations of Welsh names: Bellimore from W *Bolgros* (*bolg* 'belly' and *rhos* 'moor'), Bridstow and Peterstow, originally *Lann San Bregit* c1130 and *Lann petyr* c1150. These Welsh place-names do not necessarily prove a survival of Celtic influence from an early period. Later Welsh immigration has modified English place-names and introduced many names of a late Welsh type. Trebumfrey has replaced the *Humfreyeston* of 1292. Sellack, *Lann Sulac* c1130, was originally the name of the church. The village, existing in 1086, was *Baysham*, a name which was lost in the sixteenth century (*Beysham* alias *Cellach* c1550). Now Sellack is the village and Baysham Court a farm in the parish. In Dorston in the middle of the thirteenth century the field-names were, with one exception, English, as *Huntehulle, Benfelde, Dudintone, Marleput,* etc., whereas today they are mostly Welsh, *Llanavon, Mynyddbrith, Pwll Cam, Bedw, Pen-y-lan,* etc. Late Welsh names include Nant-y-glas-dwyr 'valley of the grey-blue river', Pentre, W *pen-tref* 'village', Perth-y-Perton, said to be W *perth-y-perten* 'thorn-bush of the smart little girl', Pont Vaen 'stone bridge', Rhiwlas 'green slope', Trevaddock and Trewaddock 'Madoc's homestead', Ty bach 'little house', Tyboobach 'goblin-house', etc.

Here we may note Ekwall's neat and apt solution of the problem of a group of Herefordshire names. The Welsh form of Leominster, *Leomynster* 10th, was *Llanllieni*. The Welsh *llan* 'church' has been replaced by OE *mynster*. Thus the name of the place where the church was situated was OW *lion* or *lian*, of which *llieni* is a plural form. This became OE *Lēon*, the old name of a district on the Arrow and the Lugg, surviving in the *Leo-* of Leominster. It occurs as *Lene*, the DB form of Eardisland and Kingsland, as *Leine* for Monkland and as *Lenehalle* for Lyonshall. All these places were within an extensive district called *llieni* 'waters, streams'. Eardisland was that portion belonging to the earl (*Erleslen* 1234), Kingsland that of the king, and Monkland that of the monks of the abbey of Conches in Normandy, whilst Leominster was the 'church within the district of the waters'. Leland writes c1550: 'Leonminstar (alias Lemster) supposed of clerkis that the old name of this toune tooke beginninge of the nunes, and was caullyd in Walche Llanllieny, idem locus vel fanum monialium, and not of a lyon that is written to have apperyd to Kynge Merwalde'. He gives us the local pronunciation, Lemster, still in common use, rejects the fabled connexion with a lion and gives us the correct Welsh form, though he misinterprets it as the 'shrine of the nuns'. Ekwall explains the name as the 'church on the streams' or 'in the district of the streams'. The latter is more correct. The church of Leominster looks down on the Lugg, but Eardisland and Kingsland are some distance away, on the Arrow. These rivers, Arrow, Lugg and Pinsley, dominate the area and are liable to sudden and extensive flooding after heavy rain or thunder-storms in the Welsh hills, particularly in winter, when extensive areas are inundated, communications cut and villages isolated.

Shropshire represents an artificial union of the *Wreocensætan* 'the dwellers near the Wrekin' and the *Magonsætan*, once a people of some importance. They seem to have had a dynasty of their own, ruling over southern Shropshire and part of Herefordshire, including lands west of Offa's Dyke which they lost when that became the frontier between Wales and England. They were the people for whom the bishopric of Hereford was created and long retained their individuality, for they sent contingents to fight against Cnut at Ashingdon in Essex in 1016. Their name means 'the dwellers in a district called *Magen*', an early form of W *maen* 'stone', used also to mean 'plain', which is now preserved in Maund Bryan and Rose Maund in Herefordshire. Welsh names are numerous in the Forest of Clun (a British river-name) and the Oswestry district, where we find such names as Llan Howell, Pant-y-Lidan, Hengoed, Nant-y-gollen, etc., due, probably, as in Herefordshire, to a late Welsh immigration. Elsewhere they are less numerous, but by no means rare, including Prees (W *pres* 'brushwood copse'), Wenlock 'white monastery', Hodnet, early Welsh (*Glyn*) *Hodnant* 'pleasant, peaceful valley', Condover and Cound, both on Cound Beck.

The British element in Cheshire is comparatively slight, but includes Crewe (cf. W *cryw* 'ford'), with the hybrids Crewood and Crowton, Ince (cf. W *ynys* 'island'), Wheelock, a river-name, 'winding', Tarvin 'boundary' and Landican 'church of St Tecan', with Audlem, Liscard and Wallasey, discussed above.[1] Mottershead in Mottram (like Mocktree, Sa) probably contains W *moch-tref* 'pig-farm'.

In Gloucestershire and Worcestershire British names are fairly common in the parts adjoining Wales and Herefordshire. The Brit *Glevum* survives in Gloucester itself; Lancaut is the 'church of St Cewydd', Penpole, earlier *Penpau*, 'end of the district', Newent, a British name corresponding to Gaulish *Novientum* (now Nogent) 'new place', and Maisemore 'large plain'.

In Worcestershire, near the Herefordshire border, we have Bredon, Brit *bre(ʒ)*, Dowles on Dowles Brook, a British river-name 'black stream', identical with Dalch and Dawlish (D) and Dowlish (So),

---

[1] *v.* pp. 82, 84.

Malvern 'bare hill', Penhull, Pensax 'Saxons' hill', with the Brit *crūc* 'hill' in Crutch, Crookbarrow Hill and Churchill. Carton, earlier *Carkedon*, probably Brit *carrec* 'cliff, rock' plus OE *dūn* 'hill', is near Mamble, which may be a British name from *mam* used in Scotland and Ireland as the name of a hill, found also in Mamhead (D), Mam Tor (Db) and Mansfield (Nt), *Mamesfeld* 1086.

Cornwall

Cornwall derives from OE *Cornwealas*, first recorded c900 as the name of the inhabitants of the peninsula, and this later became the name of the county. Up to the end of the ninth century they were called *West Wealas* 'the West Welsh'; *Cornwealas* means 'the Welsh of *Corn*', the name of the peninsula, from Brit *Cornāviā*, perhaps from *corn* 'horn', from its shape. This became MW *Cerniu*, later *Cernyw*, and Co *Kernow*, which survives in the surname *Curnow*.

There is no definite record of Roman settlement west of *Isca* (Exeter), but the county must have been occupied in part by the military, as the place-names Carlyon, Carleen and Carleon are identical in origin with Caerleon (Mon), from *Caerleghion* 'fort or camp of the legion': Maker and Magor in Camborne are identical with W *magwyr*, OW *macyrou*, OBret *macoer*, from Lat *maceria* 'wall, ruin' and may refer to Roman ruins as the discovery of a tessellated pavement at Magor in 1924 suggests there may have been a Roman villa here. *Caer* 'fort' occurs alone as Cair, Gare, Gear, in the plural in Kerrow, Keiro, Cairo, and in numerous compounds, including Carwyn 'white', Cardew, Carthew 'black', Carvean 'little', etc. In some names we have late Latin loan-words borrowed by the British: *castel* in Kestlemerris, *eglos* 'church' from Lat *ecclesia* in Egloskerry and Egloshayle 'church on the R. Hayle', an old name of the Camel estuary, *fonten* 'spring, well' in Penventon, *fos* 'ditch' in Trevose, *melin*, from a late Lat *molina* 'mill' in Tremellen, *pont* 'bridge' in Penpont, and *porth* from *portum* 'harbour' in Porthquin and Porthallow 'harbour on the R. Allow'.

In pre-Saxon Cornwall the inhabitants consisted of small tribal groups, each with its own king or chief, with a court or capital called their *lis* (W *llys*). Lestowder in St Keverne is said to have been the *pen plas* 'chief place' of a semi-legendary Teudar. Trigg, now the name of a hundred, was a district-name, *pagus Tricurius* 9th, *Trigerscīre* 1130, the district of the *Tricurii*, a tribal name found in Gaul meaning 'those with three armies', surviving as Tréguier in Brittany, and parallel with the Gaulish *Petrocorii* 'those with four armies', now Perigord in France. The *lis* of the Tricurii was probably at Helston, *Henlistone* 1086, 'old court or capital' (Co *henlis* with later addition of OE *tūn*), afterwards transferred to Lesnewth 'the new capital'. Liskeard was probably the chief place of the old district of Wivelshire.

The Tamar has always, at least since the time of Athelstan, formed the boundary between Devon and Cornwall throughout its course, except at one point, where a finger of land consisting of the parishes of North Petherwin and Werrington projects several miles into Cornwall. But the river does not form a linguistic boundary between names of English and Celtic origin. The place-names of the parishes on the west side of the Tamar are nearly as English as those on the east side except for the small area between the Ottery and the Inney, where Cornish place-names predominate right up to the Tamar. This area, under the name of *Landwiþan*, was given in 823 by king Ecgberht to the Bishop of Sherborne, and if, as is possible, it had been an ecclesiastical estate before the conquest of Cornwall, the Celtic inhabitants may have been left undisturbed. To *Landwiþan*, a British name 'the church of Wiþan', the Saxons added OE *tūn*, *Langvitetona* 1086, which has now become Lawhitton. A similar addition was made to the British name of Callington, *Celliwic*, either identical with W *celliwig* 'wood, forest' or a compound of Co *celli* 'grove' and *gwic* 'village', 'village by a grove'. It is *Cællwic* 988, *Caluuitona* 1086, *Calwintona* 1188.

In East Cornwall the English place-names are very similar to those of Devon, common elements being *bearu*,[1] *cumb*, *(ge)hæg* 'enclosure', *lacu* 'stream', *pytt* and *torr*. OE *twicene* 'cross-roads' appears as Ditchen and Titching; OE *ēa* 'stream' has the same development as in the Devon Yeo in Beryo, Treyeo; *cote*, frequent in the north-east but rare in the south-east, is liable to confusion with Co *coit* 'wood' as in Truscott 'across the wood', Lidcott, formerly *Luitcoit* 'grey wood'; *-worthy* is frequent and confused with *-ford*, as in Devon, Bulsworthy, Wishworthy, earlier *Boltesford* and *Wisheforde*, Mugford, earlier *Moggeworthi*. The prepositional *Atte(r)* 'at the' has been replaced by *Tre-* (perhaps influenced by names in *Tre-*): Tremoutha, Treforda, Treway, Treven, Tremoorland. In some names *atte* survives as *Ta-*: Tamill 'at the mill', Talhay 'at the wood or clearing' (OE *lēah*). English place-names in West Cornwall are few and scattered, as Viscar, earlier *Fursgore*, Kenap (OE *cnæpp* 'hillock').

[1] *v.* p. 34.

In West Cornwall British place-names are in a majority, including simple names like Kelly 'grove', Kestle, Carne 'rock', Preeze, Priske 'brushwood', and compounds like Dranneck, Drinnick 'place of thorns', Kelynack 'place of holly', Carwalsick 'fort in the grassy spot' (*gwelsek*), with occasional hybrids, Croftnoweth 'new croft', Anhay 'the enclosure' (the Cornish definite article plus OE (*ge*)*hæg*).

Co *bod*, earlier *bot*, and later *bos* 'house, dwelling' is found in Bodmin 'house of the monks', where there was a monastery, said to have been founded in 926 by king Æthelstan. Boscawen (cf. W *ysgawen*, Bret *scaven* 'elder-tree'), Bossiny 'house of Cini'. Boscastle is misleading. It is *Boterelescastel* 1302 'the castle of (the family of William) Boterel' (1130).

Brit *penn*, Co *pen* 'head, top, summit', also 'point, promontory' occurs twice in Penare, one at Nare Point, *Pennarð* 967, one near Mevagissey, *Penhard* 1303, both named from promontories, Co *pen ard* or *arth* 'high headland', Penryn (Co *penryn* 'promontory, cape'), Pentire Point 'end of the land', Penwith, an old name for Land's End,[1] Penzance 'holy cape, holy headland'.

Co *pol* 'pool' occurs in Polglaze (Co *glas* 'blue', 'green') and Polscoe, *Polscat* 1086, 'boat pool' (Co *scath* 'boat'). The first element of Polperro, *Portpira* 1303, and Polruan, *Porthruan* 1284, is Co *porth* 'harbour'.

Co *ros*, originally 'projection, hill, hill spur', later came to mean 'hill covered with heath' and still later 'moor' or 'heath'. Nearly all the places named from this element are on or near hills or ridges. It survives alone in Roose, Rose and Rowse. When compounded as a first element it is often reduced to *Res-* and in East Cornwall, where English early supplanted Celtic, names like at *Rosman* 'at the hill stone' survive as Tresmaine. Among the numerous examples are: Rosecare, Roskear 'hill-fort' (*caer*), Roseglos 'hill church' (*eglos*), Rosemullion 'Milian's promontory', Rosewarne 'hill with an alder-grove' (*gwern*), Treskilling, *Roskelin* 1251 'holly hill' (*celin*), Tresmarrow, *Rosmarc* 1201 'horse-hill' (*margh*); as a final element in Penrose 'end of the hill', Trerose 'homestead on the hill'. Resparva, Resparveth, Sparret and Tresparret all go back to an original *Rosperveth* 'middle hill' (Co *perveth*).

W *tref*, *tre*, Co *trev*, *tre* 'homestead, village, town' is a very common first element in Wales and Cornwall and is found also in Herefordshire and Lancashire. Cornish Tregair, Tregear, Tregarn and

[1] *v.* p. 71.

95

Tremaine are 'hamlet of the fort, rock and stone' respectively, Tremenheere, that by the menhir or long stone. Treneglos is the 'farm by the church', the *n* being a relic of the Co definite article *an*. Trenowth is 'new homestead'. Where Cornish continued to be spoken after the Saxon conquest, the name of the English owner was added to the Cornish *Tre-*: Trebursey 'homestead of *Beorhtsige*', Tredundle (*Deneweald*), Trehawke (*Heafoc*), Trehunsey (*Hūnsige*), Trekinnard (*Cyneheard*), Trevashmond (*Æscmund*), Trevollard (*Æðelweard*).[1] Such names were given by Cornish speakers, as were Carsawsen, Nansawsen and Tresawsen, respectively 'the camp, valley and farmstead of the Saxons', and Trezize and Tresayes 'homestead of the Englishman' (cf. W *Sais*). Similar compounds continued to be formed by Cornish speakers after the Norman Conquest: Trefrank, Trerank, Trink, homesteads of French tenants or owners; Ponsmayou 'Matthew's bridge', Crouse Harvey 'Harvey's cross', Penvories, olim *Ponsferris*.

In regions of mixed languages Celtic place-names were translated: Blackhay (*Haythu*), New Mill (*Melynneweth*); or partially translated, Mill Mehal (*Melynmyhal*) 'Michael's mill', Gwealgoose (*Gwaelgoyth*) 'goose field'. The difficulties of English speakers in taking over unfamiliar Cornish names produced some interesting popular etymologies: Barbican (*bar bihan* 'little summit'), Cutbrawn (*coit bran* 'crow wood') and Crumplehorn, olim *Tremylhorn*, in East Cornwall; Beersheba (*bos aber* 'dwelling by the estuary'), Cowlands (*ceunans* 'narrow valley'), Palestine (*pen lestyn* 'chief lodging-place') and Camels (*cam als* 'crooked cliff'), in West Cornwall.

Early British compounds in which the defining element came first are found in Cornwall as elsewhere: *henlis* 'old court', the original name of Helston(e), as opposed to the later Lesneweth 'new court', Hengar 'old camp', Camborne 'crooked hill'. But most Cornish place-names of British origin consist of a noun plus a defining element, as Kenwyn, lit. 'ridge white', Lizard 'court or hall high', Trenoweth 'hamlet new'. Marazion, *Marghasbigan* c1200, is a compound of Co *marchas* 'market', translated by the Latin *in Parvo Foro* (1311) and the French *Petyt Marche* (1324), 'little market'. In 1620 it occurs as *Market Jew* alias *Marasion*. Originally these names denoted two separate places, *Marcasiou juxta Marcas byghan* (1311). The first was a similar compound of Co *marchas* and *dyow*, *Marchadyou* c1200, *Markeju* c1540, 'southern market', a name which now

[1] For Cornish personal-names, *v.* pp. 67–69.

survives in Market Jew St in Penzance, leading to Marazion. Withiel was probably the name of the high upland district which separated it from Lostwithiel and may mean 'wooded upland' or 'wood of the upland' (cf. W *gwydd* 'wood', Co *gwydh* 'trees' and *iâl* 'fertile upland region'). Lostwithiel, some miles away, on the other side of this upland region, would then be 'the end of Withiel', from Co *lost* 'a tail'. Restormel is a triple compound of Co *ros* 'moor', *torr* 'mountain' and *moel* 'bare'.

Many of the well-known Cornish place-names are of obscure origin. Godolphin may contain a river-name, Bude and Falmouth take their names from the rivers on which they stand. So does Fowey, probably 'beech-river'; Fawton is a hybrid, 'farm (OE *tūn*) on the Fowey'. Helford is the 'fjord (ON *fjorðr*) of Hayle', identical with the old name of the Camel estuary in north Cornwall, probably 'salt river'. Kenidjack is a derivative of a river-name ultimately identical with that of the Kennet in Wilts and Cambridgeshire. East and West Looe are named from the R. Looe, Co *lo* 'an inlet of water, a pool', a name probably at first restricted to the mouth of the river. Launceston, *Lanscavetone* 1086, is a hybrid in which OE *tūn* has been added to an OCo *Lan* 'church', combined with a saint's name, usually taken to be that of St Stephen. Stratton is *Strætneat* c880, which means either 'the valley of the R. *Strat*' or 'the river *Strat*', an earlier name of which was *Neth*, probably identical with OIr *necht* 'clean'. *Stræt* is W *ystrad* 'valley' or Co *stret* 'stream'. This was later taken to be the name of the river, the Saxons added *-tūn* and the place was called Stratton (*Stratone* 1086).

GOIDELIC PLACE-NAMES

The vast bulk of the Celtic place-names of England were taken over by the Anglo-Saxons from speakers of Brittonic. They provide no evidence for the theory that the first Celts to settle in England were Goidels, who were later conquered by the Britons and driven westwards into Ireland. The Irish–Gaelic element in English place-names is slight. Irish monastic settlements might lead to the introduction of an occasional Irish place- or personal-name, but these were few and exceptional. Beckery near Glastonbury, mentioned in an Anglo-Saxon charter as '*Bekeria*, quae parva Ybernia dicitur', is identical with Ir *Bec-Eriu* 'Little Ireland' and suggests a colony of Irish monks at Glastonbury. Flat Holme (So), in the Bristol Channel, 'flat island' (ON *holmr*), is recorded as (*æt*) *Bradan Relice* in 918, 'the broad

Relic', from OIr *reilic* 'cemetery'. Malmesbury, *Maildufi urbs* c730, 'the city of Mailduf', contains the OIr personal-name *Maeldubh*, the name of a Scot who is said by William of Malmesbury to have founded the monastery.

But what Gaelic influence there is on our place-names is due almost entirely to the immigration of Irish–Norwegian vikings into the north-west in the tenth century. Their personal-names and the inversion-compounds of a Celtic type which they employed have been discussed above.[1] Here we are concerned only with a loan-word they had borrowed from Irish. They introduced ON *erg* 'a shieling or hill pasture' from OIr or Gaelic (MIr *airge*, Ir *airghe*, Gael *airigh*). It was used originally of a small dairy settlement with huts and pastures on a mountain-side used only in summer, but seems also to have denoted more generally 'a small dairy settlement'. It is found in Arrowe (Ch), Arras, and, in the dative plural, in Argam, Arram (ERY) and Arkholme (La). It is compounded with words denoting building materials, location or situation in Stephney (Cu), *Stavenerge* 1231 (ON *stafn* 'stack, pole'), Tirril (We), *Tyrerhge* c1189 (ON *tyri* 'dry, resinous wood'), Torver (La), *Thoruergh* c1199 (ON *torf* 'turf, peat'), possibly 'hut made of sods', Cleator (Cu), from ON *klettr* 'rock, cliff', Berrier (Cu), *Bergherge* 1166 (OE *beorg* 'hill'), Birker (Cu) 'birches', Docker (La, We), from ON *dǫkk* 'valley', Mosser (Cu) and Mozergh (We) 'moss'. It is frequently compounded with a personal-name: Battrix, WRY (ON *Boðvarr*), Coldman Hargos, NRY (OIr *Colmán*), Goosnargh, La (OIr *Gosan*), Skelsmergh, We (ON *Skjalmar*), etc.

Glendue (Nb) 'dark valley', just over the border from north Cumberland, may have been borrowed from speakers of Cumbric in the eleventh century. Both British and Goidelic personal-names are compounded in place-names which date from the eleventh and twelfth centuries.[2] The by no means inconsiderable Gaelic element in the place-names of Cumberland cannot all be due to Norwegian settlers from Ireland. It must come in part from Gaelic speakers among the immigrants from Strathclyde in the tenth and eleventh centuries. Gille son of Bueth has probably left his name in Gilsland and his father in Boothby (*Buethby* 1276). Both are mentioned in the Lanercost foundation charter. *Bueth* is a common Gaelic name in twelfth-century Cumberland, and, as Boothby is a compound of *-by*, the name must have arisen in or after the tenth century and may well be a post-Conquest formation.

[1] *v.* pp. 69–70.   [2] Cf. pp. 60, 69.

Chapter Six

THE ENGLISH ELEMENT

FOLK-NAMES

THE earliest place-names created by the Anglo-Saxons were not originally place-names in the strict sense of the word; they were folk-names; later, the district came to be called by the name of the tribe or people living there. Essex, Middlesex and Sussex really mean 'the East, Middle and South Saxons' respectively. These names were then used of the kingdoms they established and now survive as the names of counties. East Anglia is an artificial name. It was originally *Eastengle* 'the East Angles', comprising two distinct peoples, 'the North Folk' and 'the South Folk', who occupied the counties now known as Norfolk and Suffolk. Such names are well known on the Continent. The German Franken, Preussen and Sachsen, originally 'the Franks, Prussians and Saxons', came to mean Franconia, Prussia and Saxony. In France, Amiens, Arras, Rheims and Soissons derive directly from the Gaulish tribal-names *Ambiani, Atrebates, Remi* and *Suessiones*. The name of the Jutes, who settled not only in Kent but also in the Isle of Wight and southern Hampshire, was, according to Florence of Worcester, still preserved after the Norman Conquest in the New Forest, 'which in the tongue of the English is called *Ytene*'. It is found also in the tenth-century name of Bishopstoke (Ha) as *Æt Yting Stoce* and in Eadens in East Meon (Ha), *Ytedene* 1263,

99

Iteden 1453, where both institutions and archaeology have Jutish affinities.

Cornwall and Devon are English forms of British tribal-names, whilst Cumberland 'land of the *Cumbras*' contains an English form of *Cymry* 'the Welsh'. Westmorland, *Westmoringaland* 966, was the 'land of the *Westmoringas*', the people dwelling west of the Yorkshire moors. Northumberland, originally *Norphymbre* 867, 'the dwellers north of the Humber', at first referred to all the lands north of the Humber, including land north of the Tweed which was ceded to Scotland in 1018. But when Cumberland and Yorkshire acquired names of their own, *Norðhymbraland* was used only of the modern Northumberland and Durham and finally, after c1100, when Durham had become a palatinate under the Bishop of Durham, the name was restricted to the present county.

'In no part of England can the essential contrast between the age of settlement and that of consolidation be more strikingly illustrated than round the margin of the Fens, for it was there, on ground afterwards the borderland between the conflicting territorial interests of East Anglia, Mercia, and Northumbria, that the earliest Anglo-Saxon communities of the midlands had their unremembered homes. The sagas of their noble families were lost in the welter of later political discord: the settlers themselves lacked in the critical period the conservative and centralizing forces of a royal court or an episcopal *familia* which helped elsewhere to turn the local traditions into annals, and to perpetuate the memory of kings and the years of their reigns; and in default of these factors they became a people who have no memorial.'[1] What we know of these obscure tribes comes almost entirely from the enigmatical record of the ancient seventh-century tribute-list of the Mercian kings known as the Tribal Hidage which survives in a tenth-century manuscript. Many of their names are mysterious and unintelligible and the location of their homes vague and indefinite, but place-name evidence has identified some and revealed traces of distant and otherwise unknown migrations.

The *Spalde* or *Spaldas* lived in the fens of Huntingdonshire, Northamptonshire and Lincolnshire and their name survives in Spalding (L) and possibly in Spaldwick (Hu), with an offshoot at Spalford (Nt). From *Spaldas* was formed a name *Spaldingas*, either 'descendants of the *Spaldas*' or 'members of the tribe of *Spaldas*',

---

[1] R. G. Collingwood and J. N. L. Myres, *Roman Britain and the English Settlements* (Oxford, 1936), p. 383.

who may quite well have migrated from the Continent, where similar names are found in Spauwen in Holland (*Spalden* 1096) and L'Espaix in France (*Spalt* 11th). Some members of the tribe must have migrated north into Yorkshire, where we have Spaldington and Spalding Moor (ERY). Oundle (Nth) preserves the obscure name of a tribe mentioned by Bede.

The counties of Bedford and Huntingdon are of late origin, first mentioned by name in 1011, and each probably represents the district occupied by one of the Danish armies among whom the southern Danelaw was divided. The Tribal Hidage throws some light on their earlier history. The 300 families which formed the folk of the *Gifle* were certainly inhabitants of the valley of the Bedfordshire river Ivel, and their name survives in Northill and Southill (Beds), *Nortgiuele*, *Sudgiuele* 1086, though each village is a good two miles west of the river. Its name is identical with that of the Somerset Yeo, 'the forked river', which is preserved in Yeovil and in Givendale (ERY). From this the tribe was known as 'the dwellers on the river Ivel', and Northill and Southill are probably descriptive of settlements in the north and the south of their territory rather than loose appellations for villages well away from the river itself. Behind the name of Hurstingstone Hundred (Hu) lies that of the 1200 families found in the Tribal Hidage in the corrupt forms *Herefinna*, *Hersinna* and *Herstinna*. These *Hyrstingas* were so called from the ancient woodland district in which they lived, its former nature perpetuated in the surviving names of Old Hurst (*Waldhirst* 1227), Woodhurst (*Wdeherst* 1209), Upwood and Wood Walton (*Waltune* 1086, *Wodewalton* 1284, probably from *Waldtūn*), containing the OE woodland elements *wald*, *wudu* and *hyrst*. The next name in the Tribal Hidage is that of the 300 families of the *Sweordora*, probably the 'dwellers by the point at the end of the neck of land', from OE *sweora* 'neck' and *ord* 'point'. The name no longer survives, but twelfth-century documents connect it with Whittlesea Mere, old maps of which show a broadish peninsula jutting into the lake. At its north-west corner is a point of land called *Swere Point* and behind it a corner of the peninsula marked off as *Swere Hord*. Hitchin (Herts) is (*ad*) Hiccam 944–6, *Hicche* 1062, *Hichene* 1147. The first form is probably for *Hiccum*, dative plural of the tribal-name *Hicce* of the Tribal Hidage.

Ripon (WRY) preserves a tribal-name *Hrype* which Stenton considers may well go back to the fifth century. The neighbouring Ribston is possibly from OE *Hrypa stān*, a stone marking the

101

boundary of the *Hrype* or the meeting-place of the tribe. Some of the tribe migrated south to Repton (Db), *Hrypadun* c745, 'the hill of the *Hrype*', situated above the right bank of the Trent in a district where cremation-cemeteries have been found. Bede tells us that his own monastery of Jarrow (Du) was situated near the river Tyne in a place called *in Gyruum* 'among the *Gyrwe*', a tribe of whom nothing further is known. He also states that a tribe of *Gyrwe*, divided into two folks, each of 600 households, lived in the fens. According to the Ely chronicler, St Etheldreda, who was born at Exning (Sf), married Tonbertus, a *princeps* of the *Australes Girvii*, receiving the Isle of Ely as a dowry. It seems clear that these southern *Gyrwe* had an alderman of their own and that their territory included the Isle of Ely, originally part of the kingdom of East Anglia, later in Cambridgeshire, but always a distinct and separate area, under the control first of the abbot and later of the bishop of Ely, and still a separate area today, with its own County Council, quite distinct from that of Cambridgeshire. *Gyrwe* derives from an old word meaning 'mud' or 'fen' (OE *gyr*). Whether the Northumbrian folk of Jarrow had migrated north from the Fenlands or took their name from some other fen, we cannot decide.

Like the *Magensætan*, the *Hwicce* were a tribe for whom a bishopric, that at Worcester, was established. They occupied an extensive area in Gloucestershire, Worcestershire and west Warwickshire and in the eighth century numbered 7,000 tribute-paying families. They were a people of mingled Anglian and Saxon stock, forming the under-kingdom of the Hwicce, which may well have been established by Penda himself. Their rulers, variously known as kings, *reguli* 'under-kings' or *ministri*, can be traced from 675 to 777, when the last of them styled himself 'under-king of the Hwicce by the dispensation of the Lord' and Offa, king of Mercia, in the same charter, calmly corrected the title to 'my under-king, ealdorman, that is, of his own people of the Hwicce'. Their name is preserved in Wichenford (Wo), Whichford (Wa) and Wychwood (O), where the king of Mercia had granted the Bishop of Worcester ten hides in 840. Wichnor (St) points to a migration of part of the tribe from the Severn valley to the neighbourhood of Burton on Trent and Whiston (Nth) of others into Northamptonshire, whilst Witchley Green near Ketton (R), *Hwicceslea* 1072, owes its name to a solitary migrant.

Midway between Worcester and Stratford-on-Avon, a small stream, still known as Whitsun Brook (*Wixena broc* 972), owes its name to a settlement here of the *Wixan*, a tribe already divided into eastern and western sections in the eighth century. Their original home was in the fenland, in the neighbourhood of the *Gyrwe* and the *Spalde*. One branch moved up the Welland, over the watershed and down the valley of the Warwickshire Avon; another made its way south into Middlesex, where it established settlements at three places some distance apart, at Uxbridge, *Wixebrug*' c1145, at *Woxindon*' 1257, a name now preserved only in Uxendon Avenue in Harrow, and at Waxlow, *Woxeleye* 1294.

Further evidence of distant migrations of smaller groups may be found in certain village-names, in the settlement of men from Kent at Canterton (Ha) and Conderton (Wo), of men from Essex at Exton (Ha), *æt East Seaxnatune* 940, 'village of the East Saxons', of Anglians in Saxon territory at Englebourne (D) and Englefield (Berks), of East Anglians in Mercia at Engleton (St), and of Saxons in Anglian territory at Saxham (Sf), Saxton (C, WRY) and Saxondale (Nt). This evidence of somewhat extensive group-migration is a matter of some importance to the historian and the student of dialect and may be of interest to the archaeologist when his finds are less homogeneous than he would like.

Some of these tribal areas are described as *regiones* or *provinciae*, which clearly formed the fundamental divisions of the various English peoples. There appears to have been no regular English term for such an area, though *mǣgð* is used occasionally, a word originally meaning 'kindred', which had early developed the wider sense of tribe or people. This does not mean that the *regio* was composed of a related group of kinsfolk, but it does emphasise the fact that these divisions originated in tribal settlements, a fact confirmed by the names of some like *Geddingas* (now Yeading, Mx), a formation indicative of group-settlement. There are, however, a few names definitely described as *regiones*, which contain an archaic topographical term *gē* 'district', cognate with the German *gau*, already obsolete by the time of the earliest written records. It is found chiefly in Essex and Kent, but also in the names of two larger areas, both early described as *regiones* and both modern counties, Ely 'eel-district' and Surrey, *Suthrige* 722, 'the southern district', that part of the kingdom of Middlesex south of the Thames. In Kent we have Eastry 'the eastern district', Lyminge, that near the river *Limen*, the old name of the Rother, though Lyminge is not on the river, and Sturry, that on the Stour, all of which later became lathes. In Essex we have Vange, *to*

H   103

Fænge 963, 'the fen district' and an extensive area once called by the doubly archaic folk-name *Geingas* 'the dwellers in the *gē*'. In the centre of the county, south-west of Chelmsford, the DB *Ginges* included the modern parishes of Ingatestone and Fryerning, Margaretting, Mountnessing, Buttsbury, Stock, Ingrave and presumably the intervening Hutton, originally *Hou*, with a post-Conquest addition of *tūn*, and part, at least, of East Horndon, in which was *Ginge Puelle*, now Fouchers. This compound of the archaic *gē* with *-ingas*, itself evidence of high antiquity, may well carry back this folk-name to the age of the Migration.

The second element of Elsass (Alsace), earlier *Elsazzun*, 'those dwelling outside' (that is, west of the Rhine), is paralleled in England by Dorset and Somerset, where the second element is OE *sǣte* 'settlers, dwellers'. The former is *(to) Dorsǣton* in 955, 'the settlers at *Dorn*', an elliptical form of the British *Durngueir* c894, found as *Durnonovaria* in the Antonine Itinerary, lit. 'fist play' (cf. W *dwrn* 'fist' and *gwarae* 'play'), possibly with reference to the Roman amphitheatre, and Englished as *Dornwaraceaster* 864, *Dorecestre* 1086, 'the city of the dwellers at *Dorn*', now Dorchester. Somerset, *(on) Sumersǣton* 1048, 'the people of Somerset', is similarly elliptical for *Sumortūn sǣte* 'the dwellers at Somerton', *Summurtunensis paga* c894. So, too, the people of Wiltshire were called *Wilsǣton* in 800, 'settlers on the river Wylye', but here the county came to be called *Wiltunscir* (870) from its capital Wilton 'the town on the Wylye'. The same element also appears in a corrupt form in Grantchester 'dwellers on the Granta',[1] and, compounded with *tūn*, in Bilston (St), *Bilsetnatun* 996, 'village of the dwellers at *Bil*', perhaps the name of a neighbouring hill; Phepson (Wo), *Fepsetnatun* 956, which must point to a westward migration of the *Feppingas*, a Middle Anglian tribe mentioned by Bede; and in Poston (He), *Poscetnetune* 1086, *Puttestun* 1242, perhaps 'the village of the dwellers by *Puttandūn*', possibly the name of the ridge at Poston.

Just as *sǣte* is often used in names like *Peacsǣtna* 'inhabitants of the Peak', *Tomsǣtan* 'dwellers by the river Tame', *Dunsǣte* 'the hill-dwellers', i.e. the Welsh, names of peoples, which never became place-names, so OE *ware* 'dwellers' is used in *Lynware* 'the men of (King's) Lynn' and *Cæstruuarouualth* (747), with a variant *Cæstersǣta walda* (801), 'the common wood of the men of the *ceaster*', i.e. Rochester. In *Merscuuare* 'the marsh-dwellers' it was clearly used for

_____
[1] *v.* p. 25.

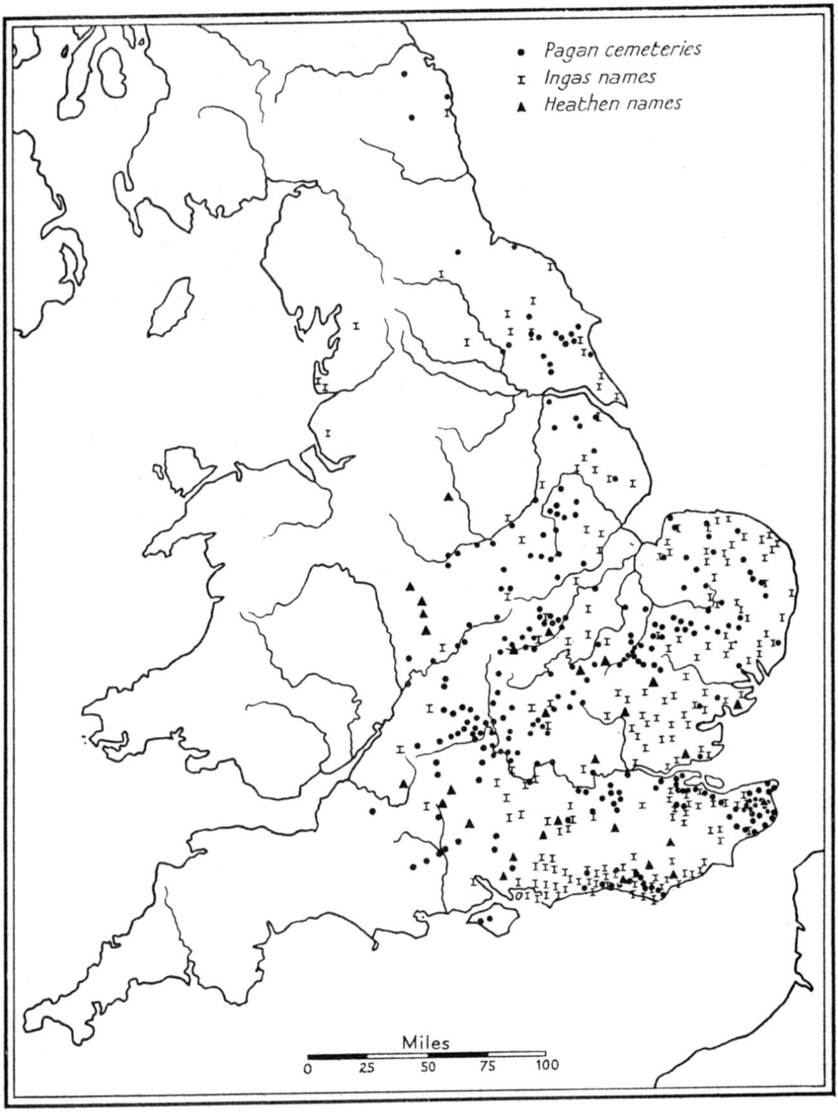
Pagan cemeteries
Ingas names
Heathen names
Miles
0
25
50
75
100

Early English Settlements

From R. G. Collingwood & J. N. L. Myres: *Roman Britain and the English Settlements* (Oxford University Press, 1936).

Romney Marsh, described here as a *regio*, but the name has not survived. Similarly, East and West Meon (Ha) are called *Meanuarorum prouincia* c730, 'the province of the dwellers in the valley of the Meon', and *Meanware mægð* c890, from OE *mægð* 'folk'. The boundaries of the people of Cliffe at Hoo near Gravesend, (*to*) *Cliua* 10th, are referred to five times in 778 in the phrase *clifwara gemære*. Whether this was used here as a place-name is not clear, but it is clearly the origin of Clewer (Berks, So), respectively *Clifwara* 1156 and *Cliveware* 1086, 'dwellers on a hill-slope'. The element is common in Kent: Canterbury, *Cantwaraburg* 754, 'fort of the men of Kent', Canter Wood in Elham, *Canterwrth'* 1292, 'enclosure of the men of Kent', Burmarsh, *Burwaramers* 'marsh of the men of the *burg*' of Canterbury, Bulverhythe (Sx), *Burewarehethe* 1229, 'harbour of the citizens' of Hastings; Felderland in Eastry, *Feldwareland* 1226, 'land of the dwellers in the open-country'; Tenterden, part of the manor of Minster in Thanet, *Tentwardene* 1179, 'swine-pasture of the men of Thanet', near which was *Tenetwara brocas* 968, and Waldershare, *Wealdwarescare* 11th, 'boundary or share of land of the dwellers in the forest'.

PLACE-NAMES IN -ingas

The ancient kings of Kent were known as the *Oiscingas*, the descendants of Oisc, son of Hengist, and those of East Anglia as the *Wuffingas*, from the grandfather of Rædwald, Wuffa, the reputed founder of the kingdom. These dynastic names are clearly patronymics, the plural of names in -*ing*, a suffix commonly used in genealogies to denote 'son of', as Wulf *Wonrēding*, also called *sunu Wonrēdes* 'son of Wonred', Æðelred *Eadgaring*, and in biblical contexts *Adaming* 'son of Adam' and *Nathaning* 'son of Nathan'. Plural formations of this kind are frequently found as place-names, often in the dative plural, *Kyteringas* 972 (Kettering, Nth), *æt Diccelingum* 880–5 (Ditchling, Sx). They originally denoted, not the place, but those who dwelt there, communities of various sizes, which were obviously much too large to be regarded as the settlements of individual families or of groups of kinsmen. The *Berecingas* of the *regio* of Barking cannot all have been blood-relations, nor can the *Rēadingas* of Reading who occupied a territory seven miles wide. There is no evidence that any of these names are patronymics, no indication of a primitive habit of settlement by families. Some of the names are toponymics, based on a place-name, and denoted the inhabitants of that particular spot, as Avening (Gl), 'dwellers by the Avon', Nazeing (Ess), 'dwellers on the ness or spur of land', and Epping 'the upland dwellers'. When combined with a personal-name, these names in -*ingas* denoted not merely the man's descendants and other kinsmen but also the whole body of his followers, free and unfree. Those covering the larger areas may contain the name of the eponymous founder of the tribe; others of these communities may represent warrior bands who proudly bore the name of the leader who had led them across the seas and had triumphantly settled them in a new land, as the *Brahhingas* 'the men of Brahha, the shining one', whose name survives in Braughing (Herts).[1]

One proof of the high antiquity of these names is the nature of the personal-names with which they are compounded. They are mostly of the short, uncompounded type which had gone out of fashion among the upper classes by the ninth century, but they are seldom found as independent names and their interpretation is difficult. For parallels we have to go to the Continent, for these personal-names had ceased to be used in England before written records began. They were the names brought over by the invaders from the Continent and died out within a few generations of the Migration. The forms of Desning (Sf) are so confused that it is uncertain whether the original name was *Deselingas* or *Deseningas*. In any case, the only possible parallels are the OHG personal-names *Dusilo* and *Taso*, both found in German place-names, but otherwise unknown in England. So, too, the personal-names lying behind Detling (K), Fletching (Sx) and Shimpling (Nf, Sf) can only be paralleled abroad. Occasionally the personal-name is dithematic, as in Godalming (Sr), from OE *Gōdhelm*, corresponding to OG *Godohelm*, Wittering (Sx), from OE *Wihthere*, and Wymering (Ha), from OE *Wīgmær*. Wallenberg explains many of these place-names as names applied to the inhabitants as a whole. Cooling (K), from OE *Cūla*, he prefers to interpret as *Cūlingas* 'the hole-dwellers', Malling as 'the crazy, foolish men', a derogatory nickname given by their neighbours to the settlers at Malling, Detling as 'the men of a lumpy, rounded stature', Rooting as 'the merry, cheerful men', and Ratling as 'the men making a rattling noise'. This last is merely absurd, but not quite so ridiculous

[1] There is a considerable literature on the subject. *v.*, e.g., E. Ekwall, *English Place-names in* -ing (Lund, 1923) and A. H. Smith, *English Place-name Elements* (Cambridge, 1956), vol. i, pp. 282–303.

as the nickname he prefers for Barming, 'the issues (from the lap), descendants'. True, he frequently offers other suggestions, but it is the nicknames he prefers. Yalding is undoubtedly OE *Ealdingas* 'the people of Ealda'. The explanation 'the old men, the chieftains' or 'the chieftain's men' is impossible; all the men of Yalding could not have been old or chieftains. Nor could the men of Malling all be crazy or those of Detling all fat and lumpy, or all those of Rooting merry. A nickname **Rōta* 'the cheerful, merry man' is possible and likely, but *Rōtingas* can only mean 'the people of a man called *Rōta*'.

Further proof of the great age of these names is that they usually denote places of some importance, parishes and villages. A surprising number have given rise to names of hundreds, a clear indication that these settlements had become of some importance in quite early days, e.g. Tendring (Ess), Poling (Sx), Cannings (W), Pickering (Y), etc. Others have decayed in the course of centuries and now survive only as the names of farms or halls, as at Weavering Street, a farm near Maidstone, Creeping Hall in Wakes Colne (Ess) and Byng, a hamlet near Wickham Market (Sf). Others have completely disappeared from the map and the exact site of some cannot be definitely determined. On the other hand, the ancient territory of the *Hrōðingas* is now represented by the eight parishes commonly referred to as the Rooth-ings, each with its own attribute, Beauchamp, Leaden, White Roding, etc. Havering (Ess) was created a Royal Liberty in the reign of Edward IV and now consists of five large parishes. The history of the *Mæcc-ingas* we shall never know. Their name survives in two Essex parishes, 25 miles apart: Matching, the normal development, and Messing, which owes its present form to Anglo-Norman pronunciation. Between them lies the parish of Mashbury, a French version of the English *Mæccean byrig* 'the stronghold of Mæcca', the eponymous founder of the tribe, whilst a neighbouring brook was once called *Massebrok*. We can hardly escape the conclusion that Mæcca and his men played no small part in the earliest settlement of Essex.

In Sussex, names in *-ingas* are thicker on the ground and were clearly the names of smaller communities who settled at suitable places which were then nearer the sea than they are today. In some instances two such settlements were made within the area of a single parish, as at West Tarring and Worthing in the parish of Broadwater and at Perching Farm in Fulking parish. The 45 such names of Sussex con-trast strongly with the 19 of Kent and the 24 of Essex, but in east Sussex we find a marked difference. The *Hæstingas* of Hastings were a tribe of such importance that a Northumbrian chronicler records the defeat of the *gens Hestingorum* by Offa in 771, and they had maintained their individuality as a separate people so effectively that as late as 1011 the Anglo-Saxon Chronicle includes the *Hæstingas* with the *Centingas* and the South Saxons in a record of peoples who by that date had been harried by the Danes. A people whose individuality could be remembered for 500 years and who, at the end of that period, could be mentioned in a national chronicle side by side with the people of Kent and the South Saxons must have been something more than a mere fragment of a larger kingdom. The few Saxon charters which have survived for Sussex provide evidence which suggests the existence of two separate dynasties in Sussex and the *Hæstingas* may well have had kings of their own. Their territory was certainly extensive. Hastingford in Hadlow Down in the Rape of Pevensey must mean 'the ford of the *Hæstingas*' and was probably so named because that was the entrance to their territory for those coming from the north-west. Far away to the east, near Wye in Kent, is the parish of Hastingleigh, which can mean nothing less than 'the wood of the *Hæstingas*'. Kent charters provide references to the bounds of the South Saxons south of Warehorne and to land of the South Saxons east of Burmarsh, neither of which can be equated with the modern division between Kent and Sussex. Hastingleigh might possibly have been a distant swine-pasture of the *Hæstingas*, but it looks as if, in the very early days of the settlement, their territory may have extended from Hastingleigh to Hastingford, including the whole of the rapes of Pevensey and Hastings. It is noteworthy that the Anglo-Saxon Chronicle does not attribute any fighting to Ælle east of Pevensey and that place-name evidence suggests that the influence of the *Hæstingas* extended over the three eastern rapes of Sussex, whilst there are certain affinities with Kent. The OE **hāð* 'heathland', as distinct from the normal *hæð*, is found only in East Sussex and Kent, and there frequently, in such names as Hoads and Hoathly in Sussex and Hoath and Hoaden in Kent. Glynde and Glyndebourne contain OE **glind* 'fence, enclosure', an element limited to East Sussex, whilst Hodshrove and Bingletts are compounded with OE **sceorf* 'steep slope' and **bing* 'hollow', elements found also in the Weald of Kent.[1] This evidence is suggestive rather than conclusive, but it seems probable that the *Hæstingas* were a tribe which came over in a body from the Continent and long maintained their individuality,

[1] *v.* A. Mawer, *Problems of Place-name Study* (Cambridge, 1929), pp. 15–19.

settling, thinly no doubt, in East Sussex and south-west Kent. Much of this territory was in the Weald which then came down to the coast at Tenterden, whilst the area south of the old river Limen, including the whole of Romney Marsh, was uninhabitable. It is noteworthy, too, that neither archaeology nor place-names provide any evidence of early settlement in south-west Kent west of the Downs. Here is Hastingleigh and, not far away, Westenhanger, a difficult and doubtful name, which may mean 'the wooded slope of the men from the west', whilst in Elham is Canter Wood 'the enclosure of the men of Kent', which it is, perhaps, not too fanciful to suggest may have been a defensive outpost to keep an eye on these men from the west in this former frontier between the *Centingas* and the *Hæstingas*.

Names in *-ingas* are found in all the eastern coastal counties from Yorkshire to Sussex. As we go inland and westwards they become less frequent. They are common in Norfolk and Suffolk and scattered throughout the East Midlands, but are curiously rare in Wessex, only four examples occurring in Berkshire and five in Hampshire. This agrees well with what is known of the course of the Saxon settlement. Kent, Essex and Sussex, where these names are frequent, were among the first areas colonised by the Saxons and the Jutes. East Anglia must have been invaded by 500 or earlier. The establishment of the kingdom of Wessex is more complicated and is still a subject of controversy. The obvious route for the invaders would appear to be up the Thames, but a good case has been made for an entry from the north by invaders who sailed into the Wash and made their way up the rivers and along the Icknield Way into north Oxfordshire. There is certainly no doubt that Jutes landed in south Hampshire in the second half of the fifth century and made their way north towards Salisbury. Only two examples are found in Oxfordshire, Filkins and Goring. Where names in *-ingas* are common, we may assume early settlement. Where they are rare or absent, settlement was later. There seems no reason to doubt Ekwall's conclusion that these names, on the whole, date from a period not much later than c500 and represent some of the original settlements of the Anglo-Saxons. In general, they agree very well with the archaeological evidence, though it is curious that Cambridgeshire with its numerous and undoubtedly early cemeteries has not a single name in *-ingas*, whilst in Essex, where names of this type are common, the archaeological evidence is scanty and disappointing.

SINGULAR NAMES IN -ing

Not infrequently it is difficult to decide whether a modern name ending in -ing was originally singular or plural. But there are many which were undoubtedly singular, particularly common nouns, often late ME formations used as names of small and unimportant places, some common also in field-names, as ME *stoccing* 'uprooting of trees', used of 'land cleared from the woods', 'clearing' as in *la Stocking* 1248 (Stocking Green, Ess); ME *stubbing*, with a similar meaning, in Stubbing (Db, Nt) and Stubbins (La); OE *cēping* 'bargaining', hence 'market-place', in Chipping (La); OE *fælging* 'fallow land', used also of a measure of land, in Falinge (La), Fallinge (Db), Fallings (St) and Felling (Du); OE **niming* 'taking', 'land taken into cultivation', in Nimmings (Wo); OE **rydding* 'clearing', common in ME and in field-names, in Reading Street (K), Redding Wood (Herts), Reddings (Wo), Riddings (Db) and Rudding (Cu).

All these are late and of no value in the discussion of Anglo-Saxon settlement. There is, however, ample evidence in OE of the existence of a singular suffix -ing, used to form place-names. Many of these names are difficult to interpret and some, like Hawkinge (K), Wantage (Berks), earlier *Wanetingc*, and Billinge (La), are pronounced with a palatal (j) sound like that in *hinge*. Various explanations of this have been offered, but it is too difficult and complicated a subject to be discussed here. Some 50 of these names are recorded in OE, of which 22 have not survived; of the rest, 16 have become parish names. Most of them originally denoted boundary marks, streams and woods; they were names of topographical features and never denoted anything more than farmsteads or small hamlets. They cannot, therefore, be used like plural names in -*ingas* as evidence for the history of the Saxon settlement. But the difficulty of explaining many of them suggests that the type was early, and this is confirmed by their distribution, chiefly in Kent, Hampshire and Essex, and in East Anglia.

Their exact meaning, too, is difficult. The suffix -*ing* appears sometimes to mean 'stream', at others nothing more than 'place'. Doulting (So) is described as a stream in an early charter and contains a British river-name, perhaps 'dirty river'. Glynch Brook (Wo) 'pure' and Guiting (Gl) 'torrent' were also stream-names. Dinting (Db) and Stowting (K) are hill-names, the former probably containing the same British name as Dent (Cu, WRY), the latter OE *stūt* 'hill'. Others contain names of plants, Clavering (Ess) 'place where clover grows', Cressing (Ess) 'cress', Docking (Nf) 'docks', Wratting (C, Sf), OE *wrætt* 'cross-wort'; Hawkinge and Ruckinge (K) may be named from birds, 'hawk-wood' and 'rook-wood' respectively, but each might contain a personal-name used as a nickname. Deeping (L) derives from an adjective *dēop*, 'the deep place', 'deep fen', and Weeting (Nf) from OE *wǣt* 'wet', 'the wet district'.

That this singular -*ing* was compounded with personal-names is made quite clear by such lost names as *to Cynewoldincge* (*Cyneweald*) and *Notfreðing* (*Notfrið*). Of these Professor A. H. Smith has recently stated that 'semantically names like Balking Brk and others which contain personal-names are just as likely to be new settlement-names formed from old folk-names'. One would like some evidence. Balking, he explains as OE *Baðalacing* 'the place of Baðulac'. It is clearly a singular name, for it appears three different times in tenth-century charters, always in a singular form. Similarly he explains Garlinge (K), Swaythling (Ha) and other names from folk-names, *Grenelingas*, etc., settlers at a place called *Grene-lēah* 'the green glade'. Garlinge near Margate is *Groenling* c824 and is clearly a singular name, as it occurs in 943 in the bounds of *North mynstre* as *op grenlinges mearce*, as far as the boundary of *grenling*. This both Ekwall and Wallenberg explain as OE *grēn-hlinc* 'green hill'. Garlinge Green in Petham is identical in origin, though it is not evidenced so early, *Grellynch'* 1327, where the second element is clearly *hlinc*. Sydling (Do), *Sidelyng* 939, 'broad hill', is derived by Smith himself from *hlinc*, an etymology confirmed by later forms, *Sidelince* 1086, *Sedelinch* 1190. These and similar names in -*ling* are clearly not derivatives of -*ing*.

NAMES IN -ingahām

Some of the early Saxon communities threw off daughter-settlements. Wokingham (Berks) was probably an offshoot of Woking (Sr), some nine miles away, and Ellingham on the Avon, north of Ringwood, *Adelingeham* 1086, 'the village of the people of Æðel', was similarly a colony of Eling (Ha), on Southampton Water, *Edlinges* 1086, *Eillinges* 1100–35, 'the people of Æðel'. These names in -*ingahām* denoted specific places where a community, closely associated with the village whose name they bore, had established their home. They are usually names of old villages and parishes and the personal-names they contain are of the same type as those found in names in -*ingas*. They are thus very old names, a little, perhaps a few generations, later than those in -*ingas*. Godmanham (ERY), 'the village of Godmund's people', which is recorded in 730 as *Godmundingaham*, was, Bede tells us, the site of a heathen temple. Short personal-names are the base of Tillingham (Ess), *Tillingeham* c610, from OE *Tila*, Walsingham (Nf), from *Wæls*, Effingham (Sr), from *Æffa*, etc.; compound personal-names are found in Letheringham (Sf), from *Lēodhere*. Walkeringham (Nt), from *Walhhere*, Leasingham (L), from *Lēofsige*, etc. Sandringham (Nf), *Santdersincham* 1086, *Sandringham* 1275, is 'Sand Dersingham', so called to distinguish it from the neighbouring Dersingham 'the village of Dēorsige's people'. Occasionally the name derives from a topographical element: Woldingham (Sr) 'village of the dwellers in the forest' (OE *wald*), Uppingham (R) 'village of the upland dwellers', Hameringham (L) 'village of the dwellers on the *hamor* or hill'.

Names in -*ingahām* are more widely spread than those in -*ingas*. Both are found in the areas of early settlement in the east, though -*ingahām* seems to have been a mark of Anglian rather than of Saxon settlement. In the south-east they are less common than -*ingas* names, only 20 being found in Kent, Surrey and Essex, but Suffolk has 16 and Norfolk 45, whilst in Lincolnshire they are more numerous (25) than those in -*ingas*. Yorkshire has 20, only four of them in the West Riding. In the midland counties they become less numerous and in Wessex are rare.

Similar compounds are found with other elements: Hallingbury and Finchingfield (Ess), Ardingly (Sx) 'the clearing of Earda's people', Rottingdean (Sx) 'the valley of Rōta's people', Wallingford (Berks) 'the ford of the people of Wealh', Abinger (Sr), *Abingewurd* 1191, 'the enclosure of Æbba's people', Bobbingworth alias Bovinger (Ess) 'enclosure of Bobba's people', Waldringfield (Sf) 'open country of Waldhere's people', Waldingfield (St) 'open country of the dwellers in the forest', Bengeo (Herts), *Beningeho* 1210, 'spur of land of the dwellers by the river Bene', Shillinglee (Sx) 'clearing of the dwellers on the shelf of land' (OE *scylf*), Vinnetrow (Sx), *Feningetrowe* 12th, 'tree of the fen-dwellers'. All these names refer to occupation of a particular spot by a group of people rather than by an individual, but some of them are obviously comparatively late, though it is unlikely that any were formed after the eighth century. Many of them occur in districts unsuitable for early occupation. Yattendon (Berks), *Yetingedene* 1220, 'valley of Gēat's people', is on the Reading Beds, a formation unattractive to early settlers, in a district which is still thickly wooded.

We cannot leave these -inga- compounds without a reference to the curious and unique name Jay Wick (Ess). It is not recorded before the fifteenth century when it is found as *Clakyngeywyk* in 1438, *Claken-jaywyke* in 1441 and *Clackyngia Wyke* in 1459. In the sixteenth century we find *Clacton Jaewyke* (1513) and the shortened *Gey wyck* (1584). Although the forms are late, there can be little doubt that this is for *Claccinga-wic* 'the dairy-farm of the people of *Clacc*', the man who gave name to Clacton. The name is probably much older than its late occurrence suggests. One could not imagine such a formation arising in the fifteenth century, nor would one expect the development of ME -*inge*- to [indʒ] which is found also in Bovinger for Bobbing-worth and in Dengie to occur so late. At one stage in its history the form *Clack-inge-wick*, with a palatal *j* sound and a syllabic *e*, seems to have been understood as *Clacken-gewick*. *Clacken* was then inter-preted as the local form of *Clacton*, and the name taken to be *Clacton Jewick* or *Jaywick*, and the *Clacton* was finally dropped.

NAMES IN -ington

Some of the numerous names ending in -*ington* undoubtedly go back to OE -*ingatūn* and are formations parallel to those in -*ingahām*. They denote villages established by communities but are somewhat later than those in -*ingham*. Sneinton appears to be a secondary settle-ment from Nottingham and Winterton, *Wintringatun* c1067, from Winteringham (L). Ovingham (Nb) is clearly 'the village of the people of Ofa'. In the same parish is Ovington. Both names are recorded late, but *Ovinton* 1201 and *Ovigton* 1242 point to a reduction from an original -*ing*- and it is a fairly safe assumption that Ovington was a colony of Ovingham. Certain examples of -*ingatūn* are: Knedlington (ERY), *Cnyllingatun* 959, 'village of the people of Cnytel'; Litlington (C), *Litlingetona* 1086, Lidlington (Beds), *Litincletone* 1086, 'village of the people of Lȳtel'; Eastrington (ERY), *Eastringatun* 959, 'farm-stead of those living to the east'; Wallington (Nf), *Wallinghetuna* 1086, 'farmstead of the dwellers by the wall', probably an embank-ment to contain the waters of the Ouse.

Many of these names appear in OE without any sign of the genitive plural: Teddington (Wo), *Teottingtun* 780 (Teotta), Liston (Ess), *Lissingtun* 995 (Lissa), Eckington (Db), *Eccingtun* 1002 (Ecca),

Orpington (K), *Orpedingtune* 1032, from a personal-name *Orped* 'the energetic'. The interpretation of these names has caused much controversy and opinions are still not agreed. One difficulty is that many OE charters are preserved only in ME copies and we cannot always be certain that the forms have been copied accurately. Teddington (Mx), e.g., is *æt Tudingatunæ* c970, clearly 'the farmstead of the people of Tuda', which must be preferred to *Tudintun* in a charter of 969 which is extant only in a copy made c1100. Benson (O) is *Bænesingtun* in the Anglo-Saxon Chronicle under the year 571 in a manuscript which cannot be earlier than the end of the ninth century. None of the numerous forms adduced in the *Place-names of Oxfordshire* shows any sign of the *-a-* of the genitive plural *-inga-* and the name is explained as 'Benesa's farm'. Ekwall prefers 'the farm of the Benesingas' and this is confirmed by the reference to the place c730 as *Banesinga villa*. Lotherton (WRY), *Lutteringtun* 963, occurs also as *Luteringatun* c1030. Neither is the pure OE form, which was probably *Hlūtringatūn* 'the farm of the Hlūtringas', the dwellers at a spring or stream called *Hlūtre* 'the clean one'. It is clear, therefore, that some of the names evidenced only late or rarely in the form *-ington* may derive from an original *-ingatūn*, but there are numerous others where this interpretation is impossible.

There is undoubted evidence for the existence in OE of a connective suffix *-ing*. In some place-names it alternates with the genitive singular, e.g., Brightwalton (Berks), *æt Beorhtwaldingtune* 939, *Bristoldestune* 1086; Tiddington (Wa), *æt Tidinctune* 969, *Tidantun* 985. *Beorhtwaldingtune* cannot have been a mere alternative for *Beorhtwaldestun* 'Beorhtwald's farm', for we find similar compounds with a woman's name and with other elements. Sinnington (NRY), *Siuerinctune, Sevenictun* 1086, and Tavistock (D), *æt Tefing stoce* c1000, denote farms 'having to do with or belonging to the rivers Severn and Tavy'. Raffling Wood (Sx) is a clear example of a late use of this connective particle. It is the wood belonging to Ratford. It is not easy to express these shades of difference shortly and clearly in modern English, but we might put it that *Beorhtwaldingatūn* would correspond to 'the Johnsons' estate', *Beorhtwaldestūn* to 'Johnson's estate' and *Beorhtwaldingtūn* to 'the Johnson estate'. Unless there is clear evidence of the medial *-inga-*, these names cannot be used as evidence of settlement by communities.

A modern name in *-ington* is not necessarily a name in *-ing-*, or even in *-tūn*. It may represent a weakening of *-an*, either the genitive of a ·

115

personal-name or an adjectival inflexion, or of some other ending, e.g.: Bullington (Ha), *Bulandun* 1002, 'hill of Bula, or of the bull'; Newington (K), *Niwantun* 11th, 'new farm'; Carsington (Db) and Cassington (O), 'cress-farm', from OE *cærsen* 'of cress'; Calvington (Sa), *Calveton* 1198, OE *calfa-tūn* 'calves' enclosure'; Donnington (Sx), *Dunketone* 966, 'Dunneca's farm'; Honington (Wa), *Hunitona* 1043, 'honey farm'; Cannington (So), *Cantuctun* c880, 'farm on the Quantocks'; Afflington (Do), *Alfrunetone* 1086, 'farm of Ælfrūn', the lady of the manor in 1066; Dennington (Sf), *Dingifetuna* 1086, 'farm of Denegifu (f)'; Garrington (K), *Garwynnetun* 11th, 'farm of Gārwynn (f)'; Strettington (Sx), *Estretementone* Hy 1, from OE *strǣt-hǣme-tūn* 'farm of the dwellers by the Roman road' (Stane Street).

RELICS OF HEATHENISM

Our knowledge of Anglo-Saxon heathenism is vague and limited. No literature has survived from the pagan period. Memories of the ancient traditions handed on by court and migrant minstrels, many of which were undoubtedly committed to writing, are to be found in works which we can still read, but their authors were Christians to whom the ancient paganism was a pernicious superstition to be stamped out for all time. The poet of Beowulf was a Christian, his subject the legendary story of heathen Germanic peoples in their far-distant home on the Continent. Many of the blurred gaps in our knowledge have been filled in from Scandinavian sources, but the connexion between English and Scandinavian heathenism belongs to a past which was already remote when the first Saxons invaded this country. Archaeology has provided abundant material bearing on the burial customs of the pagan English, but it can throw no light on their cults or the sites of their holy places. No Anglo-Saxon temple has yet been excavated. Nor can place-names throw light on the nature of pagan beliefs, but we have now a body of evidence which reveals the names of their most popular gods and locates the sites of many of their temples.

Places like Harrow, which marks the site of a heathen temple, and sites of hills and groves where Woden and Thunor were worshipped, as at Woodnesborough and Thundersley, could not have been given these names after the conversion to Christianity. They must belong to the pagan period, and their survival today is a proof that they must have been firmly established in common use so long before the conversion that they defied all the fulminations of the Church against heathen practices and pagan beliefs. The Christian missionaries could not fail to be aware of the meaning of these names; they knew that here Woden, god of the dead, and there Thunor, god of thunder, had been revered and worshipped. They might destroy the pagan altar and the heathen temple, but the name defied them. It is a remarkable fact that within a radius of some twelve miles of Canterbury, the centre from which Augustine worked, the city which quickly became the ecclesiastical capital of England, no less than four parishes still bear names which recall the worship of Woden or the site of a pagan temple.

All such names must be early. Some probably date from the period of the Migration. The latest date at which they could be established varies. In Kent such names could not have arisen after the coming of Augustine in 597. In Essex, which, it has been said, 'can fairly be called the most strongly heathen of English kingdoms', Mellitus, who had been appointed bishop of London in 601, was driven out in 616 and the East Saxons reverted to heathenism for half a century. Birinus, the first bishop of Wessex, found the West Saxons a *gens paganissima*, a description amply justified in view of the numerous heathen place-names of the kingdom. He baptised their king Cynegils in 635, but Cenwalh, his second son and successor, was still a heathen in 645. Sussex remained heathen for a generation after 655. Paganism died hard. Even in Kent, where Eorconberht, who ruled from 640 to 664, was the first king in England to order the destruction of idols, the laws of Wihtred of 685 still found it necessary to impose penalties for heathen worship.

Some 60 sites of heathen worship can now be identified, almost all included within the region enclosed south of a line from Ipswich to Stafford and east of one from Stafford to Weymouth. They are confined to areas known to have been settled early, often on hills or in clearings, near Roman roads or ancient trackways, heathen burial-grounds or villages with names of an archaic type. Of the three elements denoting 'temple', OE *ealh* survives in Alkham near Dover. More common is *hearg*, usually used of a 'hill sanctuary'. It is found in Harrowden (Beds, Nth), Harrowdown (Ess) and Arrowfield Top (Wo). In Peper Harow (Sr), as in Patchway (Sx), the first element is a personal-name, here OE *Pipper(a)*, an indication that a temple, like a Christian church in later times, could be owned by an individual. Others could take their name from the people whom they served. The original name of Harrow on the Hill (Mx) was *Gumeninga hearh* 'the sanctuary of the Gumeningas', a tribe otherwise unknown. Particularly interesting is *Besinga hearh* 'the sanctuary of the Besingas' near Farnham (Sr), the site of a heathen temple given by the unbaptised king of Wessex for the foundation of a Christian monastery. OE *wēoh, wīh* 'idol', 'shrine containing an idol', is found uncompounded in Weyhill (Ha), *Leweo* 13th, with later addition of *hill*, in Wye near Canterbury, and, in the dative plural, in Wyham (L), *Wihum* c1115. It is compounded with *dūn* 'hill' in Weedon (Bk) and Weedon Lois (Nth), but more commonly with *lēah* 'grove', as in Weeley (Ess), Whyly and Whiligh (Sx), Willey (Sr), Wheely Down (Ha) and Weoley (Wo). Other compounds are Weeford (St) and Wyville (L), *Uuiuuelle* 1106–23, 'the heathen temple by the stream'. Patchway (Sx) is 'Pæccel's temple', which, with *Cusan weoh* 'Cusa's temple', a lost place in Farnham (Ha), and Peper Harow (Sr), preserves the name of the founder or owner.

The names of *Tīw, Wōden* and *Þunor* we still use daily in Tuesday, Wednesday and Thursday. All three survive in place-names. *Tīw*, the god of war, is least common, but his name is found in Tuesley (Sr), in two lost names, *Tislea* (Ha) and *Tyesmere* (Wo), and in Tysoe (Wa), 'Tīw's spur of land'.

All the Anglo-Saxon dynasties which claimed a descent from the heathen gods trace their descent from Woden, god of the dead, especially of those slain in battle, except the kings of Essex, who claimed as their divine ancestor Seaxnet, a god of the continental Saxons. It is not surprising, therefore, that the only evidence we find for his worship among the East Saxons is in two lost field-names, *Wodnesfeld* in Widdington and *Wedynsfeld* in Theydon. Elsewhere, his name is found in place-names in the territories of each of the three peoples which composed the English nation. Among the Jutes of Kent he was worshipped at Woodnesborough and Wormshill, *Wodneshelle, Wornesell* 1275. In Wiltshire, which was not converted until after 634, we have *Wodnesdenu* in West Overton and *Wodnesbeorh*, a barrow now known as Adam's Grave in Alton Prior. The valley and the barrow are less than four miles apart and between them runs the famous earthwork once known as *Wodnes dic* (903), now as Wansdyke, and Stenton plausibly suggests that the three names probably denoted different parts of a single great sanctuary dedicated to Woden. Another sanctuary of about the same extent is probably indicated by the names Wednesbury and Wednesfield (St) in the heart of Mercia. Further north we have Wensley (Db), and in Middle Anglia, Wenslow Half Hundred (Beds).

So far as is known, Woden is the only god to whom the Anglo-Saxons attributed the making of great earthworks of forgotten origin. The name Wansdyke shows that they attributed to him the construction of the greatest linear earthwork in southern Britain. There is no direct proof that Woden was known in England, as in Scandinavia, by the byname Grim, but Ekwall has shown that the identification is highly probable. In Wiltshire there are three dykes named Grim's Ditch, of which two survive on the modern map, one recorded as *grimes dic* in 956. The same name is found also in Oxfordshire, Middlesex and Hertfordshire, whilst in Essex we have Gryme's Dyke and in Hampshire Grims Dyke. Woden's Dyke (Ha) is actually called *Grimesdich* in 1272. All these earthworks were regarded as superhuman, such as could be made only by a god, and are not, like the other names discussed, evidence that he was worshipped there. Occasionally these earthworks are regarded as the work of giants: *to ænta dic* 1026 (in King's Worthy); Andyke in Barton Stacey (Ha), *Auntediche* 13th. At a later period, such earthworks were attributed to the Devil, but the name is invariably late, an antiquarian's invention. The Cambridgeshire Devil's Dyke is not so called before the sixteenth century. Earlier it was simply *le Dyche* or *le Micheldyche*.

Thunor, god of thunder, is commemorated at least six times by reference to his sacred grove in Thunderley and Thundersley (Ess), Thursley (Sr), and in lost names in Sussex, Hampshire and Wiltshire; and also in Thunderfield (Sr), Thundridge (Herts), in the name of the Essex hundred Thurstable 'Thunor's pillar' and in that of the lost Thunderlow in the same county. In Anglian territory no evidence of his cult survives; two or three possible field-names are of doubtfu origin.

Somewhere between Eastry and Minster in Thanet once stood a barrow which marked the only place in Kent known to be associated with the worship of Thunor. It gave rise to what is, perhaps, the earliest of all the romantic stories engendered by place-names. The legend, which flourished in Kent for over 500 years, appears in several different versions, constantly embellished throughout the centuries. It begins with the bald statement in the Anglo-Saxon Chronicle under the year 640 (though this item was added much later) that two Kentish princes were murdered by Thunor. From later sources we learn that their uncle, Egbert, king of Kent, who had connived at the murder, by way of penance promised their sister Domneva that he would give her, for the endowment of a monastery, as much land as her pet doe could encompass in a single run.[1] On the appointed day, the king, accompanied by his attendants, with soldiers and monks and a crowd of people from Canterbury, followed the doe's course. When it began to include land belonging to Thunor, this man of sin and son of perdition, this limb of the devil, rushed forward on his horse and headed it off. Immediately the earth opened and man, horse and arms were engulfed and down went Thunor to join Dathan and Abiram in hell. The king ordered his body to be covered with a mighty heap of stones and passers-by called the place *Thunerhleaw*. A fifteenth-century Canterbury chronicler makes no reference to the mound, but states that the pit was still to be seen in his days and was called *Thunor hys lope*. On the strength of this statement, aided by a contemporary map, O. G. S. Crawford identified the site of the pit, by means of an air-photograph. But this appears to be a dene-hole. *Thunoreslope* is an error, not uncommon, due to misreading the Anglo-Saxon *w* in *Thunoreslowe* as *p*.

The full implications of this legend we cannot discuss here. But it seems that in their fight against the powerful paganism of this district, the Church deliberately fostered and embellished it in an attempt to destroy the cult of Thunor. No Anglo-Saxon was ever called by such a name. Thunor is used only as the name of a god, and *Thunerhleaw* must have been a place associated with his worship. The fact that Thunor is named as the murderer in the Anglo-Saxon Chronicle proves the existence of the legend in some form already before the compilation of that document in the ninth century. The purpose of the Church was so far accomplished that no further mention of the barrow occurs and its exact site is unknown. Later, the legend was elaborated as a warning to despoilers of the Church and in the latest version Thunor is castigated in the company of Simon Magus, Arians, Pelagians, Nestorians and Wycliffites, and is finally damned to all eternity as a Lollard.

There appears to be no direct evidence for the deliberate re-naming of heathen sites under Christian influence, but there are hints that this may have occurred. The place-name Godshill is found in Sussex, Hampshire and the Isle of Wight, and as Godsell in Wiltshire, whilst Gadshill is found twice in Kent, one of which is probably to be identified with *Godeshylle* recorded in a charter of 973. Similar com-

[1] This 'boundary of the liberty' is marked on the 6″ Ordnance Map of 1870.

pounds occur with other elements: Godsfield (Ha), Godswell Grove (W) and Gadsey Brook (Beds), *Godeshoslade* 1239. It would indeed be a remarkable coincidence if all these names, six of them compounded with *hill*, were to contain the personal-name *Gode*, a short form of *Godric*, *Godwine*, etc. It is inconceivable that the reference should be to the Christian Deity, as in Godstow (O), the name of a monastery. All are situated in areas of early settlement where heathen place-names might be expected and may well contain OE *god* 'a god'. It is noteworthy that the earliest forms of Wormshill (K) are *Godeselle* 1086, *Godeshelle* c1100, actual evidence for Woden himself not appearing before 1225. Woodnesborough, too, appears in DB as both *Wanesberge* and *Gollesberge*. These forms Wallenberg explains as AFr spellings with *G* for *W*, but this, if it occurs at all, is very rare.[1] Have we here a hint of the fierce conflict between Christian and heathen which underlies the legend of the Kentish Thunor? Do these forms imply that the Church did attempt, with partial success, to replace the name of the heathen Wōden by the less obnoxious *god*, which might be interpreted as God? It is not beyond the bounds of possibility. Kökeritz further suggests that the genitive plural *god(en)a* may enter such names as Godley and Godley Bridge (Sr), the former the name of a hundred, Godley (Ch) 'grove of the gods', and Godney (So), *Godeneia* 971, 'island of the gods', for which there are 'such fine Swedish parallels as *Onsön* "Woden's island" and *Torsö* "Thor's island" '. These names cannot be regarded as conclusive proof of heathen associations, but they are suggestive and might find support in Anderson's derivation of two Sussex names. Easwrithe is the name of a hundred which might mean simply 'Ēsa's thicket or copse', but it might contain OE *ēsa* (genitive plural), 'the copse of the gods', with reference to a sacred grove where the hundred met. The ancient name of the hundred of Westbourne was *Ghidenetroi*, which is found only in DB, but may well be from OE *gydenne-trēow* 'the tree of the goddess' (OE *gyden* 'goddess').

Long ago, Henry Bradley suggested that names like Swineshead, Hartshead, etc., pointed to a custom of setting up the head of an animal, or a representation of it, on a pole, to mark the place for public open-air meetings. Some of them are names of hundreds which are often named from places which have always been unimportant,

---

[1] A continental parallel is the change of the OG place-name *Wodnesberg* into *Godesberg*, cited by H. Kökeritz, *Place-names of the Isle of Wight* (1940), p. xliii, n. 86.

often in the middle of an uninhabited moor, where the men of the hundred assembled for deliberation. Later, Professor Bruce Dickins called attention to a practice of the heathen Lombards who, in the time of Tacitus and Ptolemy, were close neighbours of the Angli and the Saxones. Gregory the Great describes the slaughter by the Lombards of 40 Italian husbandmen who would not eat of flesh sacrificed to idols. After their custom they sacrificed the head of a goat to the devil, running round it in a circle and dedicating it by singing dreadful songs. They bowed their necks to it and adored it, and when their prisoners refused to do the same, they slaughtered them.

This suggests an interpretation of Gateshead, Bede's *ad caprae caput*. Adam of Bremen, describing the great festival of the Swedes held every nine years at Uppsala, noted that nine heads were offered, of every male animal with whose blood it was customary to appease the gods. Their bodies were hung in a grove near the temple. The victims mentioned were of three types, man, horse and hound. Excavations of Icelandic temples have shown that in the hall where sacrificial feasts were held were found bones of sheep, goats, oxen, swine and horses, so that it seems reasonable to add to the list of victims the ox or bull, goats, swine or boar and sheep or ram.

The name of each of these victims is found in place-names in England or Germany compounded with *head*. In England we have Manshead Hundred (Beds), Farcet (Hu), from OE *fearr* 'bull', Gateshead, Swineshead (Beds, L, Gl, Wo), Eversheads Farm (Sr), from OE *eofor* 'boar', Shepshead (Lei), Ramshead and Rampside (La). In addition, the names of the hart, badger, raven, wild cat, snake and the eagle are found in Hartshead (La, WRY), Hartside (Nb), Broxhead (Ha), Broxted (Ess), *Brochesheuot* 1086, Ravenshead (Nb), Cats Head Lodge (Nth), Worms Heath and Heronshead (Sr), *Ernesheved* 1358. The human sacrifice which accounts for Manshead is a proved Germanic custom, evidenced by Tacitus, who also describes how Germanicus, when in 15 A.D. he visited the scene of the disaster to Varus, saw human heads (doubtless of prisoners sacrificed by the victorious Germans) prominently nailed to the trunks of trees. We know, too, that human sacrifice was practised by the heathen Saxons of the fifth and sixth centuries as by the worshippers of Nerthus in the first. In some of these names, *hēafod* may be used of a hill or headland; some may contain a personal-name. Farcet is a clear example where we can have neither a personal-name nor a topographical term. It is unsafe to generalise, but some, at least, of these names may be those of places which were once the site of bloody sacrifice, where the head, human or animal, was offered to a heathen deity.[1]

PLACE-NAMES WITH CHRISTIAN ASSOCIATIONS

The laws of Æthelred and Cnut divided churches into four classes: the 'head minster' or cathedral, the 'ordinary minster', the 'lesser church' with a graveyard and the 'field church'. *Minster* is the English form (OE *mynster*) of the Latin *monasterium* and was used in OE of both monasteries and churches. Minster in Thanet and Minster in Sheppey were the sites of monasteries found respectively by the daughter and the widow of Eorconberht, king of Kent 640–664. The sense 'cathedral' survives in York Minster and Minsterworth, which belonged to St Peter's, Gloucester. Throughout the Anglo-Saxon period many districts of some size were served by 'minsters', small groups of clergy sharing a communal life and supplying the needs of the surrounding countryside from large churches, some of which survive and still preserve the name of minster. They are sometimes described from their situation, Southminster, Upminster, Emstrey (Sa), *Eiminstre* 1086, 'church on the island', and Exminster and Charminster from the rivers on which they stand. Like the 'lesser churches' these could be owned by an individual, Bedminster (So), 'Bēda's minster', Buckminster (Lei), that of Bucca, Yetminster (Do), that of Eata; sometimes with the connective *-ing*, Lyminster (Sx), *Lullyngmynster* 880 (Lulla), Pitminster (So), *Pipingmynstre* 938 (Pyppa); sometimes the owner was a woman: Beaminster (Do), *Bebingmynster* 872 (Bebbe).

Most parish churches of the medieval period belonged to the class of 'lesser churches' which had been founded by lay noblemen. The church was regarded as the founder's property, producing an income for him and his heirs, and could be let out for hire like a mill or bequeathed by will. The name of the founder or owner, sometimes a woman, is preserved in certain of their names: Thorpe Achurch (Nth), (*æt*) *Asencircan* 972–92, 'church of **Asa* (OE) or of *Ási* (ON)', Baschurch (Sa) 'church of Basa', Offchurch, Wa (Offa), Alvechurch, Wo (Ælfgýð, f), Dymchurch (K), 'church of the judge' (OE *dēma*). In

---

[1] For the survival of heathen beliefs and superstitions in medieval England, v. pp. 208, 223–4.

Layston (Herts) only the personal-name survives from *Loefstaneschirche* 12th, 'Lēofstān's church'. Wolford Farm in Dunkeswell (D) is *Wlforthe* in 1196 and 1206, but in all later forms appears with the addition of *-church*, *Wlferechirch* 1215, etc., originally 'wolf-ford', later 'church at Wolford'. The name of Wolford church is said to be 'sunk in that of Wolford Lodge. Near the house was anciently a chapel or church of which the walls partly remain.'

Even at the end of the eighth century many Christian communities of long standing were still unprovided with any form of church. Archbishop Theodore had allowed priests to say mass 'in the fields'. The 'field church' was established for communities living on lands newly brought into cultivation and had no graveyard. In Suffolk there was a parish of *Feldchirche* in 1291. It is called *Feldcherche Belstede* in 1324. In 1540 the chapel of *Velechurche* was annexed to the parish church of Washbrook. As the early name of Washbrook was Great Belstead, it would appear that this field-church was originally that of Little Belstead.

Light is thrown by place-names on the appearance and structure of these early churches. Some are self-explanatory: Ivychurch (K), Ivy Church (W); Whitchurch (Bk, D, etc.), that at Whitchurch Canonicorum (Do) being mentioned in 880, 'white' from the white limestone used as in Whithorn in Wigtownshire, 'white house', which Bede says was so called because it was built of stone; Woodchurch (Ch, K), 'wooden'. Berechurch (Ess), *Bierdecherche* 1277, was made of boards or planks, Stokenchurch (Bk), of stocks or timber; in Frome Vauchurch (Do) and Vowchurch (He), from OE *fāg* 'variegated, multicoloured', we have the equivalent of the Scottish Falkirk, the Gaelic *Egglesbrec* 'speckled church'. Were these half-timbered black-and-white churches such as are still fairly common in Cheshire? Hornchurch (Ess), *Monasterium Cornutum* 1222, *Hornedechirche* 1291, has the figure of a bull's head with horns affixed to its eastern gable, but there is no evidence that this figure is older than the end of the eighteenth century. The only early association of a horned bull's head with Hornchurch is to be found on a figure on the Prior's seal of 1384–5, a seal which apparently did not exist in 1267. The relation of the figure on the seal to the name of the church is obscure. The church may have been so called because decorated with horns and the emblem on the seal may have been in the nature of a rebus on the name 'horned church'. Honeychurch (D), *Honecherche* 1086, *Hunichirche* 1238, may be 'Huna's church', but the preponderance of forms in *Huni-*, *Huny-* suggests that the name really contains *honey* and might have been so called from the swarming of bees under the eaves of the church. Such honey-making still takes place in the church at Hartland.

Church- as a first element raises some difficult problems. Churcham (Gl) is *Hamme* in 1086; later, *church* was prefixed, *Chirchehamme* c1233, to distinguish this church in the low-lying land by the Severn from that owned by the monks at Highnam, *Hamme* 1086, *Hyne-hamme* 1100. Churchdown in the same county is *Circesdune* in 1086, *Kyrchesdon* 1190, where the high round hill was originally called Brit *Crūc*, to which an explanatory *dūn* was added. Churchfield Farm (Nth), *Ciricfeld* c964, where there was an early chapel, is 'open land by the church'. Churchstow (D), *Churechestowe* 1242 is identical in origin with Cheristow (D), *Chircstoue* 1167, where there is no conspicuous hill, but where there was an ancient chapelry dedicated to St Wenn. Both mean 'site of the church'.

It is clear that we have to do with two distinct elements: Brit *crūc* 'hill' and OE *cirice* 'church'. Both are certainly found, but forms are often difficult to distinguish and opinions differ on the relative frequency of these elements, particularly in the not uncommon place-name Churchill.[1] Both Mawer and Ekwall agree that both elements are found, but Mawer was of the opinion that 'compounds of *church* in place-names are exceedingly rare', whilst Ekwall concludes that 'the majority of the Churchills go back to OE *Cirichyll* "church hill" '. Each name must be considered in the light of the forms available and the history and topography of the place. Certainty is frequently impossible. Undoubted examples of Brit *crūc* 'hill' are: Church Hill (So), *Crichhulle* 702; Crook Hill (Db), *Cruchell'* 1199; Churchill in Malborough (D), *Curcheswille* 1201 'spring by the hill'; Christon (So), *Cyrces gemæro* 1068, *Crucheston* 1204. Certain compounds of OE *cirice* 'church' are: Charford (D), *cyric forda* 970; Cheriton (K), *Ciricetun* c1100, *Cheritun* 1158, 'church farm'; later forms like *Cherinton* 1167, *Chirintone* 1198, from OE *ciricean-tūn*, with the later forms of the Kent name, confirm this derivation for Cheriton (D, Ha, So) and Cherrington (Wa), Churston Ferrers (D), Chirton (Nb, W) and Churton (Ch). The numerous forms of Churchill (O), none, however, earlier than 1086, point clearly to a meaning 'church hill', but the old church was not on the hill. The round barrow almost on

---

[1] *v.* A. Mawer and F. M. Stenton, *Place-names of Worcestershire* (1927), 106–9; E. Ekwall, *Studies on English Place- and Personal Names* (1931), 33–54.

top of the hill suggests that the real origin may have been 'hill with a tumulus'. An illustration of the difficulty of these names is Churchstanton (D). The place was originally called *Stantone* (1086). The prefix appears in such varied forms that Mawer dissociates it from both *cirice* and *crūc* and suggests 'cherry', the place having been noted for its cherries like Cherry Hinton (C). As the addition was probably to distinguish it from Whitestanton, he adds, it can hardly be 'church', as both villages have churches. But there is in the parish a place Churchingford, *Suthchurchamford* 1386, *Churchamford* 1499. This must mean 'the ford by (*Suth*)*churcham*', that is, by the low-lying land by the Otter near the (southern) church. There are remains of an ancient church here, now part of a farm-building.

In the ninth century it is said to have been an English custom to erect a cross for the daily service of prayer on estates where there was no church. Two hundred years earlier Archbishop Theodore had enjoined that when a church had been removed to another place a cross should be erected on the site of the vanished altar. This custom will account for a few place-names containing OE *cristelmæl* 'cross, crucifix': Christian Malford (W), *Cristemaleford* 937, which became *Christine Malford* in 1374 and luckily escaped survival as *Curst Mavord* (1585); Christleton (Ch), Christmas Hill (Wa), *Cristemelhull* 1246; Kismeldon Bridge and Kersham Bridge (D), from a metathesised *cyrstelmæl*; Littleton (Ch), *Parva Christleton* 1250, where Little Christleton has been contracted to Littleton; Rowton (Ch), *Rowecristelton* 12th, a shortened form of Row ('rough') Christleton. In some names we have OE *mæl* 'a sign, a cross': Malden (Sr), Maldon (Ess), Maulden (Beds), Meldon (Nb), all OE *mældūn* 'hill with a cross'; at Trimdon (Du), *Tremeldon* 1196, the cross was made of wood (OE *trēow* 'tree'.

OE *stōw* 'place' was used of a place where people assembled and is found in hundred names like Broxtow (Nt) 'the place of Brocwulf'. It is used of the monasteries of Barking and Bury St Edmunds and survives in this sense in Stow (L), *S' Maria de Stowe* 1086, St Mary's Abbey, Stow on the Wold (Gl), Godstow (O), and Merstow Green (Wo), 'the famous monastery' of Evesham. In Plemstall (Ch), *Pleymundestowe* 1291, it is used of a hermitage where Plegmund, archbishop of Canterbury 890–914, is said to have lived as a hermit. It is used generally of a 'holy place' and is frequently compounded with a saint's name, often that of the saint to whom the church is dedicated: Halstow (D, K), Hastoe Farm (Herts), Austy Wood (Wa),

Halwestowe 'holy place', Christow (D), *Cristinestowe* 1244 (OE *crīstene* 'place hallowed by Christian associations'); Virginstow, Instow (D), *Johannesto* 1086 (St John), Jacobstow, D (St James), Wistanstow (Sa) and Wistow, Lei (St Wigstan). Hibaldstow (L) was formerly *Cecesig* 'Cec's island' where St Hygebald is said to have been buried and here *stow* probably means 'burial-place'. OE *stoc*, also vaguely meaning 'place', similarly, though less frequently, has religious associations. It is used of a Saxon monastery at Stoke by Nayland (Sf); Halstock (Do) is 'the holy place'. Saints' names were formerly part of the names of Stockwood (Do), *Stokes sancti Edwoldi* 1238; Stoke in Hartland (D), *Nistenestoch* 1086, dedicated to St Nectan; Stoke St Milborough (Sa), *Godestoch* 1086, *Stoke St Milburg* 1291; the abbess Mildburg is mentioned in a charter of 901.[1]

SECONDARY SETTLEMENT

Once the larger communities of the early Anglo-Saxon settlers were reasonably established in their new land, their two chief concerns would be defence and food-supply. They would establish a fort, as did the *Hæppingas* of Happing Hundred at Happisburgh (Nf) and the *Mæccingas* of Matching at Mashbury and would set to work to plough and sow for the next year's harvest and in the meanwhile would hunt and seek pastures and winter shelters for their cattle and sheep. They would explore their wide domains and find it desirable to give names to hills and fords, to the springs which supplied them with water, to woods where they could get timber or firewood, or where they knew they would find deer or wild-boars for food. Such names would be given gradually and spontaneously as need arose. Even in the early days of the settlement it might be found convenient for part of the community to move to new ploughlands at some distance, still preserving the group-name, and from time to time some man of importance or independence might establish a farm of his own, soon to be called after his name, or from some prominent natural feature near by. There would be a steady movement outwards towards the confines of the territory. It would be slow and gradual, depending on the rate of increase of the population and the nature of the countryside. It would be spread over generations, or even centuries, for we have ample proof that, throughout the Middle Ages, clearing of woods and draining of marshes steadily continued and

[1] For place-names referring to ecclesiastical endowments, etc., *v.* pp. 195, 216–17.

that new farmsteads and hamlets continually increased in numbers.

The general pattern is clear and from time to time we have glimpses of the process at work, but accurate dating is impossible. Innumerable places first mentioned in Domesday Book bear ancient names which must even then have been centuries old; others, we can prove, were named from men or women living in 1066. Folk-names are undoubtedly a very ancient type. A name like Sonning, on the Thames north-east of Reading, the *provincia* of the *Sunningas* 'the people of Sunna', which corresponds very closely to the medieval 'seven hundreds of Cookham and Bray', covered an area which included Sunninghill, near Ascot, and Sunningwell, near Abingdon, some 20 miles north-west of Sonning. This territory may well have lain partly on the northern bank of the Thames, for in the Oxfordshire parish of Eye and Dunsden, Sonning Eye and Sonning Common preserve the name of the tribe, although it is the secondary settlement of Sunningwell which faces them across the Thames. It is tempting, too, and perhaps not too rash an assumption, to regard the Middlesex Sunbury, 'Sunna's fort', about four miles north-east of the Thames, as an outlying fortification built by Sunna to protect the territory of his people against danger from the east. Sonning is clearly a much more ancient name than the Essex Tillingham 'homestead of the people of Tila', which was certainly in existence before 610, but was always a place-name, referring to a farm or village at a particular place. As we have seen above, Wokingham (Berks) and Ellingham (Ha) were probably daughter-settlements of Woking (Sr) and Eling (Ha).[1] Similar colonies could be sent out from Corringham (L), *Coringeham* 1086, 'village of the people of *Cora*', to Carrington (L), *Coringatun* c1067, 'outlying farm of the people of *Cora*', and from Briningham (Nf), *Bruningaham* 1086, to Brinton (Nf), *Bruntuna* 1086. Wingrave (Bk), *Withungrave* 1086, now a separate parish, was originally a grove of the *Weohthūningas*, 'the men of Weohthūn', now Wing.[2]

The root meaning of OE *stoc* was probably 'standing place' and as a place-name it may originally have been used of a place where cattle stood for milking in outlying pastures. From this developed a meaning 'cattle-farm, dairy-farm', especially an outlying one. As this grew, with the erection of sheds and other buildings, with huts and cottages for the herdsmen, the term came to be used of an outlying

[1] *v.* p. 112.

[2] Cf. also Nottingham and Sneinton, Winteringham and Winterton, Ovingham and Ovington, p. 114.

farm or small settlement from some more important place. As a place-name it is most commonly found alone as Stoke, a sure sign that such places were originally of little importance and dependent on some neighbouring village. They were so common that after the Norman Conquest it was found necessary to add some distinguishing epithet, as North and South Stoke (L), Stoke upon Trent (St), Stoney Stoke (So) and Stoke Dry (R). Adstock (Bk) was an outlying dairy-farm belonging to the Æddi whose name is preserved in the neighbouring Addington. A particularly interesting example of this sense 'outlying farm or settlement' is found already in 990 in Basingstoke (Ha), 'the *stoc* belonging to the *Basingas*', the people of *Basa*, now Basing, (*æt*) *Basengum* 871. Basing was originally the more important place, but it has now been completely eclipsed by its daughter-settlement at Basingstoke. Navestock (Ess), *Nasingestok* 967, was similarly a dependent settlement from Nazeing 'the dwellers on the ness', though it is eight miles distant on the other side of the forest ridge. Chardstock (D) was an outlier of Chard (So), less than three miles away, and Calstock (Co), *Calestoch* 1086, *Kelewystoc* 1284, a secondary settlement from *Calui*, the old name of Callington.

OE *worð*, like *tūn*, appears to have meant originally 'fence', then 'enclosure', 'enclosure round a homestead', and finally 'homestead'. It is used of places varying in size from 4 to 120 hides and sometimes of a small vill. Hurworth (Du) was an enclosure made of hurdles and Shuttleworth (Db) one that was barred or bolted. Beauworth (Ha), *Beowyrð* 938, was a bee-farm, Butterworth (La) a butter-farm, and Plumford (K), *Plumwurth* 1236, an orchard of plum-trees. The element is usually compounded with a personal-name and many of these places are recorded in Domesday Book and have become parishes: Harmondsworth (Mx), 'homestead of *Heremōd*', Rickmansworth, Herts (*Rīcmær*), Chelwood (So), *Celeworde* 1086 (*Cēola*), Duxford (C), *Dukeswrth* c950 (*Ducc*). Some are recorded early: Wandsworth (Sr), (*to*) *Wendles wurðe* 693 (*Wændel*), Isleworth (Mx), *Gislheres-uuyrth* 695 (*Gīslhere*), Hillborough (Wa), *Hildeburhwrthe* 710, where the -*worth* has been lost, only the woman's name *Hildeburg* surviving, Ashmansworth (Ha), *Æscmeres wierð* 909 (*Æscmær*), Seacourt (Berks), *Seofocanwyrð* 957 (*Seofeca*), Chelsworth (Sf), *Ceorleswyrðe* 962 (*Ceorl*). In Wardleworth (La) -*worth* has been added to the name of the neighbouring Wuerdle (*Werdull* c1180) of which it was probably a dependent farm or cattle-farm, a meaning suited to earlier compounds with a folk-name such as Abinger (Sr), Bobbingworth

(Ess),[1] Bengeworth (Wo), *Benincgurthe* 714, *Benningeorde* 1086 (*Beonna*), Worlingworth (Sf), (*et*) *Wilrincgawerþa* c1035 (*Wilhere*), Needingworth (Hu), 'enclosure or farm of Hnydda's people'. The element clearly had a long history: it is found early, compounded with personal-names of the bithematic type which long persisted, some those of women, which were not found in early place-names, as Kenilworth (Wa) (*Cynehild*), Madginford (K), *Megeldeuurthe* 832 (**Mæcghild*). Some of these places increased in importance and became parishes, others, especially in Lancashire and the West Riding, are still small single homesteads, often in remote situations. There is no example of a compound with a post-Conquest personal-name.

The Weald

In the annal for 893 the Weald is named and defined in the Anglo-Saxon Chronicle as 'the great wood which we call *Andred*'; it is said to be 120 or more miles long and 30 miles broad and in the same entry is described as a *weald* or forest. It stretched from the New Forest of Hampshire to Lympne in Kent and long served as a barrier between the early settlements of Sussex and Surrey. Its thick woodland and heavy clay soil were unattractive to early settlers, but eighth-century charters reveal that it was already being used for keeping swine and pasturing sheep, and also, presumably as a source of timber. In Kent and East Sussex and, less commonly, in the neighbouring parts of Surrey, the common term is *denn*,[2] frequent in place-names, and at times described as *denbæra* or *wealdbaera* 'woodland swine-pastures' and Latinised as *pascua porcorum*. Other animals are referred to in Cowden, Lambden and Hinksden (*hengest* 'stallion'). Five compounds of OE *scearn* 'dung, filth, mud' are found in Kent: Shardens Farm, Sherenden, Shernden (2) and Shirrenden. Many of these names, however, are compounded with rare and uncommon topographical terms and personal-names which suggest that they are much older than the eighth century. They are difficult to identify as they are merely mentioned as swine-pastures appurtenant to a particular estate and placed vaguely in the Weald. The denns of Bexley were near the Surrey border, in the neighbourhood of Hever, those of Bromley in Edenbridge, those of Halling at Speldhurst and Rusthall near Tunbridge Wells. Tenterden 'the swine pasture of the men of Thanet' ultimately became a corporate member of the Cinque Ports

[1] *v.* p. 113. [2] This must be carefully distinguished from *denu* 'valley'.

and a borough, with a mayor of its own. Wye had its woodland pastures 20 miles away, including the whole of the modern parishes of Cranbrook and Hawkhurst and part of Biddenden, whilst hundreds of years after the Norman Conquest the manor of Chilham near Canterbury still had its rights in the Weald at Headcorn, Smarden and Goudhurst. Many of these names have disappeared; many are still those of insignificant places, but some had become villages by the time of Domesday and are now names of parishes, as Benenden, Frittenden, Horsmonden, Marden, Newenden and Rolvenden.

In Sussex, *denn* is confined to the east; the corresponding term in the west is OE *fal(o)d* 'fold, small enclosure for animals', which is similarly common north of the county boundary, in the Wealden district of west Surrey. The names of these present less difficulty than those of the Kent *denns*. Sharnfold and Shernfold (Sx) are parallel to Shernden (K). Winterfold (Sx) may be contrasted with Somerden (K). The animals named are more varied: Chaffields (Sx) and Chaffolds (Sr), 'calves'; Darwell (Sx) and Durfold (Sx, Sr), 'deer'; Cowfold, Exfold ('oxen'). About one-third are compounded with a personal-name: Tedfold (*Tudda*), Woldringfold (*Wulfhere*). In Surrey, three have become parish-names, Alfold ('old fold'), Chiddingfold 'fold of the dwellers in the valley' and Dunsfold 'fold of Dunt'; in Sussex, only one, Cowfold.

Whilst the complicated story of the gradual settlement of the Weald cannot yet be told in full, place-names throw some light on the growth of these secondary settlements. Upper and Lower Beeding (Sx) are several miles apart, in detached portions of Burbeach Hundred, separated by the small hundreds of Wyndham and Tipnoak. The name is old, recorded c880 as *æt Beadingum* 'the people of *Bēada*'. It is clear that they formed a single settlement, for in the fourteenth-century Subsidy Rolls only one Beeding is mentioned, and yet some of those taxed here belonged to what is now Lower Beeding, and Upper and Lower Beeding formed a single parish until modern times. Paradoxically enough, Lower Beeding is on the higher ground and farther up-country than Upper Beeding. 'Upper' appears to denote the chief or more important part of the parish, whilst Lower Beeding, *Netherbetynges* 1279, probably formed the swine-pastures of the original settlement.

Occasionally we have an unusually early hint of the establishment of a secondary settlement which retained the original name. As early as 680 we find mention of *se northra Mundan ham* side by side with *other Mundan ham*. South Mundham is now a hamlet in the parish of North Mundham. Frequently both mother- and daughter-settlements became separate parishes. Birch (Ess) is found in DB as both *Bricceiam* and *Parva Bricceiam*; the two parishes of Great and Little Birch were still distinct as late as the eighteenth century. Chipping and High Ongar (Ess) appear in DB only under the name *Angra*, but they were probably already separate parishes, for Marden Ash in High Ongar, near the boundary of Chipping Ongar, is recorded in 1045 as *Meredene*, which can only mean 'boundary valley'.

Wisborough Green, a long, narrow parish running south for some eight miles from the Surrey border to the neighbourhood of Petworth, is a late parish made up of vills from the hundreds of Bury, West Easewrithe and Rotherbridge. It is first mentioned in 1227 and contains no place mentioned in DB. Its place-names are typically Wealden: Amblehurst, Brinkhurst and Pephurst, wooded eminences of Æmele, Brynca and Pybba; Dunhurst, Barnfold, Harsfold, Headfoldswood Farm, formerly *Hudyfolde* 1296, 'Huda's fold', Orfold 'fold by the bank' of the Arun, with a number of farms preserving the names of medieval owners. It was clearly a district of secondary settlement, of isolated and scattered homesteads, established by men of whom we know nothing but their name. But of one or two we can learn something more. Lowfold, *Lollyngfolde* 1338, contains the same personal-name as Lyminster, *Lullyngmynster* c880. The Lulla who owned this ancient church only some two miles from the sea may well have had a cattle-fold in the Weald, far away to the north.

Gunshot Common, some three miles from the Surrey border, derives from an OE *Guman scydd* 'Guma's shed or swine-cot'. The second element *scydd* is found in the names of lost swine-pastures in Kent and Oxfordshire and elsewhere in Sussex and survives in Puckshot in Haslemere (Sr), 'goblin hut', and Denshott (Sr), *Duneschedde* 1241, 'swine-cot on the hill'. The personal-name *Guma* is a short form of OE *Gumbeald*, *Gumweald*, etc., and is found in Gomsall (Sr) and in Gumber Farm in Slinfold (Sx), *Gumeworth* 1261, 'the farmstead of Guma'. Gumber is some twelve miles south-west of Gunshot, its outlying swine-pasture. Drungewick, *Duryngwyk* 1279, is the 'dairy-farm of the people of *Dēora*', who can safely be identified with the founder of Durrington (*Derentuna* 1086), almost due south and quite close to the sea.

Not far from Lyminster is Poling, an ancient name, which became also the name of the hundred. Reference to the place is late, *Palinge* t. Hy 2, *Palinges* 1199, probably 'the people of Pāl'. In the south of Wisborough Green is Pallingham Farm, *Palingham* 1199, which must denote a small settlement of men from Poling. In Rudgwick, a parish bordering on Wisborough Green, was *Pallingfold* (1593), which may well have been a fold of these same people, whilst Pallinghurst Farm in Cranleigh (Sr), not far from Pallingham, may be an extension of that settlement. In Petworth, some four miles east of Pallingham, Limbo Farm is to be identified with *Palinga schittas* 953, 'swine-pastures of the people of Poling'. The identity is confirmed by references to 'the boscage called *Imbehome* alias *Palshuddes*' 1535–40 and 'boscage called *Lymhow*' 1535. The later name derives from *Imphaghe* 1327, *Imbehawe* 1418, 'enclosure made of saplings', a likely name in this woodland area. The modern form (*Limboe* 1645) is late and may well be due to the position of the farm, just on the edge of Petworth Park, on the 'outer fringe of things'.

There can be no doubt that in this part of the Weald, as in Kent, both individuals and communities from distant vills had their cattle-farms and swine-pastures. This evidence can be supported by other scattered instances. Goringlee in Thakeham was the woodland of the people of Goring; Diddlesfold in Lurgashall contains the same personal-name as Didling 'the people of Dyddel', nearly ten miles away; Clemsfold in Slinfold, barely two miles from the Surrey border, is 'the fold of Climpe' whose name is found also in Climping, a short distance from Littlehampton. In the same parish as Clemsfold is Pensfold Farm, *Peunesfaud* 1296, 'the fold of Pefen', a personal-name found in Pevensey, *Pevenisel* 788, 'Pefen's marsh-land', but otherwise found only in Penshurst (K).[1]

On the Lower Greensand of Kent and Surrey, OE *ceart* 'a rough common overgrown with gorse, broom and bracken' is found in Chart (K, Sr), Churt (Sr), Chartham (K, Sr), Chartwell (K), Chart-land and Chocolates (Sr), *Chertelease* 1548, *Cherkeleys* 1573. The term occurs frequently in Kent charters and is occasionally described as a wood (*silva*). It may denote wasteland added to that of a settlement as at Seal Chart and Chart Sutton, but, unlike *denn* and *falod*, it adjoined the village land.

---

[1] Cf. also the interesting case of Fernhurst (Sx) and Ambersham, an outlier of Steep (Ha), in S.W. Wooldridge and F. Goldring, *The Weald* (1953), pp. 208–9. Fig. 51 ib., p. 207, shows the common woodlands of the Weald, with the areas to which they were appurtenant.

Another term common in these woodland districts is OE (ge)sell, recorded in OE only in charter place-names, chiefly in Kent and Sussex, where it is found in areas where swine-pastures were common. Its meaning appears to be 'a collection of sheds', probably for animals, later applied to the herdsmen's huts and the farms which ultimately grew up around them. The modern places are almost invariably small and insignificant. The words with which the element is compounded throw an instructive light on their origin: Breadsell (Sx), made of boards (OE bred), Bemzells (Sx), probably made of logs (OE bēam 'beam, tree-trunk'), Spilsill Court and Little Spilshill (K), made of thin boards or covered with wooden shingles (OE speld 'splinter, piece of wood'); Horsell (Sr), from OE horh 'mud'; situation is indicated in Bugsell and Buxshalls (Sx) and Bowzell (K), by the beech-tree (OE bōc), Lindsell (Ess), 'lime-tree', now a parish, Deans Hill (K), Dungesell 1225 (OE dūn 'down') and Hensill (K), 'high'; Nizel's Heath (K), 'new'; Boarzell (K) and Wethersell (Sr), where boars and sheep were kept. Only occasionally do we find a personal-name: Badsell, K (Beadda), Yorkshire (Sx), Jercneselle 1195 (Eorcon).

A similar term, OE (ge)set 'dwelling, place for animals, stable, fold', is particularly common in East Anglia. In place-names the meaning is often 'fold', but many are names of old villages, and here it may rather be 'homestead' or even 'village'. The term is found in Kent charters and in a few place-names now lost, but is rare in the Weald: Brenzett (K) 'burned', Hessett (Sf) 'hedge', Hethersett (Nf) 'heather', Elmsett (Sf), Thornsett (Db), Wintersett and Woodsetts (WRY); Bricett (Sf), from OE brīosa 'gadfly', Lissett (ERY), from OE lǣs 'meadow'. Personal-names are found occasionally: Tattersett, Nf (Tāthere), Ossett, WRY (Ōsla), Simonside, Du (Sigemund), Adsett, Gl (Ǣddi). Ekwall suggests that Wetheringsett (Sf) was a secondary settlement of the Wederingas, the people of Wetherden, and Whissonsett (Nf), Witcingkeseta 1086, of Witchingham.

OE wīc is used both of a single dwelling and a collection of dwellings, a hamlet or village, whilst place-names provide evidence that wīc came to be associated with buildings used for particular occupations and manufactures, including those used for dairy and cattle farming. The element was in general use, but was particularly common in Essex and Sussex, Wiltshire and Devonshire, and numerous unidentified field-names prove that it was long-lived. As a simplex place-name it is very common and it is difficult to decide its exact meaning: Wick (Berks, Gl, etc.), Wike (WRY), Wyke (Sr), Week

(IOW), Weeke (Ha), all from the dative singular *wīce*. Many of these simplex names later received a distinguishing addition: Wick Champflower (So), Week St Mary (Co), Wyke Regis (Do). Wick Episcopi (Wo), *Wican* 757–75, was originally plural, 'dairy farms (of the bishop)'. Like *cot*, it is also used both in the nominative and the dative plural: Wicken (C, Ess, Nth), Wyken (Wa), Wykin (Lei), Wigan (Hu), Wix (Ess).[1] Both Wycomb (Lei) and Wykeham (NRY), *Wicum* 1086, are from the dative plural. Compounds are of all kinds: Astwick (Beds), Eastwick (WRY), Westweek (D); Longwick (Bk), Fenwick (Nb), Fordwich (K), Strudgwick (Sx), from OE *strōd* 'marsh'; Alnwick (Nb) and Elswick (Du), from the rivers on which they stand; from names of plants and trees come Bromwich (St, Wa, Wo), Redwick (Gl) 'reed', Aldridge (St) 'alders', Ashwick (So), Slaughterwicks (Sr), from OE *slāh-trēow* 'sloe-tree'.

The coincidence that several places in Worcestershire and Cheshire with names ending in *-wich* were famous for their salt-works led antiquaries like Camden, who talks of 'famous salt-wiches (the original had *salsinae*) where brine or salt-water is drawne out of pittes', to assume that *wīc* meant 'salt-works'. There is no evidence for this in OE; *wīc* here means 'sheds, buildings, dwellings' associated with a trade, in these instances, salt-working. The names are parallel to those of Colwich (St), Colwick (Nt, Wo) 'charcoal', Woolwich (K) 'wool', Saltwick (Nb), and with other compounds of *salt*, Salcott (Ess), Salthouse (Nf) and Seasalter (K), *sealtern* 858 'salt-house', with later description of its site by the sea. Droitwich (Wo) was originally a building or buildings for the sale of salt, *wiccium emptorium* 716, and is called *Saltwich* in a copy of a charter of 717. The modern name does not appear before the fourteenth century and appears to be OE *drit* 'dirt', as if similar in meaning to Fullwich (Ch), near Malpas, 'foul or dirty *wīc*'. This, too, had an alternative name, *Droytwich* alias *Durtwich* in the manor of Malpas. The Cheshire Northwich and Middlewich are named from their situation; Nantwich, called simply *Wich* in DB, is *Nametwihc* in 1194, from OE *named* 'famous', and by this time the name was probably interpreted 'the famous *Wich*', 'the famous salt-works'.

Most commonly *wīc* has the sense 'dairy-farm' or 'farm where domestic animals were kept': Bulwick (Nth) 'bulls', Oxwick (Nf); Cowick (WRY), Cowick Barton (D), Cowicks (Ess), Cowix (Sr), Cowage (W), Quickbury (Ess) 'the manor-house of Cowick', 'cows';

---

[1] *v.* pp. 35–7.

Conrish (W), with Cunnage Lane leading to it, *Kunewyk* 1268 'farm of the cows', OE *cūna* (gen. plur.); Calwich (St), Chelvey (So), *Calviche* 1086, 'calf-farm'; Roderwick (L), Rotherwick (Ha), Redrick (Herts), *hrȳðer* 'cattle'; Fuge, Fuige (D), *Fuwyche* 1269 'cattle-farm (OE *fēoh* 'cattle'); Shapwick (D, Do, So), Shopwyke (Sx) 'sheep'; Gatwick (Sr), Gatewick (Sx), Gotwick (Sx) 'goats'; at times it is the product of the farm which is particularised: Butterwick (Do, Du, L, We, ERY, NRY), Cheswick (Nb, Wa), Chiswick (C, Ess, Mx) 'cheese' and Honeywick (Sx), with which we may compare Bewick (Nb, ERY) 'bee-farm'.

That *wīc*, like *denn* and *falod*, was used of a dependent farm is clear. Such names as Hackney Wick and Hampton Wick (Mx), Eton Wick and Kimble Wick (Bk) were clearly those of dairy-farms appurtenant to the village, just as Jay Wick was that of the people of Clacton, where, as late as 1729, we have a reference to farms with 'a wick or dairy of 20 cows' in St Osyth, where in the thirteenth century sheep were particularly mentioned. A grant of the king of Kent in 740 to the archbishop of Canterbury included the right to pasture 150 head of cattle (*jumentorum*) in the marsh called *biscopes uuic* which was somewhere near Lydd. In 858 Westwell near Wye was granted three wicks called *Wiwarawic* which had belonged to the men of Wye. These, too, must have been near Lydd, where the lord of Westwell held such lands several hundred years later.[1] In Sussex Gotwick in Rusper is to be identified with *gatawic* 'goats' farm', a *denn* of Washington in 947, whilst in 956 Annington, some three miles north of Shoreham, had a *denstow* called *hliþwic* 'dairy-farm on the slope', and another named *Strodwic* 'marsh dairy-farm', now represented by Lydwicke in Slinfold and Strudgwick Wood in Kirdford, a district where we have already found several denns appurtenant to settlements much farther south. Not all wicks were in marshland. Most of those in Essex lie along the Thames and the coast, especially in Canvey Island, where Camden refers to 'making cheese of ewes' milk in their little dairy houses or huts built for that purpose, which they call *wiches*', but a few, like these Wealden wicks, are on higher ground in the north-west of the county, whilst others are to be found in the Berkshire Vale of White Horse. The *wica* of Buckland are recorded in Domesday Book as rendering ten pounds of cheese, whilst the wicks of the abbey of Abingdon are carefully

[1] For wicks and sheep-farming in the North Kent marshes, *v. Archaeologia Cantiana*, vol. LXVI (1954), pp. 144–5.

enumerated in the Abingdon Chronicle. The memory of these detached dairy-farms is still preserved in such names as Fyfield Wick, Ardington Wick and Goosey Wick in the Vale, and in Bray Wick at the other end of the county. OE *berewīc* 'barley-farm' is usually used of an outlying part of an estate, often of a monastic grange and is common: Barrack (So), Barricks (Ess), Barwick (Nf, WRY), Berwick (K, Sa, W, etc.), Berwick upon Tweed, Borwick (La).

The frequency of OE *cot* 'cottage', its common occurrence alone, in such names as Cote, Coates, Cotton and Cottam,[1] and its use in the plural suggest that, as its meaning would imply, it was used of small, insignificant places in areas of secondary settlement, though some of them grew to be Domesday vills and parishes, as Alvardiscott and Luffincott (D). This is confirmed by the nature of its compounds, often descriptive of situation, Eastcott, Nethercott (D), Ascot (Berks, O), Fencote (He), Fancott (Beds), and by such names as Woodmancote (Gl, Sx), Woodmancott (Ha), recorded already in 903, 'a woodman's hut', Tocketts (NRY), *Theoscota* 1108, from OE *þēos cotu* 'the servants' huts', Swancote (Wo), Swannacott (Co), Sannacott (D), 'cottages of the herdsmen, swine-herds or of the peasants', Herdicott (D), Hurdcott (W), Hurcot, Hurcott (So), 'hut of the herdsmen'. Like *wīc*, it is associated with places of manufacture or storage of materials, Glascote (Wa), Goldsoncott (So) 'goldsmiths', Wallerscote (Ch) 'salt-boiler', and is used also of shelters for animals, Bulcote (Nt), Lamcote (Nt), Lambcourt End (Beds), Shapcott (D) 'sheep' and Swincotte (Nt). Examples are rare in OE charters, Bredicot (Wo), (*æt*) *Bradigcotan* 840, Arncot (O), (*æt*) *Earnigcotan* 983, 'huts or cottages of the people of Brāda and Earn' respectively, Armscott (Wo), (*æt*) *Eadmundescotan* 1042, 'Eadmund's cottages'. The reference is probably to outlying cattle-farms as in Burcot (Bk), a minor settlement in Bierton, itself a dependent farm of Aylesbury, from OE *byrh-tūn* 'farm of the borough'. In Devonshire one-third of the 360 names in -*cott*, contain personal-names, including those of women and ME surnames: Buzzacott (*Beorhtsige*), Sepscott (*Sæbeorht*), Iddlecott in Dolton, *Edrichescote* 1168, named from the Edric who held the manor of Dolton in 1066; Allacott (*Ælfgifu*, f), Kennacott, Kennicott (*Cēngifu*, f), Lydcott (*Lēofgȳð*, f); Brazacott (Richard *Brosia* 1330), Rabscott, *Roberdescote* 1238, Coffcott Green, *Coffyncott* 1544, from the well-known Devonshire surname *Coffin*.

v. pp. 35–7.

HABITATION-NAMES

Of the terms denoting habitation in OE the two most common and most important are *hām*[1] and *tūn*. Of these, the former is the more ancient. It is more frequently compounded with folk-names as in Hedingham (Ess) and Willingham (C, L) and is most common in East Anglia and the south-east, decreasing in frequency as we pass through the Midlands to the south-west. It was at first compounded with an uninflected adjective in Higham, but continued in use after inflected adjectives became normal, as in Henham and Newnham.[2] It is compounded with women's names, as in Alpraham, Ch (*Alhburg*), Asheldham, Ess (**Æschild*), Babraham and Wilbraham, C (**Beaduburg, Wilburg*), but never with a post-Conquest personal-name.

OE *tūn*, however, is less commonly compounded with folk-names and invariably with inflected adjectives, in Newnton, Newington and Naunton. It is more frequently compounded with women's names, Bilsington (K), *Bilsvitone* 1086 (*Bilswīþ*), Knayton (NRY), Kneeton (Nt) and Kniveton (Db), all *Cheniueton* 1086 (*Cēngifu*), Warburton Ch, (*Wǣrburg*); it is also compounded with names of Domesday tenants or under-tenants: Brigmerston, W (*Beorhtmǣr*), Osmaston, Db (*Ōsmund*), Shearston So, (*Sigerǣd*). It continued in living use, especially in the south-west, for a century or two after the Conquest.[3] The word originally meant 'fence or hedge', then 'land enclosed by a fence', and gradually, by a natural process, it came to be used of an enclosure with a building, 'a farmstead', and later 'a hamlet or village' as well as 'an estate or manor'. As more than one of these meanings existed at the same time, it is often difficult to be certain of the exact meaning of a place-name. In names like Exton and Conderton[4] it clearly means 'village'. Staverton (Nth, Sf) was originally an enclosure made of stakes (OE *stæfer*); Clayton (La, St), Girton (C, Nt) and Gretton (Gl, Nth) 'gravel', and Santon (Cu, L, Nf) 'sand', may have been enclosures, farms or even villages on these particular soils. Calverton (Nt), Cowton (NRY), Lambton (Du), Rampton (C), Shepton (So), Shipton (Do) and Swinton (La), were enclosures for animals and probably outlying, dependent farms. OE *beretūn*, frequent as Barton, originally 'barley-enclosure', was early used of a corn-farm (*villa frumentaria* 808) and as a place-name denoted the demesne farm or an outlying grange. The numerous compounds with

---

[1] To be distinguished from *hamm* 'low-lying land by a stream', 'enclosure'.
[2] *v.* p. 39.　　　　　　[3] *v.* pp. 59–60.　　　　　　[4] *v.* p. 103.

a personal-name were probably at first homesteads or farms, but very many soon became villages: Brixton, D (*Beorhtsige*), Chediston, Sf (*Cedd*), Elmstone (K), *Ailmereston* 1203 (*Æðelmǣr*), Osbaston, Lei (*Ōsbeorn*).

Another habitation-name, found in a more limited area, is OE *bōðl, bōtl, bold* 'a dwelling, dwelling-place, house', which from the first denoted a separate settlement. It is found in the North and the Midlands as Bootle (Cu, La), Bothel (Cu), Bold (La, Sa) and Buddle (Nb), and, in the dative plural, in Beadlam (NRY). As a first element it occurs in Boldon (Du) and Bottesford (L, Lei), *Budlesford* 1086, *Botlesford* c1125, and as a second element in Newbottle (Du, Nth), Nobold and Nobottle (Nth), Oxenbold (Sa), Parbold (La) pear-tree' (*peru*), Rigbolt (L) 'the wright's house', Wychbold (Wo), and, compounded with a personal-name in Lorbottle, Nb (*Lēofhere*). This element is not found in East Anglia or in the counties south of Oxfordshire and Buckinghamshire except for a few minor names in the south-west: Budleigh in Moretonhampstead (D), *Bothele* 1330, Buddlehayes (D), Buddlehay and Buddle Oak (So) and Buddle (Ha). The compound *bōðltūn* is found frequently as Bolton in Cumberland, Lancashire, Northumberland and Yorkshire. Ekwall suggests that this was a name given to a village or estate which was the centre of a comparatively large settlement, the mother village, as opposed to its daughter-settlements or outlying farms.

NATURE-NAMES

So far, we have been concerned only with place-names which prove habitation and settlement, but long before the eighth century farms and villages were taking their names from neighbouring hills, woods and fords. Redlingfield (Sf), Armingford (C) and Oddingley (Wo) were settlements of communities in the open country, near a ford and by a wood. Nature-names are more numerous in Bede than habitation-names, but that these nature-names already in the eighth century were centres of habitation is proved both by their occurrence in early charters, by occasional descriptions as a *villa* and by the OE custom of prefixing the preposition *æt* to such of these names as were habitation-sites, e.g. Bede's *Ad Baruae* for Barrow (L) and *æt Clife* for Bishop's Cleeve (Gl). Oxford was at first the name of a ford used by oxen. When, later, a village grew up near this ford, it took its name from the ford and was called 'the village at Oxford', and finally 'the village Oxford'. This prepositional use is never found with names like Rendlesham and Hauxton.

As we must rely for our information on documents not earlier than the seventh or eighth centuries it is impossible to discover exactly when nature-names began to be used for habitation-sites, but the practice was well-established in the seventh century and must be much earlier. We have seen that heathen place-names must be much older than their earliest record. The *regiones* of Lyminge (689), Surrey (722), Ely (730) and Eastry (788) must be considerably older than these dates when they are first mentioned. Similarly both habitation-names and nature-names recorded in the seventh century must by that time have been well-established: Adisham, K (616), Bookham, Sr (675), Dagenham, Ess (692); Itchenor (Sx), 'Ycca's landing-place' (683), Bapchild (K), 'Bacca's spring', (696), Banstead (Sr), 'bean-place' (675), Stodmarsh (K), 'horse-marsh' (675), Lagness (Sx), 'long pasture' (680), Everley (W), 'boar-wood' (704).

A further proof of the age of some of these names is the fact that already in the eighth century names were being changed or forgotten. In 738 we have the sole reference to a place *Andscohesham* in the *regio* of Hoo (K). The place was already called *Stokes*, 'which was of old called *Andscohesham*' and survives as Stoke, probably in origin a dependent settlement of the lost village it has superseded. So, too, in 764 we have a reference to *Æslingeham sive Freondesberiam*. Both names survive today as Islingham and Frindsbury but were clearly interchangeable in the eighth century. Islingham may have been a colony from Eastling in Faversham hundred (*Eslinges* 1086) 'the people of Esla' and Frindsbury originally merely their fort overlooking the Medway. The alternation in the names may suggest that the fort was now becoming more important than the original settlement at Islingham. An even earlier example occurs in 605, when Chislet is described as 'villam nomine *Sturigao*, alio nomine dictam *Cistelet*'. The parishes of Chislet and Sturry today are some little distance apart, both on the Stour; Sturry was originally the name of the province and came to be used of its chief village. The name was also applied to a later settlement, perhaps because it was on the Stour and the real meaning of Sturry was already forgotten. Later, the inconvenience of having two villages so close together with the same name led to the re-naming of the less important one as Chislet, a change in process but not completely established in 605. Whether Chislet means 'gravel place' or 'gravelly stream', it is clearly a nature-name.

The great age of some nature-names is proved by their etymology. Erith (K) is recorded as early as 695 as *Earhyð* and must be much older. The name is repeated in Earith (Hu), though this is not on record before the thirteenth century (*Earheth* 1260). Both must be compounds of OE *ēar* and *hȳð*, 'the muddy or gravelly landing place'; *ēar* is found only as the name of one of the runic letters in OE and in the *Runic Poem* it probably denotes 'earth'. The ON cognate *aurr* is used of wet clay or loam and also of gravel. Yarmouth (IOW) may be 'gravel harbour'.

Wilsmere Down Farm in Barrington (C), *Wlmaresdung* 13th, contains an element *dung* which has been found only here and in *Folddung*, a lost place in the same parish. This is doubtless the word *dung* recorded once in OE poetry in the sense 'subterranean chamber, dungeon', corresponding to ON *dyngja* 'woman's apartment', originally used of a room of which the lower part was underground and probably at first so called because the roof was covered with dung. MHG *tunc* was similarly used of a spinning-room, half underground. Its exact meaning as a topographical term in OE cannot now be determined, for the word was probably rare and archaic even when it was first used of this place and was soon confused with the common *dūn* 'down'. It is noteworthy that this archaic fragment of primitive Anglian speech which never came to general currency in England should appear in the name of a site in the neighbourhood of one of the most important burial-grounds in the eastern Midlands.

At times we can see the process of place-name formation at work. Carhampton (So) is (*æt*) *Carrum* 833, a nature-name identical with Carham (Nb), *Carrum* c1050, 'at the rocks'. Already c880 a neighbouring farm was called *Carumtun* 'the farm at *Carrum*'. So, too, Tiverton (D), (*æt*) *Twyfyrde* 885 'double ford', had become *Tuuertone* before 1086, 'farm (or village) at *Twyfyrde*'. Twerton (So) has the same history. Similar formations are Ashford (K), *Essetesford* 1046, 'ford at *Æsc-scēat* 'the ash-copse', Burlton (He), *Burghelton* 1242, 'farm at *Burghill*'; it is actually close to Burghill 'hill of the fort'. But Woodmansterne (Sr), *Wudemaresthorne* 1186, is more likely to mean 'Wudumǣr's thorn-bush' than 'thorn-bush by the boundary of the wood', for personal-names are frequently compounded with tree-names, as in Bisterne (Ha), 'Bīeda's thorn-bush', Burston (Bk), *Bridelestorn* 1227 (*Briddel*). Triple compounds of the type Brafferton are thus to be interpreted rather as 'farm at *Bradford*' than as 'broad

141

ford farm'; hence Dulverton (So), 'farm by *Dulverd*', 'the hidden ford', Milverton (So) and Melverley (Sa) 'farm and wood at *Milford*'. Budleigh Salterton is a very late name. It was *Saltre* in 1210, in the manor of East Budleigh, and was named from the *salterns* or salt-pans there. It is not called *Salterton* until 1667 and *Budley Salterton* in 1765.

Throughout the ME period new homesteads continued to be created as woods were cleared and marshes drained and some of the OE terms continued to be used both in place-names and in field-names, e.g. *worðig* 'enclosure' in Curworthy (*cweorn* 'mill'), Butter-bury, *Boterworthi* 1330, Neopardy (*næp* 'turnip'), Wigford, *Wigewrth* 1249 (*Wicga*), Brexworthy, *Bristeleshorda* 1086 (*Beorhtel*), Hols-worthy (*heald*), and, from medieval surnames, Derworthy (*Dyra*), Stroxworthy (*Stroke*) and Wargery, *Wadesworthe* 1574 (*Ward*), all in Devon. This element is essentially south-western, found chiefly in Devon, but also in Cornwall and Somerset. OE (*ge*)*hæg* 'enclosure' is very common in Essex, as in Cowey, Fairy Farm and Fairyhall (OE *fearh* 'pig'), the latter held by a swineherd, Likely, Lilly and Littley 'little', Oxney, and compounds with personal-names, Ed-mondsey and Domsey (Walter *Dolfin* 1291). The characteristic Devonshire plural forms Hayes and Hayne have been discussed above,[1] and other terms for newly enclosed land will be treated below.[2] A marked feature of Essex farm-names is the large number called simply after some early owner, often the man who cleared the waste and set up the homestead, e.g. Crow's Cottage, Duckett's Farm, Frost's Hall. So common are these that they have more than once ousted the original place-name.[3]

This steady increase of names proceeded at varying rates. The eight Roding parishes which once included the territory of the *Hröðingas* are mentioned as the *duae Rodinges* c1050 and in 1086 contained no Domesday vill apart from the Roding villages them-selves. Not one of the eight parishes contains an OE habitation-name in -*hām* or *tūn*. Apart from Berwick Farm, we have only such names as Rookwood Hall, Longbarns and Millhill Wood, with a host of names like Brown's Farm, Philpots and Gibb's Cottages. The small Sussex parish of Westdean, on the other hand, contains three Domesday vills, *Dene*, Charlston and Exceat, whilst Benson (O) has a DB vill Crowmarsh, Fifield 'five hides' which must date from long before the Conquest, with names like Hale, Kingsbury, Mogpits,

[1] *v.* p. 37.   [2] *v.* pp. 213–14.   [3] *v.* p. 60.

Oakley, Port Hill and Roke, and a few minor names like Turners-court, Beggarsbush Hill and Gallows Leaze.

Many places of importance bear insignificant names. Sheffield 'open country on the Sheaf' and the Yorkshire Bradford owe their growth and importance to the Industrial Revolution. Dunwich, once the seat of a bishopric with its seven churches, is now a decayed village still falling into the sea which long ago swallowed its ancient glories. Brighton dates its growth and prosperity from the days of the Regency. Its name, too, has changed. It kept its old name *Brighthelmston* 'farm of Beorhthelm' until the beginning of the nineteenth century, though there is some evidence for the use of the shorter Brighton in the seventeenth. In 1636 it was *Brighter Limeston*.

Brighton does appear in Domesday Book, but the earliest reference to Southend-on-Sea is in 1482, when it was 'a lane called Sowthende of the parish of the Blessed Mary of Pritwell'. It was an unimportant spot at the south end of Prittlewell parish, called earlier *Stratende* 'street-end'. This was the 'old town' of Southend, where the Corporation Jetty now is. The *stræt* was a highway from Prittlewell Priory to Milton and the shore, along which grain was carried for shipment to Canterbury.

Torquay is another place of modern importance but insignificant in origin and name. It is first marked as *Torre Key* on a chart of the reign of Henry VIII and is later described as 'a small village called Torkay' in 1668 and in 1670 as '*Fleete* otherwise *Torkey* within the parish of Tormohun'. An earlier reference to the place occurs in 1412, when a French ship laden with wine was seized and brought into Devon at a place called *le Getee de Torrebaie*. The name was applied at first to a quay or landing-stage perhaps built by the monks of the neighbouring Torre Abbey. The town, which covers the whole of the ancient parish of Tormoham, most of St Mary Church, and a part of Cockington, is chiefly of nineteenth-century growth. Tor-morham was simply *Torra* in 1086, and later *Torre Brywere* and *Torre Moun*, from William Briwere, whose daughter Alice married William de Mohun (1242). *Fleete*, above, is still preserved in Fleet Street, where a small stream formerly entered the sea.

PLACE-NAMES CONTAINING WOMEN'S NAMES

More than once in our discussion of various elements we have noted that some were compounded with names of women, an indication that women could own churches or lands on an equality with men. Such names are not infrequent and may be more common than appears, for in dealing with the numerous short personal-names found in place-names it is always difficult, and usually impossible, to distinguish between the names of men and women. The real derivation of Bibury (Gl), *Beaganbyrig* 721–43, which had previously no fixed name, is made clear by the statement in the charter that the land was granted to earl Leppa and his daughter *Beage*, hence 'Bēage's *burg*'. Without this information, the name might, and almost certainly would, have been interpreted as 'the *burg* of a man named *Bēaga*'. In names compounded with a bithematic personal-name, such as Wollerton (Sa), *Wluruntona* 1130–5, 'Wulfrūn's farm', there is no such ambiguity.

Few of these names can be dated exactly, but, in general, they belong to the later rather than to the earlier centuries of Anglo-Saxon history. The earliest recorded appears to be Bamburgh (Nb), found in king Alfred's translation of Bede as *Bebbanburg* 'Bebbe's fort'. The fortress was built by king Ida in 547 and is said to have been named after Bebbe, queen of Æthelfrith (593–617). Bognor (Sx), 'shore or landing-place of Bucge', a short form of some woman's name beginning or ending in *Burg*, is mentioned in a charter of 680 and Fladbury (Wo), '*burg* of Flæde', a pet-form of a feminine name like *Æðelflæd*, in one of 692. This element *burg* is not uncommonly compounded with a woman's name, as in Adderbury (O), (*æt*) *Eadburggebyrig* c950 (*Ēadburg*), Alderbury (W), (*to*) *Æðelware byrig* 972 (*Æðelwaru*), Harbury (Wa), (*æt*) *Hereburgebyrig* 1002 (*Hereburg*), Bucklebury (Berks), *Borgeldeberie* 1086 (*Burghild*). The meaning, in general, is probably 'fortified house or manor', but in Bamburgh it is clearly 'fort'. In other names it is just as certainly 'monastery'. In a charter of 681 the estate later known as (*to*) *Tettan byrg* (872–915) and now as Tetbury (Gl) is described as *prope Tettan monasterium* and is named from Tette, a sister of Ine and abbess of Wimborne. Fladbury, too, is described as a *monasterium* in an early eighth-century charter. In Domesday Book, Tolpuddle (Do) is mentioned among the possessions of Abbotsbury Abbey under the name of *Pidele*, the name of the stream on whose banks it is situated. The first syllable of the modern name, which was added later (*Tolepidele* 1212) to distinguish this from other places on the same stream, represents the name of Tola, widow of Urc, a housecarle of king Cnut, who gave Tolpuddle to the abbey. Wolverhampton (St), *æt Heantune* 985, was the *hēah tūn* or chief manor of the lady Wulfrūn who in that year gave land to

Wolverhampton church, which still preserves her name (*Wolvrene-hamptonia* 1074–85). Good Easter (Ess) is distinguished from High Easter as the part bequeathed by will to Ely by a widow Godiva (OE *Godgifu*) in the reign of Cnut.

More than 70 of these names appear in Domesday Book, but the list is not complete, for Elson in Gosport (Ha), which is not included there, is found in a charter of 948 as *Æðelswiðetuninga lea* '(wood of the people of) Æðelswīþ's village', and Wissington (Sf) in one of c995 as *Wiswypetun* (*Wīgswīþ*). Others, recorded only later, can be safely regarded as pre-Conquest in origin: Aylton (He), *Aileuetona* 1138 (*Æðelgifu*), Chellington (Beds), *Chelewentone* 1219 (*Cēolwynn*), Edburton (Sx), *Eadburgetun* c1247 (*Ēadburg*). Names of this type are found in Domesday Book scattered throughout England, as Binderton, Sx (*Beornðrȳð*), Darlton, Nt (*Dēorlufu*), Offerton, Wo (*Alhðrȳð*), Willington, Ch (*Wynnflǣd*), Wollaton, D (*Wulfgifu*). Kent, exceptionally, has some eight examples, including Elvington (*Ælfgȳð*), Garrington (*Gārwynn*), Ringleton (*Hringwynn*) and Sevington *Sǣgifu*).

As we have already seen, -*hām* was also compounded with women's names, but less frequently, as in Abram, La (*Ēadburg*), Hubberholme (WRY), *Huburgheham* 1086 (*Hūnburg*) and Worldham (Ha), *Werildeham* 1086 (*Wǣrhild*), none of which is likely to have been named after the end of the eighth century, whereas *tūn* was in common use long after the Conquest. Women's names are also found in nature-names, as in Eythorne (K), *æt Heagyðeðorne* 805–31, '*Hēahgȳð's* thornbush', Buckden (Hu), *Bugedene* 1086, 'Bucge's valley', Goodwood (Sx), *Godiuawuda* c1200 (*Godgifu*) and Allecombe (D), *Aldithecumb* 1244 (*Ealdgȳð*); in compounds with *cot* and *wīc*, as Goodcott (D), *Godevacota* 1086 and Goodwick (Beds), *Godyuewyk* Ed I, both from *Godgifu*; and fairly frequently with *lēah* 'wood': Alveley (Sa) and Aveley (Ess), both from *Ælfgȳð*, Avely Hall, Sf (*Ælfwynn*), Balterley, St (*Bealdðrȳð*), Kimberley, Nf (*Cyneburg*), Wilderley, Sa (*Wilðrȳð*). Although these names form only a small fraction of the total of English place-names, there can be no doubt that men had no monopoly in holding land and that women took their part, too, in the clearing of woods and the founding of secondary settlements.

One proof of this is the survival today, often in a corrupt form, of place-names which show that this particular land was once the dowry of some Anglo-Saxon lady. It was a custom for the husband, on the morning after the marriage, to give his wife as a 'morning

145

gift' (OE *morgen-gifu*) land which became her own property and which she could sell or bequeath by will as she wished. Apart from field-names like *Moryeve* and *Morrif* in Hampshire, Oxfordshire, Wiltshire, Surrey, Sussex, Essex, Suffolk, Cambridgeshire and Northamptonshire, the memory of this custom is preserved, despite the appearance of the modern forms, in Morgay Farm (Sx), Morghew and Murrain Wood (K), Moor Farm in Woodham Ferrers (Ess), Marraway (Wa), Mooray (W), and Morris Farm in Great Waldringfield (Sf), *Morefes*, from Henry *del Moriyeue* 1462.

LAND-TENURE AND PLACE-NAMES

A law of Edward the Elder provides penalties for those who withhold another man's rights 'either in bookland or in folkland'. The latter, 'land held according to folkright', in the ninth century denoted land from which the king drew food-rents and customary services. Land could be exempted from these public burdens only by the grant of a royal charter or *bōc*. This *bōcland* or 'bookland' could then be alienated or bequeathed by will as the grantee desired, though the burdens of serving in the fyrd and working on bridges and fortifications were reserved. The word survives in the common place-name Buckland. It is found only in the south, especially in Devon and Somerset, but does not occur north of Hertford, Buckingham and Gloucester. From its nature, *folcland* is rare as a place-name and is found only in Falklands (Wo) and Faulkland (So).

Hyde Park preserves the OE *hīd* 'a hide of land', that area of land necessary for the support of a single free family with its dependents. This was estimated at about 120 acres, but both hide and acre varied in different regions according to the productivity of the land. As a simplex place-name, Hide and Hyde are common and widespread. We find reference to fractions in Halfhide (Herts) and Half Hides (Ess) and to a combination of two hides in Toyd (W), *Tohyde* 13th. Estates of five hides (OE *fīf hide*) were of frequent occurrence among the Anglo-Saxons and from an early period this unit of five hides became the regular basis of assessment for services and payments to the king, though by the time of Domesday Book this had become artificial and obscured. Hence we have such names as the three Fifeheads of Dorset, Fivehead in Somerset, two Fifields in Oxfordshire and two in Wiltshire, two Fyfields in Berkshire and one each in Hampshire and Essex, and, more corruptly, the curious Fitzhead in Somerset, *Fifhida* 1065. Of these, some ten are mentioned in Domesday Book and seven are actually assessed at five hides. Nynehead (So) was an estate of nine hides. The north Berkshire Fyfield was the subject of royal grants in the reigns of Eadwig and Eadgar, and it is remarkable that whilst the first grants 13 hides in the vill, the second conveys no less than 25, whilst in Domesday Book its assessment is 20. It is clear that by the time of Eadwig this Fyfield had far outgrown the limits of its original five hides, a fact which suggests its name was conferred long before the tenth century. In Domesday Book, on the other hand, the Somerset Fivehead is assessed at only 1½ hides. The 10-hide unit is illustrated in Tinhead (W), and, well disguised, in Combeinteignhead and Stokeinteignhead (D), *Cumbe in Tenhide* 1227, *Stoke in Tynhide* 1279, 'the combe and the *stoc* in the Ten Hide', so called from a district of 13 manors of which the total hidage in Domesday Book was 10 hides. A still larger unit is found in Piddletrenthide (Do), one of the villages on the river Piddle or Puddle, duly assessed at 30 hides in Domesday Book. It is *Pidele Trentehydes* in 1212 and *Pudele thrittyhide* in 1314, the French *trente* surviving. In compounds we have Bulidge (W) 'bull', Nasthyde (Herts) 'east', Rashwood (Wo), *Eshide* 1221, 'ash', Hyffold and Idehurst (Sx), neighbouring places, the hide with a fold and a wooded hill, and, with a personal-name, in Budshead (D), 'St Budoc's hide' in St Budeaux parish, and Tilshead (W), *Theodulveside* 1086 (*Þēodwulf*).

Ultimately a derivative of *hīd*, OE *hīwisc* 'a household, family', later 'the measure of land that would support a family', is found only in the south-west in Hewish (So) and Huish (D, Do, So, W), and in compounds, as Bowrish (*būr* 'peasant'), Gorhuish (mud), Langage, *Langehiwis* 1086 (long), Melhuish, Mowlish (mules), Quoditch, *Quidhiwis* 1249 (*cwēad* 'dung, filth'), and Woodhuish, all in Devon.

SOCIAL CLASSES

Place-names reveal the former existence of small communities of what were clearly different classes of society, but unfortunately they cannot throw any light on the obscurities which still trouble the historian. Several of the terms are vaguely explained as 'servants or peasants', but their occurrence in the same area proves they cannot be identical in meaning. Occasionally we have reference to an official, the *ealdormann*, the king's deputy, who until the tenth century was in charge of a single shire, and who often received a grant of land for his services, as at Aldermaston (Berks) and in the lost *Aldermanbury*, the official residence in Bedford of the 'alderman' of the shire, or, in Thenford (Nth), to the thane who was assessed at five hides and had a church, a kitchen, a bell-house and a fortified dwelling-place, memories of which still survive in Belhus (Ess) and Bellhouse (Ess, NRY) and in Burgate (Ha, Sr, Sf), Boreat (D) and Buckhatch Farm (Ess). When the alderman's authority was increased to the control of several shires, the individual shire was in charge of the shire-reeve or sheriff. The estates often attached to this office are commemorated in Shrewton (W), Shroton (Do) and Shurton (So).

The numerous Knightons and Knightleys scattered throughout the west Midlands and the south-west contain OE *cniht* 'a youth, servant, soldier', in late OE 'the retainer of a royal or noble personage', but its meaning in place-names is not altogether clear. Such retainers were of some standing and may well have lived together in villages of their own. Knighton (Berks) was held in the reign of the Confessor by five freemen, that in the Isle of Wight by eight freemen, and West Knighton (Do) by two thanes, and these may represent survivals of such communities of *cnihtas*, though in 1086 all these were held by individual tenants. A meaning 'young warrior' seems also suited to Knightlow Hill (Wa), the meeting-place of Knightlow Hundred, whilst Knightwick (Wo) was probably a dairy-farm of servants of some kind attached to Worcester Cathedral. Such a meaning seems apt for compounds of *cot*, as Knightcote (Wa), Knightacott, Knightshayes and Knightshayne (D). In Knightley (Wa), Knightwood (Ha) and Night Wood (W) the meaning must remain vague.

The meaning of OE *cild* in place-names is similarly difficult to decide. In Chilton it cannot have its ordinary meaning, for 'children's village' is nonsense, whilst the interpretation of Chilford (C) as 'a ford which could be crossed by children' is difficult to accept, though 'children's spring' for Chilwell (Nt) is more likely. In the eleventh century *cild* was used as a title of honour, of the sons of royal or noble families, as well as of a sokeman, 'one under a lord's jurisdiction', and even of an attendant. It is impossible to decide between these. The common Chilton may have been a farm of men comparable in status to the drengs of the northern Danelaw, the sergeants of Norman times, or of farms allocated to younger sons whilst their father was still alive. Childerley (C) was held in 1066 by four sokemen, and Chilfrome (Do) by three thanes. OE *munuc-cild* meant 'a boy training to be a monk', and this is clearly the meaning in some of these names, for the St Albans chronicler tells us that Childwick (Herts) took its name from the younger monks, who had to be fed on milk which was produced at the farm. Other compounds are: Chilcote (Lei, Nth), Childhay (Do), Chilhampton (W), Chilthurst (Sx), Chillaton, Chilley and Chelsdon (D), *Childedon* 1242.

More often it is the lower classes whose existence is perpetuated in place-names. Particularly common are references to the churl (OE *ceorl*), the ordinary freeman who probably had a hide of land which he could inherit and leave to his children. He was not bound to the soil and could rise to the rank of a thane, but by 700 the position of many had deteriorated and they held their land of a lord and did him service. The only habitation-elements with which *ceorl* is compounded are *tūn* and *cot*, never *hām*. The significance of *ceorla-tūn* is not certain; it might be 'farmstead of the peasants' or 'peasants' enclosure', which the law stipulated must be fenced. As many Charltons are in the neighbourhood of important centres, a *ceorla-tūn* may have been land on the outskirts of an estate taken in for cultivation, fenced and allocated to peasants. It clearly denoted a community settlement as distinct from a village owned by a single lord. Charlton is common and widespread, except in the Danelaw, where the name has been Scandinavianised as Carlton. It also occurs as Charleton (D), Charlston (Sx), Chalton (Beds), Charton (D), Charaton (Co), Higher and Lower Cheriton (D), *Cherletone* 1086, and Chorlton (Ch, La, St); *ceorla-cotu* 'cottages of the churls' is found as Charlacott (D), Charlecote and Charlcote (W), and Chalcot (Wa); other compounds are: Challabrook (D), Chilbrook (Co), *Churlebroke* 1309, Charlecombe and Chilcombe (D), *Churlecombe* 1303, Charford (Wo), Charley (Herts), Charlwood (D, Sr, Sx), Chorley (La, Sa, St), Chorleywood (Herts), Churwell (WRY) and Cherville (K).

The (*ge*)*būr*, 'the peasant trembling on the verge of serfdom', was given his holding of a quarter of a hide by his lord and supplied with two oxen, one cow and six sheep as initial stock. He had seven acres already sown and was given tools for his work and utensils for his house. For this he had to pay a formidable array of rents and services, including two days' work each week, a rent of 10*d.* at Michaelmas, 23 bushels of barley and two hens at Martinmas, and a young sheep or 2*d.* at Easter. He had to take his turn in keeping watch at his lord's fold from Martinmas to Easter and to plough one acre per week in autumn. When he died, his lord was entitled to take possession of all he had. He is commemorated in a small number of place-names, but it is often difficult or impossible to decide in compounds in favour of (*ge*)*būr* as against *būr* 'cottage, bower', as in Bures (Ess) and *burh* as in Burden (Du) and Burford (Sa). Undoubted examples are: Bowrish (D), compounded with *hīwisc*, Burraton (Co, D), Bourton, Burrington and Burrowton (D). Boship Farm (Sx) is from OE *(*ge*)*būrscipe* 'a group or association of peasants', 'a township'.

OE *gafolmann 'a payer of rent or tribute' is found in Galhampton (So), Galmington (D, So), Galmpton and Gammaton (D), all farms inhabited by rent-paying peasants. OE *gafol* 'tax, tribute, rent' is used of a farm or land rented or of fords and bridges where a toll was paid: Galton (D, Do), Gavelacre (Ha), Gawlish (D), *Gavelersh* 1310, 'rented ploughland', Gawcott (Bk), Gaul Field (C), Gawbridge (So), Galford (D), Galley Wood (Sr), Galleywood Common and Gavelwood Reden (Ess).

OE *boia, of obscure origin and not recorded before 1300, is found as a first element in a number of names where it appears to mean 'boy' or 'servant'. Some of these have been derived from OE *Boia* or *Boie*, but it is inconceivable that this late and rare personal-name should be compounded 15 times with *tūn* and 7 with *cot*, apart from other compounds and field-names, many in the same district. Probably all are to be taken as parallel with Charlton and Charlcott, Chilton and Chilcot, names of farms or cottages of groups of peasants of whose exact status we are ignorant: Boyton (Sf, Ess, K, W, Co), Boyden (K), from -*tūn*, Boycott (Wo, Sa, Bk), Boycote, Boy Court, Boyke (K), *Boiwiche* 1136, Boyland (Nf), Boycombe (D), Bayford (K, So), Bycott, Bystock (D), and Byford Tye (Ess).

TRADES IN PLACE-NAMES

Trade played no great part in the activities of the early English communities, for they were almost inevitably self-sufficient. They grew their own food, their flocks and herds provided not only food but also wool and leather for clothing, and they built their own houses of timber from the nearest woods. But even at this early period they were dependent on others for salt for seasoning and to preserve meat and fish for the winter and for metals for the tools and weapons they needed. To meet these needs, a flourishing salt industry grew up on the coast and in Worcestershire and Cheshire, whilst iron was worked in the Forest of Dean and the Weald. Droitwich, Nantwich and Seasalter have been discussed above.[1] Salcombe (D) is named from a valley with a salt-water creek where salt was made and Salt (St) from a salt-pit. OE *sealtere* means both 'salt-maker' and 'salt-seller' and is used in both senses in place-names: Saltram (D), *Salterham* 1249 and Woodbury Salterton (D) were villages of salt-makers, but Salterton (W) must have been one of salt-dealers. The latter is certainly the meaning in names of roads, bridges and fords, as Salterford (Nt), Salterforth (WRY), Saltisford (Wa), which carried the salt-way from Droitwich to Warwick, and Salter's Bridge (St). Wallerscote (Ch) is 'the cottage of the salt-boiler' (OE *wællere*).

Metal-workers are commemorated by reference to the villages or dwellings in which they lived or to the smithy where they worked. The earliest reference is to Great Smeaton (NRY), *Smiþatun* 966–72, 'village of the smiths'; others are Smeaton (Co, WRY), Smeeton (Lei), Smeetham Hall (Ess), *Smedetuna* 1086, Smethcote, Smethcott (Sa), Smithacott, Smithincott and Smynacott (D) and Smethwick (Ch, St). Care is needed to distinguish names containing OE *smēðe* 'smooth', as in Smithfield (Mx) and Smithdown (La). OE *smiððe* 'smithy' survives as Smeeth and Smead in the Weald of Kent and in Smitha (D). Hammersmith (Mx) is 'the hammer smithy'. Occasional reference is found to the worker in wood, the carpenter or wright: Wrightington (La), *Wrichtington* 1202, OE *wyrhtena tūn* 'village of the wrights' and Rigbolt (L), *Writtebaud* 13th, 'the wright's dwelling'.

The earliest and most important industry was agriculture. Grants of land in early charters included a vague reference to 'fields, woods, meadows, pastures, waters, mills, fisheries, fowling places, and hunting grounds', and a host of place-names throws light on these and on soils and crops and the domestic animals bred and wild animals hunted. Numerous references to dairy and cattle-farming, etc., have been met with already.[2] The domestic animals are usually easy to recognise, Cowley (Gl), *Kulege* 1086 'cow pasture', Cowdale (Db), Cowarne (He) 'cow-house'; Oxhey (Herts), Oxley (St), Oxton (Ch, Nt); Bulcamp (Sf) 'bull enclosure', Bulkeley (Ch) 'bullock pasture'; Hardwick 'herd farm', Sheffield (Sx), *Shipfeud* 1202 'sheep-field', Sheepwash (D, Nb) 'place where sheep were washed', Sheppey

[1] v. p. 135.   [2] v. pp. 136–7.

(K), Shippea (C) 'sheep island', Shepton (So), Shipton (Do, Gl, O) 'sheep farm', Shipham (So), Shipden (Nf), Shipmeadow (Sf), Shipway (K) 'sheep road'; Swinden (Gl, WRY), Swindon (St, W), Swinghill (K), *Swinesfeld* 1202; Lambeth (Sr) 'harbour where lambs were shipped' (OE *hȳð*), Lamberhurst (K), Lambley (Nb), Lambton (Du), Lamcote (Nt). Less obvious are: Rotherfield (Ha, O, Sx) 'open land where cattle grazed' (OE *hrȳðer*), Rotherhithe (Sr), with the identical Riverhead (K), Roderwick (L), Rotherwick (Ha), Ritherhope (La); Nafford (Wo), Neatham (Ha), Natton (Gl), from OE *nēat* 'ox, cattle'; Warley and Worsley (Wo), from OE *weorf* 'draught cattle'; Wrantage (So), Wrinstead (K) and Wrenbury (Ch), from OE **wrǣna* 'stallion'; Henstridge (So), Hinksey (Berks) and Hinxhill (K), OE *hengest* 'stallion'; Enham (Ha) and Yen Hall (C), from OE *ēan* 'lamb'; OE **tacca* 'a teg, young sheep' is found in Acton (Do), *Tacatone* 1086, Tackbear (D) 'pasture', Tackley (O), Takeley and Tagley (Ess); Fairfield (Wo), *Forfeld* 817, Farwood Barton (D), *Forhode* 1086, and Forwood (Wa) are from OE *fōr* 'pig'.

Fish was not only an important article of diet in the days of regular fasts on Fridays and the numerous saints' days but also a valuable source of income to monasteries. At Ely a rent of 10,000 eels was not uncommon; on the coast the sea-fisheries produced a rent of 60,000 herrings at Dunwich. Fisherwick (St) and Fisherton (W) were villages of fishermen; Fiskerton (L, Nt) is a Scandinavian-ised form of the same name. At Shotley (Sf) there was once a hamlet called *Fyshbane*, with a road called *fysshebane weye* (1469) and *Fyshebanstrete* (1534), named, presumably, from the fish-bones scattered about. Fishwick (La) was a place where fish were sold. Fishbourne (Sx), Fishburn (Du) and Fishlake (WRY) were streams where fish were plentiful. The actual name of the fish is rarely mentioned. Ekwall explains Fornham (Sf) as the village on the trout stream, a fish found also at Troutbeck (Cu) and Trouts Dale (NRY). Whaplode (L), *Cappelad* 810, is the 'eel-pout stream'. OE *ǣl* 'eel' is found in Almer (Do), Elmer (Sx), Elton (Du) and Ely (C).

The modern *hunter* is first found in place-names: Hunston (Sf), *Hunterestun* c1095, 'the huntsman's farm', Huntercombe (O) and Hunterley (Du). In OE the usual word was *hunta* (gen. sg. *huntan*, gen. pl. *huntena*), which in the singular cannot be distinguished from *Hunta*. OE *huntena-tūn* is the source of two Huntingtons in Herefordshire, one recorded in 775, and one in Shropshire. These, with Huntley (Gl), Huntwick (WRY), Huntworth (So), probably refer to professional huntsmen, whilst Huntingford (Gl, He) are probably to be interpreted rather as fords used by people going hunting. Huntingdon (Hu), *Huntandun* 921, may be 'the huntsman's hill' or the 'hill of Hunta', a personal-name undoubtedly found in Huntingfield (Sf), *Huntingafelde* 1086. Huntington (Ch, St, NRY) and Hunton (K), all mean 'hill (*dūn*) of the huntsman or huntsmen'.

Here we may note the bee-keeper (*bícere*). So long as they got the honey from the nests of wild bees, the *bíceras* should be classed with the huntsmen. A name such as Bickershaw (La) 'wood of the *bíceras*' probably belongs here, whereas Bickerton (Ch, D, He, Nb, WRY) was a farm where bee-keepers lived and Bickerston (Nf) that of a single bee-keeper. Bickerstaffe (La) is 'the landing-place of the bee-keepers'. Other place-names testifying to the keeping of bees are Bewick (Nb, ERY), Beckett (Berks), *Becote* 1086 and Beauworth (Ha). Beeleigh (Ess) and Beoley (Wo) were woods where nests of wild bees were found. Honey, in the absence of sugar essential for sweetening and for the making of mead, in place-names refers to places where honey was found or produced, but it may denote 'sweet' land, as in Honeylands (Ess), or 'sweet' water in Honeychild (K), from OE *celde* 'spring', Honeybourne (Gl, Wo) and Honeywell (D). Honiley (Wa) was a wood where honey could be got and Honiton in South Molton (D) and Honington (Wa) were homesteads where honey was produced, but the Devon parish of Honiton, Honeywick (So) and Honington (Sf) all contain the personal-name *Hūna*.

Fullerton (Ha), *Fugelerestune* 1086, is 'the fowler's farm', Harcourt near Cleobury Mortimer (Sa), *Havretescote* 1086 'the hawker's cottage', but names such as Hawkerland (D) and Hawkhurst (Wa), *Hauekeresmor* 1315, are more likely to contain a medieval occupational surname. The bird-name is common in place-names, though we have also to reckon with the personal-name *Hafoc*: Hawkhurst (K), with the identical Haycrust (Sa), and Hawkley (Ha), were all woods where there were hawks.

To return to the huntsman. OE *ræcc* 'a hunting dog which pursues its prey by scent' is found in Rochford (Ess, Wo) and in the curious name Neroche Forest in Somerset. There appear to have been two places called *Rachich* or *Rechich*, probably from *ræcc-wíc* 'outlying farm where hunting dogs were kept'. One of these is recorded as *Nerechich* in 1236, with OE *nēarra* 'nearer' prefixed, in contrast to an unrecorded *Far Rachich* 'farther Rachich'. The modern name is a contraction of *Nerre Rachich*. For the animals they hunted, there is abundant evidence in place-names, as in Foxcote (Gl, Wa), Foxcott (Ha), Foscote (Nth), Foscott (Bk, O), and Forscote (So), 'fox-cots', which can hardly mean anything but 'foxes' burrows', Foxearth (Ess). Foxton (Du) is *Foxedene* c1170 and that in Northumberland *Foxden* 1325, so that whilst some of the numerous Foxtons may be 'homesteads infested by foxes', many, probably most, are really 'fox hill' or 'fox valley'.

Names referring to wolves are more numerous than would appear at first sight: Wolfhole Crag (La) 'wolves' valley', Wolvey (Wa), probably OE *wulf-hege*, an enclosure to protect flocks from wolves or to trap wolves, identical in meaning with Wollage Green and Woolwich Wood in Womenswold (K) and Woolpit (Sf, Sr); Wolborough (D) 'wolves' hill', Woolacombe and Wooladon (D), Wooldale (WRY), Woolden (La), Woolleigh (D), Woolley (Berks, D, Hu, WRY), Winfold Farm (C), *Wulfholes* 1205, and Wolleux (Co), *Wlfholca* c1150 'wolf-hollow'.

Most Barfords are from *bereford* 'barley-ford'. It is unlikely that bears were common in England in later Saxon times, but OE *bera* 'bear' is probably found in Barbon (We) and Barford (Sr, Wa), names recorded from the eighth century and probably of high antiquity. The boar was certainly common, *eofor* being used of the wild boar and *bār* of the domestic animal, but the distinction was not strictly kept. Everton 'boar enclosure' or 'boar farm' does not suggest the wild boar. In the genitive singular *eofor* is difficult to distinguish from *Eofor*, as in Eversden (C), Eversley (Ha) and Yearsley (NRY). Apart from Everdon (Nth) and Yaverland (IOW), it is found with names of woods in Everley (WRY) and Evershaw (Bk). OE *bār* is never compounded with *tūn* and is liable to confusion with *bær* 'bare' as in Bareleigh (Wa) and Barville (K), and with *bere* 'barley' as in Baretilt (K), *Bertilth* 1285 'barley crop'. Barlow (Db), *Barleie* 1086, Barwell (Lei), *Barwalle* 1043, and Boarzell (Sx) are certainly from *bār* 'boar', but Barley (La, WRY) and Barlow (La) are recorded too late to enable us to decide between 'boar' and 'bare'.

Deerfold (Wo), Dorfold (Ch), Durfold (Co) and Darton (WRY) were enclosures for deer, an animal which roamed the woods of Darley (Db), Durley (Ha), Durleigh (So) and Deerhurst (Gl). We find the doe in Daccombe (D) and Doepath (Nb) and the hind at Hindhead (Sr) and in the woods of Hiendley (WRY) and Hindley (La, Nb, St). At Hindlip (Wo), 'deer leap', there was probably a 'leapgate', a low gate in a fence which could be leaped by the deer when they wished to return to their enclosure' (*haga*), as at Leapgate Cottage (Wo), recorded in 980, Lypiatt (Gl), Lypiate (So) and Lippits Hill (Ess), *Lephacche* 1270. The roebuck (OE *rā*) was to be found at Rodden (So), Roecombe (Do), Rogate (Sx) and, in the genitive plural, at Rancombe and Renham (IOW) and Renhold (Beds), and the female of the roe (OE *rǣge*) at Reigate (Sr) and Rayleigh (Ess). Ekwall has shown, too, that OE *rāh-hege* 'enclosure for roe-deer' survives as Roffey (Sx), Rolphy Green (Ess) and Roughway (Ess, K), and that OE *hēa(h)dēor* 'stag, deer' is found in Hattersley (Ch), Heatherslaw (Nb) and Hethersett (Nf). Stagenhoe (Herts) was 'the spur of land where stags were to be found'.

Further evidence of the important part played by hunting among the Saxons is provided by place-names referring to traps or snares. We have already seen that a satisfactory solution of the much discussed Ludgershall can be reached by postulating an OE *lūtegār* 'trapping-spear'. Other names for traps are found in Grinsdale (Cu) and Grinshill (Sa), 'valley and hill where snares were set' (OE *grīn*), Slingley (Du), *Slingelawe* 1155, 'hill with a snare' (OE *slinge*), Snargate (K), 'gate (gap in a hedge or the like) where snares were set' (OE *sneare*), Wild Court (Berks), Monkton Wyld (Do) and Wylam (Nb), from OE *wīl* 'a trick', glossed *wocia*, in the sense 'trap, snare' and Wookey (So), from OE *wōcig* 'a snare'.

When we turn to arable farming, we find a marked scarcity of occupational terms. The only one mentioned in Domesday Book is Madresfield (Wo), *Madresfeld* 1086, which Ekwall derives from OE *mǣþere* 'mower', but Mawer and Stenton are probably correct in deriving this from OE *Mǣðhere*, along with Methersham (Sx) *Maderesham* c1185, and Mattersey (Nt), *Madressei* 1086, which Ekwall himself derives from a personal-name *Mǣþelhere*. Fortherley (Nb), *Falderle* 1208, 'wood of the folder or shepherd' and Poundisford (So) 'the pinder's ford', look like medieval place-names and may even be from surnames. An undoubted OE example is Horsington (So), *Horstenetone* 1086, from OE *horsþegna-tūn* 'village of the horsekeepers or grooms'. It is near Henstridge 'the stallion's ridge', near which was *Horspol*. Place-names compounded with OE *hors* are common: Horse Eye (Sx) 'island', Horseheath (C), Horsenden (Bk), Horsepath (O), Horsey, Horsford and Horsham (Nf), Horsley (Db, Gl, Sr), Horstead (Nf), Horsted (K, Sx), as also are compounds of *stōd* 'a stud, herd of horses': Studham (Beds), Stidham (So), Stodday (La), Studdah (NRY), from *haga* 'enclosure', Stody (Nf) from (ge)hæg 'enclosure', Stoodleigh (D), Studley (O, W, Wa, WRY).

OE stōd-fald is common in field-names and survives in Studfold (We), Stodfold (Bk), Stotfold (Beds) and Stuffle (Co). It meant 'an enclosure for a stud of horses', and when we find the Saxons calling by this name the walled Roman enclosures of Aldborough, Lympne (now Stutfall Castle) and Irthington, we must suppose that they actually used them as horse-folds, and not only these, but any earthwork which would serve the same purpose, hence such names as Wrenbury (Ch) 'stallions' fort' and Fowberry (Nb) 'foals' fort'. Thus, Ekwall's interpretation of Irthlingborough (Nth) as 'fort of the ploughmen' (OE ierþling), 'fort used by ploughmen for keeping their oxen', is extremely plausible, for on a large estate considerable space would be needed to confine several teams of eight oxen each. A similar explanation would hold good, too, for Salmonsbury (Gl), Sulmonnesburg 779, 'fort of the ploughmen' (OE sulhmann), where there is an ancient fort surrounded by an earthen rampart which encloses a wide area.

The chief crops were wheat, as at the common Wheatley, Whatley (So), Whatborough (Lei) and Whiteborough (Nt), from beorg 'hill', Whatfield (Sf), Whaddon (Bk, W) and Waddon (Wo); rye at Ryhill (ERY, WRY), Ryarsh (K), Royton (La), Ruyton (Sa), Ryton (Du, Sa, Wa), Raydon and Reydon (Sf), Roydon (Ess, Nf, Sf) and Renacres (La); barley at Barley (La), Barlow (Nb), Bearl (Nb) 'hill' and Barlinch (So); and oats at Oatlands (Sr) and Oteley (Sa), at Haverhill (Sf), from OE *hæfera and at Market Harborough. Less commonly, we find pilled oats, in which the grain is free from the husks or glumes, an inferior kind of oats little grown today, in Pillaton Hall (St), Pilatehala 1113.

Tradesmen and artisans naturally tended to drift into the towns, where their activities are often remembered in the names of streets. Some would inevitably carry on their trade in the country, where the materials they required were ready to hand. Charcoal-burners would be found in woodland areas, where we still have such names as Colerne (W), from ærn 'house', Colwich (St), Colwick (Nt) and Cowley (Db, La). But bakers would be more in demand in towns, so that Baxterley (Wa), not recorded before 1180, was probably a wood belonging to a man named Baxter. Potteries must have existed both at Potterton (WRY) and at Potterne (W) before 1086, but many of the potteries seem to be medieval. Crockerton (W) is first mentioned in 1249, whilst John and Stephen le Crokker were living in the parish in 1286 and 1289. There is a Potter's Hill close by, with brick and tile works still there. There was clearly a pottery industry here, but whether the place takes its name from an ancestor of the John and Stephen above or from the potters in general who worked here cannot be decided, nor do we know whether the name goes back beyond the Conquest. Similarly there were potters at Potterspury (Nth), but in 1086 the place was called simply *Perie* 'the peartree' and does not appear as *Potterispirye* before 1287. How old the pottery here is, we do not know. The difference was added to distinguish this from Paulerspury. Cock-a-troop Cottages in Mildenhall (W), *Crokerestrope* 1257, has every appearance of an OE name, 'the outlying farm of the potter'.

There appears to have been a soap-making industry in Saxon England, for OE *sāpere* 'soap-maker' occurs in four examples of Sapperton (Db, Gl, L, Sx), of which that in Gloucestershire is recorded in 969 as *Saperetun* 'village of the soap-makers', whilst those in Derbyshire and Lincolnshire were Domesday vills. *Tucker* 'fuller', a characteristically west-country word, appears, appropriately enough, in Tuckerton (So) and, as a medieval attribute, in Tucks Cary, *Tukares Cary* Hy 3. Hopperton (WRY) is probably 'the village of the hoopers or coopers', and Sutterton (L) that of the shoe-makers (OE *sūtere*).

Whilst we have occasional references to traders in Chapmanslade (W), Mangerton (Do) 'village of the mongers or dealers', and Mangersford (D), and the packman or pedlar in Packmanston (K), we have more evidence of the dangers they and other travellers faced from robbers and outlaws. In OE charters we have reference to valleys where thieves or robbers congregated in *þeofa cumb* and *þeofa dene*, and some of their haunts are still revealed in modern place-names: Thiefside (Cu) 'headland', Thievesdale (Nt), Thieves Gill (NRY), Dupath (Co), *Theuepath* 1175, Thuborough (D) 'thieves' hill', Evegate (K), *þeofacotan*, *-ӡadan* 993, possibly Tudeley (K), *Tivedele* 1086, *Theudelei* c1100 and Thriverton (D), *Thevedryngh* 1281, a curious name, apparently a place-name of the derisive nickname type, 'crowd of thieves'. OE *scēacere* 'robber' is almost equally common: Shackerley and Shakerley (La), 'the robbers' wood', Shackerdale (Nt), Shackerland Hall in Badwell Ash (Sf), formerly *Shakerlund* 'robbers' grove'; four examples reveal the highwaymen threatening the public roads: Sugarswell Barn (Wa), with Sugarswell

Farm (O), just over the county boundary, *Socreswell* c1180, 'the robbers' stream'; Sugarwell Farm in Hook Norton (O), *Shokere-wellemore* c1260, 'the moor by *Shokerewelle*, the robbers' stream', called also *Theroberewes Lake* c1230, about five miles south of Sugarswell Farm; Sugar Hill in Aldbourne (W), a border parish, must have been near *sceocera weye* (854), 'the robbers' road', an ancient road running along the parish boundary; and Shootersway (Herts), *Shokersweye* 1357. At Shackerstone (Lei), *Sacrestone* 1086, the man who set up the enclosure or the farm must have used it as a notorious headquarters for his depredations.

The common term in OE for 'a felon, criminal or outlaw' was *wearg*, which is found in Wreighill (Nb), *Werghill* 1293, 'felon hill' and Warnborough (Ha), *Weargeburninga gemæra* 1046, 'felon stream', originally the name of the Whitewater. Among the Anglo-Saxons, if a man were killed, it was regarded as the duty of his kindred to take vengeance on the slayer or his kindred, or to exact compensation. For this, the law fixed a *wergild* or 'man-price', varying with the social standing of the slain. But for some crimes, arson, house-breaking, open theft and treachery to one's lord, no compensation could be offered and death was the penalty, either by hanging on the gallows, by beheading, stoning or burning, or by drowning. Such names as Gallow Hill (Bk), Gallows Hill (W) and Galley Hill (Wa), sites of gallows, are common.

Warter (ERY), *Wartre* 1086, is a compound of *wearg* 'felon' and *trēow* 'tree', used of a gallows, whilst Worgret (Do), *Weregrot* 1086, *Wergerode* 1202, is a similar compound of *wearg* and *rōd* 'cross'. The significance of both names is illustrated by the words of the Holy Cross in *The Dream of the Rood*, 'they bade me bear aloft their felons', where the Cross tells of being carried from the forest and of being used to crucify malefactors. Hewstock Farm in Beaminster (Do), *Westheuedstok* 1268, is identical with Harestock (Ha), (*to*) *heafod stoccam* 854, from the common boundary-mark *hēafod-stocc* 'a stock or post on which the head of a criminal was fixed after beheading', an alternative for which is *hēafod-trēow*, a tree on which the head was fixed, as at Heavitree (D), an etymology which is confirmed when we find that the gallows formerly stood near by at Livery Dole, 'Lēofhere's share of the common field' of the parish. Popular etymology seems to have been at work early, for the place is called *Eueltrea* already in 1179 and *Heveltre* in 1286. But the punishment which has left the greatest impression on our place-names is that of drowning. Wreighill is on the Wreigh Burn 'the stream in which felons were drowned'. Warnborough takes its name from a 'felon stream' and the Waring (L), though evidenced only late, is probably an OE *Wærging 'felon stream'. It flows through Horncastle, the centre of an important franchise, just as the Wreigh Burn flows near the old town of Rothbury.

The criminals of Hastings were executed by drowning at a place called Storisdale, somewhere near Galley Hill at Bulverhythe. A river Gestlyng near Sandwich, now known as the North Stream, frequently mentioned in the fourteenth century, was, according to Dugdale, the stream 'in which such felons as were condemned to death, within the before specified Hundred [of Cornilo], ought to suffer judgement by drowning'. The Prior of Christchurch had diverted the stream in 1313 so that those condemned could not be drowned as formerly. This custom of drowning felons was common and is known to have existed in England before the Norman Conquest. The method varied. Sometimes the condemned man was tied to a stake driven into the bottom of the sea or a tidal river at low tide and left to be drowned by the incoming tide. Sometimes he was thrown into the river or the sea after his hands had been tied under his legs. In a small stream like the Wreigh Burn or the Waring, the water would be held up by a dam.

SPORTS, GAMES, ETC.

'Merry England' has become almost a synonym for the spacious days of Elizabeth I, though even then the tales of Robin Hood and his 'merry' men were centuries old. The Englishman has always had a zest for games and sport and merry-making and traces of this are inevitably found in our place-names. Such names as Butt Hill and The Butts (Wa) recall the once-popular sport of archery. The word is found only in ME and meant originally 'a mound', then the commonest sort of butts, archery butts. It is used of natural hills, Robin Hood's Butts, near Weobley (He), and also of tumuli, as Robin Hood's Butts in Otterford (So). There is also a ME butte 'a strip of land abutting on boundaries' which is common in field-names, but in innumerable parishes we still have places or fields whose names mark the sites of the old archery butts. Shooting at the popinjay and tilting at the quintain are recalled by fields named Popingeyfeld in Barking and 'place called la Quinteyne' in Warwickshire. We have a Gamenhulle (1299) in Worcestershire, 'a hill where games were played', and *Gameneslond* (1375) in Sussex, whilst the Berkshire Hundred of Ganfield, *Gamenesfelle* 1086, was a stretch of open land where games were played. The name survives in Gainfield Farm in the centre of the hundred, where five parishes meet, an eminently suitable place for sports and festivities at the meeting of the hundred. The farm is mentioned as early as 957.

The Camping Close in Histon (C) and Camping Lane in Norton (Db), now included in Sheffield, are particularly interesting names. As a field-name this occurs at Fulbourne in 1540 as *le Campingplace* and also in the Tithe Award of six other Cambridgeshire parishes and occasionally elsewhere. They derive from ME *camping* 'contending in a camp-ball or camping-ball match'. The camping close was clearly the village football-ground where was played a game with indefinite numbers on each side, somewhat similar to that which survives in the well-known Shrove Tuesday football match at Ashbourne in Derbyshire.

OE *glēam* 'merriment' appears to be the source of a few names, chiefly compounds of *ford*, near which sports were held: Glandford (Nf), Glanford Brigg, now Brigg (L), Glemham and Glemsford (Sf), three of which are certainly OE names, Curiously enough, Little Glemham was called 'Thieves' Glemham in Domesday Book. But most of the names with which we are concerned are compounds of OE *plega* 'play', with an occasional variant *plaga*. OE **pleget* 'a place for games' is found in Plaitford (Ha) and *pleg-stede* 'play-place' in Chapel Plaster (W), *Pleystede* 1268. Compounds of *plega* are: Playford (Sf), Playley Green (Wo), Plealey (Sa), Pleyton (Co) and Plyford (D); of *plaga*: Plawhatch (Sx) and Plowden (Sa). OE **pleg-stall* 'play place' is found in two Essex field-names and this is probably the source of Plaxtol (K), which is first recorded as *Plextole* in 1386. Most common of all is OE *pleg-stōw* 'sport place', 'a place where people gathered for play', glossing the Latin *amphitheatrum*, *palaestra* and *gymnasium*. Several of these modern places are in or near a large open space in the middle of the village. Some of the compounds above point to gatherings in glades or near fords. The West Ham Plaistow is still invariably pronounced *Plarstow*, a pronunciation which, with unstressed -*er* for -*ow*, has given a modern *Plaster*, which has now often been replaced by the normal spelling: Plaistow (D, Db, Ess, Sr), Playstow (Herts, K), Plaistows Farm (Herts), Plestowes (Wa), Plastow Green, Plasterhill Farm and Plestor (Ha), Plaster Down (D).

The twofold occurrence of Wakefield in Yorkshire and Northamptonshire suggests that the name is not, as has sometimes been suggested, compounded with the personal-name *Waca*, but rather with OE *wacu* 'a watch, wake' and *feld*, denoting an open piece of land where a wake was held. This meaning would also suit Wakeley (Herts), Wakebridge (Db) and the lost *Wakegreave* (Db), 'grove where wakes were held', the second element of all these finding a parallel in such names as Playley and Glandford Brigg. The sense 'wake, annual festival' is probably old and is particularly apt for the West Riding Wakefield, the home of the Towneley Plays. These do not go back to the days of the Saxons, but their importance in the later Middle Ages suggests that the annual fair itself may have been ancient and it is noteworthy that all four of these places were Domesday vills.

Chapter Seven

THE SCANDINAVIAN ELEMENT

Dane Court (K), Dane End (Beds), Danehill (Sx), Danes Brook (Bk) and such-like names have no connexion whatever with the Danes. They are dialectal forms of the common *dean* 'valley' and are limited to Kent and Essex and some neighbouring counties where ME *dene* regularly appears as *dane*. Dane John in Canterbury is a corruption of the French *donjon* which has also given us the Essex *Don Johns*, the local pronunciation of Dungeon Farm. The common desire to find Danish influence in the south is due to a misconception. The Danes who wintered in Sheppey and Thanet in 835 and 850 were plundering pirates whose sole object was loot. They came, murdered and devastated and departed with their booty. The Danish settlement was, as we shall see, the result of later and more intensive incursions, largely limited to the area which later came to be called the Danelaw.

In districts where these Scandinavians settled their influence on our place-names varied. They continued to speak their own language and where they considerably outnumbered the native Anglians they have left behind large numbers of place-names whose forms, even today, prove they were bestowed by speakers of a Scandinavian language. Where the population was more mixed, an Anglo-Scandinavian dialect developed and we find place-names, English in origin, modified by Scandinavian pronunciation, Scandinavian terms substituted for similar English terms and Scandinavian personal-names compounded with English topographical terms.

PURE SCANDINAVIAN PLACE-NAMES

A name like Bilsthorpe (Nt), *Bildestorp* 1086, is a pure Scandinavian place-name, a combination of the ODa personal-name *Bild* with *thorp*, a common Danish term for a new settlement or a farm. But Bildeston (Sf) and Bilstone (Lei), *Bildestone* 1086, though containing the same Danish personal-name, are not pure Scandinavian place-names, as they are compounded with the OE *tūn*. So, too, Grimsby (L) 'Grim's village', Haddiscoe (Nf) 'Haddr's wood' and Lowestoft (Sf), *Lothu Wistoft* 1086, 'Hloðvér's homestead', are similar compounds of a Scandinavian personal-name and a Scandinavian topographical term, whilst Eakring (Nt), ON *Eik-hringr* 'oak-circle', Rowland (Db), *Ralunt* 1086 'roe-wood', Thonock (L), 'thin oak', Thrunscoe (L) and Thurnscoe (WRY) 'thorn-wood', are pure Scandinavian compounds. Eyke (Sf) is ON *eik* 'oak', Kelham (Nt), the dative plural of ON *kiǫlr* 'keel', in the sense 'ridge', found also in Keal (L), whilst Loskay (NRY), *Loftischo* 1282, is a pure Scandinavian description, *lopt í skógi* 'the loft in the wood'. ON *hestaskeið* 'race-course' survives as Hesketh (La, NRY) and thrice as Hesket in Cumberland. Horse-racing was a favourite sport of the Scandinavians.

Undoubted proof that a place-name was given by a Scandinavian-speaker is provided by the survival of Scandinavian inflexional forms. The OSc genitive in -*ar* survives in Aismunderby (WRY), 'village of Ásmundr', Amotherby (NRY), 'village of Eymundr', Amounderness (La), 'headland of Agmundr', Helperby (NRY) and Helperthorpe (ERY) 'village and homestead of a woman named Hialp' (gen. *Hialpar*), Holderness (ERY), 'headland of the hold', a high-ranking officer in the Danelaw, Beckermet (Cu) and Beckermonds (WRY) 'meeting of the streams', Dalderby (L), 'village in a little valley' (ON *dæld*, gen. *dældar*), Litherland (La) and Litherskew (NRY), 'land and wood of the slope', and Londonthorpe (L), *Lundertorp* 1086, 'homestead by a grove'. Sawrey (La), *Sourer* 1336, is ON *saurar*, plural of *saurr* 'mud, muddy place'. Borrowdale (Cu), *Borgordale* c1170, may represent ON *borgar dalr* 'valley of the *borg* or fortress',

163

or it may be identical with Borrowdale (We), a compound of *borgar á* 'river of the fort'. Furness (La), *Futhpernessa* c1150, was originally the name of the most southerly point of the peninsula, Rampside Point. Outside Rampside is Peel Island, formerly called *Fouldray* (*Fotherey* c1327). This is ON *Fuðar-ey* 'the island of *Fuð*' (gen. *Fuðar*), a name applied to small islands, a skerry. From this, the neighbouring headland was called **Fuðarnes*, which was later applied to the whole peninsula. This ON inflexion is also used in compounds formed from older place-names: Allerdale (Cu), Ennerdale (Cu) and Nidderdale (WRY), the valley of the Ellen, Ehen and of the Nidd respectively. Such compounds are usually found in areas known to have been at least partly colonised by Norwegians and are rare in preponderatingly Danish districts. Osmotherley (La), *Asemunderlawe* 1246, is a remarkable hybrid consisting of the personal-name *Ásmundr*, in its Scandinavian genitival form *Ásmundar*, compounded with OE *hláw* 'hill'. Osmotherley (NRY), *Osmunderle* 1088, is a similar compound with OE *léah* 'wood'. These names can have originated only with a speaker of a Scandinavian language.

In Norway this *r* of the genitive was normally preserved; in Danish and Swedish it was lost, particularly before a consonant, the normal ODa genitive becoming -*a* and later -*e*. This *a* is preserved in the early forms of many English place-names and accounts for the rare appearance of -*ar* in Danish names in England: Hawerby (L), *Hawardabi* c1115, 'Haward's village', Dromonby (NRY), *Dromundeby* c1185, 'Drómund's village'. This genitive ending was also extended to Scandinavian personal-names which had a genitive in -*s* and to English personal-names compounded with a Scandinavian element: Osgodby (L, NRY), Osgoodby (NRY), *Ansgotabi* c1115; *Osgotesbi* 1086, *Angotebi* 1202 (ODa *Asgot*); Atterby (L), *Adredebi* 1185 (OE *Éadréd*), Audleby (L), *Alduluebi* 1086 (OE *Aldwulf*), Barnetby le Wold (L), *Bernodebi* 1086 (OE *Beornnóð*).

To the OE genitive in -*es* corresponds the Scandinavian genitive -*s*, without a preceding vowel. This *s* was voiceless and made a voiced consonant before it also voiceless, e.g. *v* became *f*, *d* or *ð* became *t*. This voiceless consonant was often lost, e.g. *ts* became *s*; it still remains voiceless in modern names: Braceby, L (ON *Breiðr*), Rauceby, L (ON *Rauðr*), Laceby, L (ON *Leifr*), Ulceby, L (ON *Úlfr*), Faceby, NRY (ON *Feitr*) and Skewsby (NRY), *Scoxebi* 1086 (ON *Skógsbýr* 'village in the wood').

SCANDINAVIANISED PLACE-NAMES

Sound-substitution. After the Battle of Stamford Bridge (1066) the Norwegians left Ravenser in Holderness and, according to a story in the *Heimskringla*, one of them named Styrkar, who had no clothes but a shirt and no weapon but a helm and sword, on a cold, windy evening robbed an East Riding farmer of his fur-lined jacket. Before he died, the farmer is said to have recognised Styrkar as a Norwegian by his speech. At this period the farmer himself may well have spoken an Anglo-Scandinavian dialect, but the story does illustrate the fact that the relationship between Anglian and Scandinavian was much closer than that between Brittonic and Old English. Their speech habits were similar and many words could easily be understood by either race; there would be no difficulty, for instance, in recognising the identity of meaning of OE *cyning* and ON *konungr* 'king', of *stān* and *steinn* 'stone', and of OE *wulf* and ON *úlfr* 'wolf'. But there were sounds in OE which were unfamiliar to Scandinavians and words similar in pronunciation which were liable to be misunderstood. This would be particularly common when Scandinavians settled in a district already occupied by Anglians. The victorious and dominant new-comers would impose their rule, their system of law and possibly their customs on the defeated English, but they would find it impossible to revolutionise the nomenclature of the whole area. They would be compelled to adopt the English place-names already in existence, and in so doing they would inevitably modify them in accordance with their own habits of speech, a process to which many modern place-names bear witness.

The Buckinghamshire hamlet of Skirmett occurs in 1307 as *la Skiremote* which can be nothing other than a Scandinavianising of OE *scīr(ge)mōt* 'the moot or meeting-place of the *shire* or district', with a substitution of Scandinavian *sk* for the English *sc*, pronounced *sh*, a sound not found in early Scandinavian. The etymology is confirmed by the fact that only half-a-mile from Skirmett is Fingest, the early forms of which prove that this was originally *þing-hyrst* 'the wood or wooded hill where the assembly met'. A parallel example is that of Skyrack (WRY), from OE *scīr-āc* 'shire-oak', the oak near which the wapentake actually met. Skirlaugh (ERY) is a Scandinavianisation of OE *scīr-lēah* 'bright clearing', a name found elsewhere as Shirley (Db, Ha, Sr, Wa), whilst Skirlington was probably a dependent settlement from Skirlaugh, OE *Scīrlēaingatūn*, 'village of the men of Shirley'. Both Skirlaugh and Skirlington belonged to the manor of Hornsea. Skipton (NRY) is from OE (Northumbrian) *scīp* 'sheep'; Skipwith (ERY) was OE *scīpwīc* 'sheep-farm', with the additional substitution of ON *viðr* 'wood' for OE *wīc*; Scopwick (L) is a Scandinavianised OE *scēapwīc* 'sheep-farm', whilst Skiplam (NRY), *Scipnum* 1086, is the dative plural of OE *scipen* 'shippon, cow-shed'. Shelton (Beds, Nf, Nt), 'farm on a bank or shelf', appears seven times in Cumberland and Yorkshire as Skelton, whilst OE *sceald* 'shallow', found in Shalbourne (W) and Shalford (Ess), has Scandinavian *sk* in Scaldwell (Nth) and Scalford (Lei). Similarly, the northern Keswick and the northern and midland Carlton, corresponding to the southern Cheswick, Chiswick and Charlton, and Kildwick (WRY) to Childwick (Herts), owe their initial consonant to Scandinavian which had no *ch* sound. Middop and Midhope (WRY) 'middle valley' retain the original English *d*, for which the Scandinavian *ð* has been substituted in Meathop (We) and Mythop (La).

Word-substitution. As in Skipwith, OE *wīc* has been replaced by ON *viðr* 'wood' in Tockwith (WRY). Substitution of a Scandinavian word for an English synonym is common: Braithwell (WRY), *Bradewell* 1086 (OE *brād*, ON *breiðr* 'broad'), Coniscliffe (Du), *Ciningesclif* 778, *Cuniggesclive* 1202 (OE *cyning*, ON *konungr* 'king'), Eagle (L), *Aclei*, *Aycle* 1086 (OE *āc*, ON *eik* 'oak'), Holbeck (Nt), *on holan broc* 958, *Holebek* c1180 'stream in the hollow' (OE *brōc*, ON *bekkr* 'stream'), Howden (ERY), *Æt Heafuddæne* 959, *Hovedene* 1086 (OE *hēafod*, ON *hǫfuð* 'head'), Melton (Nf), *Middilton*, *Methelton* c1060, Methwold (Nf), *Medelwolde* c1050, *Methelwalde* 1086, Methley (WRY), *Medelai* 1086, *Metheleia* c1160 (OE *middel*, ON *meðal* 'middle'), Owstwick (ERY), *Osteuuic* 1086 (OE *ēast*, ON *austr* 'east'), Rawcliffe Bank (NRY), *Roudeclif* 1086, (*in*) *Readeclive* 1108 (OE *rēad*, ON *rauðr* 'red').

In Northamptonshire we have several examples of the substitution of a Scandinavian term for an unrelated English word. Badby appears in an original charter of 944 both as *baddan byrig* and as *baddan by*, 'the fort and the village of Badda', a purely English personal-name, so that originally the name must have been OE *Baddan byrig*, his fort, now represented, probably, by Arbury Hill Camp, which already in the tenth century could be called alternatively *Baddan by*, his village. Naseby (Nth), *Navesberie* in Domesday Book, 'Hnæf's fort', and Greasby (Ch), *Gravesberie* 1086, 'the fort by a grove or trench', have both undergone the same change. Rugby (Wa), *Rocheberie* 1086, *Rokebi* Hy 2, shows a similar substitution of ON *by* for OE *byrig*. The form *Rokeby Fields* survives in the Tithe Award and is a parallel to Rokeby (NRY) and Rookby (We) which may well show the same substitution. The triple occurrence of the name suggests that the first element is rather 'rooks' than a personal-name.

This raises the problem of Ashby (Nth) and the other 16 examples of the same name scattered throughout the Danelaw, together with Asby (Cu, We). In Lincolnshire we find numerous ME forms in *Aske-* which suggest that the name might be wholly Scandinavian. Ekwall derives all from OSc *Askabý(r)* 'village where ash-trees grew', with a possible alternative in some instances of 'Aski's village'. But it should be noted that there is no evidence in Scandinavia for the formation of such compounds. Nor can we take Ashby, like Badby, as a Scandinavianisation of an English *Ashbury*, for that name is found only twice in England, in Berkshire and Devon, and it could never have been common, for there is no particular reason for associating ash-trees with old forts. Further, compounds of *by* with the names of other trees are rare. Selby (WRY) is derived by Smith from ON *selja* 'a willow' and *by*, a pure Scandinavian name, but Ekwall himself suggests that the name may be a Scandinavianised OE *Seletūn* (from *salh* 'sallow copse'), a name actually recorded in 779, and this may refer to Selby itself. Linby (Nt) is explained as 'lime-tree village'. Thornby (Nth), *Torneberie* 1086, may well be a Scandinavianised form (ON *þyrnir*) of OE *þornbyrig*, as in Thornbrough (Nb) and Thornbury (D, Gl), a fort where a thorn-hedge formed part of the defences. The numerous Willoughbys are explained by Ekwall as 'village among the willows', but he adds that it is curious that this hybrid name is so common. 'Very likely Willoughby is in most cases a Scandinavianised form of OE *Weligtūn*', a name actually found in Lincolnshire as Willoughton. It is probable that to the Scandinavians of the tenth century there appeared little, if any, difference between an English *tūn* and a Scandinavian *by* and that the terms could be used indifferently, a suggestion confirmed by the fact that Bleasby (Nt) is first recorded in a charter of 958 as *Blisetune*; Thringstone and Nailstone (Lei) and Scofton (Nt) all appear in Domesday Book with *-by*, *Trangesbi*, *Nevlebi* and *Scotebi*, whilst Holdenby (Nth) occurs as both *Aldenestone* and *Aldenesbi*. There are no unequivocal examples of the combination of *by* with a tree-name. Ashby is nearly as common a name as Ashton; Selby can be paralleled with Willoughby and Willoughton; the solitary Linby is outnumbered by the Lintons. All should probably be regarded as examples of the substitution of ON *by* for OE *tūn*.

A clear instance of the substitution of ON *kirkja* for OE *cirice* is to be found in Peakirk (Nth), *æt Pegecyrcan* 1042–66, which is also recorded in a thirteenth-century transcript of a charter of 871 in the form *Pegekyrk* and is reputed to take its name from the church founded here by St Pega, sister of St Guthlac. Other compounds of *kirk* in which the same substitution has taken place are Kirkstead (L), Kirstead (Nf), Kirkley (Sf), and probably Kirkstall (WRY). Some are pure Scandinavian names: Kirkland (La), 'church wood' (ON *lundr*), Kirkdale (La), Skewkirk (WRY), 'church in the wood', Felkirk (WRY), 'church made of boards' (ON *fjǫl*), identical in meaning with Bradkirk (La), where OE *bred* has been substituted; but others may be late names, formed after ME *kirk* had become an appellative: Kirkgate, Kirkhaugh (Nb), Kirklees (WRY).

Kirton (L, Nt, Sf) is a Scandinavianising of OE *ciric-tūn*, now Cheriton, but Kirkham and Kirkby or Kirby offer difficulties. These have been explained as Scandinavianisations of OE *ciric-hām* and *ciric-byrig* respectively, both of which are exceedingly rare. The only example of Churcham is found in Gloucestershire, where the *Church-* is a prefix added after the Conquest to an original *Hamme*. The only possible compound with *-bury* is Chirbury (Sa) and compounds of *Church-* with other elements are rare except in late names and the Churchills discussed above. Both the Lancashire and the East Riding Kirkham have forms in *-heim* such as are not uncommon in other names in *-hām*. None of these survives today, but in view of the lack of examples of the English *Churcham*, Kirkham was probably a pure Scandinavian name. So, too, with only a solitary example of *Church-bury*, it is unlikely that the many examples of Kirkby and Kirby should be Scandinavian forms of an English name. We must, therefore, regard them as pure Scandinavian names, 'the result of a deliberate naming afresh, and, further, that they must belong to a period of the Viking settlements when the Vikings had abandoned their heathenism and were ready to recognise the church as the centre of life of the district'. The forms *Chercheberie* and *Kirkeberia*, which are found for the Northamptonshire and Warwickshire names, are chance Anglicisings of a generally prevailing Scandinavian type and not a survival of an Anglian one.

Askham (Nt), like Kirkham, has been explained as a Scandinavianisation of an OE *Æschām*, but, whilst Ashton is common, no such name as *Asham* exists. The Domesday form is *Ascā*, repeated in *Askam* in 1289. This must be a pure Scandinavian name, identical with the Westmorland Askham, *Askum* 1232, from ON *askum*, the dative plural of *askr* 'at the ash trees'. We should certainly not expect -*am* in DB, but a clear parallel is found in Newsholme (ERY), *Neuhusa* 1086, 'at the new houses'.

ANGLICISING OF SCANDINAVIAN NAMES

Substitution of an English for a synonymous Scandinavian element has also taken place. Scand *austr* 'east' has been replaced by OE *ēast* in East Riding (*Oustredinc, Estreding* 1086; *Riding* is from ON *þriðiungr* 'a third part'); ON *fagr* by English *fair* in Fairwood (NRY), *Fagherwall* 1257, *Faverwald* c1300; ON *nýr* by OE *nēowe* in Newball (L), *Neobole* 963, from ON *nýbøle* 'new homestead'; ON *melr* by OE *mōr* or *mere* in Tranmere (Ch), 'cranes' sandbank'. Additional examples will be found among the early forms of names in which the substitution has not survived. In others, English and Scandinavian forms are recorded simultaneously and it is impossible to decide which is the original.

HYBRIDS

Many of the place-names discussed above are often regarded as hybrids, but it is clear that the mixture of languages is not original. A purely Scandinavian or a purely English name has been modified in the mouths of speakers of the other language. Real hybrids are not common among the old names and the names of villages except when based on an old place-name, as in Ennerdale, Nidderdale, etc. It seems clear that when the village names arose the English and the Scandinavian elements were kept apart. But in course of time a number of Scandinavian terms were adopted by the Anglians, became part of their vocabulary and were used freely like the native terms. Hence arose a number of real hybrids, names of small and insignificant places, names often found in counties where Scandinavian influence was slight but where Scandinavian words had been admitted into the local vocabulary. Hence the occurrence in Essex of such names as Biggin (ON *bigging* 'building'), Aldercar Wood

169

(ON *kjarr* 'marsh overgrown with brushwood'), and field-names such as *Thornholm, Chircheholm, Tunmanholme,* etc. (ON *holmr* 'higher ground amid marshes'), *Munekeswong* (ON *vangr* 'monks' garden'); all late and in a county where Scandinavian influence in major place-names is by no means strong. Such hybrids are rarely names of villages. We may note: Aikhead (Cu), (ON *eik* 'oak' and OE *hēafod* 'head'), Altofts (WRY) 'old tofts', Beanthwaite (La), Benwray (Cu), 'bean nook' (ON *vrá*), Coneywood Fen (C), *Cunewode* 'royal wood' (ON *konungr* 'king'), Grange Hill (C), earlier *Eegreine* 'river-fork' (OE *ēa*, ON *greinn*), Ryeholmes (Nt).

'GRIMSTON HYBRIDS'

'Grimston hybrid' is a convenient term for place-names consisting of a Scandinavian personal-name compounded with OE *-tūn*, of which Grimston is particularly common. It derives from ON *Grímr*, ODa *Grím*, and is found ten times in the counties of Yorkshire, Nottingham, Leicester, Norfolk and Suffolk. These names are usually those of villages and the great majority are mentioned in Domesday Book, a fact which proves they originated within less than two centuries of the Scandinavian settlement. As a class they belong to an early period of the settlement and are almost, but not quite, as old as names in *-by*. Their distribution, too, is interesting. They are remarkably rare in areas where, as in Lindsey and Kesteven in Lincolnshire and the Wreak Valley of Leicestershire, an impressive array of names in *-by* proves early and intensive Scandinavian settlement. Where they are common is on the fringe of such areas, in districts where Scandinavians had settled less thickly in areas already occupied by Anglians. Figures are misleading. A full assessment of their distribution and importance would involve a detailed survey of the place-names of whole counties, but we may note that while we have 10 examples in the North Riding and 14 in the East Riding, with 19 in Nottinghamshire and 11 in Derbyshire, in counties where Scandinavian settlement was less intense examples are only occasional: Cambridge has 2, Bedford and Huntingdon 1 each, with 3 in Warwickshire and 4 in Staffordshire.

The etymology of these names creates no difficulty. The personal-names are usually well known: Caxton, C (*Kakkr*), Farthingstone, Nth (ON *Farþegn*, ODa *Farthin*), Gamston, Nt (*Gamall*), Thurlaston, Wa (*Þorleifr*). The real problem is to decide the significance of such names. In theory they might denote settlements made by an individual Scandinavian in a thoroughly English neighbourhood, but this could not apply to Snibston (*Snípr*) and Bilstone (*Bildr*) in Leicestershire, where Nailstone and Thringstone could never have appeared with -*by*, and Carlton and Congerston (a Scandinavian form of OE *Cyningestūn*) could never have assumed their present forms if there had not been a considerable Scandinavian element in the local population. From their geographical position, it is most unlikely that these villages were new settlements in the Danish period. A village like Gonalston (Nt) probably denoted a village acquired by a Dane named Gunnulf at the time when the Great Army of the Danes divided out the land for settlement. There is no reason to suppose that the English peasants were displaced. The new Danish owner had an obvious interest in retaining them as a source of rents and services. The village probably had a name preserving that of the original English founder. As place-names arose spontaneously, it became convenient and customary to refer to the village by the new owner's name. 'Gunnulf's *tūn*' acknowledged the new, foreign owner, but remained an English *tūn*. Whether a village of which a Dane had become lord was called his *tūn* or his *by*, depended on local circumstances, in particular on the relative number of Danes and Englishmen in the village or its immediate neighbourhood.

SOME COMMON ELEMENTS

The element -*by* is extremely common wherever the Scandinavians settled in England, particularly in Lincolnshire, Leicestershire and the North Riding of Yorkshire. Names in -*by* imply a considerable Scandinavian-speaking population in the district. It is not necessarily, as has sometimes been suggested, a certain sign of Danish origin, for it is common in the Wirral, where the settlers were Norwegians. In Norway the word meant 'homestead', in Denmark 'a village'. In England the usual meaning is 'village', but in Spanby (L), 'shingle roof *by*', the reference must be to a single house or farmstead. In a few names it must refer to a new or secondary settlement, especially when compounded with an older place-name: Blackfordby (Lei), Saltfleetby (L), Stokesby (Nf), and in Raby (Ch, Du), '*by* on the boundary'. About two-thirds of the names are compounded with personal-names, mostly Scandinavian, as Ormesby, Nf (*Ormr*), Stainsby, Db

(*Steinn*), Freeby, Lei (ODa *Frǣthi*), Wragby, Wrawby, L (ODa *Wraghi*); the personal-name may be OIr: Lackenby, NRY (*Lochán*), Fixby, WRY (*Fíach*);[1] or OE: Ellerby (ERY, NRY), *Aluuardebi* 1086 (*Ælfweard*), Gutterby (Cu), *Godrickeby* 1235 (*Godrīc*); or a post-Conquest name: Harraby (Cu), *Henricheby* 1175 (Henry), Ponsonby, Cu (*Puncun* 1177).[2] Other compounds include: Austby, WRY (*austr* 'east'), Utterby, L ('outer', with OE *ūterra* substituted for ON *ytri*), Wetherby (WRY) 'wether', Boothby (L) 'booths', Ferriby (ERY, L) 'ferry'. Lazenby (NRY) and Lazonby (Cu) were villages of freedmen (ON *leysingr*), Thirlby (NRY), that of the thralls or serfs (ON *þrǽll*).[3]

Widely spread and next in importance is *þorp*, which was rare in Norway but common in Sweden and Denmark. In England it is common throughout the Danelaw and can be regarded as a test-word for Danish occupation. Its meaning is 'a secondary settlement', 'an outlying farmstead' or 'a small hamlet dependent on a larger place', a use clearly seen in such names as Burnham and Burnham Thorpe (Nf), Ixworth and Ixworth Thorpe (Sf), Barkby and Barkby Thorpe (Lei). Many of the thorps are of late origin and lie in low land, and the fact that the name was so often used uncompounded proves that these were small and insignificant places. Many have disappeared and many are still only small hamlets. Parish and township names number 12 in Nottinghamshire, 12 in the North Riding and 28 in the East Riding, whereas secondary names in Nottinghamshire number 27, in the North Riding 25 and in the East Riding 42. In the West Riding and Lincolnshire *thorp* is even more common in secondary names. Frequently there is more than one such name in a single parish, as Northorpe and Southorpe in Hornsea (ERY), Easthorpe and Westhorpe in Southwell (Nt). There are large groups of *Thorp* near Wakefield and Sheffield whilst in Lincolnshire at least 22 *thorps* have disappeared from the map. Occasionally we have evidence of the dependence of a *thorp* upon another place, as Ashwellthorpe (Nf), where eight acres of land were conveyed to Ashwell church c1066, whilst Littlethorpe is recorded as a *berewic* of Ripon (WRY) in Domesday Book. *Thorp* continued in use after the Conquest, for Chapelthorpe (WRY) was a chapel of ease of Sandal

[1] Cf. pp. 69–70.   [2] Cf. p. 49.

[3] Other social classes are referred to in Dringhoe (ERY), Dringhouses (WRY) and Drointon (St), from ON *drengr* 'a free tenant holding land by service, rent and military service' and in Bonbusk (Nt) and Bongate (We), from ON *bondi* peasant farmer, villein'.

church, whilst Canonthorpe (WRY) belonged to the canons of Nostell Priory, Kirkthorpe (WRY) to the church of Warmfield, and Monkthorpe (L) to the monks of Bardney.

As a first element, *thorp* is rare, as in Thorpland (Nf), except where, later, distinctive additions have been added: Thorpe on the Hill (WRY), Thorpe Market (Nf), Thorpe Acre (Lei), *Thorp Haueker* 1319, 'hawker', Thorpe in the Fallows (L), Thorpe Lubenham (Nth), *Thorp juxta Lobenham* 1285 (near Lubbenham, Lei), Thorpe in the Glebe (Nt), Thorpe by Water (R), *Thorp by the watir* 1459, near the Welland, Thorpe le Willows (NRY); Thorpe Arnold (Lei), Thorpe Mandeville (Nth) and Thorpe Stapleton (WRY), from former owners. Thorpe Morieux (Sf) is simply *Torp* in 1086; a knight's fee here was given by Warin Bussel to Ranulf de Glanvil as dower on his marriage to Gutha, Ranulf's sister, and the place was called *Thorp Bussel* in 1236 and *Githesthorp* in 1250. Gutha's son, Roger de Murious, inherited the land (called *Thorpe Muryaus* in 1291) which still preserves his name. Other compounds are: Besthorpe, Nt (OE *bēos* 'bent grass'), Grassthorpe (Nt), Skinnerthorpe (WRY); Bromkinsthorpe, Lei (ON *Brúnskinn* 'brown skin'), Oakthorpe, Lei (*Áki*), Fleecethorpe, Nt (ODa *Flik*), Edderthorpe, WRY (OE *Ēadrīc*), Yaddlethorpe, L (OE *Ēadwulf*, adopted as ON *Jádulf*); Painthorp, WRY (ME *Payn*), Perlethorpe, Nt (ME *Peverel*).

This Danish *þorp* must be carefully distinguished from OE *þrop*, *þorp*, which had a similar meaning 'hamlet', 'outlying farm'. Examples of this may occur in the Danelaw, but in the absence of forms like *throp*, this is unlikely except in border districts. In the south it is the English word, not the Danish, which is found. In Essex we have Gestingthorpe, an old village name recorded in 975, with medial *-inga-* and forms in *-throp* in 1248 and 1285, which must be regarded as a wholly English name; and Easthorpe, *Estrop* 1204, 1291, *Estthrop* 1285, clearly from *þrop*. In Southchurch near Southend we have Littlethorpe ·and Thorpehall Farm (better known today as Thorpe Bay). Both are Domesday vills (*Torpeia*, *Thorp*) and were formerly distinguished as *Northtorp* 1221 and *Suthorp* 1275; the latter is *Suth Trope* in 1286 and here, too, the names are English. But Essex was in the Danelaw, and farther north we have Thorpe-le-Soken, *Torpeia* 1119, with no form but *Thorp*. The soken was that of the Bishop of London, which included Kirby-le-Soken, a pure Scandinavian name, whilst not far away, in St Osyth, in the same hundred, is Frowick Hall, a difficult name, but probably ON

173

Fróðavík 'Fróði's creek', again purely Scandinavian. This *thorp* must be regarded as a relic of a small Scandinavian settlement near the Naze.

OE *þrop* may have persisted in Northumbria in Throphill (Nb) and Thrope (WRY); in Northamptonshire it is difficult to decide between OE *þrop* and ODa *þorp*. Where the names are compounded with Scandinavian elements or personal-names in areas with other evidence of Scandinavian settlement, they are probably from the Danish word; it is in the south-west of the county, on the borders of Warwickshire, Oxfordshire and Buckinghamshire, that the OE *-throp, -trop* is found, and there seems no reason to deny these their English origin, along with the three Warwickshire names Eathorpe, Stoneythorpe and Princethorpe. The word is not found in Kent or Sussex or in Devon and Cornwall, but occurs in the southern counties from Worcestershire to Surrey. As a simplex name it is found as Thorpe (Bk, Sr), Throop (Ha), Throope (W), Thrope (WRY), Thrup (Beds), and Thrupp (Berks, Gl, O), and in compounds: Astrop (O), Eastrip (So), Eastrop (Ha, W) 'east'; Hatherop (Gl), Heythrop (O) 'high'; Neithrop (O) 'lower'; Sedrup (Bk), Southrop (Gl), Southrope (O) 'south'; Upthorpe (Wo), Westhorpe (Bk), Westrip (Gl), Westrop (W); Brookthorpe (Gl), Eythrop (Bk) 'river' (OE *ēa*); and with personal-names in Adlestrop (Gl), Williamstrip (Gl) and Huntingtrap (Wo).

ON *topt*, ODa *toft* 'curtilage', 'plot of ground in which a dwelling stands', 'homestead', is found chiefly in Yorkshire, the East Midlands and East Anglia, suggesting a Danish rather than a Norwegian origin, but in ME it became an appellative, widely scattered, and these later names have no reference to its original distribution. It is common as Toft (C, Sf, etc.) and Tofts (ERY) and in compounds, with both significant words and personal-names: Bratoft, L (*breiðr* 'broad'), Eastoft, ERY (*eski* 'ash'), Langtoft (L, ERY), Moortoft (L); Brothertoft (L), Lowestoft (Sf).

ON *hlaða* 'barn' is found in Laithes (Cu); Lathom and Laytham (ERY), from the dative plural; and in Laithwaite (La), Newlass (NRY) and Silloth (Cu) 'sea'. ON *sætr* 'a mountain pasture, a shieling' is common in the mountainous districts of Cumberland and Westmorland, Yorkshire and Lancashire, as in Satterlowe, Satterthwaite (Cu), Seatoller (Cu), an inversion compound, 'alder-tree shieling', Appersett (NRY) 'apple-tree'; Swineside (NRY), Swinside (Cu); Summerseat (La); Earlside (Nb), Yarlside (NRY); Oughterside, Cu

(OE *Ūhtrēd*), Arkleside NRY (ON *Arnkell*), and Setmurthy (Cu) 'Murdoch's shieling'.

ON *þveit*, ODa *thwēt* is most frequent in the north-west, where some 80 examples are found in Cumberland, at least 30 in Westmorland, about 40 in Lancashire and 30 in the North Riding, whilst it is common in the western parts of the West Riding. Elsewhere in the Danelaw it is rare, only three examples occurring in the East Riding and seven in Nottinghamshire, though in both counties it is common in field-names. This distribution is probably due to the fact that the north-western counties had more forest- and waste-land to exploit than the better-developed eastern and midland counties. It has been suggested that *thwaite* is a sign of Norwegian influence, but the element was as common in Denmark as in Norway and it is found as a parish-name in Norfolk and Suffolk. In ME it was widely used as an appellative and many of the names are late. Its meaning in England is 'a clearing in woodland, probably used as meadow-land, a meadow, paddock or close': Thwaite (Nf, Sf, NRY), Thwaites (Cu), Braffords (ERY), Braithwaite (Cu, Y) 'broad' (ON *breiðr*), Easthwaite (Cu), Eastwood (Nt); Smaithwaite (Cu) 'small' (ON *smár*), Micklethwaite (Cu, WRY); Falthwaite (WRY) 'broken up for cultivation' (OE *falh*), Garfit (Nt) 'muddy' (OE *gor*); Kirkthwaite (La); Applethwaite (Cu, We), Birthwaite (WRY) 'birch' (ON *birki*); Seathwaite (Cu) 'sedge, rush' (ON *sef*), Thistlewood (Cu); Beanthwaite (La); Haithwaite (Cu), Haythwaite (NRY); Calthwaite (Cu) 'calf', Gristhwaite (NRY) 'pig' (ON *gríss*), Ickenthwaite (La) 'squirrel' (ON *ikorni*); less than one-tenth of the names contain personal-names: Gunnerthwaite, La (ON *Gunnarr*), Gunthwaite, WRY (ON *Gunnhildr* fem.); Douthwaite, NRY (OIr *Dubhán*); Godderthwaite, Cu (*Godard*).

DANISH TEST-WORDS

As we have seen already, it is frequently impossible to decide whether a particular word or personal-name is of Danish or Norwegian origin. Both *by* and *thorp* were used alike in East and West Scandinavia, whereas in England, whilst *by* was clearly used by Norwegians, *thorp* may be regarded as a sign of Danish settlement. But some few terms can definitely be assigned to one or other of these races. OESc *bōð* 'a temporary shelter', 'cow-house, herdsman's hut' became ME *bōþ(e)* modern *booth* and corresponds to OWSc *búð*. It is a Danish form which survives in Boothby (L) and is common in minor names. Similarly, for ON *holmr* the Danes had *hulm* 'island, water-meadow', found in Hulme (Ch, La, St), Levenshulme (La), Kettleshulme (Ch) and in Oldham (La), *Aldhulm* 1227 'the old holm'. Clint (WRY) is from ODa *klint* 'a hill', corresponding to ON *klettr*, found in Cleator (Cu). *Toft* is rather Danish than Norwegian.

NORWEGIAN TEST-WORDS

The Norwegian *búð* is found in Cumberland in Bewcastle, *Buthecastra* c1178, 'temporary dwellings within the lines of the Roman camp'; Bowderdale, *Beutherdalbek* 1322, ON *búðar dalr* 'valley of the booth'; Burthwaite Bridge, *Butherthwait* 1211, a similar genitival compound, 'clearing around or adjacent to a booth'. ON *holmr* 'higher dry ground amidst marshes', 'a piece of flat ground', 'an island', is exceedingly common. Forms in *hulm* are definitely Danish, but most place-names appear to be from the Norse element. The word became common outside Scandinavian areas and many of the place-names in *-holme* in the Danelaw may really be from the ODa *hulm*, its real origin being obscured by AN spellings as *holm*. In modern compounds today it often appears as *-ham*: Bromholm (Nf), Haverholme (L) 'oats', Grassoms (Cu), Soffham (ERY) 'sedge' (ON *sef*), Durham (*dūn*).

Other Norwegian test-words are OWSc *brekka* 'hill, slope', found in Breck (La, NRY, WRY); Larbrick, *Lairbrec* 'clay slope', a pure Scandinavian name, Norbreck, Scarisbrick and Warbreck 'beacon hill' (ON *varði*), all La; OWSc *gil* 'a ravine, a deep narrow valley with a stream', not used in ODa, common in the north-west, especially among the mountains of the Lakes and the Pennines settled by Norwegians. It is usually compounded with ON elements: Ragill Beck (La), 'red' (ON *rauðr*), Swarthgill (Cu), 'black, dark' (*svartr*), Gaisgill (We, WRY), 'goose' (ON *gás*), Reagill (We), 'fox' (*refr*), Rossgill (We), 'horse' (*hross*); OWSc *skáli* 'a temporary hut or shed' in Scales (Cu, La), Scholes (La, WRY), Scole (Nf), Scaleby (Cu), Scholar Green (Ch), *Scholehale* Ed I (OE *halh*), Gatesgill (Cu), 'goat' (ON *geit*), Seascale (Cu), 'sea', Summersgill (Cu), Winscales and Winskill (Cu), 'windy'; OWSc *slakki*, 'a small shallow valley, a hollow in the ground', in Slack (La, WRY), Hazelslack (We), Nettleslack (La), Witherslack (We), 'wooded'. The Irish–Scandinavian loan-word *ergh* has been dealt with elsewhere.[1]

[1] *v.* p. 98.

THE DANISH SETTLEMENT

The first Danish raiders certainly known to have visited England reached Sheppey in 835 and in the next thirty years at least twelve separate attacks on the coast are recorded. In 850 a Danish army wintered in Thanet and again in 854 in Sheppey. The first naval battle recorded in English history is that of the defeat of a Danish fleet off Sandwich in 851 by Æthelstan, under-king of Kent. All these (and others) were sporadic raids for plunder. It was not until 865 that the first serious attempt was made at settlement. In that year a great Danish army landed in East Anglia intent on conquest and settlement. It was a composite host, including numerous nobles regarded by their countrymen as kings, under a unified command, its leaders Ivar the Boneless and Halfdan, sons of Ragnar Lothbrok, the most famous viking of the ninth century. The full story of the Danish wars of conquest must be sought from the historians. Here we must confine our attention to the broad outlines necessary for the interpretation of the influence they have had on our place-names.

For twelve months these Danes remained in East Anglia, collecting horses and material for further movements and carrying out raids to subdue the neighbourhood. In 866 they moved into Northumbria and occupied York, making this their headquarters and their base. In the next few years they made ravaging expeditions into Mercia and East Anglia, where, in 869, they defeated and killed Edmund, king and future saint. Practically the whole of Eastern England was now in Danish hands. For nine years the Danish force had acted as a single military unit. In 874 it was divided into two armies, never to be reunited. In 875 Halfdan marched into Yorkshire, which he subdued, devastating Bernicia beyond the Tees and penetrating into Cumberland. In 876 he divided up the land which the Danes ploughed and tilled and the former pirates began to settle down as peaceful agriculturists.

The second army, under Guthrum, invaded Wessex but was forced in 878 to withdraw to Mercia, which was divided into two parts, one Danish, the other English, under Ceolwulf. The ravaging of the south continued until 886, when Alfred the Great made peace with Guthrum and a common boundary was fixed between their territories, from the mouth of the Thames to the Lea, along this river to Bedford, and thence along the Ouse to Watling Street. East of this was the territory later to be called the Danelaw.

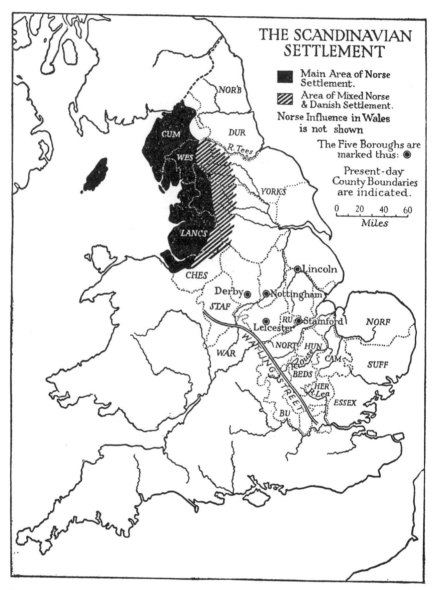

THE SCANDINAVIAN
SETTLEMENT

■ Main Area of Norse
Settlement.
▨ Area of Mixed Norse
& Danish Settlement.

Norse Influence in Wales
is not shown

The Five Boroughs are
marked thus: ◉

Present-day
County Boundaries
are indicated.

0   20   40   60
‾‾‾‾‾‾‾‾‾‾‾‾‾‾
Miles

NOR'B
CUM
DUR
R.Tees
WES
YORKS
LANCS
CHES
Lincoln
Derby◉   ◉Nottingham
STAF
RU◉ ◉Stamford   NORF
Leicester
WAR   NORT   HUN   CAM   SUFF
WATLING STREET
R.Ouse   BEDS
HER   R.Lea   ESSEX
BU

From H. C. Darby, *A Historical Geography of England* (Cambridge University Press, 1951)

There were thus three separate Scandinavian dominions: Northumbria (Yorkshire), East Anglia, occupied by the army from Cirencester in 879 and Scandinavian Mercia. Of this, little is known. It included the Five Boroughs of Lincoln, Stamford, Leicester, Derby and Nottingham, each apparently with a jarl and an army of its own. The Danish stronghold was in Northumbria. The reconquest of the Danelaw was begun by Edward, son of Alfred the Great, who gradually subjugated East Anglia and Scandinavian Mercia and, in 924, shortly before his death, was 'chosen as father and lord' by the Northumbrian peoples, whether English, Danish or Norwegian. A noteworthy feature of this reconquest is the comparatively weak resistance offered by the southernmost counties of the territory and the rapidity with which they seem to have been re-anglicised. This applies particularly to the 'Danish' regions of Buckinghamshire, to the counties of Bedfordshire, Hertfordshire and Essex, and southern Suffolk. The Scandinavian population here must have formed the minority, likely to be soon absorbed by the native majority. In Northumbria the position was very different. Up to c950 York was ruled by Scandinavian kings, some of them Norwegian Vikings from Dublin, then by its own earls, whose dependence on Wessex must have been merely nominal. In 1013, when Swein of Denmark landed at Gainsborough to conquer the whole country, he was immediately acknowledged by the men of Northumbria and Lindsey. It is the northern portion of the Danelaw which is isolated from the rest of England by its administrative, judicial and social institutions.

The distribution of Scandinavian place-names agrees, in general, pretty well with what we should expect from the historical evidence. Parish-names of Scandinavian origin are spread thickly throughout the North and East Ridings, across the Humber in Lincolnshire and Leicestershire, and less densely in Nottinghamshire. In Norfolk they are well represented; in Suffolk they are well scattered but less numerous. In the West Riding we have a band running from north Lancashire across the county to the North and East Ridings, with another farther south, from south Lancashire to Nottinghamshire. These are less dense and separated from one another and from the counties to north and south. Elsewhere in the Danelaw they are rare or non-existent. If we take the names in -by, we get a similar impression. There are about 250 of these names in Yorkshire, of which 150 are in the North Riding and 42 in the East Riding; Lincolnshire has 260, Leicestershire 58, Nottinghamshire 21, Northamptonshire

18 and Derbyshire 10. In East Anglia, Norfolk has 21, Suffolk only 3. In the southern counties of the Danelaw, Essex has only 1, whilst there is not a solitary example in Cambridgeshire, Huntingdonshire or Bedfordshire. These tests reveal the greatest Scandinavian influence in the areas settled by the three great Danish armies, in Yorkshire, Scandinavian Mercia and in East Anglia: the influence is less intensive on the borders of these areas and in the counties which were first reconquered from the Danes.

To obtain a full realisation of the strength of the Danish influence in any particular area, it is necessary to consider other elements and to take account of minor names. In Domesday Book Scandinavian names in the North Riding outnumber those of English origin, though these are not few. In the East Riding we find two Scandinavian names for every three English in Domesday Book, but if minor and later names are included we have ultimately about three Scandinavian names for every four English. But here we have also examples of word-substitution as in Howden and Owstwick and of sound-substitution in Skirlaugh and Skirlington, whilst 'Grimston hybrids' are numerous. How far English names have been replaced by Scandinavian names it is impossible to say, but the original name of Whitby was *Streonæshalch*. Even in Derbyshire, where Scandinavian influence was not strong, Derby was one of the Five Boroughs and the Danes of the neighbourhood replaced the English *Northworthig* 'north homestead' by *Deoraby* 'village with a deer park', a name of their own creation.

In Northumberland Scandinavian influence is slight, whilst in Durham a considerable number of Scandinavian names is found only in the south, near the Tees and the Wear. In 875 Halfdan had sailed up the Tyne, destroyed Tynemouth and ravaged the whole of northern Northumbria, clearly with the intention of removing any threat to the settlement of Yorkshire. In Northumberland there is no example of -*by* or of the commonest and most characteristic Scandinavian elements. The modern form of Wansbeck is misleading. Its second element is -*spic* (*Wenspic* 1137), probably 'a bridge that could be crossed by a waggon'. There is no trace of any general settlement of the countryside, though in the centre of the county we have names containing Scandinavian inflexional forms, rare Scandinavian words and rare Scandinavian personal-names, which suggest the presence of Scandinavian settlers, who seem to have settled peaceably among their English neighbours. In Durham we have eight names in -*by*, four *thorps*, one *toft*, one *garth* and two *holmes*. The modern map is again misleading. The numerous *becks* were all earlier called by the English name of *burn*, whilst Bulbeck Common is a manorial name preserving that of a Norman family from Bolbec on the Seine. The *holms*, the *carrs* and the *Newbiggins* contain elements common in the northern dialects. It is only on the borders of Yorkshire that we find names in -*by*, Aislaby, Killerby, Raby, Selaby and Ulnaby near the Tees, Ornsby, Raceby and Rumby near the Wear. There was clearly a Scandinavian settlement on a large scale, a later movement from the North Riding.

Cambridge was once the seat of a Danish army, but Scandinavian influence on its place-names is distinctly less than in Northamptonshire, though stronger than in Bedfordshire and Huntingdonshire. There is no name in -*by* in the county. Only six parish names contain Scandinavian elements—Bourn, Caxton, Conington, Croxton, Toft and Carlton, and of these only Bourn and Toft are of pure Scandinavian origin. Caxton and Croxton are 'Grimston hybrids', whilst Conington shows a substitution of ON *konungr* for OE *cyning* and Carlton is a Scandinavianisation of Charlton. It is noteworthy, too, that all six are situated on the clay which was once well-wooded and avoided by the early Anglian settlers. Denny 'island of the Danes', an English name, is certainly indicative of Scandinavian settlement, but implies that Danes were in a minority in the district. Minor names, however, and field-names provide distinct evidence, well distributed throughout the county, that the Scandinavian settlers left their mark on the vocabulary and local nomenclature of the area, but the general impression is that of the naming of minor places in a more or less settled time and the gradual replacement of English names by similar or corresponding Scandinavian ones, some of which became common even in districts where the settlement was not strong. In the parishes along the Lincolnshire border we have, e.g., a Scandinavian personal-name in Singlesole 'Singull's wood' (OE *holt* 'wood'), a pure Scandinavian name in Dowsdale 'Dúsi's valley', Scandinavian words in Flag Fen and Flegcroft (Da *flæg* 'flag, a water plant', used of a marsh where flags grew), Kirkgate, Fengate, etc. (ON *gata* 'street'), hybrids in Plain Field, *Flaynefelde* 1335, identical with Plainfield (Nb), from ON *fleinn* 'pike, arrow', either descriptive of shape or a personal-name and Fitton 'farm by the meadowland' (ON *fit*), with numerous lost field-names.

The most intensive Scandinavian settlement in the eastern Danelaw was in Lincolnshire (except in Holland) and in the Wreak valley of Leicestershire. The chief Danish settlement was not around Leicester itself. The English population in the neighbourhood of the borough seems to have been left undisturbed as at Nottingham, probably to furnish food for the army. In Nottinghamshire Scandinavian influence was scattered but fairly well distributed. Names in *-by* are few, but 'Grimston hybrids' and *thorps* are numerous, with a few Scandinavianised names like Scarrington and Screveton 'sheriff's farm'. There was a considerable but scattered Danish settlement in areas already cultivated by Anglians. In Derbyshire the Scandinavian element is much slighter than in Nottinghamshire. There is a compact group of Scandinavian names in Repton hundred, where the Danish army wintered in 874. Ingleby suggests a village of Anglians amidst an overwhelmingly Scandinavian population but Bretby and Normanton point to a later settlement of Irish Vikings. Foremark (*Fornwerk*) 'the old fortification' is a pure Scandinavian name, as is Oakthorpe [1] 'Aki's outlying farm'. Croxall and Ravenstone are hybrids and Appleby is probably a Scandinavianisation of an OE *Æppeltūn*. This was clearly a district of mixed races with a Scandinavian-speaking population, probably an overflow from Leicestershire, rather than settlers from the Danish army of Repton. Derbyshire was clearly on the fringe of the Scandinavian settlement, an area where Norwegians from Cheshire met Danes from the east, both settling in territory already occupied by the native Anglians.

The significance of Watling Street as an early boundary between English and Danish territories is well illustrated in Northamptonshire. When, in 1013, Sweyn received the submission of all the army 'north of Watling Street' it was only after he had crossed Watling Street that he began to harry the country; beyond the street the territory was English. West of Watling Street Scandinavian influence on place-names is much less than elsewhere in Northamptonshire. This area is almost entirely free from traces of Scandinavian settlement, which left some third of the county almost entirely untouched. The three northern parishes west of Watling Street are Barby, Kilsby and Ashby St Ledgers, of which Kilsby shows a Scandinavianisation of OE *Cild* and Ashby has replaced an OE *Æsctūn*, as also in Canons Ashby. Thorpe Mandeville and Abthorpe contain the English *throp*, not the Scandinavian *thorp*. Badby originally was purely English, *Badbury*. Catesby 'Káti's village' should have given an English

---

[1] Now in Leicestershire.

Cateby. The medial *s* may be due to a re-fashioning of the name on the analogy of OE genitives like *Eadmundes*. There can be no doubt that here the population was mainly English, with an admixture of Danes who had gradually spread beyond the limits of the Danelaw. Similarly in Warwickshire typically Scandinavian names are found just west of Watling Street, Monks Kirby, Rugby and Willoughby, the last two certainly refashionings of English names, with Toft and Wibtoft. There are some traces of Danish influence in Staffordshire in Croxton, Drointon and Gunston. South of the Lea, in Hertfordshire, on the English side of the boundary fixed for the Danelaw by Alfred and Guthrum, is Dacorum Hundred 'the hundred of the Danes'. The complete absence of any Danish place-name elements or personal-names in the nomenclature of the hundred shows there can never have been any intensive Danish occupation here or indeed of any other part of Hertfordshire. The name must have been given in contrast to the English hundreds of Bedfordshire and Buckinghamshire and must be due to the fact that at some time in the past the local courts, their procedure and rules of law must have been controlled by men who had taken the Danish standpoint in every conflict between Danish and English tradition. The name proves the existence of a local aristocracy of Danish birth and not the division of the countryside among the rank and file of a Danish army.

The chief Danish settlement in East Anglia was in Norfolk, where it is widely distributed but falls into two distinct areas with different characteristics. In the east, on the lower Waveney and in the Broads, we find some twenty names in *-by*, mostly pure Scandinavian names like Herringby 'Hæringr's village', Rollesby (*Hróðulfr*) and Scratby (*Skrauti* 'one given to display'), with two examples of Ashby and other typically Scandinavian names, Crostwick and Crostwight 'thwaite or clearing by a cross', Felbrigg (ON *fiol-bryggia*) 'plank bridge' and Haddiscoe 'Haddr's wood' (ON *skógr*). 'Grimston hybrids' and Scandinavianised names occur, as Thurgarton, Carleton, Keswick and Matlask (OE *mæpl-æsc* 'ash where a moot was held'), but are not characteristic. Elsewhere the only safe example of *-by* is Tyby 'Tidhe's village'; there are some twelve names in *thorp* (Gunthorpe, Ingoldisthorpe), whilst 'Grimston hybrids' are common, as Grimston, Helhoughton (*Helgi*), Scoulton (*Skúli*), etc. This would suggest that the Scandinavians settled first on the lower Waveney and then found their way up the rivers, a suggestion which does not accord with what we know of the history of the settlement. The victorious army from Cirencester would not march right through Norfolk and settle on the lower Waveney. The centre of the settlement was more probably Thetford, where the army wintered in 870. To explain this curious distribution of the place-names, Ekwall puts forward two plausible, and not mutually exclusive, explanations. The Scandinavians probably settled about equally thickly over most of the county. In most parts there was a considerable English population and the Scandinavians were not sufficiently numerous to affect the nomenclature of the district seriously except in the low-lying district of the lower Waveney, which at that time was probably only sparsely occupied. In most districts they would adopt names already in use, but when new settlements were founded, probably at a later time, these were often named by suffixing *Thorpe*, as in Burnham Thorpe. It is possible, too, that the large number of Scandinavian names on the lower Waveney may be partly due to a later influx of Scandinavian settlers, who might have been induced to come over after the army had made its conquest. As Ekwall notes, it is somewhat difficult to believe that the army can have been numerous enough to account for the very extensive Scandinavian colonisation in England, and a reinforcement by later settlers from Denmark is possible.

In Suffolk the Scandinavian element is less intensive. The names are more scattered and there are few pure Scandinavian names. There are only three names in -*by*, Ashby and Barnby, near Lowestoft, and Risby, near Bury St Edmunds, where Scandinavian influence is evident in the name of Thingoe Hundred 'the mound where the assembly met'. The chief concentration of Scandinavian place-names is in and around the island of Lothingland, between Lowestoft and Yarmouth, a low-lying area probably avoided by the early Anglian settlers. The English place-names appear to be late, Bradwell, Hopton, etc. 'Grimston hybrids' are common, Flixton, Corton, Somerleyton; Lowestoft (with a lost *Akethorpe*) and Lound are pure Scandinavian names, Kirkley and Hobland (ON *lundr*) hybrids; there are two names in -*by*. In two instances we can probably identify the man who gave his name to the place. Oulton is first mentioned in 1202 as *Aleton* 'Áli's farm'. In Domesday Book Oulton seems to have been called *Duneston*, which was held in 1066 by Ala, a man of Danish descent, whose name seems to have replaced that of the English *Dūn*. Brotherton in Hopton is not mentioned in Domesday Book, but in Browston Green in Belton, a parish bordering on

Hopton, Broder, a free man, held 60 acres as a manor, and it is not unreasonable to suppose that this man of Danish descent gave his name to Brotherton. Names in *thorp* are common in the county, but, apart from Lothingland, Scandinavian influence is scattered except in Colneis hundred, itself probably a Scandinavian name, where we have such names as Kirton, Grimston and Nacton (ON *Hnaki*).

THE NORWEGIAN SETTLEMENT

Vague and unsatisfactory as it often is in its details, the story of the Anglo-Danish conflict has been the theme of chroniclers and historians for centuries. Our knowledge of the Norwegian settlement of the north-west, on the other hand, is limited to a fragment of an obscure Irish annal, preserved only in a seventeenth-century manuscript, itself a copy of some unknown manuscript, first printed in 1860.[1] This Irish tradition seems to have originated in a contemporary chronicle of events and there appears to be no reason why we should not accept its outline of events as genuine history. Briefly, it records that the Norsemen left Ireland (probably in 902) under Ingimund, a Viking leader, and after a vain attack on north Wales, he approached Æthelflæd, sister of King Edmund and Lady of the Mercians, whose husband Æthelred was ill, and obtained permission to settle near Chester, 'where he would build huts and dwellings, for he was at this time weary of war'. But when he saw the wealth of the city and the choice land around it, he desired to possess them and he persuaded 'the chiefs of the Lochlanns and the Danes' to attack Chester. Their assault on the city failed, but that these Norsemen remained and settled in the district is abundantly proved by surviving place-names. Both Danes and Norwegians took part in the settlement. The 'Lochlanns' were the descendants of the Norwegians who had colonized Ireland in the early ninth century. They had become partly Celticised, were pagans and were joined by Irishmen known as 'Gall-Gháidhil', a term current for a short time in the ninth century for a native Irishman who had abandoned Christianity and joined the Norsemen. 'They were Scoti and foster-children to the Northmen . . . a people who had renounced their baptism, and they were usually called Northmen, for they had the customs of the Northmen, and had been fostered by them, and though the original

[1] *v.* F. T. Wainwright, *Ingimund's Invasion* (*English Historical Review*, LXIII 1948), pp. 145–169).

Northmen were bad to the churches, these were by far worse.' These Irish Norwegians had adopted Irish names, formed their patronymics in the Irish fashion, *Thorfinn mac Thore*, had borrowed Irish words and formed many of their place-names in the Irish way, with the defining element last.[1] But they had not abandoned their native language or their Norwegian personal-names. In Cheshire, ON *erg*, a borrowing of Gaelic *airigh*, MIr *airghe* 'a shieling' survives in Arrowe, where the term is found frequently in field-names like *Broad Arrowe*, *Smiths Arrowe*, etc. The mysterious Noctorum may contain OIr *cnocc* 'a hillock'. Norse elements such as *brekka*, *gil*, *slakki*, and others are found in field-names in the Wirral. The only certain example of Danish influence is Frankby, which contains the ODa *Franki*, corresponding to OWSc *Frakki*.

It is clear there was a compact colony of Scandinavians, chiefly Norwegians, in the Wirral, where there are eight names in -*by*, including West Kirby, named in distinction from an eastern *Kirby*, now Wallasey, Pensby, a hybrid, 'the village at Pen', a Celtic name, Whitby and Greasby, a Scandinavianisation of OE *Grāfes-byrig* (*Gravesberie* 1086) 'fort by the grove'. Irby is *Erberia*, *Irreby* c1100, 'fort of the Irishmen', a name given by Anglians to a settlement of Irish–Norwegian Vikings, with a later substitution of ON *by* for OE *burh* as Scandinavian speech became more common in the district. The early forms of Caldy, *Calders* 1086, *Caldera* c1245, 'cold islands', and of Red Stones, *Arnaldsheire* 1358, 'Arnald's islands', containing the ON plural *eyiar*, are evidence of the persistence of Scandinavian speech. Larton and Storton contain ON *leir* 'clay' and *stórr* 'big'. This Norwegian settlement in the west of Cheshire is separated by almost the width of the county from a small Danish settlement in the east, where we have five examples of the Danish *hulm* (Hulme, Kettleshulme, etc.), Toft, and Scandinavian personal-names in Rostherne (*Rauðr*) and Croxton (*Krókr*). These are to be associated with the Danish settlement farther north, near Manchester, and are probably due to settlements of Danes beyond the boundary fixed for Ceolwulf's English Mercia.

On the settlement of the rest of the north-west history is silent, but place-names prove its strength and its extent. It stretched along the coastal areas north of the Mersey to Westmorland and Cumberland, and east, beyond the Pennines, into the West and North Ridings of Yorkshire. In Lancashire, south of the Ribble, it is chiefly

[1] *v.* pp. 69–70.

along the coast, near and north of Liverpool, where we find traces in Roby, West Derby, Formby and Kirby, with Crosby (OIr *cros*, ON *kross*), undoubted Norse elements in Anglezark and Sholver 'the shielings of Anlaf and of Skialgr', whilst *breck*, *scale* and *slack* are common in minor and field names. Litherland is a pure Scandinavian name, ON *Hliðarland* 'wood on the slope', retaining the genitive ending *-ar*, as is Aintree (ON *eintré* 'lonely tree'), whilst Sefton is a hybrid, 'rush farm' (ON *sef*).

North of the Ribble, Norwegians settled throughout Amounderness and Lonsdale South of the Sands, in the lowlying lands near the coast and the rising land to the east. Scandinavian field-names are particularly numerous. Typically Norwegian are Grimsargh and Kellamergh 'shielings (*erg*) of Grímr and of Kelgrímr', Larbrick, Norbreck and Warbreck (*brekka*). Ireby on the Yorkshire border was a village of Irish Norwegians.

In Westmorland, in the old barony of Kendal, many typical Norwegian names are found among others of English origin. Common Norse elements occur in Haverbrack 'oat-hill' (ON *hafri*, *brekka*), Howgill, Leasgill, Mansergh 'Man's shieling' and Skelsmergh 'Skialdmar's shieling' (ON *erg*). Brigsteer is an inversion compound, 'Styr's bridge'. Norse features are found round Lowther and Ullswater in Tirril, *Tyrerhge*, a compound of ON *tyri* 'dry, resinous wood' and *erg*, Winder 'wind(y) shieling' and Reagill 'fox valley' (ON *refr* 'fox').

Irish–Norwegian influence is particularly strong in Cumberland, with inversion compounds in Aspatria 'Patrick's ash', Gillcambon 'ravine of Cambán', an OIr personal-name, Kirksanton (St Sanctán, an Irish saint), and Tarn Wadling, *Terwathelan* 1285, 'the tarn of Gwyddelan "the little Irishman" '.[1] In some of these names Scandinavian inflexions are preserved: Brotherilkeld, *Butherulkel*, an inversion compound, with the OWSc plural *búðir* 'Úlfkell's booths', a formation paralleled by Scarrowmanwick, *Scalremanoch*, containing *skálir*, the plural of OWSc *skáli* 'shepherd's summer hut', compounded with either OIr *Maenach* or *manaich*, genitive singular of *manach* 'a monk'. Common Norse elements are found in Birker 'birch shieling' (*birki*, *erg*) and Cleator 'cliff shieling' (*klettr*, *erg*); ON *gil* 'ravine, narrow valley', is common, as in Gill, Gillhead, Gillfoot, Catgill, Scale Gill, etc.; *skáli*, too, is common: Scales, Scaleby, Skelgill, Bowscale and Seascale. There are some 70 names in *-by*, including Aldby 'old village', Crosby, Langwathby 'village by the long ford', Sowerby 'farm on marshy ground'. Many of these contain OIr personal-names, others are late, containing post-Conquest names, as in Parsonby, Johnby, etc.[1]

From Cumberland and Westmorland the track of these Irish–Norwegians can be traced by place-names over the Pennines into the North Riding and from Lancashire into the West Riding of Yorkshire, where they must have been numerous in the Craven district. Here we have the Norwegian *erg* compounded with a Scandinavian personal-name in Battrix (Bǫðvarr's shieling) and Golcar (*Guthlaugr*) and with an OIr personal-name in Feizor and Fixby (*Fíach*). Other Norse elements occur in Raygill, High Scale and Scalebed. In the North Riding, in the western half, in Gilling, Richmondshire and Langbargh, there is very definite evidence of extensive Norse settlement, as well as on the coast near Whitby, the latter, no doubt, reached directly from the North Sea. These Irish Vikings, on their way east, quickly came into contact with the earlier Danish settlers and in places there was a considerable mixture of races, Norwegian, Danish and Anglian. The western limit of Danish settlement seems to have been in the neighbourhood of Danby on Ure and Danby Wiske, whilst its chief strength was in the half-circle of wapentakes round York, where *thorpes* are common, whilst the *gills* are almost entirely in the west.

The Norwegian movement from the north-west into Yorkshire culminated in 919 in the capture of York by Ragnall mac Bicloch, who was the first of a series of Irish Viking kings of York which lasted for thirty-five years, during which constant intercourse must have been maintained between Yorkshire and Ireland, with a constant increase of Irish–Norwegian settlers all along the route. In the western dales, in Lower Teesdale and in the Cleveland district the Scandinavian place-names are strikingly similar to those of the Lake District. We have pure Scandinavian names like Roxby 'Rauðr's farm', Upsall, from ON *up-salir* 'high dwellings', identical with the Swedish Uppsala, and Sowber Hill 'sunny hill' (ON *sólberg*); Scandinavian inflexions in Osmotherly, Skelderskew, ON *Skjaldarskógr* 'wood of Skjǫldr', and in the DB form of Upleatham, *Upelider* (ON *hlíðir*, nom. plur.), the modern form deriving from the dative plural *hlíðum*; OIr personal-names are found in Gatenby (*Gaithen*) and Melsonby (*Maelsuithan*); with abundant evidence of Norse

[1] *v.* pp. 49, 60.

influence in minor names and field-names. Scarborough is one of the few place-names of which we know the exact origin. From the *Kormakssaga* we learn that two brothers Thorgils and Kormak went harrying in Ireland, Wales, England and Scotland. 'They were the first men to set up the stronghold which is called Scarborough.' From two poems which Kormak addresses to his brother, we know that Thorgils was nicknamed *Skarði* 'the hare lip', hence the Scandinavian form of the name, *Skarðaborg*, found also in English as *Scartheborc* c1200, later *Scareburgh* (1414). Thorgils died in 967; the brothers' expedition to England took place immediately after their return from one to Russia in 966, so that Scarborough must have been founded late in 966 or in 967.

The mixture of races is well illustrated by such names as Danby, Normanby and Ingleby, each of which occurs three times in the North Riding. These denote villages of Danes, Norwegians and Angles and can have been given only by Scandinavians in districts where these races were in a minority. Irby is similarly a village of Irishmen, whilst Irton is the 'farm or village of the Irishmen', both emphasising that Irishmen were outnumbered in the neighbourhood, at Irby by other Scandinavians, at Irton by Anglians. There are no Normanbys in Cumberland and Westmorland, where the Scandinavian population was overwhelmingly Norse, nor are there any parallels in the East Riding, where the Scandinavians were almost entirely Danish in origin. In the West Riding we have Denaby and two examples of Denby, with another in Derbyshire. All have been tacitly accepted as synonyms with Danby, 'Denby was evidently a settlement of Danes in a predominantly English region'. If so, the name would have been bestowed on the village by speakers of English who would not have used the Scandinavian word *by*. Danes are unlikely to have named one of their own villages 'the village of the Danes'; in any case they would have used the Danish form, Danby. Denby is derived from *Dena-by* and Denaby from *Deniga-by*, both containing genitive plural forms of OE *Dene* 'a Dane', the compound being one of an English inflected form with a Scandinavian element, a type for which there is no parallel except where the first element is a personal-name. A solution of this problem may, perhaps, be found when the place-names of the West Riding have been fully surveyed.

Normanton, found four times in Nottinghamshire, thrice in Derbyshire and in Leicestershire, and also in Rutland and the West

Riding, is an English name given to a place inhabited by Norwegians in a district where Anglians were more numerous. Normanby, found four times in Lincolnshire and three times in the North Riding, was a village where Norwegians lived among an overwhelming Danish population. The distribution of these names is interesting and unexpected. They provide evidence for Norwegians in the eastern Danelaw who could hardly be Vikings from Ireland. They may have been Norwegians who had joined the armies of Halfdan and Guthrum, and the scanty evidence of their presence in the eastern Midlands may be due to the known hostility between Danes and Norwegians. The capture of York from the Danes and the establishment of a Norwegian kingdom would not conduce to friendly relations, and the Anglo-Saxon Chronicle of the tenth century not only gives proof of the internecine feuds between them but also provides evidence of similar hostility farther south. A poem interpolated in the Chronicle for the year 942 tells of the overrunning by King Edmund of Wessex of the Five Boroughs—Leicester, Lincoln, Nottingham, Stamford and Derby—and how the Danes there had previously suffered under the yoke of the Norsemen, in bonds of captivity until King Edmund redeemed them. The poem does not celebrate, as was once thought, the freeing of these boroughs by an English king from Danish tyranny, but the freeing of the comparatively christianised Danes in these boroughs from the cruel domination of later heathen Norse invaders, of whom we may, perhaps, have a reminder in the Normantons and Normanbys of this area.

HEATHENISM

Both Danes and Norwegians were heathens when they first began to settle in England, but place-names throw little light on their beliefs or their sacred places. Hoff (We) was the site of a heathen temple (ON *hof*), as was Ellough in Suffolk (ON *elgr*). The only place-name containing the name of a Scandinavian god is Roseberry Topping, a high hill on the north-western edge of Cleveland, earlier *Othenesberg*, the hill where Othin, the Scandinavian Woden, was worshipped. Plumbland (Cu), *Plumlund* 12th, 'plum-tree grove', is a compound of ON *lundr*, a term which in Sweden often denoted a place of worship, a meaning possible here, too, for Reginald of Durham tells us this was 'a grove dedicated to peace'. In England the word often means simply 'wood' and has no religious associations, but some names of wapentakes, as Aveland (L), Framland (Lei) and Wayland (Nf), ended in *lundr*, and, as *things* were often held in groves, these may have been heathen sanctuaries. ON *haugr* is a common term found also in names of wapentakes. In Greenhoe and Gallow (Nf) it must have its common sense of 'hill', but in some names the reference is to a tumulus, as at Thingoe (Sf), the mound where the *thing* met. In certain Lincolnshire hundred-names *haugr* is compounded with a personal-name found also in that of a neighbouring village, Haverstoe and Hawerby, Wraggoe and Wragby, Candleshoe and Candlesby. These hundreds took their names from moot-hills situated near the settlement of the local chieftain. In Scandinavia *things* were often held on grave-mounds, hence Wraggoe may well have been the burial-mound of Wraghi, the founder of Wragby. Other examples, *Leggeshou* and Legsby, *Katehou* and Cadeby, *Scalehau* and Scawby, may similarly bear witness to this heathen burial-custom. But it would be dangerous to assume that all compounds of *haugr* with a personal-name were proof of heathen worship.

Chapter Eight

THE FRENCH ELEMENT

THE Norman Conquest imposed on England a foreign aristocracy organised for war. It was a conquest, not a settlement or national migration. The victors at Hastings numbered little more than some 6,000 men. These Normans were descendants of Vikings whose presence in northern France had been tolerated in the hope that they would keep out others. They were the dominant race, but a minority; they remained a race of fighters, but adopted the language and religion of the country; they became Normans, Northmen by race, speaking a northern French dialect, born and bred in Normandy, a Duchy of France. In England, too, they were a dominant minority; Normans ultimately merged with the English; their language was absorbed by that of the defeated natives.

The first task of the conquerors in England was to build castles manned by Norman men-at-arms to hold down the country. English bishops and abbots were replaced by Normans. Law and administration, too, were controlled by Normans. French was the language of this ruling class, as well as of traders and merchants in the towns. French became fashionable and many people were bilingual. As late as the end of the thirteenth century, Robert of Gloucester wrote that men of rank still spoke French, although the lower classes stuck to English: 'If a man knows no French, people will think little of him.

. . . It is well known that it is the best thing to know both languages.'
The earliest proclamation in English by a King of England was that
by which, in 1258, Henry III declared his acceptance of the Provisions
of Oxford. It was also issued in French. Not until 1362, 300 years
after the Battle of Hastings, was Parliament opened in English, when
it was enacted that in future all court proceedings were to be in
English, though enrolled in Latin. Law French, however, continued
much longer and was not finally abolished until 1731. Even today
the royal assent to a bill in Parliament is given in French. All this
had a marked effect on the English language. Many French loan-
words were adopted and inflexions were considerably modified. But
here we are concerned only with the effect on place-names.

The pattern of the English countryside was largely fixed before the
Conquest. Most of our village names are to be found in Domesday
Book. Some few new villages grew up, with French names, but, in
general, what remained was the gradual clearing of woodland and
draining of marshes where new farms and hamlets were established.
One marked effect of the Norman Conquest on our place-names is
to be seen in the feudal and manorial attributes consisting of French
surnames added to English place-names which we have already discussed.[1]

The name of the Essex vill of *Fulepet* 'filthy hollow' was replaced
after 1086 by the more attractive French name Beaumont 'beautiful
hill', a name found also in Cumberland, Lancashire and Warwickshire, in Cornwall as Belmont, and, with the English pronunciation,
in Beamond End (Bk) and Beamonds (Sr). Other compounds of
bel or *beu*, revealing the French feeling for beautiful scenery, are not
uncommon; some may have been actually transferred from France:
Beachy Head (Sx) and Beauchief (Db) 'beautiful headland'; Beaudesert (St, Wa) 'beautiful waste (land)'; Beaufront Castle (Nb)
'beautiful brow'; Beaulieu (Ha), Bewdley (Wo), Bewley (Du, We)
'beautiful place'; Beaumanor (Lei) 'beautiful seat'; Beaurepaire (Ha),
Bear Park (Du), Belper (Db), Bareppa, Barripper and Bereppa (Co),
'beautiful retreat'; Beauvale (Nf) 'beautiful valley'; Belvoir (Lei) and
Bever Grange (D) 'beautiful view'; Bewbush (Sx) 'beautiful thicket';
Beamish (Du) 'beautiful mansion', identical with the French Beau-
metz. The French *bel assis* 'beautiful seat' occurs as Belasis (Du),
Bellasis (Du, Nb), Bellassize (ERY), Belsars Hill (C), Belsize (Herts,
Nth), Belsize Park (Mx) and Belsay Fields (Cu). Compounds with

[1] v. pp. 60–66.

mal are rare, but we have Malpas 'difficult passage' in Cornwall, pronounced *Mopus*, and in Cheshire and Malzeard (WRY) and Meshaw (D), *Mauessart* 1086, *mal assart* 'bad clearing'.

A site of strategic importance on the top of a precipice overlooking the Swale was chosen by Count Alan of Brittany for the castle of Richmond (Y) 'strong hill' which became the head of his honour. The Surrey Richmond was originally *Sheen*, a name surviving in East Sheen, and was a residence of the kings of England from the time of Edward I. In 1501 the palace was destroyed by fire but was rebuilt by Henry VII, who caused the name to be changed from Sheen to Richmond after his earldom of Richmond in Yorkshire. Ridgmont (Beds), earlier *Rugemund*, is a Norman–French name descriptive of the reddish sandstone ridge on which the village stands. Ridgmont (ERY) has the same meaning, with the same development. The normal form survives in Rougemont (WRY) and in the name of the Norman castle at Exeter, built on red sandstone. The Norman castle of Mountsorrel (Lei) owes its name to the pinkish granite quarried there (OFr *sorel* 'reddish-brown'). Although there are three places in France named Aigremont, no connexion can be traced between any of these and the Cumberland Egremont, so that it is probable that this is a new formation from OFr *aigre mont* 'sharp-pointed hill', an apt description of the castle site. The extensive earthworks of the Norman castle of Pleshey (Ess), which was the head of the Honour of Mandeville, derive their name from OFr *plaisseis* 'an enclosure park or forest, formed by a plashed hedge', one bent back towards the centre of an enclosure for purposes of fortification. In some instances the fence was one of living wood with interlacing branches, and in minor names, where there is no evidence of fortification, the reference must be to an enclosed park or forest. We have also a variant, OFr *plaissiet*, in Plessey (Nb), Plashet Grove (Ess), Plashett (Sx) and Plasset (Nf).

Newly established monasteries might be named from French convents. The Priory of Grosmont (NRY) 'big hill' takes its name from the mother priory of Limoges. The name of the Priory of Mount Grace (NRY) has replaced Bordleby, the ancient name of its site, as has Haltemprice (ERY), *haute emprise* 'great undertaking', which was moved to Newton shortly after its foundation in 1322. Jervaulx 'valley of the Ure' and Rievaulx 'valley of the Rye' contain OFr *vals*. Battle was named in commemoration of the Battle of Hastings. Rewley Abbey (O) 'royal place' was founded in 1281 by

Edmund, Earl of Cornwall, on land acquired by his father Richard, younger brother of Henry III, the only Englishman to become King of the Romans. Marmont Priory (C) is a name transferred from Marmonde (Lot et Garonne), whilst Kirmond le Mire (L) corresponds to the French Chèvremont and Quèvremont 'goat-hill'. ONFr *capele* 'chapel' survives in Capel (K, Sf, Sr) and Caple (He).

Minor names often recall ecclesiastical endowments: Ampers Wick (Ess) was the dairy-farm of the almoner of St Osyth's Abbey, Armoury Farm in West Bergholt (Ess) was part of the endowment of the Almonry of St John's Abbey, Colchester, The Alm'ners (Sr) of Chertsey Abbey, Anmers Farm (Berks) of Reading Abbey, Amery Court in Blean (K) of St Augustine's, Canterbury, and Upper and Lower Almonry (Sx) of Battle Abbey. Cannhall (Ess) and Ken Wood (Mx) both belonged to the *canons* of Holy Trinity Priory, Aldgate; Cannock Mill (Ess) was the dairy-farm of the canons of St John's Abbey, Colchester. Armathwaite (Cu) is 'the clearing of the hermit'; at Armitage (St), Hermitage Farm in Little Packington and Hermitage Bridge in Wootton Wawen (Wa) there were ancient hermitages; in 1406 'poor hermits of Haddenham' kept in repair the causeway over Haddenham Fen, an act of charity still recalled by the names The Hermitage in Haddenham (C) and Hermitage Sluice Bridge in Willingham; Hermit's Cave in Harthill (Db), where the hermit is mentioned in 1549, is cut from the solid rock and inside the cave still survives the partly mutilated figure of a crucifix.

SURVIVAL OF FRENCH TERMS

A French diminutive suffix survives in Claret Hall (Ess), 'Little Clare' as opposed to Clare (Sf), Hampnett (Gl), East Hampnett (Sx) and Cricket (So) 'Little *Cruc*' (hill). The Norman suffix -(i)ere, found in Normandy in such names as Quetterie and Toroudière, is found twice in England, though now well disguised. Garnons in Wormingford (Ess), *La Gernunere* (1231) 'the manor of the Gernons' was held in 1086 by Robert Gernun, in whose family it remained for 300 years. Miserden (Gl), *Musardera* 1187, 'Musard's manor' is also named from its Domesday lord. Hascoit Musard 'the dreamer' held *Grenhamstede* in 1086, an English name ousted by the Norman.

A certain number of less common French loan-words, sometimes legal terms, often referring to woodland or agriculture, are found, chiefly in minor names. Some of these, though not adopted into the

195

standard language, must have been current in popular use, at least locally. Devizes (W) is from OFr *devise* 'boundary', plural *devises*, ultimately from Lat *diuisae*, and often shortened in pronunciation to *Visez* or *Vyes*. The boundary was that between the hundreds of Potterne and Cannings which passed through the Castle, the former being chiefly in the king's hands, the latter belonging to the Bishop of Salisbury. The town of Devizes grew up round the Norman castle built by Bishop Roger in the twelfth century. The original name of Pipewell Abbey (Nth) was *Sancta Maria de Divisis*, so called because its demesne lands lay on both sides of Harpers Brook, here the boundary between the hundreds of Corby and Rothwell. Viza in Ashwater (D), the home of John *de la Vise* in 1330, Vizacombe in Inwardleigh and Vyse Wood in Morthoe all preserve the popular, shortened form which is found in surnames of the thirteenth and fourteenth centuries in Devon, Hertfordshire and Kent. Vyse Wood is on the borders of the parishes of Morthoe and West Down. The other two Devonshire places are not near a parish boundary but may have been on the dividing line between the manors of Ashwater and Henford, and Inwardleigh and Curworthy respectively.

Another French loan-word which must have had more than a local currency is ME *preye*, from OFr *pred* 'meadow', from Lat *prātum*. The earliest references to Delapre Abbey (Nth) are in Latin, *Sancte Marie de Prato* (1217); later we have the French forms *de la Preez* (1316) and *Delapre* (1328). Similarly, The Prae and Prae Wood (Herts) preserve the memory of the abbey of St Mary *de Pratis* or *Pre*, founded in 1194. The early spellings are *Preye* or *Pray*. The modern *Prae* is not found before the eighteenth century and is evidently an attempt to give a Latin appearance to a place-name adjoining Roman Verulamium. The word was common in Surrey, where we still have Pray Heath in Woking, Primemeads in Alfold (*Preystrete* 1559, *Preymead* 1775), Sudpray Farm in Worplesdon, Catsprey in Chiddingfold and field-names like Pre Mead and Pray Field in ten other parishes.

Less common, but worthy of note, are Joist Fen (C), *Agist fen*, *Gyste Fenn* (1507) and Justment (D), *Agismont* (1713), the former from ME *agist*, OFr *agister*, originally 'to admit cattle for a defined time into a forest', later 'to take in livestock to remain and feed at a certain rate', the latter from the abstract noun *justment*, *gistmont*, which came to be used of 'a piece of land of which the pasture or grazing is let'. In the court rolls of Denny (C) we find that the provosts

of the marsh in 1347 were fined 24*s.* for not mentioning the total of
the cattle in the marsh and for not making *agistment* accordingly,
whilst in 1559 an order was made that 'no man was to keep any *Geste*
Cattle in the marshes unless great neede require'. 'Joist cattle' in
Rackefenne in Littleport near Ely are mentioned in 1606, whilst part
of Wicken Fen was once called *Wicken Joyst fenn* (1708). OFr
bouverie 'ox stall' survives in Beufre (Ha), OFr *vacherie* 'dairy farm'
in Vachery (Sr) and OFr *bergerie* 'sheep-fold' in Bergerie (Ha).

AFr *assart* 'clearing in a forest', used of woodland converted into
arable by grubbing up trees and brushwood, is found in Sart Wood
and Assart Farm (Nth) and in Sart Farm (D). Other woodland terms
are found occasionally: Spinney (C, Sr), Cowdray (Sx), OFr *coudraie*
'hazel copse'; Salcey Forest (Nth), OFr *salceie* 'willow wood'; Clear
Wood (W) and Clearfields (Bk), OFr *clere* 'forest-glade'; Brail (W)
and Broyle (Sx), OFr *broile* 'a park or wood stocked with deer or
other beasts of the chase'. OFr *launde* 'forest-glade, woodland
pasture' is more common: Laund (La), Launde (Lei), Laund's Farm,
The Lawn, Lawn's Farm and Lund's Farm (Ess), Blanchland (Co,
Nb), and Kingsland (Wo). Temple Bruer (L) is from OFr *bruiere*
'heath', found also in Brewershill (Beds), Bruern (O) and Bruera (Ch),
where the French word has superseded the original English *Heath*.
Portsand Farm in Thorney (C) is identical with Postland (L) on the
other side of the Old South Eau, which is 'island called *le Purceynt*'
in 1415, from AFr *purceynt* 'enclosure', Lat *procinctus* 'girt about,
enclosed', and clearly refers to land in the marsh surrounded by
water. Purps (D) and Purprise (WRY) are from OFr *pourprise* 'close
or enclosure', a legal term used of encroachments upon the property
of a community or of the Crown.

Names like Houghton le Spring (Du), Walsham le Willows (Sf),
Capel le Ferne (K) and Bolton le Sands (La) are common and the
French *le* has often been wrongly interpreted. The full form of such
names survives in Chapel en le Frith (Db) and Brampton en le
Morthen (WRY) and was formerly often found in names in which
the preposition has now been lost. Barton le Street (NRY) is Barton
in le Strete in 1614, whilst Barton le Willows (NRY) is Barton *in the
Willos* in 1574. Thornton le Moor (NRY) is Thorinton' *in mora* in
1208 and Thornton *in the More* in 1327. These are translations of
the English form still found in Hutton in the Forest (Cu) and Norton
in the Moors (St). In early forms, Latin, English and French are used
indifferently. Thus, Thorpe le Vale (L) is to be interpreted as 'Thorpe

in the valley', Hamble le Rice (Ha) as 'Hamble in the brushwood', Walton-le-Soken (Ess) as 'Walton in the *soke* or special jurisdiction of the Bishop of London'. In the popular mind, this *le* later came to be regarded as a preposition meaning *on*, *with* or *by* and is so used in Haughton le Skerne and Preston le Skerne (Du), which are on the river Skerne, St Peter le Poor 'the church of the poor friars', St Mary le Bow built on 'bows' or arches of stone. In Marylebone (Mx) the original name of Tyburn was changed to Maryborn, from the church of St Mary, in an attempt to rid the name of its unpleasant association with the place of execution. With the loss of *r* in pronunciation, *Marybun* suggested association with Fr *bon* 'good' and popular etymology, with a gross contempt for gender, quite unnecessarily introduced the *le* under the impression that the name meant 'Mary the good'. There is no evidence that the *le* which survives in some 80 or so of these English names is in any way connected with the OFr preposition *lès* 'near' in such French place-names as Plessis-lès-Tours.

It is interesting to note how three not far-distant parishes came to be distinguished. The attribute of Ault Hucknall (Db) is OFr *haut* 'high', describing its position. Hucknall Torkard (Nt) preserves the name of Geoffrey *Torchard*, who held the manor in 1195; Hucknall under Huthwaite (Nt) was originally *Hothweit* (1208) 'hill-clearing'. Later, it came to be called *Hokenhale Houthwayte* (1330), and finally *Hukenall under Hucthwet* alias *Dirti Hukenall* (1519), English descriptions from its situation on the lower ground beneath the hill-clearing.

FRENCH INFLUENCE ON SPELLING AND PRONUNCIATION

The greatest influence of French on our place-names, however, was its effect on their written form and pronunciation. Anglo-Norman spellings are numerous and very many have not persisted, but a considerable number of English place-names still preserve French spellings and French pronunciations, particularly in districts where Norman influence was strong, in the neighbourhood of Norman castles and centres of administration, as we have already seen in our discussion of Cambridge and Grantchester. OE *Heðinningaham* 'farm of the followers of Hethin' was early reduced to Hedingham, where remains of the castle of the de Veres can still be seen; in the thirteenth century it was still further reduced to *Hengham*, just as the name of the hundred *Heðinningaford*, where the sheriff's tourn was held, is usually *Hidingford* in Doomesday Book, *Hengford* in the twelfth century, and now Hinckford.

The sound *ch* did not exist in Anglo-French before the vowels *e* and *i*. It was written *c*, pronounced *ts*, a sound soon simplified to *s* and sometimes so written. Matching and Messing (Ess) are identical in origin, OE *Mæccingas* 'the people of Mæcca', whilst the same personal name is found in Mashbury 'Mæcca's stronghold'. The French form survives in Messing and in Messings Mead Plantation in Matching; Mashbury appears frequently in the French forms *Massebirig* and *Messebire*, with a later change of *s* to *sh*; Matching preserves the English pronunciation, though it is often found in the French forms *Matcinga*, *Macinga* and *Massing*. French forms survive also in Cerne (Do), Cerney (Gl), Cippenham (Bk), identical in origin with Chippenham (C, Gl, W), Cirencester (Gl), Diss (Nf) 'ditch', Dissington (Nb), where the first element is certainly *dīc* and the whole name probably identical with Ditchampton (W), Flendish Hundred (C) 'ditch of the fugitives', named from Fleam Dyke; in Lintz and Lintzford (Du) 'hill' we have the French pronunciation of *linch*, whilst the modern spelling may be due to the tradition of a settlement of German sword-makers at Lintz Green; Whissendine (R) and Whissonsett (Nf), respectively 'the valley and the fold of the *Wicingas*'; Whissonsett may actually have been a secondary settlement of the Wicingas who gave their name to Witchingham (Nf); Sedgefield (Du), *Ceddesfeld* c1050 is 'Cedd's field', whilst Sezincote (Gl) preserves a Norman pronunciation of OE *cisen* 'gravel' and Seighford (St), *Cesterforde* 1086, is a Normanised form of Chesterford. The Norman pronunciation of *chester* is common in such names as Towcester (Nth), Wroxeter (Sa) and Craster (Nb), *Craucestr'* 1242 'crow'.[1]

Initial *s* followed by a consonant proved a difficult combination for Frenchmen, who often solved the problem by dropping the *s*. Nottingham was originally *Snotengaham* (868) 'the home of the people of Snot', a personal name meaning 'wise'. Norman influence was strong here. There was a Norman castle; Castle Gate was known alternatively as *the Fraunkisshgate* or *Frenshegate* 'Frenchmen's street', whilst the town was divided into the *burgus Francensis* or *le Frencheborgh* 'the French borough' in the neighbourhood of the castle and the *burgus Anglicus* or *Englisheburgh* 'the English borough', and from the early twelfth century onwards the name of the city appears only in its French form of Nottingham. Curiously enough,

[1] Cf. p. 26.

the daughter-settlement of *Snotington*, now Sneinton, retains its English *Sn-*, although, in compensation, it has undergone French influence of a different kind, the loss of the dental between the two vowels, as in Bainton (Nth, O), earlier *Badingtun*, Dainton (D), *Doddintune* 956, High and Low Toynton (L), *Tedintune* 1086 'farm of Tēoda' and Toynton All Saints and St Peter (L), *Totintune* 1086 'farm of Tota'. It is interesting to note that the initial consonant of Sneinton was lost in the DB form *Notintone* at a time when it was still retained in Nottingham and is still missing in Notindon Place in Sneinton. As early as 1286 there was official doubt as to the correct form, for a jury declared that 'the vill of Sneynton was never called Notington but was always Sneynton; Notington was part of the vill of Notingham'. Folk-memory was obviously at fault.

Trafford Park in Manchester preserves the name of the old manor of Trafford which was carved out of the township of Stretford, the ford where the Roman road from Chester to Manchester crosses the Mersey. The manor owes its name to the Trafford family, which itself took its surname from Stretford: Henry de Stratford (1206), Hugo de Straforde (1212). These French-speaking lords of the manor regularly spelled and pronounced their name *de Trafford* from 1200 onwards and, as the manor-house was situated at a considerable distance from the village, its name came to be dissociated from that of the village and persisted in its Normanised form, whilst the village itself preserved the English form of Stretford.

The French difficulty in pronouncing the English form of Shropshire, *Scrobbesbyrigscir*, has given us the modern (county of) Salop. The first step was to drop the *-byrig-* in the eleventh century *Scropscir*. In Domesday Book the pronunciation of *Shr-* was eased by the insertion of a vowel, *Sciropescire*. Then the initial sound was simplified to *s* and the first *r* dissimilated to *l*: *Salopescira* (1098). Salop was then used alone, although the fuller form was retained in Shropshire. Unlike Nottingham, the town kept its English form, though Norman forms were also used, *Sciropesberie* (1086), *Salopesberia* (1098). The development of the English name itself is not normal. We should have expected a modern *Shropsbury*, but the earlier *Scrobbesbyrig* seems to have become *Shrovesbury* and then *Shrowsbury*, a pronunciation still regarded as the correct one. But, on the analogy of words like *shew* and *show*, the spelling was altered to Shrewsbury.

The Norman *s* for initial *sh* survives in Selly Oak (Wo), identical with the common Shelley 'clearing on a shelf of land', that in Essex being found as *Sellege* in 1197; in Over and Nether Silton (NRY), identical with Shilton (Berks, Lei, O, Wa) 'farm on a bank or ledge'; in Singleborough (Bk) 'shingle hill' and Singleton (La), either 'farm with a shingled roof' or 'farm on shingly soil'.

For initial *Y*, a sound unknown to them, the Normans substituted *J*, which survives in Jarrow (which should have become *Yarrow*), Jesmond, *Gesemuthe* 1275, 'the mouth of the Ouse Burn', where French *-mond* 'hill' has also been substituted for *mouth*, Jagdon (Sa) 'cuckoo hill', Jevington (Sx) and Jervaulx (NRY) 'valley of the Ure', identical with Yordale (NRY).

The voiceless initial *th* of *thorn* was unknown to the Normans, who substituted *t*. This is normal in Norman personal-names of Scandinavian origin and persists in modern surnames such as Turkil and Turtle (*Thorkell*), Tustin and Tutin (*Thurstan*), Turbott and Tarbutt (*Thorbert*), etc., as well as in place-names: Turnworth (Do) 'thornbush enclosure', Torrisholme (La) 'Thorald's water-meadow', Tarleton (Gl), *Tornentone* 1086, a Norman variant of Thornton, Tusmore (O), *Toresmere* 1086 'lake haunted by a giant or demon' (OE *þyrs*). Ekwall has shown that Tarbock (La) derives from OE *þorn-brōc* 'thorn brook'. The place-name forms are occasionally *Thorbok*, but usually *Torbok*. The Norman influence is due to a Lancashire magnate, bailiff between Ribble and Mersey (1232–56), whose name is found as Henry *de Thornebroke* or *de Torbok* in the first half of the thirteenth century. East and West Horndon (Ess) appear in Domesday Book as *Torninduna*, a French pronunciation of the English *Thorndun* 'thorn hill'. With the division into two parishes, *Est-*, *Westtorndon* became *Est-*, *Westorndon*; the inevitable *Est-*, *West-orndon* was then re-spelled as East and West Horndon, through the influence of the neighbouring Horndon-on-the-Hill. The manor-house still retains the real English form, Thorndon Hall.

In names which contain two or more of the liquids *l*, *n* or *r*, loss of one or other of the consonants, dissimilation, assimilation and interchange took place in a way which defies all rules. For example, *r* has been changed to *l* in Bulphan (Ess), *Burgefen* 1246, 'the fen belonging to the *burg*', Bulstrode (Bk), *Burstroda* 1193, with a similar meaning, from OE *strōd* 'marsh', Bulverhythe (Sx), *Burewarehethe* 1229 'the hythe or landing-place of the men of the *burg*' (of Hastings), Salisbury, from OE *Searesbyrig*, and Shellingford (Berks), *Scaringaford* 931; *r* has been substituted for *n* in Durham, *Dunholm* c1000, 'hill-island'; Durham is on a hill almost surrounded by the Wear.

The English name is still used in the contracted Latin form *Dunelm* as the signature of the Bishops of Durham. A loss of *n* in the early forms persists in Dengie (Ess), *Deningei* 755, and Danbury (Ess), *Danengeberiam* 1086 'the fort and low-lying land of the Dæningas', and a similar development gives the clue to the development and modern forms of a number of difficult names in which the resulting *-iga-* abnormally becomes *-ege-*, *-ewe-*: Canewdon and Manuden (Ess), and Monewden (Sf). The development is shown most clearly in the forms of Mongeham (K), *Mundelingeham* 761, *Mundingeham* 1086, *Muningeham* 1195, *Monigeham* 1251, ¦the farm of Mundel's people' and Mongewell (O), *Mundingwillæ* 975, *Mongewel* 1086, 'the spring or stream of Munda's people'. A similar development accounts for Coney Weston (Sf), *Cunegestuna* 1086, Congerston (Lei), *Cuningestone* 1086, *Cunigeston* 1247, Coneysthorpe (NRY), *Coningestorp* 1086, Coneythorpe and Conisbrough (WRY), Conisby (L), Coniscliffe (Du), Conisford (Nf), Conishead (La), Conisholme (L), Coniston (La, ERY, WRY) and Conistone (WRY), in all of which the first element is ON *konungr* 'king' or a Scandinavian form of OE *cyning* 'king'.

In the southern counties, where *f* was pronounced *v*, *-feld* became *-veld*, later *-vell*, and was then wrongly regarded as a French name in *-ville* as in Barville (K) 'bare open-country', Clanville (Ha, So, W), and Glanvill (D), identical with Clanfield (Ha) 'clean, clear of shrubs, etc.', Enville (St) 'smooth', Longville (Sa), Marvell (IOW) 'pleasant', and Turville (Bk), identical with Therfield (Herts), from OE *þyrre* 'dry'. In the nineteenth century the French *-ville* was used to coin a few new names of a type more common in America, all hybrids, to which the French suffix was apparently supposed to add tone: Coalville (Lei), Ironville (Db), Bournville (Wa). The history of Woodville (Db) is interesting. On the 1836 Ordnance Map it is *Wooden Box Station*. A populous village of potters grew up in the neighbourhood of Butt House and was called 'Wooden-Box' or more commonly 'The Box', 'derived, as is well known, from a hut set up there for a person to sit in to receive the toll at the turnpike . . . this box was originally a port wine butt from Drakelow Hall'. In 1845 the name was changed from Wooden-Box to Woodville. It became a consolidated chapelry in 1847 and a civil parish in 1897 (PN Db 670). The Hampshire Waterlooville does not directly commemorate Wellington's victory. It grew up in the nineteenth century in the neighbourhood of an inn on the Portsmouth road called 'The Heroes of Waterloo'.

from the British spoken by Romano-Britons, but it is very doubtful whether the word was ever borrowed into Brittonic, since Welsh *caer* can hardly be derived from it. As Jackson suggests, it was probably borrowed from speakers of Latin living in the Roman towns, for which it is the OE word. Bede makes this quite clear: 'the city of *Rutubi Portus*, which by the English is corrupted into *Reptacæstir*' (now Richborough); 'a city which the English call *Hrofaescaestre* (Rochester), from one Hrof, that was formerly the chief man of it'. Hence its use as a common term in Caister (Nf), Caistor (L), Castor (Nth) and Chester le Street (Du), and in the compounds Chesterfield (Db) and Chesterford (Ess). Chester (Ch), originally named from the river Dee on which it stands and called *Deoua* by Ptolomy and *Deva* in the Antonine Itinerary, must derive from the Latin. In Bede it is called not only *ciuitas Legionum* 'city of the legions', clear evidence of the use of both Lat *ciuitas* and OE *ceaster* of Roman towns, but also *Legacaestir* and *Carlegion*, of which the former is an English translation of the Latin *castra legionum* 'camp of the legions' and the latter a Welsh translation, identical with the surviving Caerleon in Monmouthshire. By 1094 OE *Legacaestir* had been shortened to *Ceastre* in the Anglo-Saxon Chronicle and this has since survived as Chester. Such names as Doncaster, Winchester, Dorchester, etc., are hybrid formations created by the addition of this Latin loan-word (OE *ceaster*) to the Romano-British name. The appearance of a loan-word from Latin *faber* 'smith' in Faversham (*Fefres hám* 811, *Febres ham* 815) suggests a period of peaceful intercourse between the early Saxon settlers and a Romanised local population.

Lincoln was originally *Lindon*, identical with the Welsh *llyn* 'lake' (found also in King's Lynn), referring to a widening of the Witham. With the establishment here of a Roman colony, the name became *Lindum colonia* in the Ravenna Geography (c650), *Lindocolina* in Bede (c730), *Lindcylene* in the Anglo-Saxon Chronicle (942) and *Lincolnia* in Domesday Book (1086). The name is thus a Celtic–Latin hybrid borrowed from British speakers, probably in the early sixth century.

In spite of phonological difficulties, the identity of Speen (Berks) with the *Spinae* of the Antonine Itinerary seems certain. The name appears to be a Latinisation of a British name meaning 'thorn-bushes'. Aust (Gl), *Austan* 794, *Augusta* c1105, is Latin *Augusta*, but the reason for the name is unknown. Merevale (Wa), *Mirauall* 1148, *Mirevallis* 1154, appears to have been a purely Latin name, *mira uallis* 'wonderful valley', a type of name not infrequently transferred from the Continent by medieval monks. A monastery was established here in 1148. Later the name was associated with OE *myrig*, ME *miri*, *meri*, *muri* (*Mirival* 1188, *Murivale* 1316, *Merivale* 1444, *Mirrivale* alias *Merry Vale* 1733) and interpreted as a hybrid, 'merry valley'. Vaudey Abbey (L) is *Vallis Dei* 'the valley of God' in 1157; the modern form is a French translation.

Latin influence, however, is mostly evident in the feudal or descriptive attributes of parish-names. The feudal additions to a single name may vary, though they often have roughly the same meaning; the Latin attributes of many names have now been translated into English. Cerne Abbas (*Abbatis* 1291, *Monachorum* 1256) and Milton Abbas (*Abbatis* 1298) were abbeys in Dorset, whilst Winterborne Abbas (*Abbots* 1257, *Abbatis* 1341) belonged to the Abbey of Cerne. Here we now have the nominative *abbas* 'abbot' for the genitive *abbatis* 'abbot's' of the documents, corresponding to the normal Manningford Abbots (W), though we have Newton Abbot (D), *abbatis* 1241, *Abbots* 1338, *Abbas* 1387. Compton Abbas (West), in Dorset, belonged to Milton Abbey, but Compton Abbas (East), *Abbatisse* 1293, like Abbas Combe (So), *Abbatisse* 1327, was part of the possessions of the *abbess* of Shaftesbury. Here, *Abbas* is probably due to confusion of *Abbess* or *Abbess's* with the more common *Abbas* 'abbot' in other Dorset names. Popular pronunciation, especially after the dissolution of the monasteries, paid little attention to such niceties. Abbess Roding (Ess), belonging to the Abbess of Barking, is *Abbatisse* 1237, *le Abbesse* 1258, *Abbeys* 1518, *Abbasse* 1546, *Abbas* 1666, and *Abbots* 1653. A similar confusion is found in Great Wigborough (Ess), where Abbot's Hall, belonging to the same *abbess*, is *Abbesse* 1291, *Abbatisse* 1323, *Abbas* 1577. Here, the modern form is probably due to confusion with Abbot's Wick Farm in the same parish, which was owned by the Abbot of St Osyth and is always *Abbots*.

Other ecclesiastical attributes are Ashby Puerorum (L), assigned to the support of the choristers of Lincoln Cathedral (*puer* 'boy'); Zeal Monachorum (D), from the monks of Buckfast Abbey; Whitchurch Canonicorum (Do), from the canons of Salisbury Cathedral; Minchin Buckland or Buckland Sororum (So) was the site of a priory and was named from its nuns (OE *mynecen* 'nun', Lat *soror* 'sister'); Toller Fratrum (Do), to the Knights Templar; the neighbouring Toller Porcorum was famous for its pigs (*porci*), *Swynestholre* 1259, *Tolre Porcorum* 1341; Kingsbury Episcopi (So) was held by the Bishop of Bath (*episcopus*) in 1086; Bere Regis (Do), i.e. 'King's' (*rex*), was royal demesne before 1086; Lyme Regis (Do) became a royal borough in the reign of Edward I. In Bognor Regis the difference is quite recent, commemorating the convalescence there of George V in 1929.

Miscellaneous attributes are: Amney Crucis (Gl), said to be named from a cross (*crux*) in the churchyard; Blandford Forum (Do), *Cheping Blaneford* 1288, *Blaneford Forum* 1291, from its market, corresponding to the English Market Weston (Sf) and Chipping Norton (O), OE *cīeping* 'market'; Bradfield Combust (Sf) 'burnt', by the side of the more common ME *brende* in Brent Eleigh (Sf) and Brant Broughton (L); Barton in Fabis (Nt), with the English Barton in the Beans (Lei) and Thornton le Beans (NRY), with the French *le*; Marston Sicca (Gl) 'dry'. Collingbourne Ducis (W), earlier *Comitis*, was held by the earls (*comes*), later by the dukes (*dux*) of Lancaster. Easton and Weston in Gordano (So) preserve a curious Latinisation of a district-name, OE *gor-denu* 'muddy valley'.

Parishes of the same name were distinguished by reference to their size or situation. *Magna* and *Parva* are very common indeed, though now often restored to their native *Great*, occasionally *Much*, and *Little*: Chew Magna (So), Brandon Parva (Nf), Ashby Magna, Ashby Parva (Lei), Great Torrington (D), Little Gransden (C), Much Hadham (Herts), Much Dewchurch (He). Where parishes of the same name have been united, the plural name is combined with *ambo* 'both': Huttons Ambo (NRY), including High and Low Hutton, Luttons Ambo (ERY), a township combining East and West Lutton, and Wendens Ambo (Ess), from the union of Great and Little Wenden in 1662. Where parishes of different names were combined, their names are joined by *cum* 'with': Stow cum Quy (C), Stone cum Ebony (K). Situation may be indicated: Rickinghall Superior and Inferior (Sf), formerly *Upper* and *Lower*, Aston and Weston Subedge (Gl) 'at the foot of the ridge', Thorpe sub Montem (WRY), Bradwell juxta Mare (Ess) 'next the sea', Kingston juxta Yeovil (So), Weston super Mare (So) 'on the sea'; Ryme Intrinseca (Do), in contradistinction to the lost outlying manor of Ryme Extrinseca in Long Bredy. Warley Salop, formerly in Shropshire, now in Worcestershire, was so named to distinguish it from Warley Wigorn (Wo). The attributes are abbreviations of the Latin adjectives *Salopensis* and *Wigornensis* 'belonging to Shropshire and Worcestershire' respectively. Ely Porta (C) referred originally to a gate (*porta*) of the monastery preceding that of Walpole's Gate House.

Chapter Ten

FIELD-NAMES

IF we are to be accurate in our use of terms, 'field-names' should be used only of the names of enclosed areas of arable and pasture land which are never found on the Ordnance Survey maps. They are largely a creation of the post-enclosure period and belong to the late eighteenth and early nineteenth centuries. Many of them preserve ancient names of earlier and larger areas of unenclosed land, but new names had to be found for the numerous new units newly enclosed. Some were named from distinctive local features of historical or topographical interest, but very many of the names are commonplace and uninteresting, relieved from sheer monotony only by sporadic examples of rustic humour. In the parish of Barby (Northants), out of some 340 fields, 200 or more have names like *Long Close*, *Short Ground*, *Ryeland* and the like, whilst a mere 20 or 30 present any features of interest. In Cambridgeshire, surviving field-names, on the whole, lack distinction. In Newton, 22 out of 45 fields are now nameless. In Eltisley, the first six fields are simply numbered *First*, *Second Field*, etc., whilst such names as *Allotments*, *Engine Shed Field*, *Station Field* and *Tin Sheds Field* have every appearance of modernity. *Soldiers Field* was devoted to allotments for ex-service men after the 1914–18 war. In the North and East Ridings of Yorkshire modern field-names are similarly uninteresting; the numerous names of minor places found in medieval documents have been completely forgotten.

Not all these field-names are without interest. Crow Hill in Steeple Morden (Cambs) is recorded in 1380 as *Crouȝhulledowne*. The first element might be OE *crōh* 'saffron' and this seems likely when we find a *Saffron ground furlong* in the parish in 1675. But when we learn that the hill is only just south-east of a Roman cemetery where urns have been discovered, there can be little doubt that the name means 'hill where crocks were found', from OE *crōg*, *crōh* 'vessel, pitcher'. Fundamentally, there is no difference between these field-names and well-known place-names like Sheffield 'open country on the banks of the Sheaf', Bradford 'broad ford' or Bristol, earlier *brycg-stow* 'site of a bridge'. They have undergone similar changes but, as they are names of small places, used only locally, they are recorded less frequently and are more liable to be exposed to the influence of local dialect and popular etymology. In Foxton (Cambs) in 1328 was a place called *Oseloke* 'muddy enclosure'. On the Tithe Award of 1840 it appears with an intrusive *t* and a weakening of the ending, *Ostlick Meadow*. The *o* was pronounced with the long vowel which used to be common in *often* and *cross*, which could be written *orfen* or *crawss*. Today the name is *Horselick's Field*.

Still more interesting, both in development and meaning, are two Essex field-names, identical in meaning, but very different in their modern form. Quindal Hole in Stebbing is *Congeoneshole* in 1287, *Quonionshole* in 1594, *Quingeonshole* in 1595 and *Quendonshole* in 1676. Konjohns Hole in High Easter has diverged less from its original form, but at one time looked like becoming *Queen Joan's Hole*: *Canyoneshole* 1401, *Congeonshole* 1404, *Quenyonyshole* 1497, *Quenjohanyshole* 1507. Both testify to a local belief in dwarfs and changelings (AFr *cangeon*, ME *cangun*, *kongon* 'changeling'). Another example is Conjoint Lane in Tideswell (Derbyshire), *Congins Gate* 1764. Nunn Mills in Hardingstone (Northants) is *Quyn Johns* alias *Quingeons Mills* alias *Nunne Mills* in 1591 and is named from the nuns of the neighbouring Delapre Abbey. The lost alternative name, reminiscent of some of the forms above, refers here to Queen Joan of Navarre, second wife of Henry IV, whose dowry included the land on which the mills stood. Stebbing provides us with another warning that appearances are often deceptive. Gentrys is *Chelmetrewe* in 1422, 'Ceolhelm's tree'. Later forms prove the correctness of the identification: *Chemtre* 1517, *Chentrye* 1567, *Chentrees* 1598,

Gentrye 1615. But Gentries Field in Pebmarsh owes its name to the croft held by Richard Gentry in 1390, *Gentriescroft* 1583.

A preliminary report on a survey of the field-names of Lancashire and Cheshire has been published for the Lancashire Hundred of Amounderness. The names are taken from the Tithe Award Schedules of c1840 and run into tens of thousands. Most of the field-names are simple self-explanatory names which arouse little interest, names by the hundred of fields, meadows, hays and crofts distinguished by their shape, size, position, function and character, or preserving the names of owners or tenants. But they are not entirely devoid of historical interest. They may illustrate geological or soil conditions, or provide the agricultural historian with names of crops and stock and agricultural terms. The local historian will find references to old buildings, fords and other historical features, sites of vanished village crosses, forgotten village wells and mills which can be located exactly from the maps which accompany the awards. Names like *Canal Field* and *Methodist Nook* are obviously comparatively modern; some are clearly nicknames: *Hundred Acre* and *Many Days Work* for fields of only half-an-acre; *Little Breakfast* (21 acres), *Sweet Lips*, *Dirty Shanks*, *Mountain of Poverty* and *Pudding Pye*; some can be traced back to the thirteenth century. Reference is found to ancient customs: *Cuckstool Field*, *Duckstool Lindal*, *Maypole Hill* and *May Day Field*; or to local legends and superstitions: *Boggart Hole*, *Hob Croft* and *Witch Carr*. Earlier reference to witches is found in Hascombe (Sr), *Hescumb* 1232, Hescombe (So), *Hascecomba* 1086, *Hetsecumb* c1150, 'valley of the witch' (OE *hætse*), and in Hessenford (Co), from *hægtessena ford* 'ford of the witches' (OE *hægtesse*). Great and Little Abbeystead, lying in the loop of the Wyre, suggest that this may have been the original site of the Abbey of Wyresdale, founded towards the end of the twelfth century but removed within a few years to Woney on the Irish lands of its founder. But the most valuable result of this survey of modern field-names is the proof it provides of an extensive settlement in Amounderness of Scandinavians—and these Norwegians—in such numbers as to give rise to an Anglo-Scandinavian language of which distinct traces still persist after a thousand years. Some five dozen different Scandinavian elements survive in these field-names, including Norwegian test-words like *breck* 'slope, hill', *gill* 'ravine, narrow valley', *scale* 'hut' and *slack* 'valley', alongside the Irish–Norwegian *erg* 'hill-pasture'. Not a single safe example of the Danish *thorp*, *hulm* or *booth* has been noted.

Although not strictly accurate, the term 'field-name' is also used of the innumerable minor place-names found in documents of all periods, names which have seldom or never appeared on any map and have long ceased to be used. Many of them are on record only once or twice, often in obviously corrupt forms, and interpretation is difficult and frequently impossible. Consequently, it is unfortunate that in its recent volumes the Place-name Society has shown signs of abandoning its former caution in dealing with such names. Its publications are regarded as authoritative and local historians and others are liable to accept as definitive etymologies which cannot be accepted without reserve. In the *Place-names of Oxfordshire*, for example, *Cayseriswere* (p. 25) is derived from OE *Cāsere* 'Caesar', a personal-name which is found only in the genealogies of Anglo-Saxon kings, alongside mythological names like *Woden*. The place-name is not recorded before 1405 and must derive from some medieval owner with the surname which still survives as *Cayzer* or *Keysor*, found in Oxfordshire as early as 1195 in the form *le Keiser*, a nickname for one who had played the part of Caesar in some medieval pageant. The derivation of *Cositer Field* (p. 151), noted only once in 1685, from *cot-stow* 'cottage site' is improbable, if not impossible. True, the suggested element is common in Oxfordshire field-names as *Costow* and *Coster*, but the medial *i* of *Cositer* suggests other possibilities, none of which can be proved. *Jobs Balk*, *Job's Close*, *Job's Copse* and *Jobs Piddle* are cited as derogatory nicknames parallel with *Hungryhill*, *Purgatory* and *Hang-dog Leys* (p. 443). But *Jop* and *Job* are found as Christian names as early as 1185 and as surnames from 1202 onwards, and these place-names may well have been named from former owners. Jupeshill Farm in Dedham (Essex) undoubtedly owes its name to Matthew *le Jop*, who held land near by in the reign of Edward III, whilst the still surviving field-name Jobs Treat in High Easter in the same county is a corruption of *Jopp's street*, in or near which Geoffrey and John *Joppe*, between 1279 and 1337, had a croft, a garden and a cottage (*Joppescroft, -gardyn, -kot* 1338). The Cambridgeshire *Jonah's Field* must be a nickname for a piece of land which brought the farmer no luck, for *Jonah* is not a medieval surname, and consequently we cannot dismiss the possibility that *Job* was similarly applied at times to land productive of nothing but trouble and misery, but we must not ignore more prosaic possibilities.

Occasionally the scholar is rewarded by discovering in the midst of much unpromising material a field-name which helps to identify some place of historical importance. Some years ago Mr F. G. Gurney identified the *ðiodweg* in a Chalgrove charter of 926 A.D. with an unusually broad green-way in Eggington (Beds) known locally as Ede Way, which is clearly the direct descendant of the ancient name *ðiodweg*, a compound of OE *þēod* 'people, tribe', the equivalent of the Latin *via publica*, used of a public, national road and of important fords on such roads, the memory of which is still preserved in names like Thetford (C, Nf) and Tetford (L). The compound became ME *Thedewey* and later, by a common process of mis-division, *The Edewey*. Mr Gurney shows further that the ford which carried the road across the Ouzel and up the hill towards Wing is to be identified with a place *Yttingaford* mentioned in the Anglo-Saxon Chronicle under the year 900 A.D., in a deed of 1324 as *Tuttingford*, in another of 1511 as *Tyttyngford hyll* and in the Tithe Award of 1836 as *Tidenford*, a name, too, which does not appear on the map but survives locally as *Tiddingford Hill*, pronounced *Tiddenfoot* or *Tinfoot*. The initial *T*, as often, is due to the preservation of the final *t* of *æt* in *æt Yttingaford*. '(at) the ford of the *Yttingas*', a folk-name which must be associated with the personal-name underlying *Yttinges hlawe* in a Berkshire charter of 942, now Titlar Hall in Lower Appleton, with the same development of initial *T*.

It is not always possible to equate such names with a modern survival but, even so, the identification of the site, if only approximate, is of historical importance. The Anglo-Saxon Chronicle, under the year 584, states that Ceawlin, king of Wessex, and a certain Cutha fought with the Britons in the place called *Feþan leag*, where Cutha was killed, and that Ceawlin, after taking many towns and innumerable spoils of war, returned in anger to his own land. This entry was for long of little use to historians because there were conclusive etymological reasons for rejecting the various sites proposed for the battle, which included places as far apart as Faddiley in Cheshire and Fretherne in Gloucestershire. But Sir Frank Stenton noted a place-name *Fethelee*, corresponding exactly to the *Feþan leag* of the Chronicle, in a final concord of 1198 relating to Stoke Lyne in north-east Oxfordshire. This identification, suggested by the identity of names, is strongly supported both by the geographical position of *Fethelee* and by the meaning of *Feþan leag*. This is apparently a compound of OE *fēða* 'a band or troop' and *lēah* 'a wood', and it is interesting to note that *Fethelee* is definitely said to be a piece of woodland. The parish of Stoke Lyne occupies a stretch of undulating ground a few miles to the north of the belt of woodland which in early times connected the forests of the upper Thames valley with those of the East Midlands. This tract was the natural northern boundary of the districts dependent on Eynsham, Benson and Aylesbury, which, according to the Chronicle, the West Saxons had conquered from the Britons in 571. The next stage in the West Saxon advance towards the north may well have opened with a battle for the possession of the upland country immediately behind this barrier.

A similar discovery of a solitary field-name has thrown light on an obscure episode of the campaign of 1016 between Cnut and Edmund Ironside. According to the Anglo-Saxon Chronicle, Edmund, after an indecisive battle at Sherston in Wiltshire, collected a new army for the relief of London, which the Danes were then besieging. He marched to London, keeping, according to the Chronicle, north of the Thames, came 'out through *Clæighangra*', and relieved the garrison. No name corresponding to *Clæighangra* had been noticed anywhere on the probable line of Edmund's march until the editors of the *Place-names of Middlesex* discovered a reference in an Assize Roll of 1294 to a place called *Clayhangre extra villam de Toteham*, now, apparently, represented by Clayhill Farm in Tottenham, which they have reasonably identified with the *Clæighangra* of the Chronicle. It would appear, therefore, that Edmund, anxious to conceal his approach from the Danes at London, kept behind the screen of the Middlesex woodlands until he reached the line of Ermine Street at Tottenham and then descended quickly on the city. A strong argument for this identification is that it explains the surprise of the Danes at Edmund's appearance which is implied by the language of the Chronicle.

Of less importance historically, but of interest not only as identifying an unknown place in an Anglo-Saxon charter but also for its unusual development and long persistence, is the discovery of the site of *Spachrycg*. The name occurs in a charter of 814 relating to Bexley (Kent) which includes the names of the swine-pastures belonging to the estate. One of these *heanyfre* was correctly identified by Henry Bradley as Hever '(at the) high bank', the boundary of which, according to the charter, was to the east of *spachrycg*, which Wallenberg was unable to identify. In an unpublished note among the Streatfeild papers, Dr Gordon Ward notes that the place occurs in local documents as *Spokereg* in 1327 and as *Spokeregge* in 1499 and finally ran it to earth on the Tithe Map of 1841, where the name appears as *Old*

Pokerage, Old Pokerage Mead, Old Pokerage Hop Garden and *Pokerage Field*. The map makes it clear that the name originally covered an area on the border of the artificial lake in the grounds of Hever Castle, between the woodland and the water in Chiddingstone, and that the meadow and Pokerage Field are now beneath the waters of the lake. The loss of the initial *S* is uncommon and interesting and without work on local field-names and local knowledge the identity of *spachrycg* with Pokerage could not have been made.

The persistent enclosure of woodland and marshland throughout the Middle Ages is revealed not only in the names of minor places but also in numerous field-names both lost and surviving. The most common term, ME *innam* 'a piece of land taken in or enclosed', may be from ON *innám* in the North and Midlands where it survives in Inham (L), Enholmes (ERY) and Inholmes Road (Nt) and is found occasionally in Cumberland and Nottinghamshire field-names. The term is much more common in the south, where it must be from an unrecorded OE **innām*. In Sussex it survives five times as Inholms and is common in field-names in the Weald. In Surrey we have Inhams, Inholms (thrice) and Ninehams, with numerous field-names, including Inhams, Innome, Inhome, Innims, In Hams, Innams and Inghams, the earliest example being *Inname* (1218). In Essex, where in 1367 we have four references to payments of rent in Felsted 'for one Innome', it is found only in field-names, though we have an early example, *le innome* in the reign of Henry II. In Cambridgeshire it survives as Inholms and four times as Inham(s), mostly in the fenland. Elsewhere it is rare. In Bedfordshire, Hertfordshire and Surrey we have the less common OE **inning*, with a similar meaning, found occasionally in field-names and surviving in Innyngs House, Ninning's Farm and Ninnings Wood (Herts), in Ninnings *alias* Ninnets in Nazeing on the Essex side of the Lea, and in Ninneywood (Bk). In the marshes of Woolwich and Wapping *inning* was used of reclaimed marshland.

A similar Scandinavian term is ON *intak*, found in field-names in Cumberland, Nottinghamshire, Warwickshire and Yorkshire and surviving in Intake in Sheffield (pronounced *Intek*). In Amounderness Hundred (La) it is found in most townships as *Intack* and is used of land enclosed or reclaimed from moor, marsh, woodland, sea or river. It seems to have been particularly common in the eighteenth and nineteenth centuries, probably because of the numerous enclosures then made. ON *afnám* regards enclosure from the opposite point of view, land 'taken out', 'land detached from an estate', 'a plot of land newly taken into use from undeveloped land'. It survives in Avenham (La) and is fairly common in field-names in Cumberland and the East and North Ridings of Yorkshire in the forms Avenham, Ofnam and Ovenham. In Amounderness it survives as Avenham Field, High and Long Enam, Low Eanam and Evenham.

The history of two other terms for enclosure is obscure. Both are used of land enclosed from the fallow land and put under cultivation. ME *inheche*, found in field-names in Warwickshire, Wiltshire and Shropshire in the forms *Innage*, *Image*, *Inhedge*, *Innidge* and *Ennige*, has been associated with OE *hæcce* 'fence, rails', hence 'a fenced-in area'; ME *inhōke*, with the same meaning, and also of doubtful origin, has been associated with OE *hōc* 'hook' and may denote what results from a process of 'in-hooking', hooking or bringing into cultivation. It survives in Innox Mill, Ennix Wood and Ennox Wood in Wiltshire and is common in field-names in Wiltshire, Oxfordshire, Somerset and Gloucestershire as Inhooks, Innocks, Innicks, Innex, Enocks, Enock, Hinnocks and Ninnicks. Another field-name element, common in Wiltshire and Oxfordshire and found also in Somerset and Gloucestershire, ME *hecchinge*, may be related to these. It is the word *hitching*, recorded in the *English Dialect Dictionary* from Oxfordshire as used of 'part of a field ploughed and sown during the year in which the rest of the field lies fallow' and is to be associated with the word *hitch* used in Oxfordshire, Berkshire and Wiltshire of the changing of crops in an open or common field, and the term *hitchland* or *hookland* used of 'a portion of the best land in a common field, reserved for vetches, potatoes, etc., instead of lying fallow for two years'. In modern field-names it takes the form of Hitching, Hitchen, Hitchin, Hitchens, Hitchings, Hutchings, Itchen and Itchin.

Enclosures and boundaries are productive of disagreement. The best-known place-name which recalls ancient disputes is the Debateable Land in Cumberland, earlier *Threpelandes*, from OE *þrēap* 'dispute, quarrel', found also in four examples of Threapland, in Threapthwaite and in three field-names in the same county. Elsewhere we have Threapcroft and Threapland (WRY), Threaphow (La), Threapwood (Ch) and Threepwood (Nb). Fleet Farm in Harlestone (Nth) is deceptive. Its earliest form was *Flitlond*, found in field-names twice elsewhere in the county, and in *Flitlond* (Nt) and *Flitlonddene* (C), all from OE *(ge)flit* 'strike, dispute', which survives also in the place-names Flitteridge Wood (Sx), Flitteris Park (R) and

214

Flitwick (W). In Northamptonshire, too, we have place-names Flitnell Barn and Flitnells Farm, with one or two fields named *Flitnell(s)*. These are found earlier in fuller forms as *Flittenhill*, from *fliten*, the past participle of OE *flītan* 'to dispute, quarrel', found also in *Flitenlonde* (O) and *Flitenelond* (C). Many of these 'disputed lands and hills' were situated near a parish boundary. Of like meaning, but less numerous, are compounds of OE **strūt*, from *strūtian* 'to struggle'. Studborough Hill, on the boundary between Staverton and Catesby (Nth), is *Stroteberewe* and *Struteberue* in the fifteenth century, OE *strūt-beorg* 'hill of strife or contention'. It does not occur as *Studbury Hill* until 1712. Sutton Street in Bearstead (K) has undergone even greater simplification and the modern form is entirely misleading. From 1254 and throughout the fourteenth century it is spelled *Strutton* or *Strotton* and is clearly a compound of *strūt*, 'the farm of disputed ownership'. In Surrey we find field-names surviving as Stroudhams (earlier *Stroutham*) in Byfleet and Streetfield (*Strotefeld* 1312) in Titsey, both on parish boundaries. Among modern Amounderness field-names we have Stroot Wood, which has been regarded as a form of *Street* and associated with a possible Roman road. The undoubted development of *Strotefeld* to *Streetfield* in Surrey suggests caution. Earlier forms might show that some of the Lancashire field-names Street Croft and Street Field, and even Strait Meadow, may have a less obvious origin. Wrautam, on the boundary of the parish of Walsgrave on Sowe (Wa), is *Wrotholme* in 1304, with frequent *-holme* except in *le Wroutham* (1356) and *Wrouthom* (1411). The second element is certainly ON *holmr*, whilst the first would seem to be OE *wrōht* 'accusation, crime, strife', found in *wrohthangra*, a boundary-mark in an OE charter relating to Sunningwell (Berks). Both the water-meadow and the wooded hill were once objects of dispute. This same uncommon element *wroht* survives also in the field-name Wrothy in Eynsham (O), *Wrothey* 1284, *Wroghtehey* 1363, 'island of debate' or 'low-lying land in dispute', and in a lost field-name *Wroughthull* in Ashwell (Herts). Note also *Disputforlang* (c1210) in Thomley (O).

Field-names often provide us with the last trace of some manorial holding or ancient tenurial custom. Daber Noons in Duxford (C) was held in 1200 by Roger *de Abernuin*, a surname still preserved on the map in Stoke Dabernon (Sr). Pounces Garden in Clavering (Ess) recalls the one-tenth of a knight's fee held here by William *Pucyn* in 1248. St John's Ley in Ashley cum Silverley (C) was part of the possessions of the Hospital of St John of Jerusalem, and Abbots Mead in Aldenham (Herts) of those of the Abbot of Westminster; King's Close in Hexton (Herts) was held by Henry VIII for a short time after the dissolution of St Albans Abbey; Bone Wick in Redbourn (Herts) owes its name to Alexander Bone, a monk of St Albans in 1380; Mince Croft in North Weald Basset (Ess), formerly *Mynchynhopes*, belonged to the nuns (OE *myncen*) of Clerkenwell, whilst Little Lepers in Ilford, *Lepersgarden* in 1456, preserves the memory of a hospital for lepers. College Meadow in Thorpe (Sr) represents lands once held by the Dean and College of St Stephen's Westminster, whilst the fields called Upper and Lower Temple in Addington (Sr), *le Templefeld* 1320, were part of the land granted to the Knights Templar in 1232 and Great and Little Emple Marsh in Walthamstow (Ess), *Temple Marsh* 1594, were part of the Templars' lands whose name still survives in Temple Mills in Hackney on the opposite side of the Lea. More interesting than any of these is the field called Marrowbone Acre in Mitcham, earlier known as *Seyntmaryebernes*, the barns belonging to the priory of St Mary Overy in Southwark. In 1292 there is reference to a messuage and tenement in Thurleston near Ipswich called *Cristmeslond*. In addition to paying a rent of 21*d.* yearly and doing four days' work in autumn for which he received his food thrice a day, the tenant had to pay the lord of the manor a cock and three hens each Christmas, and it was clearly from this custom that the land had its name. But *Christmasyards Wood* in Trimley St Mary owes its name to its owner in 1327, John Cristemasse, whilst Christmas Hill in Bishops Itchington (Wa) has a still different origin. It is a corruption of *Cristemelhull* (1246) 'the hill on which stood a cross' (OE *cristelmæl*).

Similar problems arise with other names. Paternoster Hill in Waltham Holy Cross (Ess) was part of the endowment of the obit lands of the abbey, whereas Paternoster Heath in Tolleshunt Knights owes its name to a John Paternostere who lived here in 1448. Paternoster Bank (Berks) was the virgate in East Hendred held in the reign of Edward I by John Paternoster by service of saying a paternoster every day for the king's soul. Both tenant and land owed their names to the service. To which of these classes belongs Paternoster Field in Great Bookham (Sr), it is impossible to say.

Lands named from religious association are by no means uncommon. The modern *Holybread* is found in the fourteenth century in such field-names as *Halybredelond* and *Halebredfeld*, endowments for purchasing the holy bread distributed after the mass. Compounds of *bell* and *lamp* are particularly common, as Bell Butts, Land, Field, Acre, Meadow, Piece and Croft, Bell Lawn and Leaze, Bell Rope Field, along with Rope Croft and Rope Acre. It has been suggested that some of the Bell Fields, etc., may be named from a neighbouring inn, but this source must be rare. The influence of inn-signs on sur-names has been much exaggerated. Many of these can be shown to derive from nicknames or topographical terms long before such inn-signs were known, whilst some of the field-names occur early and for others there is no doubt of their origin. Bell Field in Blechingley (Sr) is stated in a deed of 1586 to have provided *beelropes* for the church, whilst Bell Land in Wardington (O) is described in the Enclosure Award of 1760 as the 'Allotment of the Trustees of the Curfew Bell'. The Cropredy Bell Land Trust was instituted in 1513 by Roger Lupton, vicar of Cropredy, for the keeping of the church clock and the ringing of the curfew and day bell and the rent from the land is applied to this purpose. The rent of Bellringers Close in Cubbington (Wa) was used for the upkeep of the church bells. A Northampton-shire field is *Belleropes* c1320. *Lamplands* in Steyning (Sussex) is said to have provided the lights for Steyning church and *Lamp Close* in Cheam (Sr) may have the same origin, the possibility of which is proved by the reference to *Laumpelonde* in a Cambridgeshire docu-ment of 1250, though, in the absence of early forms, we can never be quite certain that *Lamp* should not really be *Lamb*. In Bruern (O) there was once a field called *Vestry Light*.

So abundant is the field-name material available and so interesting from varied points of view are many of the names, that we can deal here only with typical selections and isolated names. Among lost field-names worthy of record we may note *le Kukkyngstole* (1414) in Takeley (Ess), *le Tombrel* (1378) in Ashwell (Herts) and *le Schel-vyngstole* (1292) in Oxford which recall the medieval punishment of scolds by ducking them in the village pond. The ducking-stool was also called a cucking-stool, a tumbrel and, less commonly, a shelving-stool. Light may be thrown on the structure or state of bridges: *Bredenebregge* (1374), made of planks; *Stonenbrig* (1277), made of stone; *Thele bridge* (1513), a plank-bridge; *la Trowenebregge* (1339), from OE *trēowen* 'made of wood'; *le Handbrigge* (13th), a bridge with a hand-rail; *la Voutbrigge* (1314), one of vaulted structure; *Stokkene-brigge* (1372), made of wooden stocks; *Fallendebregge* (1378), falling, ruinous; *Omannebrugge* (1398), one wide enough for one man only at a time; *Standefast Brigge* (15th), so narrow that traffic-blocks were frequent; *eorðbrycg* (10th) and *Eorthenbrugge* (14th), denote a causeway made of earth or turves, as in Risebridge (Ess), Rice Bridge (Sx), Rising Bridge (Nth) and Ridgebridge (Sr), from OE *hrīs* 'brushwood'.

For many field-names we have no early forms at all, and this applies particularly to names of the nickname type. Most of these are probably due to rustic humour, but the changes and corruptions which well-documented field-names have certainly undergone should lead to caution. Obreys in Theydon Garnon would most probably be regarded as a corruption of *Aubreys* but for its occurrence as *Oldburye* and *Eldebury* in 1497, clearly 'the old manor-house'. Dairy Wood in Alphamstone, *Derhaye Woode* 1508, was a 'deer-enclosure', not a dairy, whilst Great and Little Tweech in Good Easter are named from a double gate (*Twyhacche* 1453).

Lousy is fairly common in field-names and is usually regarded as a derogatory nickname. Examples are seldom early and often inconclusive, but the evidence in general suggests that the name was rare as a nickname. In modern field-names we have Lousy Acre, Close, Dell, Mead and Meadow, Lousy Lott, Lousey Leys, Lowsey Carr, Marsh and Mead, and Louseham. Louse Hall Field in Gosford (O) is *Loose Hall* in 1685, but in 1675 was *Lowse Hall* 'so called by the scholars' of Oxford, a suggestion that the unpleasant association with *louse* was a deliberate perversion of the name. Lousehill Field in Frencham (Sr) was *Losehyll* in 1570 and *Lowshill* in 1660 and is identical in origin with Loose Hills in Farnham (Sr), *Lowsehill* 1613, both from OE **hlōse-hyll* 'pigsty-hill'. The normal development of *hlōse* would be *loose*, as in Loose (Kent), hence Lousey Field in Corley (Wa), *Lucyfeld* 1411, derives from OE *hlōse-(ge)hæg-feld* 'field by or with a pigsty-enclosure', where the normal *loosy* has been associated with *Lucy* and spelled accordingly. Of similar origin is Hither Lucys in Copford (Ess), *Lowsey* 1441, whilst Lucy Croft in Birchanger, *Loosoues* 1523, and Lucys Field in Great Sampford, *Loshawe* 1300, are from *hlōse-haga*, also 'pigsty-enclosure'. This derivation from *hlōse* 'pigsty' is confirmed by the early forms of several major place-names: Lowsay in Holme St Cuthbert (Cu), *Lowsehowe* 1604, *Lowsey* 1718, *Loosey* 1648, where the second element is ON *haugr* 'hill'; Loosley Row (Bk), *Losle* 1241, *Louslerowe* 1484; Lowesmoor (Wo), *Losemere* 1270; Loseley (Sr), *Losele* 1086, *Lousle* 1288, *Louselee* 1303. A more pleasant corruption has taken place in Lordsgrove Field in

Banstead (Sr), *le Losegrovefild* 1432, 'pigsty-grove-field'. It may be that all these 'Lousy' place-names refer to pigsties.

Fillpotts is commonly regarded as a complimentary nickname, but the only early form adduced is *Fylpottes* in Hertfordshire in 1556. *Fill* was a common medieval pet-name for *Philip* and this field-name may well denote land once held by a man named *Philpot*. That is undoubtedly the origin of Upper and Lower Philpots in Ingatestone, *Phelpotesschot* 1384, *ffylpotesland* 1433.

The corruption which a field-name can undergo is well illustrated by the development of OE *gærstūn* 'grassy enclosure, paddock' to Garston, Garson, Gasson, Gassom, Gaston, Gason, Gassen, Gascon, Gaskin, Gascowing and Gascoynes in Surrey, with The Garcons, Gassons, Gayson and Garson in Wiltshire, and Gussan in Oxfordshire; and of ME *conynger* 'rabbit-warren' to Coney Burrows, Coney Fare, Fair and Fir, Coney Borough, Bowers, Furrow(s) and Farrow, Cunnyfur, Coney Yard, Coney Grove, Coneygarth, Cunnigarth, Coneygre, Coneygret and Cunneries in Essex, Cunnery and Conery in Warwickshire, Connigre, Connegre, Congreve, Conegars and Coney Gore in Wiltshire, Coney Gra, Coney Earth and Colney Burrows in Hertfordshire, Coneygear, Coney Grey, Cun-a-gree, Cunninger and Cunney Grift in Northamptonshire, and Coneygar, Coneygree and Conygree in Oxfordshire.

Among modern field-names nicknames of reproach are more common than those of praise. To the innumerable examples of Small Profits and Small Gains, Hungerdown, Hungerland, Hunger Hill and Hungry Hill (once corrupted to Hungary Hill), of which it is often recorded that 'no grass will grow here' or 'the field needs much manure', Starveall, Starvelarks, Starve Crow, Starve Goose, Starve Devil and Starvation Acre, we may add Starknaked, Rawbones, Knawbone, Fargains, Great and Little Poverty, Pinch Penny, Beastly Furlong, Breakheart, Famish Beggar, Labour in Vain, Purgatory, Hell Kitchen, Great Breakback, Grumble, Lord Helpus, Pickpocket, Frogs Abbey and Frog's Hall (used of marshy ground), Cold Comfort Farm, Greedy Guts, Lazy Leys and Skinny Flint. Honey Hole, Honeypot, Plum Pudding Hole and Pudding Bag, Glue Pot and Pastry Crust, Porridge Pot Field and Featherbed Lane (*Fetherbeddeslee* 1200), all have reference to muddy fields.

Less common are nicknames of praise, as Dripping Pan, Full Sack, Providence, Butter Leaze and Meadow, Butter Milk Field, Fill Tubs,

Fillcups, Lucky, Gods Garden, Mount Pleasant, Saucy Close, Sweet Lips, Bright Jimmy, Apple Pasty Acre. Occasional early examples of both types are found: complimentary in *Godesworlde* (1407), pasture called *Milkky* (1149), *Milkfurlong* (1312), *le Plenty* (1445), *Honeysweet Acre* (1406); derogatory in *Wabigan* (13th) 'woe-begone', field called *le Labor* (1411), *Stonimoder* (1243).

In Warwickshire we have places named Nineveh, New York, Canada, Labrador and New Zealand. Elsewhere we find numerous similar names, originally field-names, some few of which now appear on the map. Very few are recorded before the eighteenth, and the majority not earlier than the nineteenth century. They are frequently found on or near a parish boundary or in remote or out-of-the-way places and most were probably the result of a rustic sense of humour. Botany Bay is fairly common and to the farm labourer the prospect of working on this outlandish spot was as attractive as transportation to the Antipodes. Many of these names probably arose at a time when migration from the country-side to the colonies was by no means rare. Hence, such field-names as America, New England, Nova Scotia, New South Wales, Van Dieman's Land, Carolina, Virginia, Georgia, Pennsylvania, California and Quebec. New Zealand in Harpenden (Herts) is in a somewhat remote part of the parish, but Sir John Russell notes that field and name alike date from about 1880. When the land was redistributed at that time, the owner left it to the men to name it. One of them was about to migrate to New Zealand and the field was so called to commemorate the event. Some are names of distant places familiar to the rustic from church services: Jericho, Jerusalem, Nineveh, Canaan; others recall Napoleon and his exile: Corsica, Isle of Elba; or famous battles: Waterloo, Blenheim and Porto Bello, and we have even two relics of the Boer War in Spion Kop in Essex and in Oxfordshire. For others no obvious reason appears: Egypt, Bohemia, Dunkirk, China, Gibraltar, Mesopotamia, Leipsic and Moscow. But when we do succeed in finding a real reason, we are warned once more of the danger of generalisation. In Abbots Langley (Herts), Bunkers Farm and Lane, with a lost field-name *Bonckers dell* (t. Ed. VI), commemorate the possessions here of William *Bunker* (1452), whilst Bunker's Hill in Little Berkhamsted is similarly to be associated with John *Bunkere* (1429). Hence it is clear that not all the fields named Bunkers Hill owe their names to the battle of 1775. A farm named Australia in Tydd St Giles (C) was built by John Morton who was born c1840. As a young man he had made arrangements to emigrate to Australia with a friend who at the last moment refused to go. Morton saved up his money and named the house which he built Australia in memory of his disappointed ambition. Jerusalem Wood in Chippenham (C) was part of the lands of the Hospital of St John of Jerusalem in 1204. Newfoundland Well in Ilmington (Wa) is a corruption of *Newfound Well House* of the 1781 Enclosure Award and probably owed its name to a newly discovered chalybeate spring, whilst the cottages called Bermuda in Chilvers Coton in the same county were so named when Sir Edward Newdigate-Newdegate was appointed Governor of Bermuda in 1888. Maryland Point in West Ham similarly commemorates a specific connexion with America. A cluster of cottages here was built and named by a London merchant who had made a fortune in Maryland. But the association of Modder River Field in Tanworth (Wa) with its namesake is merely temporal. It owes its name to the chance that a dam in the field was being repaired when news arrived of the Battle of the Modder River. Obsolete names may, at times, throw light on the occasion of such names. Merrielands in Dagenham, then called *Cockermouth Farm*, was owned in 1823 by one Rowland Stephenson 'the Fugitive Banker'. When he went bankrupt and fled to America, the farm was sold and renamed *America Farm*, a name changed to Merrielands about 1890. Canada Allotments in Ashley (Cambs) owe their name not to remoteness but to their situation in bleak, open country. Late as they are, some of these names already appear in disguise. The old allotment ground in Loughton (Ess), originally *Botany Bay*, *The Bay* and *The Transports*, came to be pronounced *Bodney*, whilst the allotment gardens in Walthamstow 'partaking somewhat of a new settlement' were known as *Canada*, which by 1884 the local dialect had turned into *Kennedy*. A clear indication of how some of the Little Londons got their name is revealed by the history of Lunnon in Scarrington (Nt). This is not a farm but the site of a hamlet where about ten families lived as recently as 1920. The cottages were mud and thatch, and the place was often jocularly referred to as 'Little London'. As the cottages fell empty, they were condemned and became ruinous.

Certain field-name elements appear to be confined to particular districts. OE *bēan* 'bean' is found in certain widely separated place-names as Bampton (Cu, O), Banstead (Sr), Benacre (Sf), Bendish (Herts), Binstead (IOW) and Binsted (Ha, Sx), but as a field-name the element is characteristic of Northamptonshire and is found fairly frequently in Cambridgeshire, but occurs elsewhere only occasionally. In Northamptonshire *Bancroft* is fairly common as a modern field-name, whilst 'bean-land' appears frequently in a variety of forms, including Banlands, Bandlands, Bantlands, Bandilands, Ballands and Balance. On the map of Cambridgeshire we have Balland, Bancroft, Bannolds and Benwick, with field-names Bandland, Balland, Balance, Bean Lands and Balaams, with other examples from 1219 onwards which have not survived.

Pightel 'a small enclosure, croft', on the other hand, is almost entirely a field-name element and is more widely spread but is really common in only a limited area. Its ultimate origin is unknown; the earliest example, *Fullerespictel*, is found in Middlesex c1200, with *Nicholes Picthel* 1252, *Gresputhel* 13th, and *Stonipiktell* c1237. Elsewhere early examples are much less frequent. In Surrey it is very common in the modern forms *pightle*, *pikle* and *pickle* and, with nasalisation, *pinkle* and *pingle*. Similar forms are found in Cambridgeshire, where it is almost invariably compounded with an owner's name, *Rundelespitell* 1250. Elsewhere, even when medieval examples are common, modern examples are rare, as in Oxfordshire, where we still have Pinkhill Barn, Pintle Barn and Pingle's Field, with seven examples of a variant *piddle*, first noted in *Piddle pittes* (1573). In Middlesex and Essex, too, modern examples are uncommon. In the former county we find the interesting form *Walnutt Tree Pingwell* in 1602, whilst in the latter, where the term is still sufficiently well known to arouse a spirited discussion in a local periodical with the naïve suggestion that the term is a contraction of 'pig-in-the-hole', only three modern examples have been noted. In Sussex, Warwickshire and Wiltshire it is very rare; in Nottinghamshire it is rare and late in the form *pightle* and occasional *pickle*, but the nasalised *pingle* occurs in the fourteenth century and is very common in modern names. Similarly, in Northamptonshire, we have an early *Boyespythell* in 1272 and *Swynespyngel* in 1404, but it is only in later times that the element becomes common and survives as Pightle, Pikle, Pikewell, Pidell, Pittell, Pikeall, Piecull and Pingle. In Hertfordshire, too, where *Calves Pightle* is one of the commonest compounds in the Tithe Award and the term is very common today, early examples are rare, the earliest being *le Halfpightell* in 1409. Thus, except for the isolated Oxfordshire example, *pightle* would seem to be in ME a specifically south-eastern term, common in Surrey, Middlesex, Essex and Cambridgeshire. Later, it spread more widely but was never common in the north, west or south. It must be remembered, however, that we are not yet in a position to draw any final conclusions. Material varies from county to county. For some it is scanty and incomplete; for others it has yet to be collected.

Major place-names, supplemented by field-names, have identified various sites of heathen worship. We have already noted field-names in Essex which recall the persistence of rustic beliefs in dwarfs and changelings, to which we may add not only Dwariden (WRY), Dwerryhouse (La) and a lost *Dwarfholes* in Warwickshire, all derived from OE *dwerg* 'a dwarf', but also numerous field-names and certain minor place-names which reveal in their reference to goblins, giants and dragons the strong hold superstition had in all parts of the country in the Middle Ages. We are all familiar with the mischievous activities of Shakespeare's Puck, whilst, for many, Kipling's 'Puck of Pook's Hill' has long associated him with Sussex, so that it is no surprise to find his name five times on the Sussex map in Pookhill, Pookreed, Poppets, earlier *Poukeput* 'the hollow haunted by Puck or a goblin', Puckscroft and Puckstye 'goblin path', near which was also *Poukstrete*. In addition, field-names suggest that in local folk-lore Sussex was goblin-haunted to an extent without parallel elsewhere. Mills, streams, springs, lanes, hollows, nooks, hills, enclosures, meadows, clearings and land of every kind might be so haunted. Surrey has its goblin-haunted hut (Puckshot) and Hertfordshire a goblin-ridge (Puckeridge), whilst Essex had land (now Puck Lane) and near by a spring in Waltham Holy Cross, five mills, three fields, three plots and a fen all associated with goblins. Several examples occur in Cambridgeshire, but they are less numerous than we should expect in Devon; in Oxfordshire we have Poppets Hill, another Puck Lane and a lost *Poukebrugge*, and in Wiltshire, where *pūca* was common in medieval field-names, there still survive Puck Well, Puck Shipton (*Pukeshepene* 1303) 'goblin-haunted cattle-shed' and the field-names Pookscroft, Puck Hay and Pock Ridge, identical with the Hertfordshire Puckeridge; in Hampshire we have Purbrook, *Pukebrok* 1248, 'goblin-haunted brook', and Pugdells, *Pukedelle* 1263. In Parkwalls in Advent (Co), formerly *Pokewalles*, we have reference to prehistoric remains on Bodmin Moor which were supposed to be haunted by goblins. A diminutive *pūcel* 'little goblin' survives in Popple Drove (C) which is near Pock Field, Putshole in Hartland (D) and Puxley (Nth), whilst thrice we have reference to a goblin-haunted church, Pucklechurch (Gl), Pucklechurch, a field near

Lyneham Church (W) and an unidentified *Poculchurchmede* (1529) in Winterbourne Bassett, not far away.

A similar, but less common term, OE *scucca* 'evil spirit, demon, goblin', usually compounded with a word meaning 'hill' survives in Shuckstonefield and Shuckton (Db), Shugborough (St), Shuckburgh (Wa) and Shucknall (He), and, associated with water, in Shobrooke (D) and Shocklach (Ch), in the field-name Suckmoor (Wa) and the lost *Shuckelawe* c1215 (O) and *Schokepet* 1431 (C). Water-demons or kelpies (OE *nicor*) frequenting pools or streams and occasionally other places are recalled by such names as *Nikerpoll* in Savernake Forest, Sussex and Wiltshire, *Nycharpool* and *Nickerwells* (L), *Nikeresaker* (C) and *Nikersmadwe* (Ess), whilst in 1563 we have reference to the *Marmaydes Hole* in the river Colne near Colchester. A field called *Marmayden Pytte* in 1540 still survives in Bury St Edmunds as Mermaids Pits.

A belief in giants (OE *þyrs*) was also widely spread and gave rise to such names as Thirst House (Db), the name of a cave in Deep Dale where numerous prehistoric and Roman finds have been made, Thursden (La), Thursford (Nf), Thirlspot 'pot or pool', *Thursgill* 1384, *Thyrspoone* 1568 and *Thrushhowe* 1578 (Cu), Trusey Hill (ERY), Tusmore (O), Thruss Pits and Rush Pools, *Thirsepol* c1275, *Thruspole* 1565, *Thrushpulle* 1577 (Nt), *þyrspit* 872–4 BCS 537 (Wo), *þrispit* 1250 (C), *Therspettes* 1256 (Nb), *Thursput* 1280 and *Thirs-queche* 1292 'thicket' (Nt), and *Thurspyttys* 1491 (Db). In Thrushgill (La) and *Thursmare* (ERY) we have compounds of ON *þurs* 'giant' with ON *gil* 'ravine' and *marr* 'fen, marsh' respectively.

Memories of old Germanic folk-tales of buried treasure or valuable grave-goods guarded by dragons are preserved in names of hills, mounds, valleys and hollows, as Dragley (La), *Drakelow* c1270, Drakedale (NRY), Drakeholes (Nt), Drakelow (Db, Wo), Drakenage (Wa) 'edge' of a long, low hill, Drake North (W), *drakenhorde* 940–6 'dragon-hoard' and Drake Pits (WRY); in surviving field-names as Dragberry (Sr), *Drakebergh* 1384, Draker (Nt), *Drachou* t. Ed t, both 'dragon hill or mound', and in lost field-names, *Drakenhord* c1230 in Garsington and *Drakestone* (O). In Surrey the 'dragon hill' (*Draken-hull*) of 1318 in Artington is now St Catherines Hill, taking its present name from a chapel dedicated to St Catherine which stood here as early as 1202.

The collection and study of field-names is, it is clear, something more than a mere harmless pastime. Their mortality has been greater than that of the major place-names, but in origin they are similar and interpretation demands the same methods. Our treatment, selective and incomplete as it is, proves conclusively that field-names are a valuable subsidiary source for the local historian. With his special knowledge he can make identifications and provide historical and topographical information which might well elude the worker in a wider field. Occasionally he may be rewarded by a discovery of more than local importance. Material is abundant but, at present, full and detailed surveys of parish field-names are rare.

Chapter Eleven

STREET-NAMES

MANY of our ancient towns still retain the old names of some of their streets, but many old names have been replaced by more modern ones and many more have disappeared completely, especially where widening and rebuilding have taken place and new streets have been made which do not always follow the line of their predecessors. Few street-names are mentioned by name in Old English sources. No London street-name now in use is recorded before the Conquest, though some of those found in twelfth-century documents must have originated in Saxon times. A charter of 605 gives us the names of two Canterbury streets, *via of Burhgate*, now Burgate St, leading to the town gate, and *Drutingestræte*, probably Ruttington Lane, perhaps 'street of the people of *Trutinton*', a place mentioned in 1227, the etymology of which is difficult. But, as the bounds were probably not included in the original charter which survives only in a fourteenth-century copy, it is doubtful whether these street-names were actually in use as early as 605. For Winchester, a charter of 909 gives us three street-names, none of which is still in use: *þa ceap stræt* 'market street', *flæscmangerestræt* 'street of the butchers' and *scyldwyrtenastræt* 'street of the shield-makers'.

Some streets were originally markets and in the market-place different parts were distinguished by the names of the foods or pro-

226

duce sold there. The OE word for market, *cēap*, is found in Chipstead (K, Sr) and survives in the Ward of Cheap and in Cheapside and Eastcheap in London. Cheap, occasionally *Westceap*, was the chief market-place of London and also a main thoroughfare, whilst Eastcheap was both a butchers' market and a street. The name Cheapside, which has now replaced *Cheap*, is a later name, not recorded before the fifteenth century, and at first referred probably to the houses facing the market-place and later to the street. High St, Winchester, so called from c1280, has replaced the old name of *ceap stræt* (909). Wincheap St in Canterbury (*Wenchepe* 1226) 'waggon market' probably referred originally to the open space outside the town-wall at Wincheap Gate. *Riðerescæpe* (605) in the same city was a cattle-market (OE *hrīþer* 'cattle'), a name repeated in *Rother chepyng* (Ed VI), the old name for the lower part of Brook St in Warwick, from *cēping* 'market', which survives in Chipping and Chippingdale (La) and as a prefix in such names as Chipping Barnet (Mx), Chipping Campden (Gl) and Chipping Ongar (Ess). It is also found in Mealcheapen St, *Melechepyng* (1369) 'meal-market' and *Cornechepyng* (13th) 'corn-market', now Queen St in Worcester; in *Maltchepyng* (1440) 'malt-market', an earlier name for Chequer St, St Albans, named from an old inn *the Chequers*, now the Queen's Hotel, where part of Market Place was formerly *Cornechepynge* (1547) and *Crossechepynge* (1428) 'the market by the cross'; Market Place in Salisbury was *Chepyngplace* in 1357, whilst that at Warwick was *Hygh Chepyng* (Ed VI) and included *Horse Chipping* in 1656 'horse market'; in thirteenth-century Northampton we have *le Strawechepyng* 'the straw-market'. Chipper Lane in Salisbury, *Chipperystrete* 1331, *Chiperestret* 1343, varies between ME *chepere, chipere* 'market-man' and *chiperie* 'place of the market-men', formed after the fashion of *draperie* and *bocherie*, places where drapers and butchers assembled, surviving in Drapery in Northampton, Drapers Hall, Coventry, and in lost street-names in Birmingham, Nottingham, Stratford-on-Avon and Oxford, and in Butchery Green in Hertford, Butcher Row, Coventry, and in lost street-names in Hull and Northampton and in *Butchery Row*, the old name of Guildhall St, Cambridge.

Medieval tradesmen and merchants tended to congregate and live together according to their trades in streets named from the business carried on there. The shops were workshops rather than stores and retail trade was largely carried on in the market. This might be held in a market-square, as on Market Hill, Cambridge, where Market St was formerly *Cordewanaria* (1322), *Cordewanerrowe* (1348) and later *Shoomaker lane* (1574), where shoes were made of Cordovan leather. Vendors of different commodities congregated in different parts of the market: *in foro bladi* (the Cornmarket) (Hy 3), *Milkmarket* 1360, *Lethermarket* 1362, *le Maltmarket* 1389, *le Chesmarketh* 1415, *the Otemarket* 1431. Just off Market Hill was *the Pesemarket* 1485, *le Peasemarket Hyll* 1570, now Peas Hill, and near the market were *Potteresrowe* 1249, *Smitherowe* 1271, *reugio apotechariorum* 1286 'apothecaries' street', *le Lorineresrowe* 1299, where makers of metal harness-fittings lived, *le cotelerie* 1305 (cutlers), *Comberislane* 1319 (wool-combers), *le Smeremongger Rowe* 1330 (sellers of grease, lard, tallow, etc.), *le Pulterirowe* 1388, where poultry was sold, *the Botry row* 1501 (butter), *Shethers lane* 1508, *Sherrers Row* 1512 (shearers of woollen cloth), *Braderers Lane* 1516 (workers in embroidery), *the Duddrye* 1561, where woollen cloth or articles of clothing were sold, and *Brasyer Rowe* 1589 (workers in brass). Part of Market Hill was *Cooke Rowe* in 1561 and the street at a right-angle with the Market Hill was distinguished from this as *parva Cokeria* 1330, *le Petitecurye* 1344 'the little Cooks' Row' from the OFr *curie* 'kitchen', a name surviving as Petty Cury. Copenhagen St in Worcester was *Cokestrete* in 1395; there was a *Cookerewe* in Exeter called *the Cokery* in 1541, a *Cokerowe* in Peterborough in 1390, one in Ipswich in 1332, and the name survives as Cook St in Coventry. A twelfth-century Londoner has left an almost lyrical description of the attractions of the public cook-shop: 'There, daily according to the season, you may find viands, dishes roast, fried and boiled, fish great and small, the coarser food for the poor, the more delicate for the rich, such as venison and birds both big and little.' Fish St in Worcester dates from 1538, but was formerly *Corviserstret*, where the cordwainers lived and worked (ME *corviser*), whilst Little Fish St was *Huxterstrate* 'street of the petty traders' in 1232. Fisher St in Carlisle, where the fish shambles were, dates from c1300, and Fish Row in Salisbury from 1554, where there were *Fysshamels* in 1314 'fish benches or stalls'. Fishergate in York (from 1080) and Fisher Gate in Nottingham (1315) 'street of the fishermen' are from ON *gata* 'street', as is a lost *Fishmarketgat* (1307) in Beverley, where we also have reference in 1689 to the *Fish Shambles*, but a lost *Fiskergate* in Bridlington, a purely Scandinavian name from ON *fiskari* and *gata*, refers rather to the actual fishermen who lived there than to a market.

In many towns the market was held in the open street and not in a market square, hence the width of some of these streets. The medieval market at Oxford was held in High St and Cornmarket. The width of Broad St, *Horsmongeresstreta* c1235, is due to the horse-market held there, as at a lost *Horse Market* (1545) in Northampton. Sometimes there were shops or booths in the middle of the street. In Colchester the upper part of High St, near the Old Corn Exchange, was *Cornhill* in 1336, whilst from Queen St to the top of East Hill it was *Frerestret* in 1388, so named from the monastery of the Grey Friars. The middle and widest part was *le medilrowe* in the reign of Henry VII, a name due, no doubt, to a row of shops which formerly stood in the middle of this wide street. Middle Row in Stratford-on-Avon was a row of houses which formerly stood in the centre of Bridge St and were demolished in the middle of the nineteenth century.

Many of these old names are no longer remembered. In Winchester, the *flæscmangerestræt* of 909 'street of the flesh-mongers or butchers' is now St Peter St, whilst Green Croft in Salisbury has replaced the *Melemonger Strete* of 1403. But some still survive, the spicers or grocers in Spicer St, St Albans, and Spiceal St, Birmingham; sellers of Pepper in Pepper Lane, Coventry, and Pepper St, Nottingham; dealers in silks and velvets in Mercers Row in Northampton; ironmongers in Ironmonger Row in Coventry; wool-merchants in Woolmonger St, Northampton. Knifesmith Gate in Chesterfield (Db) was 'the street of the knife-smiths' or makers of knives; Saltergate was either the 'street of the salt-sellers' or the road along which salt was carried from the Cheshire salt-mines; *Soutergate* 'street of the shoe-makers' was formerly the main street of the town, part of which is now South St.

A particularly interesting survival is Waterbeer St in Exeter, *Waterberestrete* 1253, 'the street of the water-carriers'. Professional water-bearers or water-leaders were found in every town and formed one of the most ancient and poorest classes of unskilled labourers. William Waterladar' of Warwick in 1197 carted water for sale; William le Waterman of Oxford in 1249 was a water-carrier, and Richard Waterbererè of London in 1351 carried water from a spring or conduit for domestic use. In London they had their own 'Brotherhood of Saint Cristofer of the Waterberers of the Citie of London', with definite rules and ordinances. Each had his own round, like the modern milkman. Some used horses and carts, some only horses, whilst others pushed barrels on wheels or carried buckets. In Exeter, they clearly lived together in the same street.

Baxter St in Bury St Edmunds (1200), Baxter's Row in Carlisle (1380) and Baxter Gate in Hedon (1401) (ERY) were the homes of the bakers (OE *bæcestere*). In Worcester, the original thirteenth-century name has now been replaced by The Shambles. In Nottingham, the street now known as Wheelergate is mentioned in 1306 as *vicus pistorum* 'street of the bakers', a name which had been changed as early as 1395: *Baxstergate which is now called Whelewrightgate*. The king's bakehouse was in this street in 1310, but as early as 1280 property *in vico pistorum* was demised to a wheelwright, and wheelwrights must have become so much more numerous than the bakers that from 1331 the street is regularly named from them, although there was still *ye comon Bakhusse* in the street as late as 1435.

Catherine St in Salisbury is *Carterestrete* 1339, *Carternestret* 1393, *Katherine Street* 1623. The association with (St) Katherine is clearly erroneous. The name was originally 'carters' street', with the same ME weak genitive plural found also in *Carterne street* (1291), now Holloway St, in *Strikinestrete* 'bullocks' street', now Egypt Lane, and in Smythen St, *Smythenestrete* 'street of the smiths', all in Exeter. Carter Gate in Newark, Nottingham and Scarborough is also 'carters' street', from ON *gata* 'street'. Gigant St in Salisbury is *Gygornestrete* 1451, *Gigorstrete* 1455, *Giggon, Gigant* or *Gigger Street* 1808, 'street of the fiddlers', from ME *gigour* 'fiddler', with alternative forms *gigo(u)rstrete* and *gigo(u)rnestrete*, the latter a weak genitive plural form. Gluman Gate in Chesterfield, *Gleumanestrete* 13th, *Glemongate* 1345, was the 'street of the glee-men or minstrels', with a second element varying between OE *strǽt* and ON *gata*.

Trade-names still preserved in street-names include: Bridlesmith Gate in Nottingham, from a rare occupational name dating from 1304; Pilcher Gate in the same city, with a lost *Pilecher Strete* (13th) in Lewes, where lived the makers of pilches or fur-coats; Souttergate in Hedon (ERY), from ME *souter* 'shoe-maker'; Barker Gate in Nottingham, from ME *barkere* 'tanner'; Tanner St (Northampton); Lower Brook St in Winchester has replaced the old name of *Tænnere stret* (990), whilst it was not until the eighteenth century that the tenth-century *scyldwyrhtenastræt* 'street of the shield-makers' was renamed Upper Brook St; Walkergate in Beverley (OE *walcere* 'fuller' and ON *gata* 'street'); Lister Gate (Nottingham), from ME *litestere* 'dyer'; Tenters Close in Coventry and *Tenter Butts*, the old name of Stafford St in Birmingham, places where cloth was stretched; Cumbergate in Peterborough, *Comberisgate* c1250, 'street (ON *gata*) of the woolcombers'. Fletcher Gate in Nottingham and Hedon (ERY), respectively from *Flesshewergate* 1335 and *Fleshmarketgate* 1470, are both 'street of the flesh-hewers or butchers', and the weakened form *flesher* has been wrongly associated with *fletcher* 'arrow-maker'.

The medieval sports of bull- and bear-baiting are still recalled in such names as The Bullring in Birmingham and Beverley, whilst Southwark, once had its *Bulringe Alley*. Bearward St in Northampton owed its name to the 'bear ward' or 'keeper of performing bears' who lived there at least as early as 1281. Two lanes in London were similarly named at about the same time, *Berewards Lane* in Bishopsgate being now known as Hog Lane. In Nottingham *le Bereworde Gate* c1240 (ON *gata* 'street') became *Berwardlane* in the fifteenth century and is now known as Mount St. East Stockwell St in Colchester appears on Speed's map of 1610 as *S. Martins Lane* (named from St Martin's Church), but from the fourteenth to the sixteenth centuries was known as *Bereslane* and is to be associated with the Bear Stake, *le Berestake*, mentioned in the Court Rolls between 1334 and 1346. Bear Lane in Southwark is a reminder of the old Bear Gardens, but Bear Lane in Oxford was named from the Bear Inn, whilst Bear St in Barnstaple, *Barrestret* 1394, was so called from its course from the bar or barrier at the entrance to the town.

At Shrewsbury, according to the Domesday Survey, the English burgesses complained that they had to pay as much in taxation to the king as the whole town had paid in the days of Edward the Confessor, 'although the earl's castle occupies the site of 51 dwellings and another 50 are waste, and the French burgesses hold dwellings that used to pay in the old days', but were apparently then exempt. These French burgesses were one of a number of communities of Frenchmen settled in ancient boroughs after the Conquest. They were obviously there as a check against possible English disaffection and found a share in the profits of the market an attraction. Individual Frenchmen would have been unwelcome in an English borough immediately after the Conquest and so these separate communities were established, each with its own court parallel to the portmoot of the English borough, and with its own customs, particularly with regard to inheritance. Nottingham was divided into the *burgus Francensis* of the twelfth century, known also as the *burgus Gallicus* in 1240, the *Frankisburgh* in 1304 and *le Frenceborgh* 'the French borough' as late as 1384, in the neighbourhood of the Castle, and the *burgus Anglicus* (1312) or *Englisheburgh* (1384), 'the English borough'. Castle Gate was long known as *the Fraunkisshgate* (1365) or *Frenshegate* (1400) 'the French Street' because it led to the castle and the French part of the borough. Similarly, in Southampton, French St (1255) was named in contrast to *Englisschestret* (1270), now High St. French Gate in Richmond (Y) was a similar street where Frenchmen lived near a great Norman castle, whilst French Row in St Albans was near a famous monastery. There was a *Frankmannestrete* in Bury St Edmunds in 1339. In Westminster, *Petye Caleys* was where the woolstaplers from Calais resided, whilst other French merchants lived in Petty France. The mixture of races which we have already noted in Cumberland is revealed also in the street-names of Carlisle, though the evidence is less conclusive then we should like. There appears to have been confusion between the English *gate* and ON *gata* 'street'. Botchergate was originally the name of one of the city gates (*porta Bochardi* c1180, 'Bochard's gate'), but was later transferred to the street leading through the gate (*in vico Bochardi* c1245, *Bochergate-streate* 1652). English St (1794), the way to the south, led to the gate called *English Gate* in 1684, of which Denton remarks: 'In these three last and other most commendable places of the city leading to and nigh the market place and churches dwelt the chief and best citizens, natural Englishmen'. Scotch St (1786) passed through *Scotch Gate* (1794), a name said to have been used in the seventeenth century for Rickergate, 'Richard's gate', the gateway to Scotland. Irish Gate Brow was called the 'street of the Irishmen' already in 1233. According to Denton, 'In the great street now called Abbey Gate were placed the Irishmen, who dwelt there in cottages when it was waste'. George St in Oxford was *Hyrismanstrete* in 1251. Among the frequent references to Irishmen in Oxford records is one which states that in 1303, when some undergraduates were playing ball in the High St in the afternoon, three Irishmen came up and killed one of them with a knife. Flemish merchants were numerous in medieval England, as is proved by the survival of the surname *Fleming* and of Flemingate 'street of the Flemish traders' in Beverley, a name in use already in the twelfth century.

In most medieval towns the Jews lived together in their own quarter. They had filtered into England after the Conquest and, as the Church forbade Christians to engage in usury, they quickly acquired wealth by lending money in large and small sums alike and in providing capital for both trade and the building of cathedrals and monasteries. The rate of interest they charged was high. One loan of

40*s*. for 14 months cost the borrower 37*s*. 4*d*. in interest. The hatred felt for them by embittered debtors was increased by superstition and religious prejudice. Henry II protected them against their debtors and found them useful in collecting money for the Crown. In the reign of Henry III the Jewries in many towns were sacked and in 1290 Edward I finally expelled the Jews from the country, but the memory of these medieval Jews is still perpetuated in some of our towns. In London, the Jewry was a large district in the wards of Cheap and Coleman Street, including also the parish of St Laurence and Laurence Lane. As early as 1130 we find a reference to *vicus Judeorum* and in 1183 to St Olave *in iudaismo*, a name still surviving in Old Jewry, from AFr, ME *juerie* 'land of the Jews', 'the Jews' quarter'. Jewry St in Aldgate was formerly *pauperum Judaismum* (1349), *la Pore-jewerie* (1366), 'Poor Jewry'. In York, Jewbury is from ME *buri* in the sense of 'part of a town outside the borough proper'. It was the burial ground of wealthy Jews from the early part of the twelfth century. Jubbergate, probably one of the first streets built outside the city walls of York, was originally *Brettegata* (1155) 'the street of the Britons' (ON *Bretar* and *gata*), probably Cumbrian Britons who accompanied the Irish Vikings and were segregated outside the city walls, probably as slaves. Later, Jews must have concentrated here, and their name was prefixed to the old street-name, *Jubretegate* 1356, *Jubergate* 1443 'the Jews' Bretgate'. Warwick also has its Jury St, *le Iuerie* 1347, *Jury Burgage* 1525, and Winchester its Jewry St, *Geweri-strete* 1311. In Cambridge, All Saints' Passage is on the site of the old Jewry. The *vicus Judeorum* (Ed I) ran as far as the cemetery of Al Saints' Church, which was called *Omnium Sanctorum in Judaismo* as late as 1428. In Oxford, there was a Little Jewry Lane, mentioned as *parvo Judaismo* in 1285 and as *Jewrilane* in 1449. This was south of Blue Boar Lane and parallel with it, but the name is now no longer used. The Jewry was between the High St and St Aldate's St. In Nottingham, St Nicholas St was *venella Judæorum* in 1315 and was still called *Jew Lane* in 1744.

A few miscellaneous names of interest may be noted. Carfax in Oxford is *Carfox* in 1483 and *Quartervois* in 1661, a French name derived from the ME plural *carfoukes*, from OFr *carrefourcs*, from Latin *quadrifurcus* 'four-forked' and is used of a place where four roads meet. The name survives also in Carfax in Horsham (Sx) where it was *Scarfax* in 1548, and it was formerly used (*Carfoix* 1350, 1436) for the junction of High St and North and South Streets in

Exeter, whilst London had its *carfuks del ledenhalle* in 1357. Litchdon St in Barnstaple, *Lycheton* 1370, is from OE *līc-tūn* 'cemetery', and probably led to the medieval burying-ground. Lich St in Worcester, *Lychestrete* 1322, *Leech St* 1649, also from *līc* 'body', was also called *Cadiferestret* in 1337 and was clearly a 'corpse-bearer street' which led to the cemetery of the cathedral church. A similar name once existed in Coventry, *le Lychelane* 1411.

A common street-name, widely distributed over Scandinavian England, is Finkle St, which is found in Carlisle, St Bees, Workington, Kendal, York, Hull, Oakham and Bennington (L), in Finkhill St in Nottingham, Fingle St in Leverton (Nt) and in a number of lost names. The earliest examples are *Fynkhullstrete* 1370, *Fenkelstrete* 1400 (York); later examples include *Finkall Street* or *Fennel Street* 1775 (Workington). The evidence is late and inconclusive. The name might mean either 'street where *finkel* (ME *fenekel* 'fennel') was sold' (for flavouring or medical use), or 'street with a bend', from dialectal *fenkel* 'corner, bend'. Finkle St in York is a narrow, crooked lane, and many of the streets so named have a bend in them, but in view of the altered topography of the streets in many of our old towns, it is impossible to say whether the absence of a bend today is necessarily a bar to such an interpretation. Finkle St in Carlisle is now almost straight, but had an angle in it before the early nineteenth-century improvements. At the same time, it is difficult to believe that the sale of fennel should be commemorated so frequently. ME *fenkel* 'corner' is not recorded in independent use and is found in no place-name apart from these street-names. Judgement should, therefore, be suspended for the present.[1]

The City of York

York has preserved not only many of its old streets but also their ancient names, which reveal the strong Scandinavian element in the city's history. The frequent ending of *-gate* is from ON *gata* 'street'. The gates of the city were called *bars*, Bootham Bar, Micklegate Bar, Monk Bar and Walmgate Bar, from OFr *barre* 'a bar' to block the passage, a name found also in other towns, as in Temple Bar in London, North Bar in Beverley, Bargate (Newark), Bargates (Leominster), Above Bar St (Southampton), and, corrupted to Bear St in Barnstaple. Ipswich had its *Barrgate Streete* in 1485, from the west

[1] See now, E. Ekwall, *Etymological Notes on English Place-names* (Lund, 1959), pp. 47–53.

bar or gate, removed in 1780. Castlegate was the street leading to the Castle; Davygate, the street in which stood the forest court-house and prison, preserves the name of David le Iardiner, who in the early twelfth century was Royal Lardiner of the Forest of Galtres. Fossgate is the street leading to the River Foss and Gillygate that where once stood a church dedicated to St Giles. Goodramgate is purely Scandinavian, 'Guthrum's street'. Micklegate is the 'great street', and Stonegate that paved with stone. The Shambles, *Flesshamelles* 1316, was the street where butchers set up their 'flesh-benches' or stalls for the sale of meat. Other names commemorate ancient trades: Colliergate (colliers or charcoal-burners), Coppergate (ON *koppari* 'joiners'), Fishergate, Skeldergate (ON *skjaldari* 'shield-makers') and Spurriergate 'spur-makers'. Blossom St was *Blossomgate* in 1624, and in the thirteenth century *Ploxhsuaingate* 'street of the ploughswains' (ON *plóg-sveinn*) or ploughmen. It was outside the city walls. Coney St is 'king's street', from Da *kunung*. Feasegate was formerly *Fesegayle*, a purely Scandinavian name from ON *fé-hús, fjós* 'cowhouse' and *geil* 'a narrow passage', an element formerly found also in Felter Lane, *Feltergayle* 13th, 'felt-makers' passage', and in the lost *Thursgayle* c1200, 'giant's lane', from ON *þurs* 'giant'. The most curious name of all, Whip-ma Whop-ma Gate is obscure. It is not found before the sixteenth century, when it appears as *Whipnam Whapnamgate* and *Whipney-Whapneygate*, which has been associated with *whip, whipman* 'whipper', *whap* 'to bark' and *whappet* 'a small dog given to yelping'. It has been suggested that the name might be due to the local custom of dog-whipping on St Luke's Day or to the whipping-post and pillory which were situated at the end of the street.

The City of London

Most City street-names are compounded with *street* or *lane*, less commonly with *row, alley* or *hill*; *road* is not a City term. Farringdon St only becomes Farringdon Road outside the City boundary. OE *strǣt* originally meant a paved road, particularly a Roman road, but was also used of a street in a town. The laws of Henry I provided that a street should be sufficiently broad for two loaded carts to pass and for 16 armed knights to ride abreast, and streets in towns probably satisfied this requirement. A lane was much narrower, one thirteenth-century record stating that it should be wide enough for a cask of wine to be rolled along it transversely with one man on each side. Fye Foot Lane was so called because it was 5 feet broad. Other medieval City lanes are stated to have had a width of 7, 12 or 18 feet. The names of these streets and lanes varied from time to time and many of the old names have disappeared. Gresham St, e.g., first recorded in 1845 and named from Gresham College, founded in the late sixteenth century, was *Cattestrate* in 1271, *Cattonlane* 1449, *Cateaton St* 1837, with late and curious corruptions of the original 'cats' street'. Full information on such changes and on names difficult to interpret must be sought elsewhere. Here we can deal only with certain general characteristics and one or two names of interest.

It was a common practice in medieval London to name streets after the owner of some prominent house. Many of these names have been changed or have disappeared, but some persist, e.g. Philip Lane, already *Philippeslane* in 1179, although Philip cannot be identified; Gutter Lane, *Godrun lane* c1190, was named from a woman with the OE name of *Gōdrūn*; Sermon Lane, *Sarmoneres lane* Hy 3, from Adam *le Sarmoner* 'the preacher of sermons' who had a tenement here in 1228. Wingoose Alley was *Wendegoslane* in 1279, so called from a man named *Wendegos* 'turn goose', probably a derogatory nickname of the same type as *Turnbull*.

One or two of these names contain folk-names and go back ultimately to a period before the Conquest. Maiden Lane, formerly *Ing Lane*, is *Englenelane* in 1282, clearly OE *Englena lanu* 'lane of the Angles', pointing to an Anglian immigration into London. Staining Lane, *Staningelane* c1186, is to be associated with *Stæningahaga*, a place mentioned in an Anglo-Saxon writ of 1053–65, meaning 'the *haga* (town-house or hostel) of the people of Staines (Mx)'. Similarly, Basinghall St was the 'street of *Basingehawe*' (1279), either 'the street of Bassishaw ward' or 'the street by the manor of Bassishaw', 'the town-house or hostel of the Basings' who probably came here from Basing or Basingstoke (Ha). OE *haga* was not used with this special meaning after the Old English period, so that this name, like Staining Lane, is probably a pre-Conquest name.

As we have seen elsewhere, streets often took their name from the commodities sold there, as in Bread St, Milk St[1] and Old Fish St, or from the traders or dealers who lived there. In London, many of the latter type have disappeared. Roper St in Dowgate was an old name of Thames St, Pancras Lane was formerly *Nedlerslane* and Water Lane was *Sporiereslane*, where the spurriers worked. Billeter

---

[1] There is a Milk St in Exeter (Hy 2) and in Hull (1341); in Nottingham, *the Milke Cros* of 1331 is described in 1315 as 'the cross where they sell milk'.

St, *Belʒeterslane* 1298, was the 'lane of the bell-founders'. Cannon St 'street of the candle-makers' has a curious and interesting history. Originally *Candelwrichstrete* c1187, it derives from an otherwise unknown OE *candelwyrhta* 'candle-wright', for which the common term in ME was the French *chandler*. The first *r* of this early form was lost and *ht* became *c* (pronounced *k*), giving *Candelwikstrete* in the thirteenth and fourteenth centuries, which was shortened to *Canwyke strete* in the fifteenth. By 1480 this had become *Canyngesstrete* and by 1664 *Cannon-street*. Birchin Lane is another interesting and difficult name. Stow derived it from a former owner named *Birchouer*, Heuser from ME *berk-chervere* 'bark-carver' or tanner, and Bohman from OE *beorc-ceorfere* 'birch-carver'. Ekwall more plausibly explains the name as 'lane of the barbers', *Bercheruere lane* (1195) deriving from an unrecorded OE *beardceorfere* 'beard-cutter', analogous to the German *Bartscherer* 'barber'. The later development is difficult, but is clear from the forms *Bercheneslane* 1301, *Birchenlane* 1386. Fetter Lane, *Faytureslane* 1292, is from ME *faitour* 'an imposter, cheat, especially a vagrant who shams illness'.

Many names were descriptive of the condition or situation of the streets. Cross Lane was formerly *Fule-lane* in 1265 and *Fowle Lane* in the time of Stow, 'foul, dirty or evil-smelling lane'; from 1288 to 1843 King Edward St was called *Stinking lane*. Addle St is from OE *adela* 'filth, liquid manure' and Pudding Lane was so called, according to Stow, 'because the Butchers of Eastcheape have their skalding House for Hogges there, and their puddinges, with other filth of Beestes, are voided downe that way to theyr dung boates on the Thames'. In ME *pudding* had the sense 'bowels, entrails, guts'.

Fleet St and Holborn preserve the names of streams now underground. London Wall is named from the city wall, the Old Bailey from an outwork in front of the wall and Barbican from an outer fortification or defence to the city. Fenchurch St is the 'street by the church in the fen'. Gracechurch St, *Gærsecherchestrate* 1284 and still *Grasse church streete* in the sixteenth century, is named from St Benet Gracechurch, originally 'grass church', either because it stood in a grassy plot or because it was roofed with turves. The first element was associated with *grace*. In the sixteenth and seventeenth centuries the common pronunciation was *Gracious Street*. Foster Lane was the lane by the church of St Vedast (*venella Sancti Vedasti* 1275, *seint uastes lane* 1271). St Vaast (the correct French form) was Bishop of Arras who died in 539 and was popular in France, where some dozen

237

places called St Vaast preserve his name. The initial *V* was regarded as a dialectal pronunciation of *F*[1] and the name became *Seint Fastes lane* 1321, *Fasteslane* 1337. Then an intrusive *r* was added, an Anglo-Norman feature found elsewhere;[2] hence *Fasterslane* 1359, *fasterlane* 1422; the change to *Foster lane* (1428) was probably dialectal. Miles's Lane, formerly St Michael's Lane, is named from the church of St Michael Crooked Lane. *Mile(s)* was a development of *Mihel*, a common medieval form of *Michael*. Miles Coverdale, when living abroad, called himself Michael Anglus. Sise Lane, *Seint Sytheslane* 1401, is named from the church of St Benet Sherehog, which is also dedicated to St Sithe (*Seinte Site* 1363), who has usually been regarded as St Osyth but the colloquial pronunciation of St Osyth (Essex) is *Toosey*, just as St Olaf has given us Tooley St. This, with the late appearance of the name here, favours Kingsford's preference for Santa Zita of Lucca. Her worship may have been introduced into London by Lombards.

Mincing Lane is one of the few names commemorating the old religious foundations of London. It is from OE *myncen* 'nun', 'the nuns' lane', but as the name dates from at least 1189 it cannot, as suggested by Stow, refer to the nunnery of St Helen's, Bishopsgate, which was not founded until 1212. Crutched Friars, *le Crouchedfrere-strete* 1405, is named from a house of the Crutched Friars or Friars of the Holy Cross, called *the Crossed Friars* in 1533. *Crouched* is from ME *crouch* 'cross'. The Minories was an Abbey of the Minoresses, founded in 1293 for 'The Poor Sisters of Clare', called in Latin *Sorores Minores*. The street-name is late (*Minorie street* 1624).

In three names we have the ME -*bury* 'manor-house', common in Essex and Hertfordshire. Aldermanbury was the street near *Aldres-manesberi* (c1130), 'the manor of the alderman', but the reason for the name is unknown. Bucklersbury was originally a manor or tenement belonging to the family of Warin Bucherel (1104). Lothbury is a much-discussed name. In early sources it refers to a manor or district or a ward and is found both as *Lodebere* c1200, *Lothebiri* 1232, and *Lodingeberi* 1286, *Lothyngebire* 1275. These are probably OE formations from *Hloþan burg* 'manor of Hloþa' and *Hloþingaburg* 'manor of Hloþa's people or descendants'. This same use of -*bury* is found in Middlesex: Bloomsbury, *manerium de Blemund* 1274, *Blemundesberi* 1291, from the family of William Blemund (1202); Barnsbury in Islington, *Iseldon Berners* 1274, *Bernersbury* 1406, from William de

Berners (1235); Brondesbury, probably the manor of Brand, a canon of St Paul's (1180–1216); Gunnersbury, *Gounyldesbury* 1334, the manor of a woman named Gunnhild, and in Finsbury and Mapesbury.

Greater London

The street-names of Greater London are of all kinds and of all periods, preserving old place-names or even field-names, and ranging from the names of noble landlords, their relatives and possessions, to names of inns and inn-keepers, builders, battles and games, convents and theatres, men famous and obscure. Aldwych is the name given by the L.C.C. to the new street of which the eastern arm passes near the site of the old *Wiche St* (1677), earlier *Oldewiche lane* (1393), named from Aldwych 'the old dairy-farm' (1199). Long Acre was 'the pasture called *Longeacre*' in 1547. Great Windmill St was the site of *Windmill Feild* (1585) where the windmill still stood in 1650. Birdcage Walk recalls 'The Bird Cage in St James Park' (1683) where the king had an aviary.

In 1710 the manor of Marylebone was bought by John *Holles*, Duke of Newcastle, who was given that title after his marriage to a daughter and heiress of Henry *Cavendish*, 2nd Duke of Newcastle, a relative of the Duke of *Devonshire*. His daughter and heiress, *Henrietta*, married in 1713 Edward *Harley*, who in 1724 succeeded his father as Earl of Oxford, Earl *Mortimer* and Baron Harley of *Wigmore* Castle and who had property at *Wimpole* (C). The estate passed to William *Bentinck*, 2nd Duke of Portland, whose seat was at *Welbeck* and who had property at *Carburton* and *Clipstone* (Nt) through his marriage with Lady *Margaret* Cavendish Harley, daughter of the above. Their eldest daughter married the 2nd Viscount *Weymouth*. Hence the names Holles St, Cavendish Square, Devonshire St, Henrietta St, Harley St, Mortimer St, Wigmore St, Wimpole St, Bentinck St, Great Portland St, Welbeck St, Carburton St, Clipstone St, Margaret St and Weymouth St. Similar family connexions are commemorated elsewhere, including Bedford Square and Woburn Square (Holborn), Ampthill Square, Tavistock Square, Torrington Place and other neighbouring streets in St Pancras which recall the possessions of the Dukes of Bedford. But Bedford Row in Holborn, with Harpur St, were on an estate bequeathed by Sir William Harper, mayor of London 1561–2, for the foundation and endowment of a school at Bedford. Allen St in Kensington was built in 1820 by one Mr Allen.

Babmaes St in Westminster owes its name to Baptist May, Keeper of the Privy Purse to Charles II.

Red Lion Square is named from a seventeenth-century inn, Three Colt St in Stepney from an inn-sign dating from before 1683, whilst Hungerford Bridge in Westminster owes its name to an inn of a different kind, *Hungerford Inne*, a house mentioned in 1472 as formerly in the possession of Robert Hungerford, knight, Lord Hungerford. Trafalgar Square, constructed in 1829–41, commemorates Nelson's victory of 1805, whilst Wellington St, made c1830 to give approach to Waterloo Bridge, opened in 1817, was named in honour of the Duke of Wellington's defeat of Napoleon at Waterloo in 1815. Maida Vale, a street-name, though often used as if it were the name of a district, was so named from the battle of Maida in Italy (1806) in distinction from *Maida Hill* (1817), preserved in Maida Hill West.

Occasionally an early name has survived. Knightsbridge is found in the reign of Edward the Confessor as *Cnihtebricge* 'the bridge of the young men' who may have been responsible for the upkeep or the defence of this bridge over the Westbourne stream where it is crossed by the Great West Road. Leather lane in Holborn, *Le Vrunelane* 1233, *Louerone lane* 1306, has no connexion with leather, but preserves an OE woman's name *Lēofrūn*. Lots Rd in Chelsea crosses land called *lez lotte* in 1544 and recalls the 'lots' of ground over which the parishioners had Lammas rights. Lambs Conduit St commemorates the public spirit of William Lamb, a citizen of London, who made a new conduit here in 1577. Peerless St in Finsbury is interesting both for its origin and its form. Stow tells us that it took its name from 'one other cleare water called *Perillous pond*, because diuerse youthes swimming therein have been drowned'. It is called *Parlous Pond* in Middleton's *Roaring Girl* (1611) and *Peerless Pool* on a map of 1799. Theobalds Rd is so called because it was the way along which James I rode on his way from Whitehall to Theobalds (Herts). And so we might continue endlessly with scraps of family history and with reminders of what London once was when saffron grew in a garden of Ely House still called Saffron Hill, transformed by Cockney dialect and the parish clerk into *Suffering Hill* in 1750, of the Adelphi, christened in Greek by its builders the Adams *brothers* (Gk ἀδελφοί), and of Soho Square, where hunting took place in 1562. The theory that the name was an old hunting cry is supported by this and by the fact that the name was first given to certain fields, later built over.

But the legend that the name was taken from the Duke of Monmouth's battle-cry at Sedgemoor in 1685 is disproved by the existence of the place-name in 1632. It was rather the house of the Duke which stood here which suggested his battle-cry. But space will permit of further reference only to three much-discussed names.

The original name of Pall Mall was *Spittelstrete* (1222) because it led to St James's Hospital. The modern name occurs as *Pall Mall Walk* in 1650 and *Pell Mell* in 1659. It is named from a game, from Italian *palla* 'a ball' and *maglio* 'a mallet', which reached England by way of OFr *palemaille*, described by Cotgrave as 'a game wherein a round box bowle is with a mallet strucke through a high arch of yron (standing at either end of an alley one) which he that can do at the fewest blowes, or at the number agreed on, winnes'. When the *Pall-Mall* became a residential street, the new Mall was constructed in the Park itself.

The earliest reference to Piccadilly is *Pickadilly Hall in St Martin in the Fields* (1623), where, says Kingsford, the name is applied to 'a range of houses extending up the east side of Windmill Street, whence it came to be applied generally to the neighbouring district and more particularly to the gaming house and ordinary at Shaver's Hall. In none of these uses did it apply to any part of the street now called Piccadilly'. As long ago as 1656, Blount mentions two possible derivations, based on the supposition that the name is to be associated with *piccadil*, used in the seventeenth century of 'a border of cut work inserted on the edge of an article of dress, especially on a collar or ruff, later transferred to the collar itself'. He suggested that the ordinary called *Pickadilly* might have been so called because it was then 'the outmost or *skirt* house of the suburbs that way' or from the fact that a certain tailor who built it 'got much of his estate by Pickadillies which in the last age were much worn in England'. That such a nickname is quite possible is proved by the statement in 1636 that 'Simone Austbiston's house is newly christened. It is called Shaver's Hall as other neighbouring places thereabout are nicknamed Tart Hall and Pickadel Hall.' The name of the Hall was soon applied to the district and then to the street. This was first known as *Portugal Street*, from Catharine of Braganza, queen of Charles II, and is *Piccadilly Street alias Portugal Street* in 1685.

Pimlico Rd in Westminster is called *Strumbelo* in 1746, south-east of the earlier *Rombelowe Feilds* (1614). *Rombelowe* was originally a meaningless refrain to a sea-chanty and came to be used as a comic

241

place-name as in the *londe of Rombelowe* (1530) and *Rumbelow fayr* (1549). The modern name is derived from the name of the district, *Pimplico* (1630). There was a similar place-name in Hoxton, surviving in Pimlico Walk, *Pimlyco or Runne Redcap* 1609, *Pimlico House* 1742, *Pimlico Gardens* 1799. A clue to the origin of the name is found in a rare pamphlet, *Newes from Hogsdon* (1598), 'Have at thee then, my merrie boyes, and hey for old Ben Pimlico's nut browne.' It would appear that Ben Pimlico was a well-known Hoxton inn-keeper whose name was later given to his house. The Westminster name, applied to a district almost uninhabited before the nineteenth century, was presumably transferred from that at Hoxton, though actual proof is not forthcoming.

FOR FURTHER READING

Vol. I, Pt. I of the publications of the English Place-name Society (EPNS), *Introduction to the Survey of English Place-names*, by A. Mawer and F. M. Stenton (Cambridge, 1924), contains a series of essays by experts on the various aspects of the subject. Though written as a preliminary to the survey, the book is still sound and reliable. For a full and detailed treatment of the elements found in place-names, reference should now be made to Vols. XXV and XXVI, A. H. Smith's *English Place-name Elements* (Cambridge, 1956), which contains a useful introduction.

The most complete reference-book for the chief English place-names (towns, parishes, etc.), with an invaluable introduction, is E. Ekwall's *The Concise Oxford Dictionary of English Place-names* (4th ed., Oxford, 1960). The fullest treatment of the place-names of the counties will be found in the county volumes of the EPNS, each containing an important historical introduction. Those already published are:

A. Mawer and F. M. Stenton: II *Buckinghamshire* (1925), III *Bedfordshire and Huntingdonshire* (1926), IV *Worcestershire* (1927), VI, VII *Sussex* (1929–30).

A. H. Smith: V *North Riding of Yorkshire* (1928), XIV *East Riding of Yorkshire* (1937), XXX–XXXVII *West Riding of Yorkshire* (1961–3).

J. E. B. Gover, A. Mawer and F. M. Stenton: VIII, IX *Devon* (1931–2), X *Northamptonshire* (1933), XI *Surrey* (1934), XIII (*Warwickshire* (1936), XV *Hertfordshire* (1938), XVI *Wiltshire* (1939), XVII *Nottinghamshire* (1940), XVIII *Middlesex* (1942).

P. H. Reaney: XII *Essex* (1935), XIX *Cambridgeshire and the Isle of Ely* (1943).

A. M. Armstrong, A. Mawer, F. M. Stenton and Bruce Dickins: XX, XXI XXII *Cumberland* (1950–2).

M. Gelling: XXIII, XXIV *Oxfordshire* (1953–4).

K. Cameron: XXVII, XXVIII, XXIX *Derbyshire* (1959).

For other counties the best volumes available are: A. T. Bannister, *Herefordshire* (Cambridge, 1916); W. H. Duignan, *Staffordshire* (London, 1902); E. Ekwall, *Lancashire* (Manchester, 1922); A. Fägersten, *Dorset* (Uppsala, 1933); A. Goodall, *South-West Yorkshire* (Cambridge, 1914); H. Kökeritz, *Isle of Wight* (Uppsala, 1940); A. Mawer, *Northumberland and Durham* (Cambridge, 1920); F. W. Moorman, *West Riding of Yorkshire* (Leeds, 1910); W. W. Skeat, *Suffolk* (Cambridge, 1913); F. M. Stenton, *Berkshire* (Reading, 1911); J. K. Wallenberg, *Kentish Place-names* (Uppsala, 1931), *Place-names of Kent* (Uppsala, 1934).

Chapter II

Simeon Potter's *Our Language* (Pelican Books, 1950) includes useful chapters on Old English, Scandinavian and French, and Etymology and Meaning, with an excellent treatment of Sounds and Spellings and a brief chapter on Names of Persons and Places. The standard work on English Pronunciation is Daniel Jones's *An Outline of English Phonetics* (6th. ed. London, 1940). A. Mawer's *Problems of Place-name Study* (Cambridge, 1929) is valuable for its discussion of methods and problems.

Chapter IV

Information about personal-names is scattered. The best brief account is Sir Frank Stenton's *Personal Names in Place-names* (EPNS I), and, for women's names, his *The Place of Women in Anglo-Saxon Society* (*Trans. Royal Hist. Soc.*, 4th Ser., 1943). The post-Conquest survival of OE and Scandinavian personal-names is discussed in the Introduction to P. H. Reaney's *Dictionary of British Surnames* (London, 1958). For a discussion of Scandinavian and 12th century personal-names, reference may be made to Stenton's *The Danes in England* (2nd Impr., Oxford, 1957) and *The Danish Settlement of Eastern England* (*Trans. Royal Hist. Soc.* 4th Ser., XXIV, 1942).

Chapter V

E. Ekwall, *The Celtic Element* (EPNS I, 1920).
Scandinavians and Celts in the North-west of England (Lund, 1918).
English River-Names (Oxford, 1928).
J. E. B. Gover, *Cornish Place-names* (*Antiquity* II, 1928), 319–27.
The Element Ros in Cornish Place-names (*London Medieval Studies*, V, 1938), 249–64.
K. Jackson, *Language and History in Early Britain* (Edinburgh, 1953).
F. M. Stenton, *England in the Sixth Century* (*Trans. Royal Hist. Soc.*, 4th Ser. XXI, 1939).

Chapter VI

H. Bradley, *English Place-names* (*Essays and Studies*, English Assoc., I (1910); reprinted in *The Collected Papers of Henry Bradley*, Oxford, 1928).
B. Dickins, *English Names and Old English Heathenism* (*Essays and Studies*, English Assoc., XIX, Oxford, 1934).
Place-names formed from Animal-Head Names (*Place-names of Surrey*, EPNS XI, Cambridge, 1934).
E. Ekwall, *English Place-names in* -ing (Lund, 1923).
Names of Trades in English Place-names (in *Historical Essays in Honour of James Tait*, Manchester, 1933).
A. H. Smith, *Place-names and the Anglo-Saxon Settlement* (British Academy, Oxford, 1956).

F. M. Stenton, *The English Element* (EPNS I, 1924).
The English Occupation of Southern Britain (*Trans. Royal Hist. Soc.*, 4th Ser., XXII, 1940).
S. W. Wooldridge, *The Anglo–Saxon Settlement* (H. C. Darby, *Historical Geography of England*, Cambridge, 1951).

Chapter VII

G. Barnes, *The Evidence of Place-names for the Scandinavian Settlements in Cheshire* (*Trans. Lancs and Ches. Antiq. Soc.*, LXIII, 1954).
E. Ekwall, *The Scandinavian Element* (EPNS I, 1924).
The Scandinavian Settlement (H. C. Darby, *Historical Geography of England*, Cambridge, 1951).
H. Lindkvist, *Middle-English Place-names of Scandinavian Origin*, (Uppsala, 1912).
F. M. Stenton, *The Danish Settlement of Eastern England* (*Trans. Royal Hist. Soc.*, 4th Ser., XXIV, 1942).
The Danes in England (Oxford, 1927).
F. T. Wainwright, *Early Scandinavian Settlement in Derbyshire* (*Trans. Derbyshire Arch. and Nat. Hist. Soc.*, XX, 1947).
The Scandinavians in Lancashire (*Trans. Lancs. and Ches. Antiq. Soc.*, LVIII, 1948).

Chapter VIII

The standard work on Anglo–Norman Influence on English Place-names is R. E. Zachrisson's *Anglo–Norman Influence on English Place-names* (Lund, 1919). Briefer, and more accessible, is his *The French Element* (EPNS I), where James Tait's *The Feudal Element* gives a good general outline but needs revision in some details and can be much expanded from the county volumes.

Chapter X

W. Fraser, *Field-names in South Derbyshire* (Ipswich, 1947). The introductory matter is of general interest.
A. Mawer, *The Study of Field-names in relation to Place-names* (in *Historical Essays in Honour of James Tait*, Manchester, 1933).
J. G. O'Leary, *Dagenham Place-names* (Dagenham, 1958).
P. H. Reaney, *Place-names of Walthamstow* (Walthamstow, 1930).
F. T. Wainwright, *Field-names* (*Antiquity* XVII, 1943).
Field-names of Amounderness Hundred (*Trans. Hist. Soc. Lancs. and Ches.*, XCIX, 1945).
The Scandinavians in Lancashire (*Trans. Lancs. and Ches. Antiq. Soc.*, LVIII, 1948).

Chapter XI

The volumes of the Place-name Society include the street-names of the chief towns; those in Greater London will be found in the volumes for Middlesex and Surrey. For the City of London, the latest and most reliable book is E. Ekwall's *Street-names of the City of London* (Oxford, 1954), which discusses the value of earlier work.

ADDENDA

K. Cameron, *English Place-names* (London, 1961).

G. J. Copley, *Names and Places* (London, 1963).

E. Ekwall, *English Place-names in* -ing (2nd ed., Lund, 1962).

J. Irwin, *Place-names of Edenbridge* (Edenbridge and District Historical Society, 1964).

K. I. Sandred, *English Place-names in "-stead"* (Uppsala, 1963).

G. Turville-Petre, *Thurstable*, in *English and Medieval Studies Presented to J. R. R. Tolkien*, ed. N. Davis and C. L. Wrenn (London, 1962).

F. T. Wainwright, *Archaeology and Place-names and History* (London, 1962).

[None of these books have been used here.]

From time to time articles on Place-names appear in Philological Journals published in England, Germany, Holland, Sweden and America. Also in *Onoma, Antiquity* and *Names* (Journal of the American Name Society), in the Transactions of Archaeological and Historical Societies and in collections of essays and studies. Only a selection can be given here:

G. Barnes, *Some Characteristics of Cheshire Place-names* (Lancs. Dial. Soc., 1956).

K. Cameron, *A note on the Celtic element in English Place-names* (Jnl. Derby. Arch. and Nat. Hist. Soc., no. 79, 1959).

P. Clemoes, *The Anglo-Saxons . . . Studies presented to Bruce Dickins* (London, 1959). Includes:

    K. Cameron, *An Early Mercian Boundary in Derbyshire: The Place-name Evidence*. And

    A. H. Smith, *Two Notes on some West Yorkshire Place-names*.

Bruce Dickins, *English Place-name Studies since 1901* (*Antiquity*, 1963).

M. Gelling, *Some notes on the place-names of Birmingham and the surrounding district* (Birm. Arch. Soc., vol. 72, 1954).

Place-names and Anglo-Saxon Paganism (Univ. Birm. Hist. Jnl., 1961).

C. Hart, *Place-names derived from the 'Solandae' of St Paul's* (*Notes and Queries*, vol. 202, 1957).

C. F. C. Hawkes, *The Jutes of Kent* (in *Dark-Age Britain: Studies presented to E. T. Leeds*, ed. D. B. Harden, London, 1956).

Simeon Potter, *Cheshire Place-names* (Trans. Hist. Soc. Lancs. and Ches., vol. 106).

South-west Lancashire Place-names (ibid., 1959).

P. H. Reaney, *The Face of Essex: A Study in Place-names* (Essex Review, 1948).

Gernon, Garland and Garnish (Trans. Essex Arch. Soc., vol. XVII).

Land-owners and Place-names (ibid.).

The Place-names of Suffolk (The Village, vol. 10, 1955).

Place-names and Early Settlement in Kent (Arch. Cant., vol. LXXVI, 1961).

F. S. Scott, *The Place-names of Derbyshire* (Jnl. Derby. Arch. and Nat. Hist. Soc., no. 79, 1959).

G. R. Stewart, *Leah, Woods and Deforestation as an influence on Place-names* (Names, vol. 10, 1962).

F. L. Utley, *The Linguistic Component of Onomastics* (Names, vol. 11, 1963).

C. L. Wrenn, *The Place-name Bristol* (Names, vol. 5, 1957).

The following will be found useful in tracing articles:

W. Bonser, *An Anglo-Saxon and Celtic Bibliography* (*450–1087*), Oxford, 1957.

Index of Subjects

adjectives, inflexion, 39–40
afnám, 213
aldermann, 147–8
Anglo-Norman spelling and pronunciation, 8, 26, 72, 73–4, 80, 198–202
Anglo-Saxon settlement, 90, 92, 110; Devon, 86; secondary settlement, 127–37
article, definite, 37–8

bēan, 221–2
bearu, 34
bee-keeping, 153
beorg, 34
bōcland, 146
bod, bos, 67, 95
*boia, 150
booth, 175, 176
bōðl, bōtl, bold, 139
bridges, 217–18
British language, 87
Britons, survival of, 83–5, 86–7; bilingual, 87–8
burg, burh, 33–4, 144
bury, 34, 238
by, 171–2

cald, 47
calf, 47
camping, 160
cangeon, 208
carfax, 233–4
ceaster, 26, 79–80, 199, 203–4
Celtic compounds, 87, 96; elements, 74–5, 77, 81, 86–7, 92–6; personal-names, 64, 66–70; Cumbric, 98; Irish, 69–70, 97–8; place-names, distribution of, 88–90; Cheshire, 84, 92; Cornwall, 93–7; Devonshire, 85–7; Gloucestershire, 92; Herefordshire, 90–2; Shropshire, 92; Worcestershire, 92–3
ceorl, 149
*cēto-, 74
chalk, 47
chart, 133
cheap, 227
chipping, 227
Christian associations, 123–7

church, 123–6
cild, 148–9
cniht, 148
consonantal changes, 40–2
conynger, 219
cote, 35–7, 137
criminals, 157–9
cristel-mæl, 126, 216
crūc, 75, 125
customs, old, 209, 217

dane, 45, 162
Danish inflexions, 164; test-words, 175–6; personal-names, 57; settlement, 177–84; Cambridgeshire, 181; Derbyshire, 182; Durham, 180–1; Lincolnshire, 181–2; Norfolk, 183–4; Northants, 182–3; Northumberland, 180; Notts, 182; Suffolk, 184–5; Yorkshire, 180
dative plural, 35, 36, 37, 135; singular, 34, 36, 37, 38
denn, 130–1
devise, 196
dialect, 6, 43–8
dragons, 224
dwarfs, 208, 223

ēa, 37, 45
eccles, 81
ecclesiastical endowments, 195, 215–17
ēg, 37–8
erg, 98, 186
etymologies, popular, 1–5, 10, 14–16, 28, 53, 88, 91, 96, 198

fann, 45
farming, 131, 133, 135–7, 151–2, 155–6
feudal names, 60–6, 205–6
field church, 124
field-names, 207–25; Lancashire, 209; of historical importance, 210–11
finkle, 234
folcland, 146
fold, 131–2
folk-names, 99–110, 127–8, 236
forest-names, 74, 82
French language in England, 6, 7, 192–3; (en) le, 197–8; place-names, 193–7; burgesses, 199, 231–2

*gafolmann, 150
games, 159–61
garston, 219
*gē, 103–4
(ge)būr, 149–50
(ge)flit, 214–5
(ge)hæg, 37, 142
genitive plural, 38; singular, 33–4
(ge)sell, 134
(ge)set, 134
giants, 224
gill, 176
'Grimston hybrids', 170–1
group migration, 101–3

habitation-names, 30, 127–30, 138–9
halh, 32–3
hām, 39, 138
*hāð, 45, 109
hearh, 117–8
heathenism, Anglo-Saxon, 116–23;
  Scandinavian, 190–1
hīd, 146–7
hill-names, 73–5
hitching, 214
hīwisc, 147
hlaða, 174
holm, 176
hybrids, Celtic, 74, 75, 88, 92, 94, 95,
  204; Scandinavian, 169–71

inflexions, Old English, 9, 10, 32–40,
  53; Scandinavian, 163–4, 186, 187
-ing, 111–12
-ingahām, 112–13
-ingas, 106–10, 112–13
-ington, 114–16
inheche, 214
inhōke, 214
innam, 213
*inning, 213
inorganic r, 48, 237–8
intak, 213
inversion compounds, 69–70, 187

jewries, 232–3

land tenure, 146–7
Latin attributes, 205–6; influence,
  203–6; names, 203–4
lousy, 218–19

markets, 226–9
minster, 123
morgen-gifu, 145–6
mynydd, 74

nature-names, 30, 32–4, 74–5, 139–41,
  145
nicknames, 65, 209, 210, 218–21

nominative plurals, 36, 37
Norwegian inflexions, 164, 186, 187;
  settlement, 98, 185–90; Cheshire,
  186; Cumberland, 187–8; Lancashire, 186–7; Westmorland, 187;
  Yorkshire, 188–9; test-words, 98,
  176

penn, 75, 95
personal-names: Breton, 60, 64; Celtic,
  64, 66–7, 69; Cornish, 67–8; Danish,
  57; Irish, 64, 69–70, 172, 187;
  Norman-French, 49, 59–60, 64–5;
  Old English, 49, 50–5, 59, 64; survival of, 54–5, 59; unrecorded, 53–5,
  107–8; Scandinavian, 49, 55–9, 64;
  in Normandy, 56; bynames, 58–9;
  post-Conquest, 49, 60, 172; women's
  names, 59, 143–5
pightel, 222–3
plurals, strong and weak, 37; v. dative,
  genitive, nominative
pol, 95
prepositions, 30–2, 37–8, 94
preye, 196
principles of place-name study, 17–19
pronunciation, 6, 7, 17
Puck, 223–4

river-names, 71–2, 75–9, 89, 97, 111;
  back-formations, 77; lost, 77;
  sacred, 77–9
Romano-British towns, 79–80, 104, 204
ros, 75, 95

sǣte, 104
sǣtr, 174–5
Scandinavian elements, 171–5; hybrids
  169–71; inflexions, 163–4, 187,
  188; personal-names, 55–9, 64, 69;
  place-names Anglicised, 169; pure
  Scandinavian place-names, 163–4;
  settlement: Danish, 162, 177–84;
  Norwegian, 185–90
Scandinavianised place-names, 165–9
scucca, 224
scydd, 132–3
social classes, 147–50, 172
sound-substitution, 165–6
spelling, 5–7, 8, 12–13, 18, 28–9
stoc, 127, 128–9
stōdfold, 156
stow, 11, 126–7
street-names, 226–42; Barnstaple, 231,
  234; Beverley, 228, 230, 231, 232;
  Birmingham, 229, 230, 231; Bury St
  Edmunds, 230, 232; Cambridge,
  227–8, 233; Canterbury, 226, 227;
  Carlisle, 228, 230, 232, 234; Chesterfield, 229, 230; Colchester, 229, 231;

Coventry, 227, 230, 234; Exeter, 228, 229, 230, 233; Hedon, 230, 231; Hertford, 227; Horsham, 233; London: City, 227, 231, 233, 235–9; Greater London, 239–42; Newark, 230; Northampton, 227, 229, 231; Nottingham, 228, 229, 230, 231, 233, 234; Oxford, 229, 231, 232, 233; Peterborough, 228, 230; Richmond, 232; St Albans, 227, 232; Salisbury, 227, 228, 229, 230; Scarborough, 230; Southampton, 232; Stratford on Avon, 229; Warwick, 227, 233; Winchester, 226, 227, 229, 230, 233; Worcester, 227, 228, 230, 234; York, 228, 233, 234–5

*strūt, 215

superstitious beliefs, 208, 209, 223–4

surnames in place-names, 50, 59, 60–6

thane, 148

thorp, 172–4

threap, 214

thwaite, 175

þyrs, 224

toft, 174

topography, 19–21

trade-names, 150–1, 156–7, 228–31, 235, 236–7

tref, 67, 95–6

tūn, 39, 59, 60, 63–4, 138, 170–1

voiced f, 48; s, 47–8

vowel shortening, 40

wald, 45

ware 'dwellers', 104–6

Weald, The, 130–4

wella, 46

wēoh, wīh, 118

wīc, 134–7

word-substitution, 166–7

worð, 129–30

worðig, 142

wroht, 215

Index of Place-names

Abbas Combe (So), 205
Abbess Roding (Ess), 205
Abbot's Hall (Ess), 205
Abbot's Wick Fm (Ess), 205
Abinger (Sr), 113, 129
Ab Kettleby (Lei), 57
Abram (La), 41, 145
Abthorpe (Nth), 182
Acaster Malbis (WRY), 65
Ackton (WRY), 40
Acomb (Nb, NRY, WRY), 35, 44
Acton, 40; (Do), 38, 152
Adam's Grave (W), 118
Adderbury (O), 144
Addington (Bk), 129
Adisham (K), 140
Adlestrop (Gl), 38, 174
Adsett (Gl), 134
Adstock (Bk), 129
Afflington (Do), 59, 116
Aglionby (Cu), 60
Aike (ERY), 44
Aikhead (Cu), 170
Ailby (L), 57
Aintree (La), 187
Aire, R., 83
Aislaby (Du), 58, 181
Aismunderby (WRY), 163
Akeman Street, 2
Alby (Nf), 57
Aldborough (Nf), 156
Aldby (Cu), 188
Alde, R. (Sf), 77
Aldeburgh (Sf), 77
Alderby (W), 144
Aldercar Wood (Ess), 169
Aldermaston (Berks), 148
Alderton (Nth), 49
Aldridge (St), 135
Alexanderhayes (D), 37
Alfold (Sr), 131
Alkham (K), 117
Allacott (D), 137
Allecombe (D), 145
Allerdale (Cu), 164
Allonby (Cu), 49, 60
Almer (Do), 152
Alm'ners, The (Sr), 195
Almonry, Upper, Lower (Sx), 195
Alnwick (Nb), 135
Alphamstone (Ess), 13
Alpraham (Ch), 138
Alresford (Ha), 53
Alston (Cu, D), 42
Alstonby (Cu), 56
Alstone (Gl, St), 42
Althorpe (L), 57

Altofts (WRY), 170
Alvardiscott (D), 137
Alvechurch (Wo), 123
Alveley (Sa), 145
Amblehurst (Sx), 132
Ambleside (We), 41
Amery Court (K), 195
Amney Crucis (Gl), 206
Amotherby (NRY), 163
Amounderness (La), 163, 209, 213–4, 215
Ampers Wick (Ess), 195
Andover (Ha), 77
Andyke (Ha), 119
Anglezark (La), 187
Anhay (Co), 95
Anmers Fm (Berks), 195
Annington (Sx), 136
Anton, R. (Ha), 77
Apethorpe (Nth), 57
Appersett (NRY), 174
Appleby (Db), 182
Applethwaite (Cu, We), 175
Arbury Hill Camp (Nth), 166
Archenfield (He), 90
Ardingly (Sx), 113
Ardington Wick (Berks), 137
Argam (ERY), 98
Arkholme (La), 98
Arkleside (NRY), 175
Arlington (D), 42
Armathwaite (Cu), 195
Armingford (C), 139
Armitage (St), 195
Armoury Fm (Ess), 48, 195
Armscott (Wo), 137
Arncott (O), 137
Arracott (D), 38
Arram (ERY), 98
Arras (ERY), 98
Arrowe (Ch), 98, 186
Arrowfield Top (Wo), 117
Arun, R. (Sx), 77
Asby (Cu, We), 167
Ascot (Berks, O), 45, 137
Ascott (Bk), 45
Asgarby (L), 58
Ashbury (Berks, D), 167
Ashby (Nf), 167, 183; (Sf), 184
Ashby Magna, Parva (Lei), 206
Ashby Puerorum (L), 205
Ashby St Ledgers (Nth), 167, 182
Ashdown (Berks), 53
Asheldham (Ess), 138
Ashfield, 40
Ashford (K), 141; (Mx), 18, 81
Ashington (So), 32
Ashley, 40

Ashmansworth (Ha), 129
Ashton, 168
Ashton-under-Lyne (La), 82
Ashwater (D), 64
Ashwell (Nf), 172
Ashwellthorpe (Nf), 172
Ashwick (So), 135
Askham (Nt, We), 169
Aslockton (Nt), 49, 58
Aspatria (Cu), 70, 187
Aspinwall (La), 46
Assart Fm (Nth), 197
Asselby (ERY), 57
Astall (O), 45
Astcote (Nth), 45
Astey (Beds), 45
Astle (Ch), 45
Astley (La, Sa), 45
Aston, 45
Aston Subedge (Gl), 206
Astrop (O), 174
Astwell (Nth), 45
Astwick (Beds), 45, 135
Astwood (Bk, Wo), 45
Atterby (L), 164
Audleby (L), 164
Audlem (Ch), 82, 92
Ault Hucknall (Db), 198
Aust (Gl), 204
Austby (WRY), 172
Austle (Co), 60
Australia (C), 220
Austy Wood (Wa), 126
Aveland (L), 191
Aveley (Ess), 145
Avely Hall (Sf), 145
Avenham (La), 214
Avening (Gl), 107
Averingdown (Bk), 55
Avon, R., 77
Axe, R., 77
Aylesbury (Bk), 137
Aylton (He), 145
Azores (D), 55

Babraham (C), 138
Badby (Nth), 166, 182
Baddow (Ess), 77
Badsell (K), 134
Bainton (Nth, O), 200
Balking (Berks), 112
Balland (C), 222
Balterley (St), 145
Bamburgh (Nb), 144
Bampton (Cu, O), 221
Bancroft (C), 222
Bank Barn (C), 21
Bannolds (C), 222
Banstead (Sr), 140, 221
Bapchild (K), 140
Barbican (Co), 96
Barbon (We), 154
Barby (Nth), 182, 207
Bareleigh (Wa), 154
Bareppa (Co), 193
Baretilt (K), 154
Barford (Sr, Wa), 154
Barkby (Lei), 57, 172
Barkby Thorpe (Lei), 172

Barkestone (Lei), 57
Barking (Ess), 1, 106
Barkston (L, WRY), 57
Barley (Lei, WRY), 154, 156
Barlinch (So), 156
Barlow (Db, La), 154; (Nb), 156
Barming (K), 108
Barnby (Sf), 184
Barnetby le Wold (L), 164
Barnfold (Sx), 132
Barnsbury (Mx), 238
Barnwell (C), All Saints (Nth), 15
Barr, Great (St), 75
Barrack (So), 137
Barricks (Ess), 137
Barriper (Co), 193
Barrow, 34
Barrow upon Humber (L), 34, 139
Barton, 138
Barton in Fabis (Nt), 206
Barton in the Beans (Lei), 206
Barton le Street (NRY), 197
Barton le Willows (NRY), 197
Barugh (NRY, WRY), 34
Barville (K), 154, 202
Barwell (Lei), 154
Barwick (Nf, WRY), 137
Barwick in Elmet (WRY), 83
Baschurch (Sa), 123
Basford (Nt), 54
Basing (Ha), 54, 129, 236
Basingstoke (Ha), 54, 129, 236
Bath (So), 35
Battersby (NRY), 58
Battersea (Sr), 41
Battle (Sx), 194
Battrix (WRY), 98, 188
Baxterley (Wa), 156
Bayford (K, So), 150
Baysham Court (He), 91
Beachy Head (Sx), 193
Beaconsfield (Bk), 53
Beadlam (NRY), 139
Beaminster (Do), 123
Beamish (Du), 193
Beamond End (Bk), 193
Beamonds (Sr), 193
Bean, R. (Herts), 79
Beanthwaite (La), 170, 175
Beara, Beare (D), 35
Bearl (Nb), 156
Bear Park (Du), 193
Beauchamp Roding (Ess), 108
Beauchief (Db), 193
Beaudesert (St, Wa), 193
Beaufront Castle (Nb), 193
Beaulieu (Ha), 193
Beaumanor (Lei), 193
Beaumont (Ess), 193
Beaurepaire (Ha), 193
Beaute Fm (K), 30
Beauvale (Nf), 193
Beauworth (Ha), 129, 153
Beckermet (Cu), 163
Beckermonds (WRY), 163
Beckery (So), 97
Beckett (Berks), 153
Bedminster (So), 123
Bedruthan (Co), 67

Beeding, Upper, Lower (Sx), 131
Beeleigh (Ess), 153
Beer, Beera, Beere (D), 35
Beer Hackett (D), 64
Beersheba (Co), 96
Beesons, The (C), 32
Beggarsbush Hill (O), 143
Belasis (Du), 191
Belhus (Ess), 148
Bellasis (Du, Nb), 193
Bellassize (ERY), 193
Bellhouse (Ess, NRY), 148
Bellimore (He), 90
Bellingham (W), 52
Belmont (Co), 193
Belper (Db), 193
Belsars Hill (C), 193
Belsay Fields (Cu), 193
Belsize (Herts, Nth), 193
Belsize Park (Mx), 193
Belstead (Sf), 124
Belvoir (Lei), 193
Bembridge (IOW), 31
Bemzells (Sx), 134
Benacre (Sf), 221
Bendish (Herts), 221
Benenden (K), 131
Bengeo (Herts), 79, 113
Bengeworth (Wo), 130
Bennington (Herts), 79
Benson (O), 115, 142
Bentley Pauncefote (Wo), 65
Benwell (Nb), 31
Benwick (C), 223
Benwray (Cu), 170
Beoley (Wo), 153
Bephillick (Co), 68
Berechurch (Ess), 124
Bereppa (Co), 193
Bere Regis (Do), 205
Bergerie (Ha), 197
Berkshire, 82
Berrick Salome (O), 66
Berrier (Cu), 98
Berrow (Wo), 34
Berry (D), 35
Berrynarbor (D), 33, 64
Berry Pomeroy (D), 33
Berwick, 137; Fm (Ess), 142
Berwick Maviston (Sa), 65
Berwick upon Tweed, 137
Beryo (Co), 94
Besthorpe (Nt), 173
Bestwall (Do), 32
Betton-in-Hales (Sa), 82
Beufre (Ha), 197
Bever Grange (D), 193
Bewbush (Sx), 193
Bewcastle (Cu), 176
Bewdley (Wo), 193
Bewick (Nb, ERY), 136, 153
Bewley (Du, We), 193
Bexley (K), 130, 212
Bibbill Fm (ERY), 33
Bibury (Gl), 144
Bicester (O), 26, 42
Bickershaw (La), 153
Bickerstaffe (La), 153
Bickerston (Nf), 153

Bickerton, 153
Biddenden (K), 131
Biddick (Du), 30
Bierton (Bk), 137
Biggin (Ess), 169
Bigods (Ess), 60
Bildeston (Sf), 163
Billinge (La), 111
Billingshurst (Sx), 52
Bilsington (K), 138
Bilsthorpe (Nt), 163
Bilston (St), 104
Bilstone (Lei), 163, 171
Binderton (Sx), 145
Bindon Abbey (Do), 31
Bingletts (Sx), 109
Binstead (IOW), 221
Binsted (Ha, Sx), 221
Birch (Ess), 132
Birdsall (ERY), 32
Birkby (Cu, La, Y), 85
Birker (Cu), 98, 187
Birmingham, 41
Birthwaite (WRY), 175
Bishop's Cleeve (Gl), 139
Bishopstoke (Ha), 99
Bisterne (Ha), 141
Blackberry (Lei), 34
Blackborough (D), 34
Blackfordby (Lei), 171
Blackhay (Co), 96
Blackmanston (K), 59
Blackwater, R. (Ess), 77
Blamster's Hall (Ess), 61
Blanchland (Co, Nb), 197
Blandford Forum (Do), 206
Blansby (NRY), 58
Blean (K), 82
Bleasby (Nt), 167
Blencarn (Cu), 87
Bloomsbury (Mx), 238
Boarhunt (Ha), 34
Boarzell (K), 134; (Sx), 154
Bobbingworth (Ess), 113, 114, 129
Bodbrane (Co), 67
Bodilly (Co), 68
Bodmin (Co), 95
Bognor Regis (Sx), 144, 206
Bold (La, Sa), 139
Boldon (Du), 139
Bolnhurst (Beds), 38
Bolton, 139
Bolton le Sands (La), 197
Bonbusk (Nt), 172
Bongate (We), 172
Bookham (Sr), 140
Boothby (Cu), 98; (L), 172, 175
Bootle (Cu, La), 139
Boreat (D), 148
Borrowdale (Cu, We), 163, 164
Borwick (La), 137
Boscastle (Co), 61, 95
Boscawen (Co), 95
Boship Fm (Sx), 150
Bossiny (Co), 95
Boswase (Co), 67
Boswhiddle (Co), 68
Boswyn (Co), 67
Bothel (Cu), 139

INDEX OF PLACE-NAMES

Bottesford (L, Lei), 139
Boucherne (Ess), 47
Bourn (C), 181
Bournville (Wa), 202
Bourton (D), 150
Bovinger (Ess), 113, 114
Bowcombe (IOW), 31
Bowderdale (Cu), 176
Bowood (Do), 31
Bowrish (D), 147, 150
Bowscale (Cu), 187
Bowzell (K), 134
Boycombe (D), 150
Boycote (K), 150
Boycott (Wo, Sa, Bk), 150
Boy Court (K), 150
Boyden (K), 150
Boyke (K), 150
Boyland (Nf), 150
Boyton (Co, Ess, K, Sf, W), 150
Braceby (L), 164
Bradfield Combust (Sf), 206
Bradford (WRY), 143, 208
Bradkirk (La), 168
Bradney Fm, Ho (C), 20
Bradwall (Ch), 46
Bradwell (Sf), 184
Bradwell juxta Mare (Ess), 206
Brafferton (NRY), 141
Braffords (ERY), 175
Brail (W), 197
Brain, R. (Ess), 77
Braintree (Ess), 66, 77
Braithwaite (Cu, Y), 175
Braithwell (WRY), 166
Brampton Bryan (He), 64, 90
Brampton en le Morthen (WRY), 197
Brandon Parva (Nf), 206
Bran End (Ess), 45
Branksome (Do), 66
Brannetts (Ess), 45
Branscombe (D), 66
Brant Broughton (L), 206
Branxton (Nb), 66
Bratoft (L), 174
Braughing (Herts), 107
Bray (D), 75
Braydon Hook (W), 22
Bray Wick (Berks), 137
Brazacott (D), 137
Breadon (D), 87
Breadsell (Sx), 134
Breazle (D), 86
Breck (La, NRY, WRY), 176
Bredicote (Wo), 137
Bredon (Wo), 75, 88, 92
Breedon on the Hill (Lei), 75
Brent Eleigh (Sf), 206
Brentwood (Ess), 203
Brenzett (K), 134
Bret, R. (Sf), 77
Bretby (Db), 85, 182
Brettanby (NRY), 70
Brettargh Holt (La), 85
Brettenham (Sf), 77
Bretton (Db, WRY), 85
Brewershill (Beds), 197
Brexworthy (D), 142
Bricett (Sf), 134

Bricklehampton (Wo), 42
Bridgerule (D), 64
Bridgwater (So), 64
Bridstow (He), 11, 90
Brigg (L), 160
Brighstone (IOW), 42
Brighthampton (O), 42
Brightlingsea (Ess), 8–10
Brighton (Sx), 42, 143
Brightwalton (Berks), 115
Brigmerston (W), 59, 138
Brigsteer (We), 187
Brill (Bk), 75
Brimstone Hill (Ess), 61
Briningham (Nf), 128
Brinkhurst (Sx), 132
Brinton (Nf), 128
Briscoe (Cu), 85
Brislington (So), 42
Bristol, 208
Briston (Nf), 77
Britwell Salome (O), 66
Brixton (D), 139; (IOW), 42
Broadfans (Ess), 45
Broadwindsor (Do), 23
Brockhampton (He), 90
Brocklesby (L), 58
Bromholm (Nf), 176
Bromkinsthorpe (Lei), 173
Bromley (K), 130
Bromwich (St, Wa, Wo), 135
Brondesbury (Mx), 239
Brookthorpe (Gl), 174
Broomfield, 30
Brotherilkeld (Cu), 70, 187
Brothertoft (L), 174
Brotherton (Sf), 184
Brough, 33
Brown's Fm (Ess), 142
Broxhead (Ha), 122
Broxted (Ess), 122
Broxtow (Nt), 126
Broyle (Sx), 197
Bruera (Ch), 197
Bruern (O), 197
Bryn (Sa), 75
Brynn (La), 75
Buckden (Hu), 145
Buckhatch Fm (Ess), 148
Buckland, 136, 146
Buckland Sororum (So), 205
Bucklebury (Berks), 144
Buckminster (Lei), 123
Buddle (Ha, Nb), 139
Buddlehay (So), 139
Buddlehayes (D), 139
Buddle Oak (So), 139
Bude (Co), 97
Budleigh (D), 139
Budleigh Salterton (D), 142
Budshead (D), 147
Bugsell (Sx), 134
Bulbeck Common (Du), 181
Bulcamp (Sf), 151
Bulcote (Nt), 36, 137
Bulidge (W), 147
Bulkeley (Ch), 151
Bullington (Ha), 116
Bulmer (Ess), 38

Bulphan (Ess), 45, 201
Bulstrode (Bk), 201
Bulsworthy (Co), 94
Bulverhythe (Sx), 106, 159, 201
Bulwick (Nth), 135
Bunkers Fm (Herts), 220
Bunker's Hill (Herts), 220
Burbage (Db, Lei, W), 33
Burcot (Bk), 137
Burden (Du), 150
Bure (Ha), 30
Bure, R. (Nf), 77
Bures (Ess), 150
Burford (Sa), 33, 150
Burgate (Ha, Sr, Sf), 148
Burgh, 33; (Nf), 77; (Sr), 34
Burgham (Sr), 33
Burgh Apton (Nf), 34
Burghill (He), 33, 141
Burghley (Nth), 33
Burham (K, Sr), 33
Burley (Ha, R), 33
Burlton (He), 141
Burnham (L), 35; (Nf), 172
Burnham Thorpe (Nf), 172, 184
Burraton (Co, D), 150
Burrington (D), 150
Burrough Green (C), 33
Burrow (La), 33
Burrowton (D), 150
Burslem (St), 82
Burstead (Ess), 33
Burston (Bk), 141
Burthwaite Bridge (Cu), 176
Burton Agnes (ERY), 64
Burton End (C), 31
Burton Joyce (Nt), 34
Burton on Trent (St), 34
Burwash (Sx), 33
Burwell (C, L), 33
Bury (Hu, La, Sf), 33
Butterbury (D), 142
Butterwick, 136
Butterworth (La), 129
Butt Hill (Wa), 159
Butts, The (Wa), 159
Buttsbury (Ess), 104
Buxshalls (Sx), 134
Buzzacott (D), 137
Bycott (D), 150
Byfleet (Sr), 30
Byford Tye (Ess), 150
Bygrave (Herts), 30
Byng (Sf), 108
Bystock (D), 150
Bythorn (Hu), 30

Cadeby (L, Lei, WRY), 58, 191
Caerleon (Mon), 93, 204
Caerwent (Mon), 80
Cair (Co), 93
Cairo (Co), 93
Caister (Nf), 80, 204
Caistor (L), 204
Calcote (W), 47
Caldecote (C, Nf, Wa), 47
Calder (La, Y), 77
Caldwall (Wo), 46
Caldy (Ch), 186

Calke (Db), 47
Callington (Co), 94, 129
Callow (Db), 47
Calstock (Co), 129
Calthwaite (Cu), 47, 178
Calveley (Ch), 47
Calverley (WRY), 38, 47
Calverton (Bk, Nt), 38, 47, 138
Calvington (Sa), 47, 116
Calwich (St), 47, 136
Cam (Gl), 77
Cam Beck (Cu), 77; R. (C), 26
Camborne (Co), 96
Cambridge (C), 25–6, 181
Camel, R. (Co), 129
Camels (Co), 96
Camping Close (C), 160
Camping Lane (Db), 160
Candlesby (L), 191
Candleshoe (L), 191
Canewdon (Ess), 202
Cannhall (Ess), 195
Cannings (W), 108
Cannington (So), 116
Cannock Mill (Ess), 195
Canons Ashby (Nth), 182
Canonthorpe (WRY), 173
Canterbury (K), 80, 106
Canterton (Ha), 103
Canter Wood (K), 106, 110
Canvey Island (Ess), 136
Capel (K, Sf, Sr), 195
Capel le Ferne (K), 197
Caple (He), 195
Caradoc (He), 90
Cardew (Co), 93
Careby (L), 58
Cargenwyn (Co), 68
Cargo (Cu), 75
Carham (Nb), 35, 141
Carhampton (So), 141
Cark (La), 75
Carleby (L), 59
Carleen (Co), 93
Carleon (Co), 93
Carleton (Nf), 183
Carley (D), 86
Carlisle (Cu), 79
Carlton, 149, 166, 171; (C), 181
Carlton Colville (Sf), 65
Carlton Curlieu (Lei), 66
Carlyon (Co), 93
Carne (Co), 95
Carnetley (Cu), 69
Carperby (NRY), 70
Carrington (L), 128
Carrock Fell (Cu), 75
Carsawsen (Co), 96
Carsington (Db), 116
Carthew (Co), 93
Carthorpe (NRY), 58
Cartmel (La), 85
Carton (Wo), 93
Carvean (Co), 93
Carveddras (Co), 68
Carwalsick (Co), 95
Carwinley (Cu), 69
Carwyn (Co), 93
Cassington (O), 116

Castle Hewin (Cu), 69
Castor (Nth), 204
Catesby (Nth), 182
Catgill (Cu), 187
Cats Head Lodge (Nth), 122
Catsprey (Sr), 196
Caudle (C), 47
Cauldwell (Beds, Nt), 47
Caulke (Nt), 47
Cawkwell (L), 47
Caxton (C), 170, 181
Caythorpe (ERY, L, Nt), 58
Cerne (Do), 199
Cerne Abbas (Do), 205
Cerney (Gl), 199
Chadbury (Wo), 66
Chaddesden (Db), 66
Chaddleworth (Berks), 66
Chadkirk (Ch), 66
Chadlington (O), 66
Chadshunt (Wa), 66
Chadstone (Nth), 66
Chadsworth (Sr), 66
Chadwell (Ess), 47
Chadwich (Wo), 66
Chadwick (La, Wo), 66
Chaffields (Sx), 131
Chaffolds (Sr), 131
Chalcot (W), 47; (Wa), 149
Chaldecotts (W), 47
Chaldon (Do, Sr), 47
Chalfield (W), 47
Chalfont (Bk), 66
Chalford (O), 66
Chalgrave (Beds), 47
Chalk (K, W), 47
Challabrook (D), 149
Challacombe (D), 47
Challock (K), 47
Chalton (Beds), 149; (Ha), 47
Chalvey (Bk, So), 47
Chapel en le Frith (Db), 197
Chapel Grove (C), 21
Chapel Plaster (W), 160
Chapelthorpe (WRY), 172
Chapmanslade (W), 157
Charaton (Co), 149
Chard (So), 129
Chardle (C), 47
Chardstock (D), 129
Chardwell (Ess), 47, 48
Charford (D), 125; (Wo), 149
Charlacott (D), 149
Charlcote (W), 149
Charlcott (Sa), 150
Charlecombe (D), 149
Charlecote (W), 149
Charleton (D), 149
Charley (Herts), 149
Charlston (Sx), 142, 149
Charlton, 149, 150, 166
Charlton Musgrave (So), 66
Charlwood (D, Sr, Sx), 149
Charminster (Do), 123
Chart (K, Sr), 133
Chartham (K, Sr), 133
Chartland (Sr), 133
Charton (D), 149
Chart Sutton (K), 133

Chartwell (K), 133
Chatham (Ess, K), 74
Chattenden (K), 74
Chatwall (St), 46
Chawleigh (D), 47
Chawton (Ha), 47
Cheadle (Ch, La), 74
Chediston (Sf), 139
Cheetham (La), 74, 81
Cheetwood (La), 81, 88
Cheldon Barton (D), 66
Chelfham (D), 47
Chellington (Beds), 145
Chelmer, R., 77
Chelmsford (Ess), 77
Chelsdon (D), 149
Chelsworth (Sf), 129
Chelvey (So), 136
Chelwood (So), 129
Cheristow (D), 125
Cheriton (D, Ha, K, So), 125, 168;
 Higher, Lower (D), 149
Cheriton Bishop, Fitzpaine (D), 62
Cherrington (Wa), 125
Cherry Hinton (C), 126
Chertsey (Sr), 66
Cherville (K), 149
Chester (Ch), 204
Chesterfield (Db), 204
Chesterford (Ess), 199, 204
Chester le Street (Du), 204
Chesterton (C), 25
Cheswick (Nb, Wa), 136, 166
Chew Magna (So), 206
Chiddingfold (Sr), 131
Chiddingly (Sx), 74
Chideock (Do), 74
Chilbrook (Co), 149
Chilcombe (D), 149
Chilcote (Lei, Nth), 149, 150
Childerley (C), 38, 148
Childhay (Do), 149
Childwall (La), 46
Childwick (Herts), 149, 166
Chilford (C), 148
Chilfrome (Do), 76, 149
Chilham (K), 131
Chilhampton (W), 149
Chillaton (D), 149
Chilley (D), 149
Chillington (D), 66
Chiltern (O), 82
Chilthurst (Sx), 149
Chilton, 148, 150
Chilwell (Nt), 148
Chingford (Ess), 2
Chippenham (C, Gl, W), 199
Chipping (La), 111, 227
Chipping Barnet (Mx), 227
Chipping Campden (Gl), 227
Chippingdale (La), 227
Chipping Norton (O), 206
Chipping Ongar (Ess), 132, 227
Chipstead (K, Sr), 227
Chirbury (Sa), 168
Chirton (Nb, W), 125
Chislet (K), 140
Chiswick (C, Ess, Mx), 136, 166
Chithurst (Sx), 74

Chitterne (W), 74
Chittoe (W), 74
Chocolates (Sr), 133
Cholash (D), 47
Cholwell (So), 47
Chorley (La, Sa, St), 149
Chorleywood (Herts), 149
Chorlton (Ch, La, St), 149
Choulden (W), 47
Christchurch (Ha), 31
Christian Malford (W), 126
Christleton (Ch), 126
Christmas Hill (Wa), 126
Christon (So), 75, 125
Christow (D), 127
Churcham (Gl), 125, 168
Churchdown (Gl), 125
Churchfield Fm (Nth), 125
Church Hill (So), 125
Churchill, 75, 93, 125, 168
Churchingford (D), 126
Church Lawton (Ch), 82
Churchstanton (D), 126
Churchstow (D), 125
Churston Ferrers (D), 62, 125
Churt (Sr), 133
Churton (Ch), 125
Churwell (WRY), 149
Chute (W), 74
Cippenham (Bk), 199
Cirencester (Gl), 73, 199
Clacton (Ess), 114
Clanfield (Ha), 202
Clanville (Ha, So, W), 202
Clare (Sf), 195
Claret Hall (Ess), 195
Clavering (Ess), 112
Claxby (L), 58
Claxton (Du, Nf, NRY), 58
Claycoton (Nth), 36
Clayhill Fm (Mx), 212
Claythorpe (L), 58
Clayton (La, St), 138
Clearfields (Bk), 197
Clear Wood (W), 197
Cleator (Cu), 98, 176, 187
Clemsfold (Sx), 133
Clevancy (W), 64
Clewer (Berks, So), 106
Cliffe at Hooe (K), 106
Climping (Sx), 133
Clint (WRY), 176
Clippesby (Nf), 58
Clipston (Nt, Nth), 58
Clipstone (Nf, Nt), 58
Clixby (L), 58
Clumber (Nt), 75
Clun Forest (Sa), 92
Clun, R. (Sa), 75
Coalville (Lei), 202
Coat (So), 36
Coate (W), 36
Coates (L, Nt, Sx), 36, 137
Coatham (NRY), 36
Coatham Mandeville (Du), 36
Cock-a-troop Cottages (W), 157
Cockayne Hatley (Beds), 61
Cocker (Beck) (Cu, Du, La), 19
Cockerham (La), 19

Cockermouth (Cu), 19
Cockersand (La), 19
Cockerton (Du), 19
Coedmoor (He), 87
Coffcott Green (D), 137
Colchester (Ess), 79, 80
Coldham (Ess), 47
Cold Kirby (NRY), 57
Coldman Hargos (NRY), 70, 98
Coldwell (Nb), 47
Colerne (W), 156
Collecot (D), 47
Collingbourne Ducis (W), 206
Colne, R. (Ess, Herts), 75, 76
Colne Engaine (Ess), 62, 75
Colneis (Sf), 185
Colwall (He), 46
Colwich (St), 135, 156
Colwick (Nt, Wo), 135, 156
Combeinteignhead (D), 147
Combe Martin (D), 61
Commondale (NRY), 70
Compton Abbas (Do), 203
Compton Dando (So), 61–2
Compton Greenfield (Gl), 66
Compton Verney (Wa), 65
Conder (La), 77
Conderton (Wo), 103, 138
Condover (Sa), 77, 92
Coneysthorpe (NRY), 202
Coneythorpe (WRY), 202
Coney Weston (Sf), 202
Coneywood Fen (C), 170
Congerston (Lei), 171, 202
Conington (C), 181
Conisbrough (WRY), 202
Conisby (L), 202
Coniscliffe (Du), 166, 202
Conisford (Nf), 202
Conishead (La), 202
Conisholme (L), 202
Coniston (La, ERY, WRY), 202
Conistone (WRY), 202
Conrish (W), 136
Cooling (K), 107
Corby (Cu), 70
Cornwall, 93
Corringham (L), 128
Corstone (D), 60
Corton (Sf), 59, 184
Cote (O), 36, 137
Coton (C, Nth, Lei), 36
Coton in the Elms (Db), 36
Cotswolds, The, 45
Cottam (La, ERY), 36, 137
Cottarson Fm (D), 37
Cotton (Db, Sf), 37, 137
Cotton Abbots (Ch), 36
Cotton End (Nth), 36
Cound (Sa), 92
Countisbury (D), 87
Coupal's Fm (Ess), 60
Cowage (W), 135
Cowarne (He), 151
Cowdale (Db), 151
Cowden (K), 130
Cowdray (Sx), 197
Cowesby (NRY), 58
Cowey (Ess), 142

256

Cowfold (Sx), 131
Cowick (WRY), 135
Cowick Barton (D), 135
Cowicks (Ess), 135
Cowix (Sx), 135
Cowlands (Co), 96
Cowley (Db, La), 156; (Gl), 151
Cowton (NRY), 138
Crabb Marsh (C), 21
Crabwall (Ch), 46
Cranbrook (K), 131
Craster (Nb), 199
Cray, R. (K), 76, 77
Creech (Do, So), 75
Creechbarrowhill (Do), 87
Creech St Michael (Do), 87
Creeping Hall (Ess), 108
Cressing (Ess), 112
Crewe (Ch), 84, 92
Crewkerne (So), 75
Crewood (Ch), 92
Crich (Db), 75
Crichel (Do), 75, 88
Cricket (So), 195
Cripstone (Co), 60
Crockerton (W), 156
Croftnoweth (Co), 95
Crook (D, Do), 75
Crookbarrow Hill (Wo), 93
Crook Hill (Db), 125
Crosby (Cu), 188; (La), 187
Crosby Ravensworth (We), 64
Crostwick (Nf), 183
Crostwight (Nf), 183
Crouse Harvey (Co), 96
Crowborough (St, Sx), 34
Crow Hill (C), 208
Crowmarsh (O), 142
Crow's Cottage (Ess), 142
Crowton (Ch), 92
Croxall (Db), 182
Croxton (C), 181; (Ch), 186; (St), 183
Croydon (C), 40
Croydon Wilds (C), 46
Cruchfield (Berks), 75
Crumplehorn (Co), 96
Crutch (Wo), 75, 93
Crux Easton (Ha), 64
Cruxton (Do), 59
Cubbington (Bk, Wa), 51
Cubwell (Db), 51
Cuddesdon (O), 52
Culcheth (La), 74
Culgaith (Cu), 74
Culham (Berks), 47
Culvert's Fm (Ess), 60
Cumberland, 69, 100
Cumrew (Cu), 87
Cunnage Lane (W), 136
Curworthy (D), 142
Cutbrawn (Co), 96

Daccombe (D), 154
Dacorum Hundred (Herts), 183
Daffaluke (He), 90
Dagenham (Ess), 140
Dainton (D), 200
Dalch (D), 92
Dalderby (L), 163

Dalemain (Cu), 70
Dalston (Mx), 42
Danaway (K), 45
Danbury (Ess), 202
Danby (NRY), 189
Danby on Ure (NRY), 188
Danby Wiske (NRY), 188
Dane Court, End, Fm, Ho, 45, 162
Danehill (Sx), 45, 162
Danehurst (Sr), 45
Dane John (K), 162
Danes Brook (Bk), 162
Danhill (Sx), 45
Darent, R. (K), 76, 77
Darlaston (St), 42
Darley (Db), 154
Darliston (St), 42
Darlton (Nt), 145
Darmsden (Sf), 40
Dart, R., 77
Darton (WRY), 154
Darwell (Sx), 131
Dawlish (D), 92
Deans Hill (K), 134
Debateable Land. The (Cu), 214
Deben, R. (Sf), 77
Debenham (Sf), 77
Dee, R., 79
Deeping (L), 112
Deerfold (Wo), 154
Deerhurst (Gl), 154
Delapre Abbey (Nth), 196
Denaby (WRY), 189
Denbury (D), 86
Denby (Db, WRY), 189
Dengie (Ess), 114, 202
Dennington (Sf), 116
Denny (C), 181
Denshott (Sr), 132
Dent (Cu, WRY), 111
Deptford (K, W), 41
Derby, 180
Derrington (St), 42
Dersingham (Nf), 113
Derwent, R., 77
Derworthy (D), 142
Desning (Sf), 107
Detling (K), 107
Deveral (Co), 76
Deverill (W), 76, 77
Devil's Dyke (C), 119
Devizes (W), 196
Devon, 85
Devy, R., 77
Dewchurch (He), 67
Diddington (Hu), 42
Diddlesfold (Sx), 133
Didling (Sx), 133
Dinmore (He), 90
Dinting (Db), 111
Dipton (Nb), 40
Diss (Nf), 199
Dissington (Nb), 199
Ditchampton (W), 199
Ditchen (Co), 94
Ditchling (Sx), 106
Docker (La, We), 98
Docking (Nf), 112
Doddington (C, K, L, Nth), 42

257

Dodington (Gl, Sa, So), 42
Doepath (Nb), 154
Dogs, Isle of, 1, 2
Domsey (Ess), 142
Doncaster (WRY), 80, 204
Donnington (Sx), 116
Dorchester (Do), 104, 204
Dore (He), 77
Dorfold (Ch), 154
Dorset, 104
Dorston (He), 91
Dotton (D), 42
Doulting (So), 111
Dour, R. (K), 77
Douthwaite (NRY), 175
Dove, R., 77
Dovehirn (L), 47
Dovenby (Cu), 70
Dover (K), 77, 80, 88
Dover Beck (Nt), 77
Doverdale (Wo), 77
Dowles (Brook) (Wo), 92
Dowlish (So), 92
Downham, 5
Dowsdale (C), 181
Dowthwaite (WRY), 70
Dragley (La), 224
Drakedale (NRY), 224
Drakeholes (Nt), 224
Drakelow (Db, Wo), 224
Drakenage (Wa), 224
Drake North (W), 224
Drake Pits (WRY), 224
Dranneck (Co), 95
Drayton Parslow (Bk), 48
Dringhoe (ERY), 172
Dringhouses (WRY), 172
Drinnick (Co), 95
Drointon (St), 172, 183
Droitwich (Wo), 135, 151
Dromonby (NRY), 164
Drungewick (Sx), 132
Duckett's Fm (Ess), 142
Duddington (Nth), 42
Duggleby (ERY), 70
Dulverton (So), 142
Dunchideock (D), 86
Dungeon Fm (Ess), 162
Dunham, 5
Dunhurst (Sx), 132
Dunmail Raise (Cu), 69
Dunmow (Ess), 5
Dunnington (ERY), 42
Dunsfold (Sr), 131
Dunstall, 4
Dunterton (D), 86
Dunton (Bk), 5, 42
Dunton Basset (Lei), 61
Dunwich (Sf), 20, 88, 143
Dupath (Co), 157
Durfold (Co), 154; (Sr, Sx), 131
Durham, 100, 176, 201
Durleigh (So), 154
Durley (Ha), 154
Durrington (Sx), 132
Duxford (C), 129
Dwariden (WRY), 223
Dwerryhouse (La), 223
Dymchurch (K), 123

Eadens (Ha), 99
Eagle (L), 166
Eakring (Nt), 163
Eardisland (He), 91
Earith (Hu), 141
Earlsbury (Ess), 34
Earls Colne (Ess), 62, 75
Earlside (Nb), 174
Easby (NRY), 57
East Anglia, 99.
Eastbridge, 45
Eastbury (Ess), 34, 45
Eastchurch (D), 32
Eastcott (D), 45, 137
East Horndon (Ess), 104
Easthorpe (Ess), 173; (Nt), 172
Easthwaite (Cu), 175
Eastington (D, Do, Gl, Wa), 32
Eastling (K), 140
Eastoft (ERY), 174
Easton, 32
Easton in Gordano (So), 206
East Riding, 169
Eastrington (ERY), 114
Eastrip (So), 174
Eastrop (Ha, W), 174
Eastry (K), 103, 119, 140
East Sheen (Sr), 194
East Wall (Sa), 46
Eastwick (WRY), 135
Eastwood, 32; (Nt), 175
Easwrithe (Sx), 121
Eathorpe (Wa), 174
Ecchinswell (Ha), 81
Eccles (K, Db, La, Nf), 81
Ecclesall (WRY), 81
Ecclesbourne (Db), 81
Ecclesfield (WRY), 81
Eccleshall (Wa), 81
Eccleshill (La, WRY), 81
Eccleston (Ch, La), 81
Eccleswall (He), 81
Eckington (Db), 114
Edburton (Sx), 145
Edderthorpe (WRY), 173
Eden, R. (K), 77
Edenbridge (K), 77, 130
Edenhall (Cu), 33
Ede Way (Beds), 38, 211
Edith Weston (R), 64
Edmondsey (Ess), 142
Edmondthorpe (Lei), 30
Edwardstone (Sf), 30
Effingham (Sr), 113
Egloshayle (Co), 93
Egloskerry (Co), 93
Egremont (Cu), 194
Elbridge (K), 38
Eling (Ha), 112, 128
Ellel (La), 33
Ellenby (Cu), 60
Ellerby (ERY, NRY), 172
Ellingham (Ha), 112, 128
Ellough (Sf), 190
Elmer (Sx), 152
Elmet (WRY), 83
Elmsett (Sf), 134
Elmstone (K), 139
Elson (Ha), 145

Elstree (Herts), 38, 41
Elswick (Du), 135
Eltisley (C), 207
Elton (Du), 152
Elvington (K), 145
Ely (C), 14, 103, 140, 152
Ely Porta (C), 206
Emstrey (Sa), 123
Englebourne (D), 103
Englefield (Berks), 103
Engleton (St), 103
English Bicknor (He), 90
Enham (Ha), 152
Enholmes (ERY), 213
Ennerdale (Cu), 164, 169
Ennix Wood (W), 214
Ennox Wood (W), 214
Enville (St), 202
Epping (Ess), 21, 107
Erith (K), 141
Escombe (Du), 35
Esk, R., 77
Essex, 99
Eton Wick (Bk), 136
Etwall (Db), 46
Evegate (K), 38, 157
Evercreech (So), 75
Everdon (Nth), 154
Everley (W), 140; (WRY), 154
Eversden (C), 154
Evershaw (Bk), 154
Eversheads Fm (Sr), 122
Eversley (Ha), 154
Everton (Beds, La, Nt), 154
Ewyas (He), 90
Exceat (Sx), 142
Exe, R., 77
Exelby (NRY), 57
Exeter (D), 26, 80, 93
Exfold (Sx), 131
Exhall (Wa), 81
Exminster (D), 123
Exning (Sf), 102
Exton (Ha), 103, 138
Eyam (Db), 35
Eye Kettleby (Lei), 57
Eyke (Sf), 163
Eythorne (K), 145
Eythrop (Bk), 174

Faceby (NRY), 58, 164
Faddiley (Ch), 211
Fairfield (Wo), 152
Fairwood (NRY), 169
Fairy Fm (Ess), 142
Fairyhall (Ess), 142
Falinge (La), 111
Falklands (Wo), 146
Fallinge (Db), 111
Fallings (St), 111
Falmouth (Co), 97
Falthwaite (WRY), 175
Fambridge (Ess), 45
Fan (Ess), 45
Fancott (Beds), 137
Fandown (Ess), 45
Fanners (Ess), 45
Fanns (Ess), 45
Farcet (Hu), 122

Farmbridge (Ess), 45, 48
Farnborough (Berks, K), 30, 34
Farnham (Sr), 118
Farnley Tyas (WRY), 65
Farthingstone (Nth), 170
Farwood Barton (D), 152
Faulkland (So), 146
Faunstone (D), 60
Faversham (K), 204
Fawley (He), 90
Fawton (Co), 97
Feeringbury (Ess), 34
Feizor (WRY), 70, 188
Felbrigg (Nf), 183
Felderland (K), 106
Felkirk (WRY), 168
Felling (Du), 111
Fencote (He), 137
Fengate (C), 181
Fenham (Nb), 35
Fenwick (Nb), 135
Ferriby (ERY), 172
Fiddlers Dykes (Nf), 48
Fidler's Hall (Sf), 48
Fifehead (Do), 146
Fifield (O, W), 142, 146
Filkins (O), 110
Filston Hall (K), 48, 60
Finborough (Sf), 34
Finburgh (St), 34
Finchale (Du), 40
Finchingfield (Ess), 113
Findon Hill (Du), 15
Finedon (Nth), 18
Fingest (Bk), 165
Fishbourne (Sx), 152
Fishburn (Du), 152
Fisherton (W), 152
Fisherwick (St), 152
Fishlake (WRY), 152
Fishwick (La), 152
Fiskerton (L, Nt), 152
Fitton (C), 181
Fitzhead (So), 146
Fivehead (So), 146, 147
Fixby (WRY), 70, 172, 188
Fladbury (Wo), 144
Flag Fen (C), 181
Flat Holme (So), 97
Fleam Dyke (C), 199
Fleecethorpe (Nt), 57, 173
Fleet Fm (Nth), 214
Flegcroft (C), 181
Flendish Hundred (C), 199
Fletching (Sx), 107
Flitnell Barn (Nth), 215
Flitnells Fm (Nth), 215
Flitteridge Wood (Sx), 214
Flitteris Park (R), 214
Flitwick (W), 215
Flixborough (L), 57
Flixter (Nt), 57
Flixton (La, Sf, ERY), 57, 184
Fonston (Co), 60
Fordwich (K), 135
Foremark (Db), 182
Formby (La), 187
Fornham (Sf), 152
Forscote (So), 154

Fortherley (Nb), 155
Forwood (Wa), 152
Foscote (Nth), 154
Foscott (Bk, O), 154
Fouchers (Ess), 104
Four Wantz (Ess), 45
Fowberry (Nb), 34, 156
Fowe's Fm (Ess), 48, 61
Fowey (Co), 97
Foxcote (Gl, Wa), 154
Foxcott (Ha), 154
Foxearth (Ess), 154
Foxton (Du, Nb), 154
Framland (Lei), 191
Frankby (Ch), 186
Freeby (Lei), 172
Fretherne (Gl), 211
Frindsbury (K), 140
Frittenden (K), 131
Frome (Do, He, So), 76
Frome Vauchurch (Do), 47, 76, 124
Frost's Hall (Ess), 142
Frowick Hall (Ess), 173
Fryerning (Ess), 104
Fuge (D), 136
Fuige (D), 136
Fulking (Sx), 108
Fullerton (Ha), 153
Fullwich (Ch), 135
Furness (La), 164
Fyfield (Berks, Ess, Ha), 146, 147
Fyfield Wick (Berks), 137

Gadsey Brook (Beds), 121
Gadshill (K), 120
Gainfield Fm (Berks), 160
Gaisgill (We, WRY), 176
Galford (D), 150
Galhampton (So), 150
Gallant's Cottages (Ess), 61
Galley Hill (Sx), 158; (Wa), 159
Galley Wood (Sr), 150
Galleywood Common (Ess), 150
Gallow (Nf), 191
Gallow Hill (Bk), 158
Gallows Hill (W), 158
Gallows Leaze (O), 143
Galmington (D, So), 150
Galmpton (D), 150
Galton (D, So), 150
Gamblesby (Cu), 69
Gambuston (D), 60
Gammaton (D), 150
Gamston (Nt), 170
Ganarew (He), 90
Ganfield (Berks), 160
Gare (Co), 93
Garfit (Nt), 175
Garlands (Fm) (Ess), 61
Garlinge (Green) (K), 112
Garnetts (Ess), 61
Garnish Hall (Ess), 61
Garnons (Ess), 61, 195
Garrington (K), 116, 145
Gatenby (NRY), 70, 188
Gatesgill (Cu), 176
Gateshead (Du), 122
Gatewick (Sx), 136
Gatwick (Sr), 136

Gaul Field (C), 150
Gavelacre (Ha), 150
Gavelwood Reden (Ess), 150
Gawbridge (So), 150
Gawcott (Bk), 150
Gawlish (D), 150
Gear (Co), 93
Gernon Bushes (Ess), 61
Gestingthorpe (Ess), 173
Gibb's Cottages (Ess), 142
Gill (Cu), 187
Gillcamban (Cu), 70, 187
Gillfoot (Cu), 187
Gillhead (Cu), 187
Gilsland (Cu), 98
Girton (C, Nt), 138
Givendale (ERY), 101
Glandford (Nf), 160
Glanford Brigg (L), 160
Glanvill (D), 202
Glascote (Wa), 36, 137
Glassonby (Cu), 69, 70
Glassthorpehill (Nth), 58
Glemham (Sf), 160
Glemsford (Sf), 160
Glendhu (Cu), 87
Glendue (Nb), 98
Gloucester, 26, 80, 92
Glynch Brook (Wo), 111
Glynde (Sx), 109
Glyndebourne (Sx), 109
Goadby Marwood (Lei), 65
Godalming (Sr), 107
Godderthwaite (Cu), 175
Godley (Ch, Sr), 121
Godley Bridge (Sr), 121
Godmanham (ERY), 113
Godney (So), 121
Godolphin (Co), 97
Godsell (W), 120
Godsfield (Ha), 121
Godshill (Ha, IOW, Sx), 120
Godstow (O), 121, 126
Godswell Grove (W), 121
Golcar (WRY), 188
Goldsoncott (So), 137
Gomsall (Sr), 132
Gonalston (Nt), 58, 171
Gonerby (L), 58
Goodcott (D), 59, 145
Good Easter (Ess), 145
Goodwick (Beds), 145
Goodwood (Sx), 145
Goosey Wick (Berks), 137
Goosnargh (La), 98
Gorhuish (D), 147
Goring (O), 110; (Sx), 133
Goringlee (Sx), 133
Gorleston (Sf), 19
Gotwick (Sx), 136
Goudhurst (K), 131
Grange Hill (C), 170
Granta, R., 76, 89
Grantchester (C), 25–6, 104
Grassoms (Cu), 176
Grassthorpe (Nt), 173
Greasby (Ch), 166, 186
Great Torrington (D), 206
Greenberry (Ess), 34

Greenhoe (Nf), 191
Gretton (Gl, Nth), 138
Greysouthen (Cu), 70
Grimsargh (La), 187
Grimsby (L), 163
Grim's Ditch (W), 119
Grims Dyke (Ha), 119
Grimston (Nf), 170, 183; (Sf), 185
Grindle (Sa), 41
Grinsdale (Cu), 155
Grinshill (Sa), 155
Gripstone (D), 59
Gristhwaite (NRY), 175
Grosmont (NRY), 194
Gryme's Dyke (Ess), 119
Guiting (Gl), 111
Gumber Fm (Sx), 132
Gunby (ERY), 58
Gunnersbury (Mx), 239
Gunnerthwaite (La), 175
Gunnerton (Nb), 58
Gunshot Common (Sx), 132
Gunston (St), 183
Gunthorpe (Nf), 183; (Nt), 58
Gunthwaite (WRY), 175
Gunwalloe (Co), 68
Gutterby (Cu), 172
Gwealgoose (Co), 96

Hackney Wick (Mx), 136
Haddiscoe (Nf), 163, 183
Haddon, 41
Hadleigh, 41
Haighton (La), 33
Hail(e) (Cu, ERY), 33
Haithwaite (Cu), 175
Halam (Nt), 33
Hale (Mx), 32, 33; (O), 142
Hales (Nf, Sa, Wt, Wo), 33
Halfhide (Herts), 146
Half Hides (Ess), 146
Hallam (Db), 33
Hallaton (Lei), 33
Halling (K), 54, 130
Hallingbury (Ess), 54, 113
Hallington (L), 54
Halloughton (Nt, Wa), 33
Hallow (Wo), 32
Hallows (La), 33
Halsall (La), 33
Halstock (Do), 127
Halstow (D, K), 126
Haltemprice (ERY), 194
Halton (La, L, Sa, WRY), 33
Halwill (D), 46
Hamble le Rice (Ha), 198
Hameringham (L), 113
Hammersmith (Mx), 151
Hampnett (Gl, Sx), 195
Hampton Lucy (Wa), 39
Hampton Lovett (Wo), 39
Hampton Wick (Mx), 136
Hamsey (Sx), 19
Handley (Ch, Db, Do, Nth), 40
Hanley (St, Wo), 40
Happing (Nf), 127
Happisburgh (Nf), 127
Harbury (Wa), 144

Harcourt (Sa), 153
Hardingstone (Nth), 52
Hardwick, 151
Hareby (L), 58
Harestock (Ha), 158
Harmes Fm (Ess), 48
Harmondsworth (Mx), 129
Harpson (D), 60
Harraby (Cu), 172
Harrietsham (K), 49
Harringay (Mx), 26–30
Harrowbarrow (Co), 34
Harrowden (Beds, Nth), 117
Harrowdown (Ess), 117
Harrow on the Hill (Mx), 116, 118
Harsfold (Sx), 132
Hartshead (La, WRY), 121, 122
Hartside (Nb), 122
Hascombe (Sr), 209
Haslam (La), 35
Hastingford (Sx), 109
Hastingleigh (K), 109
Hastings (Sx), 108, 159
Hastoe Fm (Herts), 126
Hatherop (Gl), 174
Hatley St George (C), 65
Hatley Wilds (C), 46
Hattersley (Ch), 155
Hatton, 41
Haugh (La), 33
Haughton (Ch, L, La), 33
Haughton le Skerne (Du), 33, 198
Haulgh (La), 33
Hauxton (C), 140
Haverbrack (We), 157
Haverhill (Sf), 156
Haverholme (L), 176
Havering-atte-Bower (Ess), 55, 108
Haveringland (Nf), 55
Haversham (Bk), 55
Haverstoe (L), 191
Hawerby (L), 164, 191
Hawkerland (D), 153
Hawkhurst (K), 131, 153; (Wa), 153
Hawkinge (K), 111, 112
Hawkley (Ha), 153
Hawksworth (WRY), 30
Hawne (Wo), 33
Haycrust (Sa), 153
Haydon (W), 40
Haydon Bridge (Nb), 40
Hayes (D), 37
Hayne (D), 37
Haythwaite (NRY), 175
Hazelslack (We), 176
Headcorn (K), 131
Headfoldswood Fm (Sx), 132
Heal (D), 33
Healaugh (NRY), 40
Heale (W), 32
Healey (La, Nb, Y), 40
Heanton (D), 39
Hearndon Wood (Bk), 55
Heatherslaw (Nb), 155
Heaton (La, Nb, WRY), 39
Heavitree (D), 158
Hedingham (Ess), 138, 198
Heeley (WRY), 40
Hele (D), 33

Helford (Co), 97
Helhoughton (Nf), 183
Helion Bumpstead (Ess), 65
Helperby (NRY), 163
Helperthorpe (ERY), 163
Helsted (K), 44
Helston (Co), 94, 96
Hempton (O), 39
Hengar (Co), 96
Hengoed (Sa), 92
Henham (Ess, Sf), 39, 138
Henley, 40
Hensall (WRY), 32
Hensill (K), 134
Henstridge (So), 152, 155
Henton (O), 39
Henwood (D), 30
Herdicott (D), 137
Hermitage, The (C), 195
Hermitage Bridge, Fm (Wa), 195
Hermitage Sluice Bridge (C), 195
Hermit's Cave (Db), 195
Herne (K), 47
Heron (Ess), 47
Heronshead (Sr), 122
Herringby (Nf), 183
Herrison (Do), 60
Hersham (Sr), 55
Herstmonceux (Sx), 47, 64
Hertford, 30
Hescombe (So), 209
Hesket (Cu), 163
Hesketh (La, NRY), 163
Hessenford (Co), 209
Hessett (Sf), 134
Heswall (Ch), 46
Hethersett (Nf), 134, 155
Hever (K), 130, 212
Hewish (So), 147
Hewstock Fm (Do), 158
Heythrop (O), 174
Hibaldstow (L), 127
Hide, 146
Hiendly (WRY), 154
Higham, 39, 138
Higham (Gl), 125
Higham Upshire (K), 39
High Easter (Ess), 145
High-hoad (Sx), 45
High Ongar (Ess), 132
High Scale (WRY), 188
Hillborough (Wa), 129
Hill Farrance (So), 65
Hilton (NRY), 44
Hinckford (Ess), 199
Hindhead (Sr), 154
Hindley (La, Nb, St), 154
Hindlip (Wo), 154
Hinksden (K), 130
Hinksey (Berks), 152
Hinton, 39
Hinton Admiral (Ha), 39, 65
Hinton Martell (Do), 39
Hinxhill (K), 152
Hipperholme (WRY), 35
Hirst (Nb, WRY), 47
Hitchin (Herts), 35, 101
Hoad (K), 45
Hoaden (K), 45, 109

Hoades (K), 45
Hoadley (Sx), 45
Hoads (Sx), 45, 109
Hoards (Sx), 45
Hoath (K, Sx), 45, 109
Hoathly (Sx), 45, 109
Hobland (Sf), 184
Hoddern (Sx), 45
Hode (K), 45
Hodnet (Sa), 92
Hodore (Sx), 45
Hodsherf (Sx), 45
Hodshrove (Sx), 45, 109
Hoff (We), 190
Holbeck (Nt), 166
Holdenby (Nth), 167
Holderness (ERY), 163
Hollafrench (Co), 63
Holland (Ess), 44
Hollow Wood (Nth), 33
Holme Lacy (He), 61
Holsworthy (D), 142
Holwill (D), 46
Honeybourne (Gl, Wo), 153
Honeychild (K), 153
Honeychurch (D), 124
Honeylands (Ess), 153
Honeywell (D), 153
Honeywick (So), 153; (Sx), 136
Honiley (Wa), 153
Honington (Sf), 153; (Wa), 116, 153
Honiton (D), 153
Hope Mansell (He), 65
Hopperton (WRY), 157
Hopton (Sf), 184
Hornchurch (Ess), 124
Horndon, East, West (Ess), 201
Horndon-on-the-Hill (Ess), 201
Hornsey (Mx), 26–30
Horse Eye (Sx), 155
Horseheath (C), 155
Horsell (Sr), 134
Horselunges (Sx), 64
Horsenden (Bk), 155
Horsepath (O), 155
Horsey (Nf), 155
Horsford (Nf), 155
Horsham (Nf), 155
Horsington (So), 155
Horsley (Db, Gl, Sr), 155
Horsmonden (K), 131
Horstead (Nf), 155
Horsted (K, Sx), 155
Hothe (K), 45
Hothfield (K), 45
Houghton, Little (La), 33
Houghton le Spring (Du), 197
Howden (ERY), 166, 180
Howgill (We), 187
Hoyland (WRY), 44
Hubberholme (WRY), 145
Hucknall Torkard (Nt), 198
Hucknall under Huthwaite (Nt), 198
Huish (D, Do, So, W), 147
Hull (Wo), 47
Hulls (Wa), 47
Hulme (Ch, La, St), 176, 186
Hulton (La), 47; (St), 44
Hunston (Sf), 152

Huntercombe (O), 152
Hunterley (Du), 152
Huntingdon (Hu), 101, 153
Huntingfield (Sf), 153
Huntingford (Gl, He), 153
Huntington (Ch, St, NRY), 153; (He, Sa), 152
Huntingtrap (Wo), 174
Huntley (Gl), 152
Hunton (K), 153
Hunt's Hall (Ess), 60
Huntwick (WRY), 209
Huntworth (So), 152
Hurcott (So), 137
Hurdcott (W), 137
Hurn (Ha, Nth), 47
Hurst (Wo), 47
Hurstingstone (Hu), 101
Hurstpierpoint (Sx), 64
Hurworth (Du), 129
Hutton (Ess), 104
Hutton in the Forest (Cu), 197
Huttons Ambo (NRY), 206
Huyton (La), 47
Hyde, 146
Hyde Park (Lo), 146
Hyffold (Sx), 147
Hythe (Ess), 47

Ickenthwaite (La), 175
Iddlecott (D), 137
Idehurst (Sx), 147
Ilford (Ess), 77
Ilketshall (Sf), 57
Impney (Wo), 41
Ince (Ch), 92
Indicleave (D), 31
Indicombe (D), 30
Indio (D), 30
Ingarsby (Lei), 58
Ingatestone (Ess), 104
Ingleby (Db), 182; (NRY), 189
Ingoldisthorpe (Nf), 58, 183
Ingoldmells (L), 58
Ingrave (Ess), 104
Inham (L), 213
Inhams (C, Sr), 213
Inholmes (C, Sr, Sx), 213
Inholmes Road (Nt), 213
Innox Mill (W), 214
Innyngs House (Herts), 213
Instow (D), 127
Intake (WRY), 213
Ipswich, 15
Irby (Ch), 186; (NRY), 189
Ireby (La), 187
Ironville (Db), 202
Irthington (Cu), 156
Irthlingborough (Nth), 156
Irton (NRY), 189
Isaacby (Cu), 60
Isleworth (Mx), 129
Islingham (K), 140
Itchenor (Sx), 140
Ivel, R. (Beds), 101
Ivy Church (W), 124
Ivychurch (K), 124
Ixworth (Thorpe) (Sf), 172

Jacobstow (D), 127
Jagdon (Sa), 201
Jarrow (Du), 102, 201
Jay Wick (Ess), 114, 136
Jerusalem Wood (C), 221
Jervaulx (NRY), 194, 201
Jesmond (Nb), 201
Jesson Fm (K), 60
Jevington (Sx), 201
Johnby (Cu), 49, 60, 188
Johnstone (D), 60
Joist Fen (C), 196
Jolby (NRY), 49
Jordanthorpe (Db), 49
Jupeshill Fm (Ess), 210
Jurston (D), 60
Justment (D), 196

Keal (L), 163
Kearby (WRY), 57
Kearton (NRY), 57
Kedleston (Db), 57
Keiro (Co), 93
Keisby (L), 58
Kelham (Nt), 163
Kellamarsh (La), 57
Kellamergh (La), 187
Kelly (Co), 95; (D), 86
Kelynack (Co), 95
Kempsford (Gl), 41
Kenap (Co), 94
Kenderchurch (He), 67
Kenidjack (Co), 97
Kenilworth (Wa), 130
Kenn (D, So), 71
Kennacott (D), 137
Kennet, R. (C, W), 97
Kennicott (D), 137
Kent, 71
Kentchurch (He), 67
Ken Wood (Mx), 195
Kenwyn (Co), 96
Kerrow (Co), 93
Kersham Bridge (D), 126
Keskadale (Cu), 57
Kestle (Co), 95
Kestlemerris (Co), 93
Keswick (Cu), 166; (Nf), 183
Ketsby (L), 57
Kettering (Nth), 106
Kettlebaston (Sf), 57
Kettleby (L), 57
Kettleshulme (Ch), 57, 176, 186
Kettlestone (Nf), 49, 57
Kettlethorpe (L, ERY), 57
Kexbrough (WRY), 58
Kexby (L), 58
Kexmoor (WRY), 57
Keyston (Hu), 57
Kildwick (WRY), 166
Kilforge (He), 90
Kilgram (NRY), 57
Kilham (Nb, ERY), 35
Killerby (Du), 181
Kilsby (Nth), 182
Kilpeck (He), 90
Kimberley (Nf, Nt, Wa), 42, 145
Kimble Wick (Bk), 136

Kingsbury (O), 142
Kingsbury Episcopi (So), 205
Kingsheanton (D), 39
Kingsland (He), 91; (Wo), 197
King's Lynn (Nf), 104, 204
Kingston juxta Yeovil (So), 5, 206
Kinver (St), 73, 75
Kirby (Ch, La, Y), 168, 187
Kirby Bellars (Lei), 65
Kirby-le-Soken (Ess), 173
Kirby Muxloe (Lei), 57
Kirkandrews (Cu), 70
Kirkbride (Cu), 70
Kirkby, 168
Kirkdale (La), 168
Kirkgate (C), 168, 181
Kirkham, 168
Kirkhaugh (Nb), 168
Kirkland (La), 168
Kirklees (WRY), 168
Kirkley (Sf), 168, 184
Kirkoswald (Cu), 70
Kirksanton (Cu), 70, 187
Kirkstall (WRY), 168
Kirkstead (L), 168
Kirkthorpe (WRY), 173
Kirkthwaite (La), 175
Kirmond le Mire (L), 195
Kirstead (Nf), 168
Kirton (L, Nt, Sf), 168, 185
Kismeldon Bridge (D), 126
Knayton (NRY), 138
Knedlington (ERY), 114
Kneeton (Nt), 138
Knell (Sx), 47
Knightacott (D), 148
Knightcote (Wa), 148
Knightley (Wa), 148
Knightlow Hill (Wa), 148
Knighton (Berks, IOW), 148
Knighthayes (D), 148
Knightshayne (D), 148
Knightwick (Wo), 148
Knightwood (Ha), 148
Kniveton (Db), 138
Knockholt (K), 37

Laceby (L), 164
Lackenby (NRY), 70, 172
Laconby (Cu), 70
Lagness (Sx), 140
Laithes (Cu), 174
Laithwaite (La), 174
Lambcourt End (Beds), 137
Lambden (K), 130
Lamberhurst (K), 152
Lambeth (Sr), 152
Lambley (Nb), 152
Lambton (Du), 138, 152
Lamcote (Nt), 36, 137, 152
Lamellan (Co), 68
Lancaster (La), 80
Lancaut (Gl), 67, 92
Landewednack (Co), 68
Landican (Ch), 84, 92
Land's End (Co), 72
Langage (D), 147
Langtoft (L, ERY), 174
Langton Herring (Do), 61

Langwathby (Cu), 188
Lanivet (Co), 87
Larbrick (La), 176, 187
Larton (Ch), 186
Lathom (ERY), 174
Lattersey (C), 33
Launceston (Co), 97
Laund (La), 197
Launde (Lei), 197
Laund's Fm (Ess), 197
Lavant, R. (Sx), 76
Lawhitton (Co), 94
Lawn, The (Ess), 197
Lawn's Fm (Ess), 197
Layer Breton, de la Haye, Marney
  (Ess), 61
Layston (Herts), 124
Laytham (ERY), 174
Lazenby (NRY), 172
Lazonby (Cu), 172
Lea, R., 76, 79
Leaden Roding (Ess), 108, 203
Lealholme (NRY), 35
Leam (Nb), 35
Leam, R., 77
Leapgate Cottage (Wo), 155
Leasgill (We), 187
Leasingham (L), 113
Leeds (K), 83; (WRY), 83
Legsby (L), 191
Leicester, 26, 182
Leigh Sinton (Wo), 32
Lemon, R., 77
Leominster (He), 91
Lesneweth (Co), 96
Lesnewth (Co), 94
Lesteuder (Co), 67
Lestowder (Co), 93
Letheringham (Sf), 113
Levenshulme (La), 176
Lidcott (Co), 94
Lidham (St), 35
Lidlington (Beds), 114
Likely (Ess), 142
Lilly (Ess), 142
Limbo Fm (Sx), 133
Limehurst (La), 82
Linby (Nt), 167
Lincoln, 204
Lindon (Wo), 35
Lindsell (Ess), 134
Linkinhorne (Co), 68
Linshields (Nb), 19
Linton, 168
Lintz (Du), 199
Lintzford (Du), 199
Lippering (Sx), 52
Lippitts Hill (Ess), 155
Liscard (Ch), 75, 84, 92
Liskeard (Co), 94
Lissett (ERY), 134
Liston (Ess), 114
Litherland (La), 163, 187
Litherskew (NRY), 163
Litlington (C), 114
Little Gransden (C), 206
Littlethorpe (Ess), 173; (WRY), 172
Littleton (Ch), 126
Littley (Ess), 142

Livery Dole (D), 158
Lizard (Co), 96
Llancloudy (He), 67
Llandinabo (He), 67
Llanfair (He), 90
Llanfrother (He), 90
Llan Howell (Sa), 92
Londesborough (ERY), 58
London, 71, 79
Londonthorpe (L), 163
Longbarns (Ess), 142
Long Clawson (Lei), 58
Longden (Sa), 40
Longdon upon Tern (Sa), 40
Longmynd (Sa), 74
Longville (Sa), 202
Longwick (Bk), 135
Lonsdale (NRY), 58
Looe, East, West (Co), 97
Loose (K), 218
Loosley Row (Bk), 218
Lorbottle (Nb), 139
Loseley (Sr), 218
Loskay (NRY), 163
Lostwithiel (Co), 97
Lotherton (WRY), 23, 115
Lothingland (Sf), 185
Lound (Sf), 184
Lovistone (D), 50
Lowesmoor (Wo), 218
Lowestoft (Sf), 163, 174, 184
Lowfold (Sx), 132
Lowsay (Cu), 218
Ludgershall (Bk, W), 22, 155
Luffincott (D), 137
Lugg, R. (He), 77
Luggershall (Gl), 22
Lullingstone (K), 52
Lumbercote (ERY), 36
Lund's Fm (Ess), 197
Lunnon (Nt), 221
Lurgashall (Sx), 22
Lusby (L), 58
Lutterworth (Lei), 23
Luttons Ambo (ERY), 206
Lydcott (D), 137
Lydd (K), 35, 136
Lydiard Millicent (W), 65
Lydwicke (Sx), 136
Lyham (Nb), 35
Lyme (La), 82
Lyme Handley (Ch), 82
Lyme Regis (Do), 206
Lyminge (K), 77, 103, 140
Lyminster (Sx), 123, 132
Lymn, R., 77
Lympne (K), 77, 80, 88, 156
Lyonshall (He), 91
Lypiate (So), 155
Lypiatt (Gl), 155
Lytchett (Do), 74, 97

Macclesfield Forest, 82
Madginford (K), 130
Madresfield (Wo), 155
Magor (Co), 93
Maisemore (Gl), 87, 92
Maker (Co), 93
Malden (Sr), 40, 126

Maldon (Ess), 40, 126
Mallerstang (Cu), 75
Malling (K, Sx), 54, 107
Malmesbury (W), 98
Malpas (Ch, Co), 194
Malvern (Wo), 75, 87, 93
Malzeard (WRY), 194
Mamble (Wo), 93
Manhead (D), 93
Mam Tor (Db), 93
Mancetter (Wa), 26, 79
Manchester (La), 79, 81
Mangersford (D), 157
Mangerton (Do), 157
Mankinholes (WRY), 70
Manningford Abbots (W), 205;
Bohun, 65
Mansergh (We), 187
Mansfield (Nt), 93
Manshead (Beds), 122
Manuden (Ess), 202
Maplesden (Sx), 53
Marazion (Co), 96
Marden (K), 131
Marden Ash (Ess), 132
Margaretting (Ess), 104
Market Harborough (Lei), 156
Market Jew St (Co), 97
Market Weston (Sf), 206
Mark Hall (Ess), 61
Marles Fm (Ess), 48
Marmont Priory (C), 195
Marraway (Wa), 146
Marston Sicca (Gl), 206
Marsworth (Bk), 48, 52
Martindale (We), 40
Martyr Worthy (Ha), 65
Marvell (IOW), 202
Maryland Point (Ess), 221
Marylebone (Mx), 198, 239
Mascallsbury (Ess), 34
Mashbury (Ess), 108, 127, 199
Massingham (Nf), 52
Matching (Ess), 108, 127, 199
Matlask (Nf), 183
Mattersey (Nt), 155
Maughonby (Cu), 69
Maulden (Beds), 126
Maund Bryan (Sa), 92
Mawgan (Co), 68
Meathop (Wa), 166
Medway, R. (K), 76
Meend (Gl, He, Sa), 74
Melchet (Ha), 74, 75
Meldon (Nb), 126
Melhuish (D), 147
Mell House (Ess), 47
Mellor (Db, La), 75
Melmerby (Cu, La), 70
Melsonby (NRY), 70, 188
Melton (Nf), 166
Melton Mowbray (Lei), 61
Melverley (Sa), 142
Mendip (So), 74
Meon, East, West (Ha), 106
Merevale (Wa), 204
Mermaids Pits (Sf), 224
Merrielands (Ess), 221
Merstow Green (Wo), 126

Merthen (Co), 87
Meshaw (D), 194
Messing (Ess), 108, 199
Messingham (L), 52
Methersham (Sx), 155
Methley (WRY), 166
Methwold (Nf), 166
Mevagissey (Co), 68
Michaelstow (Ess), 11
Micklethwaite (Cu, WRY), 175
Middlesex, 99
Middlewich (Ch), 135
Middop (WRY), 166
Midhope (WRY), 166
Mile End (Ess), 45
Millhill Wood (Ess), 142
Mill Mehal (Co), 96
Milton Abbas (Do), 205
Milton Bryant (Beds), 64
Milton Malzor (Nth), 65
Milverton (So), 142
Minchin Buckland (So), 205
Mindrum (Nb), 74
Minehead (So), 74
Minn (Ch), 74
Minster (K), 123
Minsterworth (Gl), 123
Minton (Sa), 74
Miserden (Gl), 195
Moccas (He), 75, 90
Mocktree (Sa), 92
Modbury (D, Do), 34
Mogpits (O), 142
Monewden (Sf), 202
Mongeham (K), 202
Mongewell (O), 202
Monkland (He), 91
Monksbury (Ess), 34
Monks Kirby (Wa), 183
Monkthorpe (L), 173
Monkton Wyld (Do), 155
Montacute (So), 203
Moor Fm (Ess), 146
Mooray (W), 146
Moortoft (L), 174
Morchard (D), 74
Moresby (Cu), 60
Morfe (St), 73
Morgay Fm (Sx), 146
Morghew (K), 146
Morris Fm (Sf), 146
Morton Bagot (Wa), 61
Mosser (Cu), 98
Mottershead (Ch), 92
Mottram (Ch), 92
Mount Grace (NRY), 194
Mountnessing (Ess), 104
Mountshayne (D), 60
Mountsorrel (Lei), 194
Mowlish (D), 147
Mozergh (We), 98
Much Dewchurch (He), 206
Much Hadham (Herts), 206
Mugford (Co), 94
Mullion (Co), 68
Mundham, North, South (Sx), 132
Murrain Wood (K), 146
Myland Lodge (Ess), 45
Mylor (Co), 68

Mynde (He), 74
Myndtown (Sa), 74
Myne, East, West (So), 74
Mythop (La), 166

Nacton (Sf), 185
Nafferton (Nb, ERY), 59
Nafford (Wo), 152
Nailstone (Lei), 167, 171
Naldretts (Sx), 37
Nansawsen (Co), 96
Nantwich (Ch), 135, 151
Nant-y-glas-dwyr (He), 91
Nant-y-gollen (Sa), 92
Naseby (Nth), 166
Nash, 37
Nasthyde (Herts), 37, 147
Nasty (Herts), 37
Natton (Gl), 152
Naunton (Gl, Wo), 40, 138
Navestock (Ess), 129
Nayland (Sf), 37
Nazeing (Ess), 107, 129
Neatham (Ha), 152
Nechells (St, Wa), 37
Needingworth (Hu), 130
Neigh Bridge (W), 38
Neithrop (O), 174
Nelmes (Ess), 37
Nempnett (So), 37
Nene, R., 20
Neopardy (D), 142
Neroche Forest (So), 153
Nethercott (D), 137
Nettleslack (La), 176
Newball (L), 169
Newbold Verdon (Lei), 65
Newbottle (Du, Nth), 139
Newbury (Ess), 34
Newcastle-under-Lyme (St), 82
Newenden (K), 131
Newent (Gl), 92
New Forest, 99
Newfoundland Well (Wa), 221
Newington, 40, 116, 138
Newlass (NRY), 174
Newmarket (Sf), 203
New Mill (Co), 96
Newnham, 39, 138
Newnton (W), 40, 138
New River (Mx), 28
Newsham (L, NRY), 35
Newsholme (ERY, WRY), 35, 169
Newton (C), 207; (Sf), 19
Newton Abbot (D), 205
Newton Toney (W), 65
Nidderdale (WRY), 164, 169
Night Wood (W), 148
Nill Well (C), 47
Nimmings (Wo), 111
Ninehams (Sr), 213
Ninneywood (Bk), 213
Ninning's Fm (Herts), 213
Ninnings (Wood) (Ess, Herts), 213
Nipnose (Sr), 33
Nizel's Heath (K), 134
Noakes, 37
Nobold (Nth), 139
Nobottle(Nth), 139

Noctorum (Ch), 186
Noke, 37
Norbreck (La), 176, 187
Norfolk, 99
Normanby (NRY), 189
Normanton, 182, 189
Norrington (Herts, W, Wo), 32
Norsey Wood (Ess), 48
North Hills (C), 32
Northill (Beds), 101
Northolt (Mx), 33
Northorpe (ERY), 172
North Stream (K), 159
Northumberland, 100
Northway (D), 31
Northwich (Ch), 135
Norton, 32
Norton Fm (Wo), 32
Norton-in-Hales (Sa), 82
Norton in the Moors (St), 197
Norton Malreward (So), 65
Norway (D), 31
Notindon Place (Nt), 200
Nottingham, 114, 199
Nun Coton (L), 36
Nuneham, 39
Nunn Mills (Nth), 208
Nye (So), 38
Nyland (Do), 37
Nymet Tracy (D), 87
Nymph (D), 87
Nymphsfield (Gl), 87
Nympton (D), 87
Nynehead (So), 147

Oake (So), 40, 44
Oaken (Sa), 35
Oakerthorpe (Db), 57
Oakley (O), 143
Oakthorpe (Lei), 173, 182
Oatlands (Sr), 156
Occold (Sf), 40
Oddingley (Wo), 139
Offchurch (Wa), 123
Offerton (Wo), 145
Oldham (La), 176
Old Heath (Ess), 47
Old Hurst (Hu), 45, 101
Old Hythe Meadow (Ess), 47
Orchard (Do), 74
Ore, R. (Sf), 77
Orfold (Sx), 132
Ormesby (Nf), 171
Ornsby (Du), 181
Orpington (K), 115
Orwell (Sf), 15, 77
Osbaston (Lei), 139
Osgarthorpe (Lei, WRY), 58
Osgodby (L, ERY, NRY), 58, 164
Osgoodby (NRY), 58, 164
Osmaston (Db), 59, 138
Osmotherley (La, NRY), 58, 164, 188
Ossett (WRY), 134
Oteley (Sa), 156
Oughterside (Cu), 174
Oulton (Sf, WRY), 57, 184
Oundle (Nth), 101
Ouse, R. (C, Hu), 20
Ouston (Du, Nb), 57

Ovingham (Nb), 114
Ovington (Nb), 114
Owstwick (ERY), 166, 180
Oxenbold (Sa), 139
Oxford, 139
Oxhey (Herts), 151
Oxley (St), 151
Oxney (Ess), 142
Oxton (Ch, Nt), 151
Oxwick (Nf), 135

Pachesham (Sr), 54
Packington (Lei, St, Wa), 54
Packmanston (K), 157
Packmores (Wa), 54
Packsfield (IOW), 54
Packwood (Wa), 54
Paddle Brook (Wa), 54
Padworth (Berks), 30
Paglesham (Ess), 54
Painthorpe (WRY), 173
Pakefield (Sf), 54
Pakenham (Sf), 54
Palestine (Co), 96
Pallingham Fm (Sx), 133
Pallinghurst Fm (Sr), 133
Pangbourne (Berks), 18
Panshill (Bk), 40
Pant, R. (Ess), 76
Pant-y-Lidan (Sa), 92
Papworth Everard, St Agnes (C), 64
Parbold (La), 139
Parkwalls (Co), 223
Parsloes (Ess), 48
Parsonby (Cu), 188
Paschoe (D), 54
Pashley (Sx), 54
Patcham (Sx), 54
Patchecott (D), 54
Patchendon (Herts), 54
Patchill (D), 54
Patching (Ess, Sx), 54
Patchway (Sx), 54, 117, 118
Paternoster Bank (Berks), 216
Paternoster Heath (Ess), 216
Paternoster Hill (Ess), 216
Paulerspury (Nth), 157
Paxcroft (W), 54
Paxford (Wo), 54
Paxlet (W), 54
Peakirk (Nth), 168
Peel Island (La), 164
Penare (Co), 95
Pencoyd (He), 90
Pendlebury (La), 75, 81
Pendle Hill (La), 75
Pendleton (La), 75, 81
Penge (Sr), 74
Pengethley (He), 90
Penhill (D), 87, 88; (NRY), 75
Penhull (Wo), 93
Penkridge (St), 75
Penpole (Gl), 92
Penpont (Co), 93
Penquit (D), 86
Penquite (D), 86
Penrose (Co), 95
Penryn (Co), 95
Pensax (Wo), 75, 93
Pensby (Ch), 186

Pensfold Fm (Sx), 133
Penshurst (K), 133
Pentire Point (Co), 95
Pentre (He), 91
Penventon (Co), 93
Penvories (Co), 96
Penwith (Co), 71, 95
Penzance (Co), 95
Peper Harow (Sr), 117, 118
Pephurst (Sx), 132
Peppering (Sx), 52
Perching Fm (Sx), 108
Perlethorpe (Nt), 173
Perth-y-Perton (He), 91
Peterstow (He), 11, 90
Petham (K), 47
Petherick, Little (Co), 68
Petlands (K, Sx), 47
Petley (Sx), 47
Pett (K, Sx), 47
Petworth (Sx), 47, 133
Pevensey (Sx), 133
Phepson (Wo), 104
Phillow's Fm (Ess), 48
Philpots (Ess), 142
Pickering (NRY), 108
Piddle or Puddle, R. (Do), 147
Piddle Brook (Wo), 80
Piddletrenthide (Do), 147
Pillaton Hall (St), 156
Pilt Down (Sx), 13
Pipewell Abbey (Nth), 196
Pitminster (So), 123
Plain Field (C), 181
Plainfield (Nb), 181
Plaistow (D, Db, Ess, Sr), 160
Plaistows Fm (Ha), 160
Plaitford (Ha), 160
Plashet Grove (Ess), 194
Plashett (Sx), 194
Plasset (Nf), 194
Plaster Down (D), 160
Plasterhill Fm (Ha), 160
Plastow Green (Ha), 160
Plawhatch (Sx), 160
Plaxtol (K), 160
Playford (Sf), 160
Playley Green (Wo), 160
Playstow (Herts, K), 160
Plealey (Sa), 160
Plemstall (Ch), 126
Plenmeller (Nb), 75
Pleshey (Ess), 194
Plessey (Nb), 194
Plestor (Ha), 160
Plestowes (Wa), 160
Pleyton (Co), 160
Plowden (Sa), 160
Plumbland (Cu), 190
Plumford (K), 129
Plyford (D), 160
Pock Field (C), 223
Polglaze (Co), 95
Poling (Sx), 108, 132
Polkinghorne (Co), 67
Polperro (Co), 95
Polruan (Co), 95
Polscoe (Co), 95
Ponsmayou (Co), 96

Ponsonby (Cu), 172
Pontefract (WRY), 203
Pont Vaen (He), 91
Pookhill (Sx), 33, 223
Pookreed (Sx), 223
Poor Park (Ess), 61
Poppets (Sx), 223
Poppets Hill (O), 223
Popple Drove (C), 223
Porthallow (Co), 93
Port Hill (O), 143
Porthquin (Co), 93
Portsand Fm (C), 197
Portsmoorhall (Ess), 48
Postland (L), 197
Poston (He), 104
Potterne (W), 156
Potter's Hill (W), 157
Potterspury (Nth), 157
Potterton (WRY), 156
Poundisford (So), 155
Prae Wood (Herts), 196
Pray Heath (Sr), 196
Prees (Sa), 92
Preeze (Co), 95
Preston Gubbals (Sa), 64
Preston le Skerne (Du), 198
Primemeads (Sr), 196
Princethorpe (Wa), 174
Priske (Co), 95
Prittlewell (Ess), 143
Probus (Co), 68
Puckeridge (Herts), 223
Puck Lane (Ess, O), 223
Pucklechurch (Gl), 223
Puckscroft (Sx), 223
Puck Shipton (W), 223
Puckshot (Sr), 132, 223
Puckstye (Sx), 223
Puck Well (W), 223
Pugdells (Ha), 223
Pulston (Do), 60
Purbrook (Ha), 223
Purfleet (Ess), 1
Purprise (WRY), 197
Purps (D), 197
Putshole (D), 223
Puxley (Nth), 223
Puxton (So), 50

Quarlston (Do), 60
Quickbury (Ess), 34, 135
Quoditch (D), 147

Rableyheath (Herts), 32
Rabscott (D), 60, 137
Raby (Ch, Du), 171, 181
Raceby (Du), 181
Rackham (Sx), 19
Rae Burn (Cu), 45
Raffling Wood (Sx), 115
Ragill Beck (La), 176
Raithby (L), 58
Rampside (La), 122
Rampside Point (La), 164
Rampton (C), 138
Ramsey (Hu), 15
Ramshead (La), 122
Rancombe (IOW), 155

Rashwood (Wo), 147
Ratford (Sx), 115
Ratling (K), 107
Rauceby (L), 164
Ravenshead (Nb), 122
Ravenstone (Db), 182
Rawcliffe Bank (NRY), 166
Rawstone (D), 60
Ray (W), 37
Raydale (NRY), 45
Raydon (Sf), 156
Raygill (WRY), 188
Ray Island (Ess), 38
Raylees (Nb), 45
Rayleigh (Ess), 155
Rea (Wo), 37
Reading (Berks), 106
Reading Street (K), 111
Reagill (We), 176, 187
Rearsby (Lei), 58
Reculver (K), 19, 80
Redden (Ess), 47
Reddings (Wo), 111
Redgeland (Sx), 47
Redlingfield (Sf), 139
Redrick (Herts), 136
Red Stones (Ch), 186
Redvales (La), 33
Redwick (Gl), 135
Reigate (Sr), 155
Renacres (La), 156
Rendlesham (Sf), 14, 54, 140
Renham (IOW), 155
Renhold (Beds), 155
Repton (Db), 102
Resparva (Co), 95
Resparveth (Co), 95
Restormel (Co), 97
Rewley Abbey (O), 194
Reydon (Sf), 156
Rhee (C), 37
Rhiwlas (He), 91
Ribston (WRY), 101
Richardson (W), 60
Richborough (K), 80, 204
Richmond (Sr, Y), 194
Rickerby (Cu), 60
Rickinghall Inferior, Superior (Sf), 206
Rickmansworth (Herts), 129
Riddings (Db), 111
Ridgebridge (Sr), 218
Ridgmont (Beds, ERY), 194
Rievaulx (NRY), 194
Rigbolt (L), 139, 151
Rill (D), 38
Ringleton (K), 145
Ripon (WRY), 35, 101
Risby (Sf), 184
Risebridge (Ess), 218
Rising Bridge (Nth), 218
Ritherhope (La), 152
Rivar (W), 38
Rivenhall (Ess), 33
River (Sx), 38
Riverhead (K), 152
River Hill (K), 38
Roall (WRY), 32
Robin Hood's Butts (He, So), 159
Roby (La), 187

Rochester (K), 80, 88, 104, 204
Rochford (Ess), 153
Rock (Wo), 38
Rockell's Fm (Ess), 60
Rodden (So), 155
Roderwick (L), 136, 152
Rodge (Wo), 47
Roding (Ess), 108, 142
Roding, R., 77
Roecombe (Do), 45, 155
Roffey (Sx), 155
Rogate (Sx), 155
Roke (O), 143
Rokeby (NRY), 167
Rollesby (Nf), 183
Rolphy Green (Ess), 155
Rolvenden (K), 131
Rom, R. (Ess), 77
Roman Bank (C), 20
Romanby (NRY), 58
Romford (Ess), 77
Romney Marsh (K), 106
Rook (D), 38
Rookby (We), 167
Rookwood Hall (Ess), 142
Roos (ERY), 75
Roose (Co), 95; (La), 75
Roothings, The (Ess), 108
Rooting (K), 107, 108
Rose (Co), 95
Roseberry Topping (NRY), 190
Rosecaddon (Co), 67
Rosecare (Co), 95
Roseglos (Co), 95
Rose Maund (He), 92
Rosemullion (Co), 95
Rosewarne (Co), 95
Roskear (Co), 95
Ross (He, Nb), 75
Rossgill (We), 176
Rostherne (Ch), 186
Rother, R. (K, Sx), 77
Rotherfield (Ha, O, Sx), 152
Rotherhithe (Sr), 152
Rotherwick (Ha), 136, 152
Rottingdean (Sx), 113
Rougemont (WRY), 194
Roughway (Ess, K), 155
Rowberrow (So), 34
Rowland (Db), 163
Rowse (Co), 95
Rowton (Ch), 126
Roxby (NRY), 188
Roydon (Ess, Nf, Sf), 156
Royton (La), 156
Ruckinge (K), 112
Rudding (Cu), 111
Rudge (Gl, Sa, Wo), 47
Rudgwick (Sx), 47
Rugby (Wa), 167, 183
Rugg's Place (Wo), 47
Rull (D), 38, 47
Rumby (Du), 181
Rush Pools (Nt), 224
Rusthall (K), 130
Ruyton (Sa), 156
Ryal (Nb), 40
Ryarsh (K), 156
Rye (Sx), 37

Rye End (Herts), 38
Rye Fm (Wo), 38
Ryeholmes (Nt), 170
Rye House (Herts, K), 38
Ryhill (ERY, WRY), 156
Ryme Intrinseca (Do), 206
Ryton (Du, Sa, Wa), 156

Saffron Walden (Ess), 84
Saham Toney (Nf), 65
St Blazey (Co), 68
St Breward (Co), 68
St Budeaux (D), 147
St Catherines Hill (Sr), 224
St Devereux (He), 67
St Endellion (Co), 68
St Erth (Co), 68
St Eval (Co), 68
St Germans (Co), 68
St Gluvias (Co), 68
St Issey (Co), 68
St Ives (Co), 68
St Just (Co), 68
St Kevern (Co), 68
St Kew (Co), 68
St Mawes (Co), 68
St Neot (Co), 68
St Nighton (Co), 68
St Veep (Co), 68
St Wenn (Co), 68
St Weonards (He), 67
Salcey Forest (Nth), 197
Salcombe (D), 151
Salcott (Ess), 36, 135
Salisbury, 201
Salmonby (L), 58
Salmonsbury (Gl), 156
Salome Wood (Hu), 35
Salop, 200
Salt (St), 151
Salterford (Nt), 151
Salterforth (WRY), 151
Salter's Bridge (St), 151
Salterton (W), 151
Saltfleetby (L), 171
Salthouse (Nf), 135
Saltisford (Wa), 151
Saltram (D), 151
Saltwick (Nb), 135
Sampford, 40
Sampford Courtney (D), 65
Sandal (WRY), 172
Sandford, 40
Sandringham (Nf), 113
Sannacott (D), 137
Santon, 40; (Cu, L, Nf), 138
Sapcott (Wo), 36
Sapperton (Db, Gl, L, Sx), 157
Sarson (Ha), 50
Sart Fm (D), Wood (Nth), 197
Satterlowe (Cu), 174
Satterthwaite (Cu), 174
Sawbridgeworth (Herts), 18
Sawrey (La), 163
Sawtry All Saints, St Andrew, St Judith (Hu), 64
Saxham (Sf), 103
Saxondale (Nt), 103
Saxton (C, WRY), 103

Scaldwell (Nth), 166
Scalebed (WRY), 188
Scaleby (Cu), 176, 187
Scale Gill (Cu), 187
Scales (Cu, La), 176, 187
Scalford (Lei), 166
Scamblesby (L), 58
Scammonden (WRY), 58
Scarborough (NRY), 58, 189
Scarisbrick (La), 176
Scarrington (Nt), 182
Scarrowmanwick (Cu), 187
Scarsdale (Db), 58
Scawby (L), 191
Scholar Green (Ch), 176
Scholes (La, WRY), 176
Scofton (Nt), 167
Scole (Nf), 176
Scopwick (L), 166
Scoulton (Nf), 183
Scratby (Nf), 183
Screveton (Nt), 182
Scunthorpe (L), 58
Seacourt (Berks), 129
Sea Field (C), 21
Seal Chart (K), 133
Seasalter (K), 135, 151
Seascale (Cu), 176, 187
Seathwaite (Cu), 175
Seatoller (Cu), 174
Sedgeberrow (Wo), 34
Sedgefield (Du), 199
Sedrup (Bk), 174
Sefton (La), 187
Seighford (St), 199
Selaby (Du), 181
Selby (WRY), 167
Sellack (He), 91
Selly Oak (Wo), 200
Selwood Forest (So), 87
Sepscott (D), 137
Setmurthy (Cu), 70, 175
Sevington (K), 145
Sezincote (Gl), 199
Shackerdale (Nt), 157
Shackerland Hall (Sf), 157
Shackerley (La), 157
Shackerstone (Lei), 158
Shadwell (Ess), 47
Shakerley (La), 157
Shalbourne (W), 166
Shalford (Ess), 166
Shapcott (D), 137
Shapwick (D, Do, So), 136
Shardens Fm (K), 130
Sharnfold (Sx), 131
Shearston (So), 59, 138
Shebbear (D), 34
Sheepwash (D, Nb), 151
Sheffield (Sx), 151; (WRY), 143, 208
Shelley (Ess), 200
Shellingford (Berks), 201
Shelton (Beds, Nf, Nt), 166
Sheppey (K), 151
Shepshead (Lei), 122
Shepton (So), 138, 151
Sherbarrow (WRY), 34
Sherburn in Elmet (WRY), 83
Sherenden (K), 130

Shernden (K), 130, 131
Shernfold (Sx), 131
Shillinglee (Sx), 113
Shilton (Berks, Lei, O, Wa), 201
Shimpling (Nf, Sf), 107
Shipbourne (K), 40
Shipden (Nf), 40, 152
Shipham (So), 152
Shiplake (O), 40
Shipmeadow (Sf), 40, 152
Shippea (C), 152
Shipton (Do, Gl, O), 138, 152
Shipton Bellinger (Ha), 65
Shipway (K), 40, 152
Shirley (Db, Ha, Sr, Wa), 165
Shirrenden (K), 130
Shobrooke (D), 224
Shocklach (Ch), 224
Sholver (La), 187
Shootersway (Herts), 158
Shopwyke (Sx), 136
Shotley (Sf), 152
Shrewsbury (Sa), 200
Shrewton (W), 148
Shropshire, 200
Shroton (Do), 148
Shuckburgh (Wa), 224
Shucknall (He), 40, 224
Shuckstonefield (Db), 224
Shuckton (Db), 224
Shugborough (St), 224
Shurton (So), 148
Shuttleworth (Db), 129
Siddington (Gl), 32
Sigglesthorne (ERY), 58
Sigston (NRY), 57
Sileby (Lei), 58
Silloth (Cu), 174
Silton, Nether, Over (NRY), 201
Simonside (Du), 134
Sindon's Mill (Wo), 32
Singleborough (Bk), 201
Singlesole (C), 181
Singleton (La), 201
Sinnington (NRY), 115
Sixpenny Handley (Wo), 75
Skeeby (NRY), 58
Skelderskew (NRY), 188
Skelgill (Cu), 187
Skelsmergh (We), 98, 187
Skelton (Cu, Y), 166
Skewkirk (WRY), 168
Skewsby (NRY), 164
Skidby, (ERY), 58
Skinnerthorpe (WRY), 173
Skiplam (NRY), 166
Skipton (NRY), 166
Skipwith (ERY), 166
Skirlaugh (ERY), 165, 180
Skirlington (ERY), 165, 180
Skirmett (Bk), 165
Skyrack (WRY), 165
Slack (La, WRY), 176
Slaughterwicks (Sr), 135
Slingley (Du), 155
Slingsby (NRY), 58
Sloothby (L), 59
Smaithwaite (Cu), 175
Smarden (K), 131

Smead (K), 151
Smeaton (Cu, NRY, WRY), 151
Smeeth (K), 151
Smeetham Hall (Ess), 151
Smeeton (Lei), 151
Smethcote (Sa), 151
Smethcott (Sa), 151
Smethwick (Ch, St), 151
Smitha (D), 151
Smithacott (D), 151
Smithdown (La), 151
Smithfield (Mx), 151
Smithincott (D), 151
Smynacott (D), 151
Snargate (K), 155
Sneinton (Nt), 114, 200
Snibston (Lei), 59, 171
Sodington (Wo), 32
Soffham (ERY), 176
Solihull (Wa), 47
Somerby (L, Lei), 57
Somerden (K), 131
Somerleyton (Sf), 57, 184
Somersby (L), 57
Somerset, 104
Somerton (Sf), 57; (So), 104
Sonning (Berks), 128
Sonning Common, Eye (O), 128
Southall (Mx), 33, 41
Southend-on-Sea (Ess), 143
Southill (Beds), 101
Southington (Ha), 32
Southminster (Ess), 123
Southorpe (ERY), 172
Southrop (Gl), 174
Southrope (O), 174
Southway (D), 31
Sower Hill (NRY), 188
Sowerby (Cu), 188
Spain's Hall (Ess), 61
Spalding (L), 100
Spalding Moor (ERY), 101
Spaldington (ERY), 101
Spaldwick (Hu), 100
Spalford (Nt), 100
Spanby (L), 171
Sparret (Co), 95
Speen (Berks), 204
Speldhurst (K), 130
Spilsby (L), 59
Spilshill, Little (K), 134
Spilsill Court (K), 134
Spinney (C, Sr), 197
Stagenhoe (Herts), 155
Staines (Mx), 236
Stainsby (Db), 171
Stanford, 40
Stanley, 40
Stanton, 40
Stanway, 40
Staverton (Nf, Sf), 138
Stephney (Cu), 98
Stidham (So), 155
Stock (Ess), 104
Stockham (Ch), 35
Stocking Green (Ess), 111
Stockwood (Do), 127
Stodday (La), 155
Stodfold (Bk), 156

271

Stodmarsh (K), 140
Stody (Nf), 155
Stogursey (So), 64
Stoke (K), 140; North, South (L), 129
Stoke Bliss (Wo), 65
Stoke by Nayland (Sf), 127
Stoke Dabernon (Sr), 215
Stoke Damarel (D), 65
Stoke Doyle (Nth), 62
Stoke Dry (R), 129
Stoke Edith (He), 64
Stoke Farthing (W), 65
Stoke in Hartland (D), 126
Stokeinteignhead (D), 147
Stoke Lyne (O), 211
Stokenchurch (Bk), 124
Stoke Orchard (Gl), 61
Stoke St Milborough (Sa), 127
Stokesby (Nf), 171
Stoke upon Trent (St), 129
Stondon (Beds, Ess), 40
Stone, 4
Stone cum Ebony (K), 206
Stoney Stoke (So), 129
Stoneythorpe (Wa), 174
Stonham (Sf), 40
Stonton (Lei), 40
Stoodleigh (D), 156
Storton (Ch), 186
Stotfold (Beds), 156
Stour, R., 72
Stourpaine (Do), 64
Stow (L), 126
Stow cum Quy (C), 206
Stow on the Wold (Gl), 126
Stowting (K), 111
Stratford Toney (W), 65
Stratton (Co), 97
Stretford (La), 200
Strethall (Ess), 40
Strettington (Sx), 116
Strickstenton (Co), 68
Stroxworthy (D), 142
Strudgwick Wood (Sx), 135, 136
Stubbing (Db, Nt), 111
Stubbins (La), 111
Studborough Hill (Nth), 215
Studdah (NRY), 155
Studfold (We), 156
Studham (Beds), 155
Studley (O, W, Wa, WRY), 156
Stuffle (Co), 156
Sturry (K), 103, 140
Stutfall Castle (K), 156
Sudbourne (Sf), 41
Sudbury (Db, Sf), 34, 41
Sudpray Fm (Sr), 196
Suffield, 41
Suffolk, 41, 99
Sugar Hill (W), 158
Sugarswell Barn, Fm (Wa, O), 157
Sugarwell Fm (O), 158
Summerseat (La), 174
Summersgill (Cu), 176
Sunbury (Mx), 128
Sunninghill (Berks), 128
Sunningwell (Berks), 128
Surrey, 103, 140
Sussex, 99

Sutterton (L), 157
Sutton, 32, 41
Sutton Benger (W), 65
Sutton Maddock (Sa), 64
Sutton Mandeville (W), 62
Sutton Street (K), 215
Swaffham Bulbeck (C), 65
Swale, R. (K), 77
Swancote (Wo), 137
Swannacott (Co), 137
Swarthgill (Cu), 176
Swaythling (Ha), 112
Swincotte (Nt), 137
Swinden (Gl, WRY), 152
Swindon (St, W), 152
Swineshead (Beds, Gl, L, Wo), 121, 122
Swineside (NRY), 174
Swinghill (K), 152
Swinside (Cu), 174
Swinton (La), 138
Sydenham Damarel (D), 65
Sydling (Do), 112

Tackbear (D), 152
Tackley (O), 152
Tagley (Ess), 152
Takeley (Ess), 152
Taldbridge (La), 38
Talhay (Co), 94
Tamill (Co), 94
Tarbock (La), 201
Tarleton (Gl), 201
Tarn Wadling (Cu), 69, 187
Tarrant Crawford (Do), 63
Tarrant Hinton (Do), 63
Tarrant Keynston (Do), 64
Tarrant Launceston (Do), 63
Tarrant Monkton (Do), 63
Tarrant Rawston (Do), 63
Tarrant Rushton (Do), 63-4
Tarrant St (Arundel), 77
Tarvin (Ch), 92
Tattersett (Nf), 134
Tavistock (D), 115
Teddington (Mx), 2, 66, 115; (Wo), 2, 114
Tedfold (Sx), 66, 131
Teigngrace (D), 64
Temple Bruer (L), 197
Temple Mills (Mx), 216
Tendring (Ess), 108
Tenterden (K), 106, 130
Terley (D), 38
Tetbury (Gl), 144
Tetford (L), 211
Thames, R., 71, 72
Thedden (Ha), 22
Thenford (Nth), 22, 148
Therfield (Herts), 202
Thet, R. (Nf), 77
Thetford (C, Nf), 77, 211
Theydon (Ess), 22
Thiefside (Cu), 157
Thievesdale (Nt), 157
Thieves Gill (NRY), 157
Thimbleby (L), 41
Thingoe (Sf), 184, 191
Thirkleby (ERY, NRY), 57
Thirlby (NRY), 172
Thirlspot (Cu), 224

Thirst House (Db), 224
Thirtleby (ERY), 57
Thistlewood (Cu), 175
Tholthorpe (NRY), 58
Thonock (L), 163
Thoralby (NRY), 57
Thorganby (L), 57
Thorlby (WRY), 57
Thormanby (NRY), 57
Thornaby on Tees (NRY), 57
Thornbrough (Nb), 167
Thornbury (D, Gl), 167
Thornby (Nt), 167
Thorndon Hall (Ess), 201
Thornholme (ERY), 35
Thornsett (Db), 134
Thornthorpe (ERY), 57
Thornton le Beans (NRY), 206
Thornton le Moor (NRY), 197·
Thorpe (Bk, Sr), 174
Thorpe Achurch (Nth), 123
Thorpe Acre (Lei), 173
Thorpe Arnold (Lei), 173
Thorpe Bay (Ess), 173
Thorpe Bulmer (Du), 66
Thorpe by Water (R), 173
Thorpehall Fm (Ess), 173
Thorpe in the Fallows (L), 173
Thorpe in the Glebe (Nt), 173
Thorpe-le-Soken (Ess), 173
Thorpe le Vale (L), 197
Thorpe le Willows (NRY), 173
Thorpe Lubenham (Nth), 173
Thorpe Mandeville (Nth), 173, 182
Thorpe Market (Nf), 173
Thorpe Morieux (Sf), 173
Thorpe on the Hill (WRY), 173
Thorpe Stapleton (WRY), 173
Thorpe sub Montem (WRY), 206
Thorpland (Nf), 173
Threapcroft (WRY), 214
Threaphow (La), 214
Threapland (Cu, WRY), 214
Threapthwaite (Cu), 214
Threapwood (Ch), 214
Threepwood (Nb), 214
Thringstone (Lei), 167, 171
Thrislington (Du), 42, 58
Thriverton (D), 157
Throop (Ha), 174
Throope (W), 174
Thrope (WRY), 174
Throphill (Nb), 174
Throxenby (NRY), 58
Thrumpton (Nt), 57
Thrunscoe (L), 163
Thrup (Beds), 174
Thrupp (Beds, Gl, O), 174
Thrushgill (La), 224
Thrussington (Lei), 42, 58
Thruss Pits (Nt), 224
Thruxton (Ha, He), 57
Thuborough (D), 157
Thulston (Db), 58
Thunderfield (Sr), 41, 119
Thunderley (Ess), 119
Thunderlow (Ess), 119
Thundersley (Ess), 116, 119
Thundridge (Herts), 119

Thurcaston (Lei), 57
Thurgarton (Nf), 57, 183
Thurgoland (WRY), 57
Thurlaston (Lei, Wa), 57, 170
Thurlby (L), 58
Thurleigh (Beds), 37
Thurloxton (So), 57
Thurlston (Sf, WRY), 58
Thurmaston (Lei), 58
Thurnscoe (WRY), 163
Thursden (La), 224
Thursford (Nf), 224
Thursley (Sr), 119
Thurstable (Ess), 119
Thurstaston (Ch), 42, 49, 58
Thurston (Sf), 42, 58
Thuxton (Nf), 42, 58
Thwaite (Nf, Sf, NRY), 175
Thwaites (Cu), 175
Tiddingford (Bk), 38, 211
Tiddington (Wa), 115
Tillingham (Ess), 113, 128
Tilshead (W), 147
Timsbury (Ha, So), 34
Tinhay (D), 31
Tinhead (W), 147
Tipperton (Co), 38
Tirril (We), 98, 187
Titching (Co), 94
Titlar Hall (Berks), 211
Tiverton (D), 141
Tocketts (NRY), 137
Tockwith (WRY), 166
Toddington (Beds), 66
Toft, 174; (C), 181; (Ch), 186; (Wa), 183
Tofts (ERY), 174
Toller Fratrum, Porcorum (Do), 205
Tolleshunt D'Arcy (Ess), 63; Major, 64
Tolpuddle (Do), 144
Tonbridge (K), 4–6
Tonwell (Herts), 4
Tooting (Sr), 2
Tormorham (D), 143
Torquay (D), 143
Torrisholme (La), 57, 201
Torver (La), 98
Toton (Nt), 57
Towcester (Nth), 199
Towthorpe (ERY), 57
Towton (WRY), 57
Toxteth (La), 57
Toyd (W), 146
Toynton, High, Low (L), 200
Toynton All Saints, St Peter (L), 200
Trafford Park (La), 200
Trago (Co), 68
Tranmere (Ch), 169
Traymill (D), 38
Treable (D), 86
Treales (La), 85
Trebeigh (Co), 86
Trebick (D), 86
Treblethick (Co), 67
Trebowland (Co), 68
Trebumfrey (He), 91
Trebursey (Co), 96
Tredown (D), 38
Tredrustan (Co), 67
Tredudwell (Co), 67

273

Tredundle (Co), 96
Treforda (Co), 94
Trefrank (Co), 96
Tregaddock (Co), 67
Tregair (Co), 95
Tregardock (Co), 67
Tregarn (Co), 95
Tregaswith (Co), 67
Tregear (Co), 95
Tregenna (Co), 67
Tregerrick (Co), 68
Tregonning (Co), 67
Trehawke (Co), 96
Trehill (D), 38
Trehunsey (Co), 96
Trekernell (Co), 68
Trekinnard (Co), 96
Trelew (Co), 67
Trellian (Co), 68
Trellick (D), 86
Tremaine (Co), 96
Tremellen (Co), 93
Tremenheere (Co), 96
Tremoorland (Co), 94
Tremoutha (Co), 94
Trenearne (Co), 67
Treneglos (Co), 96
Trenoweth (Co), 96
Trenowth (Co), 96
Trent, R., 72
Trerank (Co), 96
Trerose (Co), 95
Tresadderne (Co), 68
Tresamble (Co), 68
Tresawle (Co), 68
Tresawsen (Co), 96
Tresayes (Co), 96
Tresillian (Co), 67
Treskilling (Co), 95
Tresmaine (Co), 95
Tresmarrow (Co), 95
Tresparret (Co), 95
Trevaddock (Co), 91
Trevanion (Co), 67
Trevarthian (Co), 67
Trevashmond (Co), 96
Treveal (Co), 67
Trevellick (Co), 67
Treven (Co), 94
Treveryan (Co), 68
Trevescan (Co), 67
Trevillian (Co), 68
Trevillis (Co), 68
Trevollard (Co), 96
Trevose (Co), 93
Trewaddock (Co), 91
Treway (Co), 94
Trewerry (Co), 67
Trewether (Co), 68
Trewhiddle (Co), 68
Treyeo (Co), 94
Treyseck (He), 90
Trezize (Co), 96
Trigg (Co), 93
Trimdon (Du), 126
Trink (Co), 96
Troutbeck (Cu), 152
Trouts Dale (NRY), 152
Trudnoe (Co), 67

Truscott (Co), 94
Trusey Hill (ERY), 224
Tubney (O), 52
Tuckerton (So), 157
Tucks Cary (So), 157
Tuddenham (Nf, Sf), 30, 66
Tudeley (K), 157
Tudhoe (Du), 66
Tudworth (WRY), 66
Tuesley (Sr), 118
Tugby (Lei), 57
Tunbridge Wells (K), 5, 7
Tunstall, 4
Tunstead (Db, La, Nf), 4
Tunworth (Ha), 4
Turnerscourt (O), 143
Turnworth (Do), 201
Turville (Bk), 202
Tusmore (O), 201, 224
Tweenaways (D), 31
Twerton (So), 141
Twineham (Sx), 31
Twinney Creek (K), 31
Twinyeo (D), 31
Two Bridge (Ess), 5
Twyford (Wo), 22
Twyning (Gl), 31
Ty bach (He), 91
Tyboobach (He), 91
Tyburn (Mx), 198
Tyby (Nf), 183
Tysoe (Wa), 118

Ulceby (L), 164
Ulnaby (Du), 181
Underhill (K), 31
Underly (He), 31
Underriver (K), 31
Underskiddaw (Cu), 31
Upleatham (NRY), 188
Upminster (Ess), 123
Upnor (K), 31
Uppingham (R), 113
Upsall (NRY), 188
Upthorpe (Wo), 174
Upton Hellions (D), 65
Upton Wold (Wo), 45
Upwood (Hu), 101
Usk, R., 77
Utterby (L), 172
Uxbridge (Mx), 103
Uxendon (Mx), 103

Vachery (Sr), 197
Vacye (Co), 63
Vange (Ess), 45, 48, 103
Vanhurst (Sr), 48
Vann (Sr), 48
Varncombe (Sx), 48
Varndean (Sx), 48
Varracombe (D), 47
Vasterne (W), 48
Vaudey Abbey (L), 205
Venmore (Ess), 48
Venn (D), 47; (W), 48
Venniscombe (IOW), 48
Venns (Sx), 48
Venny (W), 48
Verney (Sr), 48

Verridge (Sx), 48
Verwood (Do), 48
Vexour (K), 48
Vielstone (D), 60
Vinnetrow (Sx), 113
Virginstow (D), 127
Virley (Ess), 63
Viscar (Co), 94
Viza (D), 196
Vizacombe (D), 196
Voaden (D), 47
Vobster (So), 47
Volehouse (D), 47
Voucher's Fm (Ess), 48
Vowchurch (He), 47, 124
Vox End (Sx), 48
Vuggles Fms (Sx), 48
Vyse Wood (D), 196

Waddon (Wo), 156
Wakebridge (Db), 161
Wakefield (Nth, WRY), 161
Wakeley (Herts), 161
Wakes Colne (Ess), 62, 75
Walbrook (Lo), 84
Walcott (Nf), 84
Walden (Herts), 84
Waldershare (K), 106
Waldingfield (St), 113
Waldringfield (Sf), 113
Wales (WRY), 83
Waleswood (WRY), 83
Walford (He), 90
Walfords (Ess), 84
Walkeringham (Nf), 113
Walland (D), 86
Wallasey (Ch), 84, 92, 186
Wallerscote (Ch), 137, 151
Wallingford (Berks), 113
Wallington (Nf), 114
Wallingwells (Nt), 46
Wallover (D), 86
Walltown (Sa), 46
Wall under Haywood (Sa), 46
Walpole (Sf), 84
Walpole St Peter's, St Andrew (Nf), 21, 84
Walreddon (D), 86
Walsham le Willows (Sf), 197
Walsingham (Nf), 113
Walsoken (Nf), 21, 84
Walter Hall (Ess), 13, 84
Walthamstow (Ess), 10–14
Walton (Cu, Sf), 84
Walton Hall (La), 85
Walton-le-Soken (Ess), 198
Walton on the Naze (Ess), 84
Walworth (Sr), 84
Wandle, R. (Sr), 77
Wandsworth (Sr), 77, 129
Wansbeck (Nb), 180
Wansdyke (W), 118, 119
Wantage (Berks), 111
Warbreck (La), 176, 187
Warburton (Ch), 138
Wardleworth (La), 129
Warehorne (K), 109
Wargery (D), 142
Waring (L), 159

Warley Salop, Wigorn (Wo), 152, 206
Warnborough (Ha), 158, 159
Warnell (Cu), 40
Warter (ERY), 158
Washbrook (Sf), 124
Washington (Sx), 136
Watchet (So), 74
Waterlooville (Ha), 202
Waterston (Do), 60
Waterthorpe (Db), 47
Watling Street, 162
Waxlow (Mx), 103
Wayland (Nf), 191
Weald, 46
Weald, The (K, Sx), 46, 130
Weaverthorpe (ERY), 59
Weavering Street (K), 108
Wednesbury (St), 118
Wednesfield (St), 118
Weedon (Bk), 118
Weedon Lois (Nth), 118
Weeford (St), 118
Week (IOW), 135
Weeke (Ha), 135
Week St Mary (Co), 135
Weeley (Ess), 118
Weeting (Nf), 112
Weildbarns (Ess), 46
Welborne (NRY), 46
Weldon (Nth), 46
Welham (Nt), 46
Well (NRY, Sx), 46
Wells (Nf), 46
Welsh Bicknor (He), 90
Wendens Ambo (Ess), 206
Wendover (Bk), 87
Wenlock (Sa), 92
Wensley (Db), 119
Wenslow (Beds), 119
Weoley (Wo), 118
Westbourne (Sx), 121
Westbury Wild (Bk), 46
Westdean (Sx), 142
West Derby (La), 187
Westenhanger (K), 110
Westhorpe (Bk), 174; (Nt), 172
Westhoughton (La), 33
West Kirby (Ch), 186
West Knighton (Do), 148
Westlaby (L), 59
Westleton (Sf), 59
Westmorland, 100
Weston Corbett (Ha), 62
Weston in Gordano (So), 206
Weston Patrick (Ha), 64
Weston Subedge (Gl), 206
Weston super Mare (So), 206
Westrip (Gl), 174
Westrop (W), 174
West Tarring (Sx), 108
West Walton (Nf), 21, 84
Westweek (D), 135
Westwell (K), 136
Westwood (Court) (K), 32
Wetherby (WRY), 172
Wetherden (Sf), 134
Wetheringsett (Sf), 134
Wethersell (Sr), 134
Weyhill (Ha), 118

Whaddon (Bk, W), 156
Whaplode (L), 152
Wharram Percy (ERY), 61
Whatborough (Lei), 156
Whatfield (Sf), 156
Whatley (So), 156
Wheatley (Ess, Y), 156
Wheelock (Ch), 92
Wheely Down (Ha), 118
Whicham (Cu), 18
Whichford (Wa), 102
Whiligh (Sx), 118
Whissendine (R), 199
Whissonsett (Nf), 134, 199
Whiston (Nth), 102
Whitby (Ch), 186; (NRY), 180
Whitchurch (Bk, D), 124
Whitchurch Canonicorum (Do), 124, 205
Whiteborough (Nt), 156
White Colne (Ess), 62, 75
Whiteoxmead (So), 49
White Roding (Ess), 108
Whitestanton (D), 126
Whitmore (St), 82
Whitsun Brook (Wo), 102
Whyly (Sx), 118
Wibtoft (Wa), 183
Wichenford (Wo), 102
Wichnor (St), 102
Wick (Berks, Gl), 134
Wick Champflower (So), 135
Wicken (C, Ess, Nth), 135
Wicken Fen (C), 197
Wick Episcopi (Wo), 135
Wield (Hu), 46
Wigan (Hu), 135; (La), 85
Wigford (D), 142
Wiggonby (Cu), 60, 85
Wight, Isle of, 71
Wike (WRY), 134
Wilbraham (C), 138
Wilcombe (D), 46
Wilcot (W), 46
Wild (Herts, Bk, Nth), 46
Wild Court (Berks), 155
Wilderley (Sa), 145
Wiley (W), 77
Will (D), 46
Willey (Sr), 118
Willhayne (D), 46
Williamstrip (Gl), 174
Willingham (C, L), 138
Willington (Ch), 145
Willoughby (Wa), 167, 183
Willoughton (L), 167
Wilsmere Down Fm (C), 141
Wilton (So, W), 46, 104
Wiltown (D), 46
Wiltshire, 104
Winchester, 80, 204
Winder (We), 187
Windersome (ERY), 35
Windsor (Berks, Co, D, Do), 23
Winfold Fm (C), 154
Wing (Bk), 128
Wingrave (Bk), 128
Winscales (Cu), 176
Winskill (Cu), 176

Winsor (Co, D, Ha), 23
Winterbourne Abbas (Do), 205
Winterbourne Dauntsey, Earls, Gunner (W), 62
Winterfold (Sx), 131
Winteringham (L), 114
Wintersett (WRY), 134
Winterton (L), 114
Wisbech (C), 20
Wisborough Green (Sx), 132
Wishworthy (Co), 94
Wiske, R., 77
Wissington (Sf), 145
Wistanstow (Sa), 127
Wistow (Lei), 127
Witchingham (Nf), 134, 199
Witchley Green (R), 102
Witherslack (We), 176
Withiel (Co), 97
Wittering (Sx), 107
Wix (Ess), 135
Woden's Dyke (Ha), 119
Woking (Sr), 112, 128
Wokingham (Berks), 112, 128
Wolborough (D), 154
Wold (C), 45
Woldingham (Sr), 113
Woldringfold (Sx), 131
Wolds (L, Wa, Y), 45
Wolfhole Crag (La), 154
Wolford Fm (D), 124
Wollage Green (K), 154
Wollaton (D), 145
Wollerton (Sa), 144
Wolleux (Co), 154
Wolverhampton (St), 144
Wolvey (Wa), 154
Woodbridge, 40
Woodbury Salterton (D), 151
Woodchurch (Ch, K), 124
Woodditton (C), 203
Woodford, 40
Woodhuish (D), 147
Woodhurst (Hu), 101
Woodmancote (Gl, Sx), 137
Woodmancott (Ha), 137
Woodmansterne (Sr), 141
Woodnesborough (K), 116, 118, 121
Woodredon (Ess), 47
Woodsetts (WRY), 134
Woodsome (WRY), 35
Woodville (Db), 202
Wood Walton (Hu), 101
Wookey (So), 155
Wool (Do), 64
Woolacombe (D), 154
Wooladon (D), 154
Woolbridge (Do), 46
Woolcombe (Do), 46
Wooldale (WRY), 154
Woolden (La), 154
Woolleigh (D), 154
Woolley (Berks, D, Hu, WRY), 154; (So), 46
Woolpit (Sf, Sr), 154
Woolston (D, Ha, So), 42; (Ess), 13
Woolstone (Berks, Bk), 42
Woolwich (K), 135
Woolwich Wood (K), 154

Wootton Wawen (Wa), 64
Worcester, 26, 80
Worgret (Do), 158
Worldham (Ha), 145
Worlingworth (Sf), 130
Wormleighton (Wa), 51
Worms Heath (Sr), 122
Wormshill (K), 118, 121
Worsley (La), 81; (Wo), 152
Worsthorne (La), 55
Worston (La), 55
Worthing (Sx), 55, 108
Worthington (La, Lei), 55
Wothersome (WRY), 35
Wragby (L), 172, 191
Wraggoe (L), 191
Wrantage (So), 152
Wratting (C, Sf), 112
Wrautam (Wa), 215
Wrawby (L), 172
Wreigh Burn (Nb), 159
Wreighill (Nb), 158, 159
Wrekin (Sa), 74, 92
Wrenbury (Ch), 152, 156
Wrightington (La), 151
Wrinstead (K), 152
Wroxeter (Sa), 26, 74, 79, 199
Wuerdle (La), 129
Wychbold (Wo), 139
Wychwood (O), 102
Wycomb (Lei), 135
Wye (K), 118, 131, 136
Wyham (L), 118
Wyke (Sr), 134
Wykeham (NRY), 135
Wyken (Wa), 135
Wyke Regis (Do), 135
Wykin (Lei), 135
Wylam (Nb), 155
Wymering (Ha), 107
Wyre (La), Forest, Piddle (Wo), 80
Wyresdale (La), 80
Wyville (L), 118

Yafforth (NRY), 45
Yaddlethorpe (L), 173
Yaldham (K), 45
Yalding (K), 45, 108
Yalland (D), 45
Yarlet (St), 45
Yarlside (NRY), 174
Yarm (NRY), 35
Yarmouth (IOW), 141; Great (Nf), 19
Yarnacombe (D), 45
Yarnaford (D), 45
Yarner (D), 45
Yarnicombe (D), 45
Yarninknowle (D), 45
Yarnscombe (D), 45
Yattenden (Berks), 113
Yaverland (IOW), 154
Yeading (Mx), 103
Yearsley (NRY), 154
Yeavering (Nb), 3–4
Yelland (D), 45
Yelloways (D), 45
Yellowland (D), 45
Yendamore (D), 31
Yen Hall (C), 45, 152
Yeo (D), 45; R. (So), 101
Yeovil (So), 101
Yetminster (Do), 123
Yollacombe (D), 45
Yonderlake (D), 31
Yondhill (D), 31
Yordale (NRY), 201
York, 24, 79
Yorkshire (Sx), 134
Youlden (D), 45
Youldon (D), 45

Zeal (D), 48
Zeal Monachorum (D), 205
Zeals (W), 48
Zeaston (D), 48
Zelah (Co), 48
Zell House Fm (Ha), 48